lonely planet

Mediterranean
Europe
PHRASEBOOK & DICTIONARY

Acknowledgments

Associate Publisher Mina Patria
Managing Editor Bruce Evans
Editors Kate Mathews, Mardi O'Connor
Series Designer Mark Adams
Managing Layout Designer Chris Girdler
Layout Designer Carol Jackson
Production Support Larissa Frost

Thanks

Sasha Baskett, Melanie Dankel, Brendan Dempsey, Ben Handicott, James Hardy, Sandra Helou, Nic Lehman, Annelies Mertens, Wayne Murphy, Naomi Parker, Trent Paton, Piers Pickard, Branislava Vladisavljevic

Published by Lonely Planet Publications Pty Ltd
ABN 36 005 607 983

3rd Edition – February 2013
ISBN 978 1 74179 006 1
Text © Lonely Planet 2013
Cover Image Outdoor cafe, Oia Town, Santorini, Cyclades, Greece
Michele Falzone/AWL Images©

Printed in China   10 9 8 7 6 5 4 3 2 1

Contact lonelyplanet.com/contact

MIX
Paper from
responsible sources
FSC™ C021741

acknowledgments

This book is based on existing editions of Lonely Planet's phrasebooks as well as new content. It was developed with the help of the following people:

- Anila Mayhew for the Albanian chapter
- Gordana Ivetac and Ivan Ivetac for the Croatian chapter
- Michael Janes for the French chapter
- Thanasis Spilias for the Greek chapter
- Karina Coates, Pietro Iagnocco and Susie Walker for the Italian chapter
- Liljana Mitkovska for the Macedonian chapter
- Robert Landon and Anabela de Azevedo Teixeira Sobrinho for the Portuguese chapter
- Urška Pajer for the Slovene chapter
- Marta López for the Spanish chapter
- Arzu Kürklü for the Turkish chapter

Thank you to Floriana Badalotti (Italian), Gina Tsarouhas (Greek), Gus Balbontin (Spanish), Jean-Pierre Masclef (French), William Gourlay (Turkish) and Yukiyoshi Kamimura (Portuguese) for additional language expertise.

contents

Mediterranean Europe

Baltic Sea

Latvia

Lithuania

Belarus

Russia

Kazakhstan

Poland

Ukraine

Slovakia

Moldova

Hungary

Romania

SERBIA ✪ Belgrade

BOSNIA-
HERCEGOVINA

MONTE-
NEGRO Kosova

✪ Skopje

MACEDONIA

✪ Tirana

ALBANIA

Thessaloniki

GREECE

Aegean
Sea

✪ Athens

Izmir

Sea of Crete

Crete

EAN   SEA

Libya

Bulgaria

● Istanbul

✪ Ankara

TURKEY

BLACK SEA

Georgia

Armenia

Iran

Syria

Iraq

CYPRUS

● Nicosia
(Lefkosia)

Lebanon

Israel &
the
Palestinian
Territories

Jordan

Saudi
Arabia

Egypt

■ Spanish
■ Turkish

*Note: Language areas are approximate only.
For more details see the relevant introduction.*

EUROPE

mediterranean europe – at a glance

One of the most rewarding things about travelling around Mediterranean Europe is the rich variety of cuisine, customs, architecture and history. The flipside of course is that you'll encounter a number of very different languages. Most languages spoken in Mediterranean Europe belong to what's known as the Indo-European language family, believed to have originally developed from one language spoken thousands of years ago. Luckily for English speakers, most of these languages also use Roman script.

The Romance languages (French, Italian, Spanish and Portuguese) all developed from Vulgar Latin, which spread through Western Europe during the rule of the Roman Empire. The freedom with which English has borrowed Latin-based vocabulary means you'll quickly recognise many words from these languages. The Slavic languages are a branch of the Indo-European language family and share a large amount of basic vocabulary. Macedonian and Serbian which were traditionally associated with the Orthodox Church use the Cyrillic alphabet, while Croatian and Slovene, which were influenced by the Catholic Church, use the Roman alphabet. Albanian and Greek both form single branches of the Indo-European language family. Finally, Turkish is part of the Ural-Altaic language family, which includes languages spoken from the Balkan Peninsula to northeast Asia. Arabic script was replaced by Roman script for Turkish in the early 20th century.

did you know?

- The European Union (EU) was established by the Maastricht Treaty in 1992. It developed from the European Economic Community, founded by the Treaty of Rome in 1957. Since the 2007 enlargement, it has 27 member states and 23 official languages.
- The EU flag is a circle of 12 gold stars on a blue background – the number 12 representing wholeness.
- The EU anthem is the 'Ode to Joy' from Beethoven's Ninth Symphony.
- Europe Day, 9 May, commemorates the 1950 declaration by French Foreign Minister Robert Schuman, which marks the creation of the European Union.
- The euro has been in circulation since E-Day, 1 January 2002. The euro's symbol (€) was inspired by the Greek letter epsilon (ε) – Greece being the cradle of European civilisation and ε being the first letter of the word 'Europe'.
- The Eurovision Song Contest, held each May, has been running since 1956. For the larger part of the competition's history, the performers were only allowed to sing in their country's national language, but that's no longer the case.

Albanian

albanian alphabet

A a a	*B b* b	*C c* ts	*Ç ç* ch	*D d* d	*Dh dh* dh
E e e	*Ë ë* uh	*F f* f	*G g* g	*Gj gj* dy	*H h* h
I i ee	*J j* y	*K k* k	*L l* l	*Ll ll* ll	*M m* m
N n n	*Nj nj* ny	*O o* o	*P p* p	*Q q* ty	*R r* r
Rr rr rr	*S s* s	*Sh sh* sh	*T t* t	*Th th* th	*U u* oo
V v v	*X x* dz	*Xh xh* j	*Y y* ew	*Z z* z	*Zh zh* zh

albanian

GJUHA SHQIPE

ALBANIAN
gjuha shqipe

introduction

Albanian (*gjuha shqipe* dyoo·ha shtyee·pe) is one of the oldest Indo-European languages, generally considered the only descendant of Illyrian, the language of the ancient inhabitants of the Balkans. With no close relatives and constituting a branch of its own, it's a proud survivor of the Roman, Slavic and Ottoman influxes and a European linguistic oddity on a par with Basque.

Albanian's position on the edge of the turbulent and multilingual Balkans means that it's been influenced by many languages. Some similarities with Romanian, for example, suggest that the two languages were closely related and that their speakers interacted even in pre-Roman times. The Romans, who established control over the present-day Albania by 167 BC and ruled for the next five centuries, left their mark on the vocabulary and structure of the language. After the division of the Roman Empire in AD 395, Albanians fell within the realm of Byzantium and Greek Orthodox culture. The interaction with Bulgarian and Serbian began after the arrival of the Slavs to the Balkans in the 6th century. With the Ottoman conquest in 1479 Turkish and Arabic influences were added to the mix.

There are two main dialects of Albanian – Tosk (with about 3 million speakers in southern Albania, Greece, Italy and Turkey) and Gheg (spoken by about 2.8 million people in northern Albania, Kosovo and the surrounding areas of Serbia, Montenegro and Macedonia). Tosk is the official language of Albania and is also the variety used in this phrasebook.

Not surprisingly, Albanian has been written in various alphabets since the earliest written records from the 15th century. A single-sentence baptismal formula dating from 1462 and a Catholic prayer book from 1555 were both written in the Roman alphabet, which was mainly used for the Gheg dialect during the 17th and 18th centuries. The Tosk dialect, on the other hand, was originally written in the Greek alphabet. However, during the Ottoman rule, texts in both varieties were often in Arabic script (also used for Turkish). Even Cyrillic script was occasionally in use. This orthographic confusion was finally settled by the Manastir Congress in 1908, which adopted a modified Roman alphabet as the standard written form of Albanian.

Even though many Albanians speak English, you'll find attempts to communicate in Albanian are welcomed. Discovering some of the mysteries of this intriguing language will be rewarding – try learning a few of the 27 words Albanian has for 'moustache' or the other 27 used for 'eyebrows'!

pronunciation

vowel sounds

The Albanian vowel system is relatively easy to master, as the sounds mostly have equivalents in English.

symbol	english equivalent	albanian example	transliteration
a	father	*pak*	pak
ai	aisle	*çaj*	chai
e	bet	*pse*	pse
ee	see	*klima*	*klee*·ma
ew	ee pronounced with rounded lips	*dy*	dew
ia	tiara	*djali*	*dia*·lee
o	pot	*mosha*	*mo*·sha
oo	zoo	*jug*	yoog
uh	ago	*vëlla*	vuh·*lla*

word stress

For the vast majority of words in Albanian, the main stress falls on the last syllable of a word (or the last stem of a compound word). In a sentence, the main stress generally falls on the last word of a phrase. In our coloured pronunciation guides, the stressed syllable is always in italics.

consonant sounds

The Albanian consonant sounds shouldn't present many problems for English speakers. Note that 'rr' and 'll' are pronounced stronger than when they're written as single letters.

symbol	english equivalent	albanian example	transliteration
b	bed	*bukë*	*boo*-kuh
ch	cheat	*çaj, qen*	chai, chen
d	dog	*disa*	dee·*sa*
dh	that	*bardhë*	bar·*dhuh*
dy	joke	*gjalpë, xhami*	*dyal*·puh, *dya*-mee
dz	adds	*nxehtë*	n·*dzeh*-tuh
f	fat	*frenat*	*fre*-nat
g	go	*gisht*	geesht
h	hat	*hundë*	*hoon*-duh
k	kit	*raki*	ra-*kee*
l	lot	*omletë*	om-*le*-tuh
ll	strong l	*llum*	lloom
m	man	*muze*	moo-*ze*
n	not	*sapun*	sa-*poon*
ny	canyon	*një*	nyuh
p	pet	*po*	po
r	run	*ari*	a-*ree*
rr	strong r	*rrotë*	*rro*-tuh
s	sun	*sot*	sot
sh	shot	*shesh*	shesh
t	top	*tani*	ta-*nee*
th	thin	*uthull*	oo-*thooll*
ts	hats	*cili*	*tsee*-lee
v	very	*veri*	ve-*ree*
y	yes	*jo*	yo
z	zero	*zarf*	zarf
zh	pleasure	*bizhuteri*	bee-*zhoo*-te-*ree*

basics

language difficulties

Do you speak English?
A flisni anglisht?   a *flees*·nee ang·*leesht*

Do you understand?
A kuptoni?   a koop·*to*·nee

I (don't) understand.
Unë (nuk) kuptoj.   oo·nuh (nook) koop·*toy*

What does (*vrapoj*) mean?
Ç'do të thotë fjala (vrapoj)?   chdo tuh *tho*·tuh *fya*·la (vra·*poy*)

How do you ...?	*Si ...?*	see ...
pronounce this	*shqiptohet kjo*	shcheep·*to*·het kyo
write (*atje*)	*shkruhet fjala (atje)*	shkroo·het *fya*·la (at·ye)

Could you please ...?	*..., ju lutem.*	... yoo *loo*·tem
repeat that	*Përsëriteni*	puhr·suh·*ree*·te·nee
speak more slowly	*Flisni më*	*flees*·nee muh
	ngadalë	nga·*da*·luh
write it down	*Shkruajeni*	shkroo·*a*·ye·nee

---

essentials

Yes.	*Po.*	po
No.	*Jo.*	yo
Please.	*Ju lutem.*	yoo *loo*·tem
Thank you	*Faleminderit*	fa·le·meen·*de*·reet
(very much).	*(shumë).*	(*shoo*·muh)
You're welcome.	*S'ka përse.*	ska puhr·*se*
Excuse me.	*Më falni.*	muh *fal*·nee
Sorry.	*Më vjen keq.*	muh vyen kech

numbers

0	zero	ze·ro	17	shtatëmbë-	shta·tuhm·buh·	
1	një	nyuh		dhjetë	dhye·tuh	
2	dy	dew	18	tetëmbë-	te·tuhm·buh·	
3	tre/tri m/f	tre/tree		dhjetë	dhye·tuh	
4	katër	ka·tuhr	19	nëntëmbë-	nuhn·tuhm·buh·	
5	pesë	pe·suh		dhjetë	dhye·tuh	
6	gjashtë	dyash·tuh	20	njëzet	nyuh·zet	
7	shtatë	shta·tuh	21	njëzet e një	nyuh·zet e nyuh	
8	tetë	te·tuh	30	tridhjetë	tree·dhye·tuh	
9	nëntë	nuhn·tuh	40	dyzet	dew·zet	
10	dhjetë	dhye·tuh	50	pesë-	pe·suh·	
11	njëmbë-	nyuhm·buh·		dhjetë	dhye·tuh	
	dhjetë	dhye·tuh	60	gjashtë-	dyash·tuh·	
12	dymbë-	dewm·buh·		dhjetë	dhye·tuh	
	dhjetë	dhye·tuh	70	shtatë-	shta·tuh·	
13	trembë-	trem·buh·		dhjetë	dhye·tuh	
	dhjetë	dhye·tuh	80	tetë-	te·tuh·	
14	katërmbë-	ka·tuhrm·buh·		dhjetë	dhye·tuh	
	dhjetë	dhye·tuh	90	nëntë-	nuhn·tuh·	
15	pesëmbë-	pe·suhm·buh·		dhjetë	dhye·tuh	
	dhjetë	dhye·tuh	100	njëqind	nyuh·cheend	
16	gjashtëmbë-	dyash·tuhm·buh·	1000	një mijë	nyuh mee·yuh	
	dhjetë	dhye·tuh				

time & dates

What time is it?	Sa është ora?	sa uhsh·tuh o·ra
It's one o'clock.	Ora është një.	o·ra uhsh·tuh nyuh
It's (two) o'clock.	Ora është (dy).	o·ra uhsh·tuh (dew)
Quarter past (one).	(Një) e një çerek.	(nyuh) e nyuh che·rek
Half past (one).	(Një) e gjysmë.	(nyuh) e dyews·muh
Quarter to (eight).	(Tetë) pa një çerek.	(te·tuh) pa nyuh che·rek
At what time ...?	Në çfarë ore ...?	nuh chfa·ruh o·re ...
At ...	Në ...	nuh ...
am	paradite	pa·ra·dee·te
pm	mbasdite	mbas·dee·te

Monday	e hënë	e *huh*-nuh
Tuesday	e martë	e *mar*-tuh
Wednesday	e mërkurë	e muhr-*koo*-ruh
Thursday	e enjte	e *eny*-te
Friday	e premte	e *prem*-te
Saturday	e shtunë	e *shtoo*-nuh
Sunday	e diel	e *dee*-el

January	janar	ya-*nar*
February	shkurt	shkoort
March	mars	mars
April	prill	preell
May	maj	mai
June	qershor	cher-*shor*
July	korrik	ko-*rreek*
August	gusht	goosht
September	shtator	shta-*tor*
October	tetor	te-*tor*
November	nëntor	nuhn-*tor*
December	dhjetor	dhye-*tor*

| What date is it today? | Sa është data sot? | sa uhsh-tuh *da*-ta sot |
| It's (10 October). | Është (dhjetë tetor). | uhsh-tuh (dhye-tuh te-*tor*) |

| since (May) | që në (maj) | chuh nuh (mai) |
| until (June) | deri në (qershor) | de-ree nuh (cher-*shor*) |

next week	javën e ardhshme	ya-vuhn e *ardh*-shme
next month	muajin e ardhshëm	moo-a-yeen e *ardh*-shuhm
next year	vitin e ardhshëm	vee-teen e *ardh*-shuhm

last ...	... e kaluar	... e ka-*loo*-ar
night	mbrëmjen	*mbruhm*-yen
week	javën	*ya*-vuhn
month	muajin	*moo*-a-yeen
year	vitin	*vee*-teen

yesterday/tomorrow ...	dje/nesër ...	dee-e/ne-suhr ...
morning	në mëngjes	nuh muhn-*dyes*
afternoon	mbasdite	mbas-*dee*-te
evening	në mbrëmje	nuh *mbruhm*-ye

weather

What's the weather like?	Si është koha?	see uhsh-tuh ko-ha
It's ...	Koha është ...	ko-ha uhsh-tuh ...
cold	e ftohtë	e ftoh-tuh
hot	e nxehtë	e ndzeh-tuh
raining	me shi	me shee
snowing	me borë	me bo-ruh
sunny	me diell	me dee-ell
warm	e ngrohtë	e ngroh-tuh
windy	me erë	me e-ruh
spring	pranverë f	pran-ve-ruh
summer	verë f	ve-ruh
autumn	vjeshtë f	vyesh-tuh
winter	dimër m	dee-muhr

border crossing

I'm here ...	Jam këtu ...	yam kuh-too ...
on business	me punë	me poo-nuh
on holiday	me pushime	me poo-shee-me
I'm here for ...	Do të qëndroj për ...	do tuh chuhn-droy puhr ...
(10) days	(dhjetë) ditë	(dhye-tuh) dee-tuh
(two) months	(dy) muaj	(dew) moo-ai
(three) weeks	(tri) javë	(tree) ya-vuh

I'm going to (Tirana).
Do të shkoj në (Tiranë). do tuh shkoy nuh (tee-ra-nuh)

I'm staying at the (Hotel Tirana).
Po qëndroj te (hotel Tirana). po chuhn-droy te (ho-tel tee-ra-na)

I have nothing to declare.
S'kam asgjë për të deklaruar. skam as-dyuh puhr tuh de-kla-roo-ar

I have something to declare.
Dua të deklaroj diçka. doo-a tuh de-kla-roy deech-ka

That's (not) mine.
(Nuk) Është e imja. (nook) uhsh-tuh e eem-ya

transport

tickets & luggage

Where can I buy a ticket?
Ku mund të blej një biletë?   koo moond tuh bley nyuh bee-*le*-tuh

Do I need to book a seat?
A duhet të bëj rezervim?   a *doo*-het tuh buhy re-zer-*veem*

One ... ticket	*Një biletë ...*	nyuh bee-*le*-tuh ...
(to Shkodër),	*(për në Shkodër),*	(puhr nuh *shko*-duhr)
please.	*ju lutem.*	yoo *loo*-tem
one-way	*për vajtje*	puhr *vai*-tye
return	*kthimi*	*kthee*-mee

I'd like to ... my	*Dua ta ... biletën*	*doo*-a ta ... bee-*le*-tuhn
ticket, please.	*time, ju lutem.*	*tee*-me yoo *loo*-tem
cancel	*anuloj*	a-noo-*loy*
change	*ndryshoj*	ndrew-*shoy*
collect	*marr*	marr
confirm	*konfirmoj*	kon-feer-*moy*

I'd like a ... seat,	*Dua një vend ...,*	*doo*-a nyuh vend ...
please.	*ju lutem.*	yoo *loo*-tem
nonsmoking	*ku s'pihet duhan*	koo *spee*-het doo-*han*
smoking	*ku pihet duhan*	koo *pee*-het doo-*han*

How much is it?
Sa kushton?   sa koosh-*ton*

Is there air conditioning?
A ka ajër të kondicionuar?   a ka *a*-yuhr tuh kon-*dee*-tsee-o-noo-ar

Is there a toilet?
A ka banjë?   a ka *ba*-nyuh

How long does the trip take?
Sa zgjat udhëtimi?   sa zdyat oo-dhuh-*tee*-mee

Is it a direct route?
A është linjë direkte?   a *uhsh*-tuh *lee*-nyuh dee-*rek*-te

I'd like a luggage locker.
Dua një kyç për valixhet.   *doo*-a nyuh kewch puhr va-*lee*-dyet

My luggage has been ...	*Valixhet e mia ...*	va-*lee*-dyet e *mee*-a ...
damaged	*janë dëmtuar*	*ya*-nuh duhm-*too*-ar
lost	*kanë humbur*	*ka*-nuh *hoom*-boor
stolen	*i kanë vjedhur*	ee *ka*-nuh *vye*-dhoor

getting around

Where does flight (728) arrive/depart?
Ku mbërrin/niset linja   koo *mbuh*-rreen/*nee*-set *lee*-nya
(728)?   (shta-tuh-*cheend* e *nyuh*-zet e te-tuh)

Where's (the) ...?   *Ku është ...?*   koo *uhsh*-tuh ...
   arrivals hall   *salla e mbërritjes*   *sa*-lla e mbuh-*rree*-tyes
   departures hall   *salla e nisjes*   *sa*-lla e *nee*-syes
   duty-free shop   *dyqani pa taksa*   dew-*cha*-nee pa *tak*-sa
   gate (12)   *hyrja*   *hew*-rya
      (dymbëdhjetë)   (dewm-buh-*dhye*-tuh)

Is this the ... to   *Është ... për në*   *uhsh*-tuh ... puhr nuh
(Durrës)?   *(Durrës)?*   (*doo*-rruhs)
   boat   *kjo anija*   kyo a-*nee*-ya
   bus   *ky autobusi*   kew a-oo-to-*boo*-see
   plane   *ky aeroplani*   kew a-e-ro-*pla*-nee
   train   *ky treni*   kew *tre*-nee

What time's   *Në ç'orë vjen*   nuh *cho*-ruh vyen
the ... bus?   *autobusi ...?*   a-oo-to-*boo*-see ...
   first   *i parë*   e *pa*-ruh
   last   *i fundit*   e *foon*-deet
   next   *tjetër*   *tye*-tuhr

At what time does it arrive/leave?
Në ç'orë arrin/niset?   nuh *cho*-ruh a-*rreen*/*nee*-set

How long will it be delayed?
Sa do të vonohet?   sa do tuh vo-*no*-het

What station/stop is this?
Cili stacion është ky?   *tsee*-lee sta-tsee-*on* *uhsh*-tuh kew

What's the next station/stop?
Cili është stacioni tjetër?   *tsee*-lee *uhsh*-tuh sta-tsee-*o*-nee *tye*-tuhr

Does it stop at (Vora)?
A ndalon në (Vorë)?   a nda-*lon* nuh (*vo*-ruh)

Please tell me when we get to (Kruja).
Ju lutem më tregoni kur të arrijmë në (Krujë).
yoo *loo*-tem muh tre-*go*-nee koor tuh a-*rrey*-muh nuh (*kroo*-yuh)

How long do we stop here?
Për sa kohë do ndalojmë këtu?
puhr sa *ko*-huh do nda-*loy*-muh kuh-*too*

Is this seat available?
I lirë është ky vendi?
ee *lee*-ruh uhsh-tuh kew *ven*-dee

That's my seat.
Ky është vendi im.
kew uhsh-tuh *ven*-dee eem

I'd like a taxi ...	*Dua një taksi ...*	doo-a nyuh tak-*see* ...
at (9am)	*në orën (nëntë paradite)*	nuh o-ruhn (*nuhn*-tuh pa-ra-*dee*-te)
now	*tani*	ta-*nee*
tomorrow	*nesër*	*ne*-suhr

Is this taxi available?
Është bosh kjo taksia?
uhsh-tuh bosh kyo tak-*see*-a

How much is it to ...?
Sa kushton për të vajtur në ...?
sa koosh-*ton* puhr tuh *vai*-toor nuh ...

Please put the meter on.
Ju lutem ndizeni matësin e kilometrave.
yoo *loo*-tem ndee-ze-nee *ma*-tuh-seen e kee-lo-*me*-tra-ve

Please take me to (this address).
Ju lutem më çoni te (kjo adresë).
yoo *loo*-tem muh *cho*-nee te (kyo a-*dre*-suh)

Please ...	*Ju lutem ...*	yoo *loo*-tem ...
slow down	*uleni*	*oo*-le-nee
	shpejtësinë	shpey-tuh-*see*-nuh
stop here	*ndaloni këtu*	nda-*lo*-nee kuh-*too*
wait here	*prisni këtu*	*prees*-nee kuh-*too*

car, motorbike & bicycle hire

I'd like to hire a ...	*Dua të marr me qira një ...*	doo-a tuh marr me chee-*ra* nyuh ...
bicycle	*biçikletë*	bee-chee-*kle*-tuh
car	*makinë*	ma-*kee*-nuh
motorbike	*motor*	mo-*tor*

with ...	me ...	me ...
a driver	shofer	sho·*fer*
air conditioning	ajër të	*a*·yuhr tuh
	kondicionuar	kon·*dee*·tsee·o·noo·ar
antifreeze	kundërngrirës	koon·duhr·*ngree*·ruhs
snow chains	zinxhira për borë	zeen·*dyee*·ra puhr bo·ruh

How much for	Sa kushton	sa koosh·*ton*
... hire?	për një ...?	puhr nyuh ...
hourly	orë	*o*·ruh
daily	ditë	*dee*·tuh
weekly	javë	*ya*·vuh

air	ajër m	*a*·yuhr
oil	vaj m	vai
petrol	benzinë f	ben·*zee*·nuh
tyres	goma f	*go*·ma

I need a mechanic.
Më duhet një mekanik.   muh *doo*·het nyuh me·ka·*neek*

I've run out of petrol.
Më ka mbaruar benzina.   muh ka mba·*roo*·ar ben·*zee*·na

I have a flat tyre.
Më ka rënë goma.   muh ka ruh·nuh *go*·ma

directions

Where's the ...?	Ku është ...?	koo *uhsh*·tuh ...
bank	banka	*ban*·ka
city centre	qendra e qytetit	*chen*·dra e chew·*te*·teet
hotel	hoteli	ho·*te*·lee
market	tregu	*tre*·goo
police station	rajoni i policisë	ra·*yo*·nee ee po·lee·*tsee*·suh
post office	posta	*pos*·ta
public toilet	banja publike	*ba*·nya poo·*blee*·ke
tourist office	zyra turistike	*zew*·ra too·rees·*tee*·ke

Is this the road to (Berat)?
A është kjo rruga për në (Berat)?   a *uhsh*·tuh kyo *rroo*·ga puhr nuh (be·*rat*)

Can you show me (on the map)?
A mund të ma tregoni (në hartë)?   a moond tuh ma tre·*go*·nee (nuh *har*·tuh)

What's the address?
Cila është adresa?   tsee·la *uhsh*·tuh a·*dre*·sa

How far is it?
Sa larg është?   sa larg *uhsh*·tuh

How do I get there?
Si mund të shkoj atje?   see moond tuh shkoy at·*ye*

Turn ...	*Kthehuni ...*	*kthe*·hoo·nee ...
at the corner	*te qoshja e rrugës*	te *chosh*·ya e *rroo*·guhs
at the traffic lights	*te semafori*	te se·ma·*fo*·ree
left/right	*majtas/djathtas*	*mai*·tas/*diath*·tas

It's ...	*Është ...*	*uhsh*·tuh ...
behind ...	*prapa ...*	*pra*·pa ...
far away	*larg*	larg
here	*këtu*	kuh·*too*
in front of ...	*përpara ...*	puhr·*pa*·ra ...
left	*majtas*	*mai*·tas
near (to ...)	*afër ...*	*a*·fuhr ...
next to ...	*ngjitur me ...*	*ndyee*·toor me ...
on the corner	*te qoshja*	te *chosh*·ya
opposite ...	*përballë ...*	puhr·*ba*·lluh ...
right	*djathtas*	*diath*·tas
straight ahead	*drejt*	dreyt
there	*atje*	at·*ye*

by bus	*me autobus*	me a·oo·to·*boos*
by taxi	*me taksi*	me tak·*see*
by train	*me tren*	me tren
on foot	*në këmbë*	nuh *kuhm*·buh

north	*veri*	ve·*ree*
south	*jug*	yoog
east	*lindje*	*leen*·dye
west	*perëndim*	pe·ruhn·*deem*

Hyrje/Dalje	hewr·ye/dal·ye	Entrance/Exit
Hapur/Mbyllur	ha·poor/mbew·lloor	Open/Closed
Ka vende	ka ven·de	Rooms Available
Nuk ka vende	nook ka ven·de	No Vacancies
Informacion	een·for·ma·tsee·on	Information
Rajoni i policisë	ra·yo·nee ee po·lee·tsee·suh	Police Station
E ndaluar	e nda·loo·ar	Prohibited
Banjat	ba·nyat	Toilets
Burra	boo·rra	Men
Gra	gra	Women
Nxehtë/Ftohtë	ndzeh·tuh/ftoh·tuh	Hot/Cold

accommodation

finding accommodation

Where's a ...?	Ku ka një ...?	koo ka nyuh ...
camping ground	vend kampimi	vend kam·pee·mee
guesthouse	bujtinë	booy·tee·nuh
hotel	hotel	ho·tel
youth hostel	fjetore për të rinj	fye·to·re puhr tuh reeny

Can you	A mund të më	a moond tuh muh
recommend	rekomandoni	re·ko·man·do·nee
somewhere ...?	një vend ...?	nyuh vend ...
cheap	të lirë	tuh lee·ruh
good	të mirë	tuh mee·ruh
nearby	këtu afër	kuh·too a·fuhr

I'd like to book a room, please.
Dua të rezervoj një dhomë,
ju lutem.

doo·a tuh re·zer·voy nyuh dho·muh
yoo loo·tem

I have a reservation.
Kam bërë rezervim.

kam buh·ruh re·zer·veem

My name is ...
Unë quhem ...

oo·nuh choo·hem ...

accommodation – ALBANIAN

23

Do you have a ... room?	A keni një dhomë ...?	a ke·nee nyuh dho·muh ...
single	teke	te·ke
double	dopjo	dop·yo
twin	dyshe	dew·she

How much is it per ...?	Sa kushton për një ...?	sa koosh·ton puhr nyuh ...
night	natë	na·tuh
person	njeri	nye·ree

Can I pay ...?	A mund të paguaj me ...?	a moond tuh pa·goo·ai me ...
by credit card	kartë krediti	kar·tuh kre·dee·tee
with a travellers cheque	çek udhëtimi	chek oo·dhuh·tee·mee

I'd like to stay for (two) nights.
Dua të qëndroj (dy) net.   doo·a tuh chuhn·droy (dew) net

From (2 July) to (6 July).
Nga (dy korriku) deri më (gjashtë korrik).   nga (dew ko·rree·koo) de·ree muh (dyash·tuh ko·rreek)

Can I see it?
A mund ta shoh?   a moond ta shoh

Am I allowed to camp here?
A mund të bëj kampim këtu?   a moond tuh buhy kam·peem kuh·too

Is there a camp site nearby?
A ka vend kampimi këtu afër?   a ka vend kam·pee·mee kuh·too a·fuhr

requests & queries

When/Where is breakfast served?
Kur/Ku shërbehet mëngjesi?   koor/koo shuhr·be·het muhn·dye·see

Please wake me at (seven).
Më zgjoni në orën (shtatë), ju lutem.   muh zdyo·nee nuh o·ruhn (shta·tuh) yoo loo·tem

Could I have my key, please?
Dua çelësin, ju lutem.   doo·a che·luh·seen yoo loo·tem

Can I get another (blanket)?
A mund të më jepni një (batanije) tjetër?   a moond tuh muh yep·nee nyuh (ba·ta·nee·ye) tye·tuhr

Is there a/an ...?	A ka ...?	a ka ...
elevator	ashensor	a·shen·*sor*
safe	kasafortë	ka·sa·*for*·tuh

The room is too ...	Dhoma është shumë e ...	*dho*·ma *uhsh*·tuh *shoo*·muh e ...
expensive	shtrenjtë	shtreny·tuh
noisy	zhurmshme	zhoorm·shme
small	vogël	vo·guhl

The ... doesn't work.	Është prishur ...	*uhsh*·tuh *pree*·shoor ...
air conditioning	ajri i kondicionuar	*ai*·ree ee kon·*dee*·tsee·o·noo·ar
fan	ventilatori	ven·tee·la·*to*·ree
toilet	banja	*ba*·nya

This ... isn't clean.	Ky ... nuk është i pastër.	kew ... nook *uhsh*·tuh ee *pas*·tuhr
pillow	jastëk	yas·*tuhk*
sheet	çarçaf	char·*chaf*
towel	peshqir	pesh·*cheer*

checking out

What time is checkout?
Në çfarë ore është çrregjistrimi?
nuh *chfa*·ruh *o*·re *uhsh*·tuh chrre·dyees·*tree*·mee

Can I leave my luggage here?
A mund t'i lë valixhet këtu?
a moond tee luh va·*lee*·dyet kuh·*too*

Could I have my ..., please?	A mund të më jepni ..., ju lutem?	a moond tuh muh *yep*·nee ... yoo *loo*·tem
deposit	paratë e depozituara	pa·*ra*·tuh e de·po·zee·*too*·a·ra
passport	pasaportën	pa·sa·*por*·tuhn
valuables	gjërat e mia	dyuh·rat e *mee*·a

communications & banking

the internet

Where's the local Internet café?
Ku është qendra lokale koo *uhsh*-tuh *chen*-dra lo-*ka*-le
e internetit? e een-*ter*-ne-teet

How much is it per hour?
Sa kushton për një orë? sa koosh-*ton* puhr nyuh *o*-ruh

I'd like to ... *Dua të ...* *doo*-a tuh ...
   check my email *kontrolloj postën* kon-tro-*lloy pos*-tuhn
          time elektronike *tee*-me e-lek-tro-*nee*-ke
   get Internet access *futem në internet* *foo*-tem nuh een-*ter*-net
   use a printer *përdor një printer* puhr-*dor* nyuh *preen*-ter
   use a scanner *përdor një skaner* puhr-*dor* nyuh *ska*-ner

mobile/cell phone

I'd like a mobile/cell phone for hire.
Dua të marr me qira një *doo*-a tuh marr me qee-*ra* nyuh
telefon celular. te-le-*fon* tse-loo-*lar*

I'd like a SIM card for your network.
Dua të blej një kartë SIM *doo*-a tuh bley nyuh *kar*-tuh seem
për rrjetin tuaj. puhr *rrye*-teen *too*-ai

What are the rates?
Sa është tarifa? sa *uhsh*-tuh ta-*ree*-fa

telephone

What's your phone number?
Sa e ke numrin e telefonit? sa e ke *noom*-reen e te-le-*fo*-neet

The number is ...
Numri është ... *noom*-ree *uhsh*-tuh ...

Where's the nearest public phone?
Ku ka telefon publik këtu afër? koo ka te-le-*fon* poob-*leek* kuh-*too a*-fuhr

I'd like to buy a phonecard.
Dua të blej një kartë telefonike. *doo*-a tuh bley nyuh *kar*-tuh te-le-fo-*nee*-ke

I want to ...	Dua të ...	doo·a tuh ...
call (Singapore)	telefonoj (Singaporin)	te·le·fo·noy (seen·ga·po·reen)
make a local call	bëj një telefonatë lokale	buhy nyuh te·le·fo·na·tuh lo·ka·le
reverse the charges	anuloj tarifat	a·noo·loy ta·ree·fat

How much does a (three)-minute call cost?

Sa kushtojnë (tri) minuta në telefon?

sa koosh·toy·nuh (tree) mee·noo·ta nuh te·le·fon

How much does each extra minute cost?

Sa kushton çdo minutë shtesë?

sa koosh·ton chdo mee·noo·tuh shte·suh

(100) lek per minute.

(Njëqind) lekë minuta.

(nya·cheend) le·kuh mee·noo·ta

post office

I want to send a ...	Dua të dërgoj një ...	doo·a tuh duhr·goy nyuh ...
fax	faks	faks
letter	letër	le·tuhr
parcel	pako	pa·ko
postcard	kartolinë	kar·to·lee·nuh

I want to buy a/an ...	Dua të blej një ...	doo·a tuh bley nyuh ...
envelope	zarf	zarf
stamp	pullë	poo·lluh

Please send it (to Australia) by ...	Ju lutem dërgojeni (në Australi) me ...	yoo loo·tem duhr·go·ye·nee (nuh a·oos·tra·lee) me ...
airmail	postë ajrore	pos·tuh ai·ro·re
express mail	postë ekspres	pos·tuh eks·pres
registered mail	letër rekomande	le·tuhr re·ko·man·de
surface mail	postë të rregullt	pos·tuh tuh rre·goollt

Is there any mail for me?

A më ka ardhur ndonjë letër?

a muh ka ar·dhoor ndo·nyuh le·tuhr

bank

Where's a/an ...?	Ku ka një ...?	koo ka nyuh ...
automated teller machine	makinë automatike për të holla	ma·*kee*·nuh a·oo·to·ma·*tee*·ke puhr tuh *ho*·lla
foreign exchange office	zyrë për këmbim valute	*zew*·ruh puhr kuhm·*beem* va·*loo*·te

I'd like to ...	Dua të ...	*doo*·a tuh ...
Where can I ...?	Ku mund të ...?	koo moond tuh ...
arrange a transfer	të bëj një transferim	tuh buhy nyuh trans·fe·*reem*
cash a cheque	thyej një çek	*thew*·ey nyuh chek
change a travellers cheque	thyej një çek udhëtimi	*thew*·ey nyuh chek oo·dhuh·*tee*·mee
change money	këmbej valutën	kuhm·*bey* va·*loo*·tuhn
get a cash advance	marr para në avancë	marr pa·*ra* nuh a·*van*·tsuh
withdraw money	bëj tërheqje parash	buhy tuhr·*hech*·ye pa·*rash*

What's the ...?	Sa është ...?	sa *uhsh*·tuh ...
charge for that	tarifa për këtë	ta·*ree*·fa puhr kuh·*tuh*
commission	komisioni	ko·mee·see·*o*·nee
exchange rate	kursi i këmbimit	*koor*·see ee kuhm·*bee*·meet

It's ...	Është ...	*uhsh*·tuh ...
(12) lek	(dymbëdhjetë) lekë	(dewm·buh·*dhye*·tuh) *le*·kuh
free	falas	*fa*·las

What time does the bank open?

Në ç'orë hapet banka? nuh *cho*·ruh *ha*·pet *ban*·ka

Has my money arrived yet?

A kanë mbërritur paratë e mia? a *ka*·nuh mbuh·*rree*·toor pa·*ra*·tuh e *mee*·a

sightseeing

getting in

What time does it open/close?
Në ç' orë hapet/mbyllet?
nuh *cho*·ruh ha·pet/*mbew*·llet

What's the admission charge?
Sa kushton bileta e hyrjes?
sa koosh·*ton* bee·*le*·ta e *hewr*·yes

Is there a discount for students/children?
A bëni zbritje për
studentët/fëmijët?
a *buh*·nee *zbree*·tye puhr
stoo·*den*·tuht/fuh·*mee*·yuht

I'd like a ...	*Desha një ...*	*de*·sha nyuh ...
catalogue	*broshurë*	bro·*shoo*·ruh
guide	*manual*	ma·noo·*al*
local map	*hartë lokale*	*har*·tuh lo·*ka*·le

I'd like to see ...	*Dua të shikoj ...*	*doo*·a tuh shee·*koy* ...
What's that?	*Ç'është ajo?*	*chuhsh*·tuh *a*·yo
Can I take a photo?	*A mund të bëj*	a moond tuh buhy
	fotografi?	fo·to·gra·*fee*

tours

When's the next ...?	*Kur është ...?*	koor *uhsh*·tuh ...
day trip	*udhëtimi tjetër*	oo·dhuh·*tee*·mee *tye*·tuhr
	ditor	dee·*tor*
tour	*udhëtimi tjetër*	oo·dhuh·*tee*·mee *tye*·tuhr
	turistik	too·rees·*teek*

Is ... included?	*A përfshihet ...?*	a puhr·*fshee*·het ...
accommodation	*fjetja*	*fye*·tya
the admission	*tarifa e*	ta·*ree*·fa e
charge	*regjistrimit*	re·dyees·*tree*·meet
food	*ushqimi*	oosh·*chee*·mee
transport	*transporti*	trans·*por*·tee

How long is the tour?
Sa zgjat udhëtimi turistik?
sa zdyat oo·dhuh·*tee*·mee too·rees·*teek*

What time should we be back?
Në ç'orë duhet të kthehemi?
nuh *cho*·ruh *doo*·het tuh *kthe*·he·mee

sightseeing

castle	*kështjellë* f	kuhsh·*tye*·lluh
church	*kishë* f	*kee*·shuh
main square	*shesh kryesor* m	shesh krew·e·*sor*
monastery	*manastir* m	ma·nas·*teer*
monument	*monument* m	mo·noo·*ment*
mosque	*xhami* f	dya·*mee*
museum	*muze* m	moo·*ze*
old city	*qyteti i vjetër* m	chew·*tet* ee *vye*·tuhr
ruins	*rrënoja* f	rruh·*no*·ya
stadium	*stadium* m	sta·dee·*oom*
statue	*statujë* f	sta·*too*·yuh

shopping

enquiries

Where's a ... ?	*Ku është ...?*	koo uhsh·tuh ...
bank	*banka*	*ban*·ka
bookshop	*libraria*	lee·bra·*ree*·a
camera shop	*dyqani i aparatëve*	dew·*cha*·nee e a·pa·*ra*·tuh·ve
	fotografikë	fo·to·gra·*fee*·kuh
department store	*dyqani i veshjeve*	dew·*cha*·nee ee *vesh*·ye·ve
grocery store	*ushqimorja*	oosh·chee·*mor*·ya
market	*tregu*	*tre*·goo
newsagency	*agjencia e lajmeve*	a·dyen·*tsee*·a e *lai*·me·ve
supermarket	*supermarketi*	soo·per·*mar*·ke·tee

Where can I buy (a padlock)?
Ku mund të blej (një dry)?   koo moond tuh bley (nyuh drew)

I'm looking for ...
Po kërkoj për ...   po kuhr·*koy* puhr ...

Can I look at it?
Ta shikoj pak?   ta shee·*koy* pak

Do you have any others?
A keni të tjera?   a *ke*·nee tuh *tye*·ra

Does it have a guarantee?
A ka garanci? — a ka ga·ran·*tsee*

Can I have it sent abroad?
A mund ta dërgoj jashtë shtetit? — a moond ta duhr·*goy* yash·tuh shte·teet

Can I have my ... repaired?
A mund të ma riparoni ...? — a moond tuh ma ree·pa·*ro*·nee ...

It's faulty.
Është prishur. — uhsh·tuh *pree*·shoor

I'd like ..., please.	*Desha ..., ju lutem.*	de·sha ... yoo *loo*·tem
a bag	*një çantë*	nyuh *chan*·tuh
a refund	*kthim të parave*	ktheem tuh pa·*ra*·ve
to return this	*ta kthej këtë*	ta kthey kuh·*tuh*

paying

How much is it?
Sa kushton? — sa koosh·*ton*

Can you write down the price?
A mund ta shkruani çmimin? — a moond ta *shkroo*·a·nee *chmee*·meen

That's too expensive.
Është shumë shtrenjtë. — uhsh·tuh *shoo*·muh *shtreny*·tuh

What's your lowest price?
*Cili është çmimi më i
ulët që ofroni?* — *tsee*·lee uhsh·tuh *chmee*·mee muh ee
oo·luht chuh o·*fro*·nee

I'll give you (five) lek.
Do t'ju jap (pesë) lekë. — do tyoo yap (*pe*·suh) *le*·kuh

There's a mistake in the bill.
Është gabim fatura. — uhsh·tuh ga·*beem* fa·*too*·ra

Do you accept ...?	*A pranoni ...?*	a pra·*no*·nee ...
credit cards	*karta krediti*	*kar*·ta kre·*dee*·tee
debit cards	*karta debitore*	*kar*·ta de·bee·*to*·re
travellers cheques	*çeqe udhëtimi*	*che*·che oo·dhuh·*tee*·mee

I'd like ..., please.	*Dua ..., ju lutem.*	*doo*·a ... yoo *loo*·tem
a receipt	*një faturë*	nyuh fa·*too*·ruh
my change	*kusurin*	koo·*soo*·reen

clothes & shoes

Can I try it on?	*A mund ta provoj?*	a moond ta pro-*voy*
My size is (40).	*Numri im është (dyzet).*	*noom*-ree eem *uhsh*-tuh (dew-*zet*)
It doesn't fit.	*Nuk më nxë.*	nook muh ndzuh
small	*e vogël*	e *vo*-guhl
medium	*mesatare*	me-sa-*ta*-re
large	*e madh*	e *ma*-dhe

books & music

I'd like a ...	*Dua një ...*	*doo*-a nyuh ...
newspaper	*gazetë*	ga-*ze*-tuh
(in English)	*(në anglisht)*	(nuh an-*gleesht*)
pen	*stilolaps*	stee-lo-*laps*

Is there an English-language bookshop?	*A ka ndonjë librari të gjuhës angleze?*	a ka *ndo*-nyuh lee-bra-*ree* tuh *dyoo*-huhs an-*gle*-ze
Can I listen to this?	*A mund ta dëgjoj këtë?*	a moond ta duh-*dyoy* kuh-*tuh*

photography

Can you ...?	*A mund ...?*	a moond ...
burn a CD from my memory card	*të djeg një CD nga karta ime e memorjes*	tuh *dee*-eg nyuh tsuh duh nga *kar*-ta ee-me e me-mor-*yes*
develop this film	*ta laj këtë film*	ta lai kuh-*tuh* feelm
load my film	*fus filmin*	foos *feel*-meen

I need a ... film for this camera.	*Më duhet një film ... për këtë aparat fotografik.*	muh *doo*-het nyuh feelm ... puhr kuh-*tuh* a-pa-*rat* fo-to-gra-*feek*
colour	*me ngjyra*	me *ndyew*-ra
slide	*diapozitiv*	dee-a-po-zee-*teev*
(200) speed	*me shpejtësi (dyqind)*	me shpey-tuh-*see* (dew-*cheend*)

When will it be ready?	*Kur do të jetë gati?*	koor do tuh *ye*-tuh *ga*-tee

meeting people

greetings, goodbyes & introductions

Hello.	Tungjatjeta.	toon·dya·*tye*·ta
Hi.	Ç'kemi.	chke·mee
Good night.	Natën e mirë.	na·tuhn e *mee*·ruh
Goodbye/Bye.	Mirupafshim.	mee·roo·*paf*·sheem
See you later.	Shihemi më vonë.	shee·*he*·mee muh *vo*·nuh
Mr	Zotëri	zo·tuh·*ree*
Mrs	Zonjë	zo·nyuh
Miss	Zonjushë	zo·*nyoo*·shuh
How are you?	Si jeni/je? pol/inf	see ye·nee/ye
Fine, thanks.	Mirë, faleminderit.	mee·ruh fa·le·meen·*de*·reet
And you?	Po ju/ti? pol/inf	po yoo/tee
What's your name?	Si quheni?	see *choo*·he·nee
My name is ...	Unë quhem ...	oo·nuh *choo*·hem ...
I'm pleased to	Gëzohem që u	guh·*zo*·hem chuh oo
meet you.	njohëm.	*nyo*·huhm
This is my ...	Ky është ...	kew *uhsh*·tuh ...
boyfriend	i dashuri im	ee *da*·shoo·ree eem
brother	vëllai im	vuh·*lla*·ee eem
daughter	vajza ime	*vai*·za ee·me
father	babai im	ba·*ba*·ee eem
friend	shoku im m	*sho*·koo eem
	shoqja ime f	*sho*·chya ee·me
girlfriend	e dashura ime	e *da*·shoo·ra ee·me
husband	burri im	*boo*·rree eem
mother	nëna ime	*nuh*·na ee·me
partner (intimate)	partneri im m	part·*ne*·ree eem
	partnerja ime f	part·*ne*·rya ee·me
sister	motra ime	*mot*·ra ee·me
son	djali im	*dia*·lee eem
wife	gruaja ime	*groo*·a·ya ee·me
Here's my ...	Ja ...	ya ...
address	adresa ime	ad·*re*·sa ee·me
email address	adresa ime e	ad·*re*·sa ee·me e
	emailit	ee·*mey*·leet

What's your ...?	Cila është ...?	tsee-la uhsh-tuh ...
address	adresa juaj	ad-re-sa yoo-ai
email address	adresa juaj e emailit	ad-re-sa yoo-ai e ee-mey-leet

Here's my ...	Ja ...	ya ...
fax number	numri im i faksit	noom-ree eem ee fak-seet
phone number	numri im i telefonit	noom-ree eem ee te-le-fo-neet

What's your ...?	Cili është ...?	tsee-lee uhsh-tuh ...
fax number	numri juaj i faksit	noom-ree yoo-ai ee fak-seet
phone number	numri juaj i telefonit	noom-ree yoo-ai ee te-le-fo-neet

occupations

What's your occupation?	Ç' punë bëni?	chpoo-nuh buh-nee

I'm a/an ...	Jam ...	yam ...
artist	artist/artiste m/f	ar-teest/ar-tees-te
businessperson	biznesmen m	beez-nes-men
	biznesmene f	beez-nes-me-ne
manual worker	punëtor/punëtore m/f	poo-nuh-tor/poo-nuh-to-re
office worker	nëpunës m	nuh-poo-nuhs
	nëpunëse f	nuh-poo-nuh-se
student	student/studente m/f	stoo-dent/stoo-den-te
tradesperson	tregtar/tregtare m/f	treg-tar/treg-ta-re

background

Where are you from?	Nga jeni?	nga ye-nee

I'm from ...	Jam nga ...	yam nga ...
Australia	Australia	a-oos-tra-lee-a
Canada	Kanadaja	ka-na-da-ya
England	Anglia	an-glee-a
New Zealand	Zelanda e Re	ze-lan-da e re
the USA	Shtetet e Bashkuara	shte-tet e bash-koo-a-ra

Are you married?	A jeni i martuar? m	a ye-nee ee mar-too-ar
	A je e martuar? f	a ye e mar-too-ar
I'm married.	Jam i/e martuar. m/f	yam ee/e mar-too-ar
I'm single.	Jam beqar/beqare. m/f	yam be-char/be-cha-re

age

How old ...?	Sa vjeç ...?	sa vyech ...
are you	jeni/je pol/inf	ye·nee/ye
is your daughter	është vajza	uhsh·tuh vai·za
	juaj/jote pol/inf	yoo·ai/yo·te
is your son	djali juaj/yt pol/inf	dia·lee yoo·ai/ewt

I'm ... years old.
Jam ... vjeç. yam ... vyech

He/She is ... years old.
Ai/Ajo është ... vjeç. a·ee/a·yo uhsh·tuh ... vyech

feelings

I'm (not) ...	(Nuk) Kam ...	(nook) kam ...
Are you ...?	Po ju a keni ...?	po yoo a ke·nee ...
cold	ftohtë	ftoh·tuh
hot	vapë	va·puh
hungry	uri	oo·ree
thirsty	etje	et·ye

I'm (not) ...	(Nuk) Jam ...	(nook) yam ...
Are you ...?	Po ju a jeni ...?	po yoo a ye·nee ...
happy	i/e gëzuar m/f	ee/e guh·zoo·ar
OK	mirë	mee·ruh
sad	i/e mërzitur m/f	ee/e muhr·zee·toor
tired	i/e lodhur m/f	ee/e lo·dhoor

entertainment

going out

Where can I find ...?	Ku mund të gjej ...?	koo moond tuh dyey ...
clubs	një klub	nyuh kloob
gay venues	vendtakim për	vend·ta·keem puhr
	homoseksualë	ho·mo·sek·soo·a·luh
pubs	një bar	nyuh bar

I feel like going	Dua të shkoj në . . .	doo·a tuh shkoy nuh . . .
to a/the . . .		
concert	koncert	kon·tsert
movies	kinema	kee·ne·ma
restaurant	restorant	res·to·rant
theatre	teatër	te·a·tuhr

interests

Do you like . . .?	A ju pëlqen . . .?	a yoo puhl·chen . . .
I (don't) like . . .	(Nuk) Më pëlqen . . .	(nook) muh puhl·chen . . .
art	arti	ar·tee
cooking	gatimi	ga·tee·mee
movies	kinemaja	kee·ne·ma·ya
reading	leximi	le·dzee·mee
sport	sporti	spor·tee
travelling	udhëtimi	oo·dhuh·tee·mee

Do you like to . . .?	A ju pëlqen të . . .?	a yoo puhl·chen tuh . . .
dance	vallëzoni	va·lluh·zo·nee
go to concerts	shkoni në koncerte	shko·nee nuh kon·tser·te
listen to music	dëgjoni muzikë	duh·dyo·nee moo·zee·kuh

food & drink

finding a place to eat

Can you	A mund të më	a moond tuh muh
recommend a . . .?	rekomandoni një . . .?	re·ko·man·do·nee nyuh . . .
bar	bar	bar
café	kafene	ka·fe·ne
restaurant	restorant	res·to·rant

I'd like . . ., please.	Dua . . ., ju lutem.	doo·a . . . yoo loo·tem
a table for (four)	një tavolinë për	nyuh ta·vo·lee·nuh puhr
	(katër veta)	(ka·tuhr ve·ta)
the nonsmoking	një vend ku	nyuh vend koo
section	ndalohet duhani	nda·lo·het doo·ha·nee
the smoking	një vend ku	nyuh vend koo
section	lejohet duhani	le·yo·het doo·ha·nee

ordering food

breakfast	mëngjes m	muhn-dyes
lunch	drekë f	dre-kuh
dinner	darkë f	dar-kuh
snack	zemër f	ze-muhr

| What would you recommend? | Çfarë më rekomandoni? | chfa-ruh muh re-ko-man-do-nee |

I'd like (the) ..., please.	Më silni ..., ju lutem.	muh seell-nee ... yoo loo-tem
bill	faturën	fa-too-ruhn
drink list	listën e pijeve	lees-tuhn e pee-ye-ve
menu	menunë	me-noo-nuh
that dish	atë gjellën	a-tuh dye-lluhn

drinks

(cup of) coffee/tea ...	(filxhan) kafe/çaj ...	(feel-dyan) ka-fe/chai ...
with milk	me qumësht	me choo-muhsht
without sugar	pa sheqer	pa she-cher

| (orange) juice | lëng (portokalli) m | luhng (por-to-ka-llee) |
| soft drink | pije joalkolike f | pee-ye yo-al-koo-lee-ke |

... water	ujë ...	oo-yuh ...
boiled	i valuar	ee va-loo-ar
mineral	gline mineral	glee-ne mee-ne-ral

in the bar

I'll have ...	Dua ...	doo-a ...
I'll buy you a drink.	Do t'ju/të të qeras me një pije. pol/inf	do tyoo/tuh tuh che-ras me nyuh pee-ye
What would you like?	Çfarë dëshironi?	chfa-ruh duh-shee-ro-nee
Cheers!	Gëzuar!	guh-zoo-ar

a bottle/glass of beer	një shishe/gotë birrë	nyuh shee-she/go-tuh bee-rruh
cocktail	koktej m	kok-tey
cognac	konjak m	ko-nyak
a shot of (whisky)	një gllënjkë (uiski)	nyuh glluhny-kuh (oo-ees-kee)

a bottle/glass	një shishe/gotë	nyuh shee·she/go·tuh
of ... wine	verë ...	ve·ruh ...
red	të kuqe	tuh koo·che
sparkling	me shkumë	me shkoo·muh
white	të bardhë	tuh bar·dhuh

self-catering

What's the local speciality?
Cili është specialiteti vendas?   tsee·lee uhsh·tuh spe·tsee·a·lee·te·tee ven·das

How much is (a kilo of cheese)?
Sa kushton (një kilogram djathë)?   sa koosh·ton (nyuh kee·lo·gram dia·thuh)

I'd like ...	Dua ...	doo·a ...
(100) grams	(njëqind) gram	(nyuh·cheend) gram
(two) kilos	(dy) kile	(dew) kee·le
(three) pieces	(tri) copa	(tree) tso·pa
(six) slices	(gjashtë) feta	(dyash·tuh) fe·ta

Less.	Më pak.	muh pak
Enough.	Mjaft.	myaft
More.	Më shumë.	muh shoo·muh

special diets & allergies

Is there a vegetarian restaurant near here?
A ka ndonjë restorant   a ka ndo·nyuh res·to·rant
vegjetarian këtu afër?   ve·dye·ta·ree·an kuh·too a·fuhr

Could you prepare	A mund të përgatisni	a moond tuh puhr·ga·tees·nee
a meal without ...?	një gjellë pa ...?	nyuh dye·lluh pa ...
butter	gjalpë	dyal·puh
eggs	vezë	ve·zuh
meat stock	lëng mishi	luhng mee·shee

I'm allergic to ...	Kam alergji ndaj ...	kam a·ler·dyee ndai ...
dairy produce	bulmetrave	bool·me·tra·ve
gluten	glutenit	gloo·te·neet
MSG	msg-së	muh·suh·guh·suh
nuts	arrave	a·rra·ve
seafood	prodhimeve të detit	pro·dhee·me·ve tuh de·teet

menu decoder

burani f	boo·ra·*nee*	dish of spinach, rice & other greens
byrek m	bew·*rek*	filo pastry stuffed with cheese or spinach
çomlek m	chom·*lek*	meat & onion stew
djathë i fërguar m	*dia*·thuh ee fuhr·*goo*·ar	fried cheese
dollma me lakër f	doll·*ma* me *la*·kuhr	stuffed cabbage leaves
fërgesë f	fuhr·*ge*·suh	rich beef stew with cheese
fërgesë Tirane f	fuhr·*ge*·suh tee·*ra*·ne	dish of offal, eggs & tomatoes
filetë peshku me arra f	fee·*le*·tuh *pesh*·koo me *a*·rra	fish fillet with nuts
gjel deti m	dyel *de*·tee	turkey
hallvë f	*hall*·vuh	dessert with fried almonds in syrup
jani me fasule f	ya·*nee* me fa·*soo*·le	thick bean soup
japrakë me mish m pl	ya·*pra*·kuh me meesh	vine leaves stuffed with meat & rice
kadaif m	ka·da·*eef*	pastry soaked in sugar syrup & flavoured with nuts
kukurec m	koo·koo·*rets*	roasted entrails of sheep or goat
kurabie f	koo·ra·*bee*·e	oval-shaped biscuits
lakror misri m	lak·*ror* mees·ree	corn pie
midhje në verë të bardhë f pl	*mee*·dhye nuh *ve*·ruh tuh *bar*·dhuh	mussels in white wine
mish qingji m	meesh *cheen*·dyee	fried veal with walnuts
musaka me patate f	moo·sa·*ka* me pa·*ta*·te	potato casserole
omëletë me djathë f	om·*le*·tuh me *dia*·thuh	cheese omelette
paidhaqe f	pai·*dha*·che	grilled lamb ribs
pastiço me djathë f	pas·*tee*·cho me *dia*·thuh	pie with noodles, cheese, eggs & meat

patate të skuqura f pl	pa-*ta*-te tuh skoo-choo-ra	*fried potatoes*
patëllxhane të mbushura m pl	pa-tuhll-*dya*-ne tuh mboo-shoo-ra	*stuffed eggplants*
peshk i pjekur m	peshk ee *pye*-koor	*grilled fish*
petulla me kos f pl	pe-too-lla me kos	*pancakes with yogurt*
pulë e pjekur me oriz f	poo-luh e *pye*-koor me o-*reez*	*fried chicken with rice*
pulë me arra f	poo-luh me *a*-rra	*fried chicken with walnuts*
qefull i furrës m	*che*-fooll ee *foo*-rruhs	*baked mullet*
qofte f	*chof*-te	*meatballs*
romstek m	rom-*stek*	*mincemeat patties*
rosto me salcë kosi f	*ros*-to me *sal*-tsuh *ko*-see	*roast beef with sour cream*
sallatë me fasule f	sa-*lla*-tuh me fa-*soo*-le	*bean salad*
shishqebap m	sheesh-che-*bap*	*grilled meat on a skewer*
speca të mbushur m pl	*spe*-tsa tuh mboo-shoor	*stuffed peppers*
spinaq me kos m	spee-*nach* me kos	*spinach with yogurt*
supë me barishte f	soo-puh me ba-*reesh*-te	*vegetable soup*
supë me patate e lakër f	soo-puh me pa-*ta*-te e *la*-kuhr	*potato & cabbage soup*
tarator m	ta-ra-*tor*	*yogurt & cucumber salad*
tavë Elbasani f	*ta*-vuh el-ba-*sa*-nee	*baked lamb with yogurt, eggs & rice*
tavë kosi f	*ta*-vuh *ko*-see	*baked lamb with yogurt*
tavë me peshk f	*ta*-vuh me peshk	*fish casserole*
tavë me presh f	*ta*-vuh me presh	*baked leeks with ground meat*
turli perimesh m pl	toor-*lee* pe-*ree*-mesh	*sautéed vegetables (potatoes, tomatoes, eggplant & peppers)*

emergencies

basics

Help!	Ndihmë!	ndeeh-muh
Stop!	Ndal!	ndal
Go away!	Ik!	eek
Thief!	Hajdut!	hai-doot
Fire!	Zjarr!	zyarr
Watch out!	Kujdes!	kooy-des

Call ...!	Thirrni ...!	theerr-nee ...
a doctor	doktorin	dok-to-reen
an ambulance	ambulancën	am-boo-lan-tsuhn
the police	policinë	po-lee-tsee-nuh

It's an emergency!
Është urgjente! — uhsh-tuh oor-dyen-te

Could you help me, please?
A mund të më ndihmoni, ju lutem? — a moond tuh muh ndeeh-mo-nee yoo loo-tem

I have to use the telephone.
Më duhet të përdor telefonin. — muh doo-het tuh puhr-dor te-le-fo-neen

I'm lost.
Kam humbur rrugën. — kam hoom-boor rroo-guhn

Where are the toilets?
Ku janë banjat? — koo ya-nuh ba-nyat

police

Where's the police station?
Ku është rajoni i policisë? — koo uhsh-tuh ra-yo-nee ee po-lee-tsee-suh

I want to report an offence.
Dua të bëj një denoncim. — doo-a tuh buh-ee nyuh de-non-tseem

I have insurance.
Kam sigurim. — kam see-goo-reem

I've been ...	Më kanë ...	muh ka-nuh ...
assaulted	sulmuar	sool-moo-ar
raped	përdhunuar	puhr-dhoo-noo-ar
robbed	plaçkitur	plach-kee-toor

I've lost my ...	*Kam humbur ...*	kam *hoom*-boor ...
My ... was/were stolen.	*Ma/M'i vodhën ...* sg/pl	ma/mee *vo*-dhuhn ...
backpack	*çantën e shpinës* sg	chan-tuhn e *shpee*-nuhs
bags	*çantat* pl	chan-tat
credit card	*kartën e kreditit* sg	*kar*-tuhn e kre-*dee*-teet
handbag	*çantën e dorës* sg	*chan*-tuhn e *do*-ruhs
jewellery	*bizhuteritë* pl	bee-zhoo-te-*ree*-tuh
money	*paratë* pl	pa-*ra*-tuh
passport	*pasaportën* sg	pa-sa-*por*-tuhn
travellers cheques	*çeqet e*	*che*-chet e
	udhëtimit pl	oo-dhuh-*tee*-meet
wallet	*kuletën* sg	koo-*le*-tuhn

I want to contact my ...	*Dua të lidhem me ... time.*	doo-a tuh lee-dhem me ... *tee*-me
consulate	*konsullatën*	kon-soo-*lla*-tuhn
embassy	*ambasadën*	am-ba-*sa*-duhn

health

medical needs

Where's the nearest ...?	*Ku është ... më i afërt?*	koo *uhsh*-tuh ... muh ee *a*-fuhrt
dentist	*dentisti*	den-*tees*-tee
doctor	*doktori*	dok-*to*-ree
hospital	*spitali*	spee-*ta*-lee
(night)	*farmacisti*	far-ma-*tsees*-tee
pharmacist	*(i natës)*	(ee *na*-tuhs)

I need a doctor (who speaks English).
Kam nevojë për një mjek
(që flet anglisht).
kam ne-*vo*-yuh puhr nyuh myek
(chuh flet an-*gleesht*)

Could I see a female doctor?
A mund të vizitohem te
një mjeke?
a moond tuh vee-zee-*to*-hem te
nyuh *mye*-ke

I've run out of my medication.
Më është mbaruar ilaçi.
muh *uhsh*-tuh mba-*roo*-ar ee-*la*-chee

symptoms, conditions & allergies

| I'm sick. | Jam i/e sëmurë. m/f | yam ee/e suh·*moo*·ruh |
| It hurts here. | Më dhemb këtu. | muh dhemb kuh·*too* |

I have (a) ...		
asthma	Jam me azëm.	yam me *a*·zuhm
bronchitis	Jam me bronkit.	yam me bron·*keet*
constipation	Jam bërë kaps.	yam *buh*·ruh kaps
cough	Jam me kollë.	yam me *ko*·lluh
diarrhoea	Më shkon bark.	muh shkon bark
fever	Kam temperaturë.	kam tem·pe·ra·*too*·ruh
headache	Kam dhimbje koke.	kam *dheem*·bye *ko*·ke
heart condition	Jam me zemër.	yam me ze·*muhr*
nausea	Më përzihet.	muh puhr·*zee*·het
pain	Kam dhimbje.	kam *dheem*·bye
sore throat	Më dhembin grykët.	muh *dhem*·been *grew*·kuht
toothache	Më dhemb dhëmbi.	muh dhemb *dhuhm*·bee

I'm allergic to ...	Kam alergji ndaj ...	kam a·ler·*dyee* ndaj ...
antibiotics	antibiotikëve	an·tee·bee·o·*tee*·kuh·ve
anti-inflammatories	ilaçeve	ee·*la*·che·ve
	antipezmatuese	an·tee·pez·ma·*too*·e·se
aspirin	aspirinës	as·pee·*ree*·nuhs
bees	bletëve	*ble*·tuh·ve
codeine	kodinës	ko·*dee*·nuhs
penicillin	penicilinës	pe·nee·tsee·*lee*·nuhs

antiseptic	antiseptik m	an·tee·sep·*teek*
bandage	fasho f	*fa*·sho
condoms	prezervativ m	pre·zer·va·*teev*
contraceptives	kontraceptiv m	kon·tra·tsep·*teev*
diarrhoea medicine	ilaç për diarrenë m	ee·*lach* puhr dee·a·*rre*·nuh
insect repellent	ilaç insektlargues m	ee·*lach* een·sekt·lar·*goo*·es
laxatives	laksativ m	lak·sa·*teev*
painkillers	ilaç kundër dhimbjes m	ee·*lach* koon·duhr *dheem*·byes
rehydration salts	kripëra rihidruese f pl	kree·*puh*·ra ree·hee·*droo*·e·se
sleeping tablets	hape gjumi f pl	*ha*·pe *dyoo*·mee

english–albanian dictionary

Albanian nouns in this dictionary have their gender indicated by ⓜ (masculine) or ⓕ (feminine). If it's a plural noun, you'll also see pl. Adjectives are given in the masculine form only. Words are also marked as a (adjective), v (verb), sg (singular), pl (plural), inf (informal) or pol (polite) where necessary.

A

accident *aksident* ⓜ ak-see-dent
accommodation *vend për të fjetur* ⓜ vend puhr tuh fye-toor
adaptor *adaptor* ⓜ a-dap-tor
address *adresë* ⓕ ad-re-suh
after *pas* pas
air-conditioned *me ajër të kondicionuar* me a-yuhr tuh kon-dee-tsee-o-noo-ar
airplane *aeroplan* ⓜ a-e-ro-plan
airport *aeroport* ⓜ a-e-ro-port
Albania *Shqipëri* ⓕ shchee-puh-ree
Albanian (language) *gjuha shqipe* ⓕ dyoo-ha shchee-pe
Albanian a *shqip* shcheep
alcohol *alkool* ⓜ al-kol
all *gjithë* dyee-thuh
allergy *alergji* ⓕ a-ler-dyee
ambulance *ambulancë* ⓕ am-boo-lan-tsuh
and *dhe* dhe
ankle *thembër* ⓕ them-buhr
arm *krah* ⓜ krah
ashtray *tavëll duhani* ⓕ ta-vuhll doo-ha-nee
ATM *makinë automatike për të holla* ⓕ ma-kee-nuh a-oo-to-ma-tee-ke puhr tuh ho-lla

B

baby *bebe* ⓕ be-be
back (body) *shpinë* ⓕ shpee-nuh
backpack *çantë shpine* ⓕ chan-tuh shpee-ne
bad *keq* kech
bag *çantë* ⓕ chan-tuh
baggage claim *tërheqje e bagazhit* ⓕ tuhr-hech-ye e ba-ga-zheet
bank *bankë* ⓕ ban-kuh
bar *bar* ⓜ bar
bathroom *banjë* ⓕ ba-nyuh
battery *bateri* ⓕ ba-te-ree
beautiful *i bukur* ee buh-koor
bed *krevat* ⓜ kre-vat
beer *birrë* ⓕ bee-rruh

before *përpara* puhr-pa-ra
behind *mbrapa* mbra-pa
bicycle *biçikletë* ⓕ bee-chee-kle-tuh
big *i madh* ee madh
bill *faturë* ⓕ fa-too-ruh
black *i zi* ee zee
blanket *batanije* ⓕ ba-ta-nee-ye
blood group *grup gjaku* ⓜ groop dya-koo
blue *blu* bloo
boat *anije* ⓕ a-nee-ye
book (make a reservation) v *rezervoj* re-zer-voy
bottle *shishe* ⓕ shee-she
bottle opener *hapës shishesh* ⓕ ha-puhs shee-shesh
boy *djalë* ⓜ dia-luh
brakes (car) *frena* ⓕ pl fre-na
breakfast *mëngjes* ⓜ muhn-dyes
broken (faulty) *i prishur* ee pree-shoor
bus *autobus* ⓜ a-oo-to-boos
business *biznes* ⓜ beez-nes
buy *blej* bley

C

café *kafene* ⓕ ka-fe-ne
camera *aparat fotografik* ⓜ a-pa-rat fo-to-gra-feek
camp site *vend kampimi* ⓜ vend kam-pee-mee
cancel *anuloj* a-noo-loy
can opener *hapës konservash* ⓕ ha-puhs kon-ser-vash
car *makinë* ⓕ ma-kee-nuh
cash *të holla* ⓕ pl tuh ho-lla
cash (a cheque) v *thyej (një çek)* thew-ey (nyuh chek)
cell phone *telefon celular* ⓜ te-le-fon tse-loo-lar
centre *qendër* ⓕ chen-duhr
change (money) v *këmbej (para)* kuhm-bey (pa-ra)
cheap *i lirë* ee lee-ruh
check (bill) *faturë* ⓕ fa-too-ruh
check-in *regjistrohem* re-dyees-tro-hem
chest *kraharor* ⓜ kra-ha-ror
child *fëmijë* ⓕ fuh-mee-yuh
cigarette *cigare* ⓕ tsee-ga-re
city *qytet* ⓜ chew-tet
clean a *i pastër* ee pas-tuhr

A

DICTIONARY

44

closed *mbyllur* mbew-lloor
coffee *kafe* ① ka-fe
coins *monedha* ① pl mo-*ne*-dha
cold a *i ftohtë* ee ftoh-tuh
collect call *telefonatë e paguar nga marrësi* ①
te-le-fo-*na*-tuh e pa-*goo*-ar nga *ma*-rruh-see
come *vij* veey
computer *kompjuter* ⓜ kom-*pyoo*-ter
condom *prezervativ* ⓜ pre-zer-va-*teev*
contact lenses *lente kontakti* ① pl len-*te* kon-*tak*-tee
cook v *gatuaj* ga-too-ai
cost *kosto* kos-*to*
credit card *kartë krediti* ① *kar*-tuh kre-*dee*-tee
cup *gotë* ① *go*-tuh
currency exchange *këmbim valute* ⓜ
kuhm-*beem* va-*loo*-te
customs (immigration) *doganë* ① do-*ga*-nuh

D

dangerous *i rrezikshëm* ee rre-zeek-shuhm
date (time) *datë* ① *da*-tuh
day *ditë* ① *dee*-tuh
delay *vonesë* ① vo-ne-suh
dentist *dentist* ⓜ den-*teest*
depart *nisem* nee-sem
diaper *pelenë* ① pe-*le*-nuh
dictionary *fjalor* ⓜ fya-*lor*
dinner *darkë* ① *dar*-kuh
direct *drejt* dee-*rekt*
dirty *i pistë* ee pees-*tuh*
disabled *invalid* een-va-*leed*
discount *zbritje* ① zbree-tye
doctor *doktor* ⓜ dok-*tor*
double bed *krevat dopjo* ⓜ kre-*vat* dop-yo
double room *dhomë dopjo* ① *dho*-muh dop-yo
drink *pije* ① *pee*-ye
drive v *i jap makinës* ee yap ma-kee-nuhs
drivers licence *patentë shoferi* ① pa-*ten*-tuh sho-*fe*-ree
drug (illicit) *drogë* ① *dro*-guh
dummy (pacifier) *biberon* ① bee-be-*ron*

E

ear *vesh* ⓜ vesh
east *lindje* ① leen-dye
eat *ha* ha
economy class *klasë ekonomike* ①
kla-suh e-ko-no-*mee*-ke
electricity *elektricitet* ⓜ e-lek-tree-tsee-*tet*
elevator *ashensor* ⓜ a-shen-*sor*

email *email • postë elektronike*
ee-meyl • *pos*-tuh e-lek-tro-*nee*-ke
embassy *ambasadë* ① am-ba-*sa*-duh
emergency *urgjencë* ① oor-*dyen*-tsuh
English (language) *anglisht* ang-*leesht*
entrance *hyrje* ① hewr-ye
evening *mbrëmje* ① mbruhm-ye
exchange rate *kurs këmbimi* ⓜ koors kuhm-*bee*-mee
exit *dalje* ① dal-ye
expensive *i shtrenjtë* ee shtreny-tuh
express mail *postë ekspres* ① *pos*-tuh eks-*pres*
eye *sy* ⓜ sew

F

far *larg* larg
fast *shpejt* shpeyt
father *baba* ⓜ ba-*ba*
film (camera) *film* ⓜ feelm
finger *gisht* ⓜ geesht
first-aid kit *kuti e ndihmës së shpejtë* ①
koo-*tee* e ndeeh-muhs suh shpey-tuh
first class *klas i parë* ⓜ klas ee *pa*-ruh
fish *peshk* ⓜpeshk
food *ushqim* ⓜ oosh-*cheem*
foot *këmbë* ① *kuhm*-buh
fork *pirun* ⓜ pee-*roon*
free (of charge) *falas* fa-las
friend *shok/shoqe* ⓜ/① shok/*sho*-che
fruit *frutë* ① *froo*-tuh
full *plot* plot
funny *për të qeshur* puhr tuh *che*-shoor

G

gift *dhuratë* ① dhoo-*ra*-tuh
girl *vajzë* ① vai-zuh
glass (drinking) *gotë* ① *go*-tuh
glasses *syze* ① pl *sew*-ze
go *shkoj* shkoy
good *mirë* mee-ruh
green *jeshil* ye-*sheel*
guide *shoqërues* ⓜ sho-chuh-roo-es

H

half *gjysmë* ① dyews-muh
hand *dorë* ① do-ruh
handbag *çantë dore* ① chan-tuh do-re
happy *i gëzuar* ee guh-*zoo*-ar
have *kam* kam

he *ai* a-ee
head *kokë* ① ko-kuh
heart *zemër* ③ ze-muhr
heat *nxehtësi* ① ndzeh-tuh-*see*
heavy *i rëndë* ee *ruhn*-duh
help v *ndihmoj* ndeeh-*moy*
here *këtu* kuh-*too*
high *lart* lart
highway *rrugë kryesore automobilistike* ①
  rroo-guh krew-e-*so*-re a-oo-to-mo-bee-lees-*tee*-ke
hike v *eci në natyrë* e-tsee nuh na-*tew*-ruh
holiday *pushime* ⑩ pl poo-*shee*-me
homosexual *homoseksual* ho-mo-sek-soo-*al*
hospital *spital* ⑩ spee-*tal*
hot *i nxehtë* ee ndzeh-tuh
hotel *hotel* ⑩ ho-*tel*
hungry *i uritur* ee oo-ree-toor
husband *burrë* ⑩ boo-*rruh*

I

I *unë* oo-nuh
identification (card) *kartë identifikimi* ①
  kar-tuh ee-den-tee-fee-kee-mee
ill *i sëmurë* ee suh-*moo*-ruh
important *i rëndësishëm* ee ruhn-duh-see-shuhm
included *përfshihet* puhr-fshee-het
injury *lëndim* ⑩ luhn-*deem*
insurance *sigurim* ⑩ see-goo-*reem*
Internet *internet* ⑩ een-ter-*net*
interpreter *përkthyes* ⑩ puhr-*kthew*-es

J

jewellery *bizhuteri* ① pl bee-zhoo-te-*ree*
job *punë* ① poo-nuh

K

key *çelës* ⑩ che-luhs
kilogram *kilogram* ⑩ kee-lo-*gram*
kitchen *kuzhinë* ① koo-zhee-nuh
knife *thikë* ① thee-kuh
Kosovo *Kosovë* ① ko-so-vuh

L

laundry (place) *lavanteri* ① la-van-te-*ree*
lawyer *avokat* ⑩ a-vo-*kat*
left (direction) *majtas* mai-tas

left-luggage office *zyra për lënien e valixheve* ①
  zew-ra puhr luh-nee-en e va-lee-dye-ve
leg *këmbë* ① kuhm-buh
lesbian *lezbiane* lez-*bee*-a-ne
less *më pak* muh pak
letter (mail) *letër* ① le-tuhr
lift (elevator) *ashensor* ⑩ a-shen-*sor*
light *dritë* ① dree-tuh
like v *pëlqej* puhl-*chey*
lock *kyç* ⑩ kewch
long *i gjatë* ee dya-tuh
lost *i humbur* ee hoom-boor
lost-property office *zyra e sendeve të humbura* ①
  zew-ra e sen-de-ve tuh *hoom*-boo-ra
love v *dashuroj* da-shoo-*roy*
luggage *valixhe* ① va-lee-dye
lunch *drekë* ① dre-kuh

M

mail *postë* ① pos-tuh
man *burrë* ⑩ boo-rruh
map *hartë* ① har-tuh
market *treg* ⑩ treg
matches *shkrepëse* ① shkre-puh-se
meat *mish* ⑩ meesh
medicine *ilaç* ee-*lach*
menu *menu* ① me-*noo*
message *mesazh* ⑩ me-*sazh*
milk *qumësht* ① choo-muhsht
minute *minutë* ① mee-noo-tuh
mobile phone *telefon celular* ⑩ te-le-*fon* tse-loo-*lar*
money *para* ① pa-*ra*
month *muaj* ⑩ moo-ai
morning *mëngjes* ⑩ muhn-*dyes*
mother *nënë* ① nuh-nuh
motorcycle *motor* ⑩ mo-*tor*
motorway *autostradë* ① a-oo-tos-*tra*-duh
mouth *gojë* ① go-yuh
music *muzikë* ① moo-zee-kuh

N

name *emër* ⑩ e-muhr
napkin *pecetë* ① pe-*tse*-tuh
nappy *pelenë* ① pe-*le*-nuh
near *afër* a-fuhr
neck *qafë* ① cha-fuh
new *i ri* ee ree
news *lajm* ⑩ laim
newspaper *gazetë* ① ga-ze-tuh

night *natë* ① *na*-tuh
no *jo* yo
noisy *i zhurmshëm* ee zhoorm-shuhm
nonsmoking *ku ndalohet duhani*
   koo nda-*lo*-het doo-*ha*-nee
north *veri* ⓜ ve-*ree*
nose *hundë* ① *hoon*-duh
now *tani* ta-*nee*
number *numër* ⓜ *noo*-muhr

O

oil (engine) *vaj* ⓜ vai
old *i vjetër* ee vye-tuhr
one-way ticket *biletë vetëm për vajtje* ①
   bee-*le*-tuh ve-tuhm puhr *vai*-tye
open a *i hapur* ee ha-poor
outside *jashtë* yash-tuh

P

package *pako* ① *pa*-ko
paper *letër* ① *le*-tuhr
park (car) v *parkoj* par-*koy*
passport *pasaportë* ① pa-sa-*por*-tuh
pay *paguaj* pa-*goo*-ai
pen *stilolaps* ⓜ stee-lo-*laps*
petrol *benzinë* ① ben-*zee*-nuh
pharmacy *farmaci* ① far-ma-*tsee*
phonecard *kartë telefonike* ① *kar*-tuh te-le-fo-*nee*-ke
photo *fotografi* ① fo-to-gra-*fee*
plate *pjatë* ① *pya*-tuh
police *polici* ① po-lee-*tsee*
postcard *kartolinë* ① *kar*-to-*lee*-nuh
post office *postë* ① *pos*-tuh
pregnant *shtatzënë* shtat-*zuh*-nuh
price *çmim* ⓜ chmeem

Q

quiet *i qetë* i *che*-tuh

R

rain *shi* ⓜ shee
razor *brisk* ⓜ breesk
receipt *faturë* ① fa-*too*-ruh
red *i kuq* ee kooch
refund *kthim parash* ① ktheem pa-*rash*
registered mail *letër rekomande* ①
   le-tuhr re-ko-man-*de*

rent v *marr me qira* marr me *chee*-ra
repair v *riparoj* ree-pa-*roy*
reservation *rezervim* ① re-zer-*veem*
restaurant *restorant* ⓜ res-to-*rant*
return v *kthej* kthey
return ticket *biletë kthimi* ① bee-*le*-tuh *kthee*-mee
right (direction) *djathtas* diath-*tas*
road *rrugë* ① *rroo*-guh
room *dhomë* ① *dho*-muh

S

safe a *i sigurt* ee *see*-goort
sanitary napkin *pecetë higjienike* ①
   pe-*tse*-tuh hee-dyee-e-*nee*-ke
seat *vend* ⓜ vend
send *dërgoj* duhr-*goy*
service station *pikë karburanti* ①
   pee-kuh kar-boo-*ran*-tee
sex *seks* ⓜ seks
shampoo *shampo* ① *sham*-po
share (a dorm) *marr (dhomë) bashkë*
   marr (*dho*-muh) *bash*-kuh
shaving cream *pastë rroje* ① *pas*-tuh *rro*-ye
she *ajo* a-yo
sheet (bed) *çarçaf* ⓜ char-*chaf*
shirt *këmishë* ① kuh-*mee*-shuh
shoes *këpucë* ① kuh-*poo*-tsuh
shop *dyqan* ⓜ dew-*chan*
short *i shkurtër* ee *shkoor*-tuhr
shower *dush* ⓜ doosh
single room *dhomë teke* ① *dho*-muh *te*-ke
skin *lëkurë* ① luh-*koo*-ruh
skirt *fund* ⓜ foond
sleep v *fle* fle
slowly *me ngadalë* me nga-*da*-luh
small *i vogël* ee *vo*-guhl
smoke (cigarettes) v *pij cigare* peey tsee-*ga*-re
soap *sapun* ⓜ *sa*-poon
some *disa* dee-*sa*
soon *së shpejti* suh *shpey*-tee
south *jug* ⓜ yoog
souvenir shop *dyqan suvenireshn* ⓜ
   dew-*chan* soo-ve-nee-*resh*
speak *flas* flas
spoon *lugë* ① *loo*-guh
stamp *pullë* ① *poo*-lluh
stand-by ticket *biletë rezervë* ① bee-*le*-tuh re-zer-*vuh*
station (train) *stacion (treni)* ⓜ sta-*tsee*-on (*tre*-nee)
stomach *stomak* ⓜ sto-*mak*
stop v *ndaloj* nda-*loy*

(bus) stop *stacion (autobusi)* ⓜ
sta-tsee-*on* (a-oo-to-*boo*-see)
street *rrugë* ① *rroo*-guh
student *student/studente* ⓜ/① stoo-*dent*/stoo-*den*-te
sun *diell* ⓜ dee-*ell*
sunscreen *krem mbrojtës* ⓜ krem *mbroy*-tuhs
swim v *notoj* no-*toy*

T

tampons *tampona* ① pl tam-*po*-na
taxi *taksi* ① tak-*see*
teaspoon *lugë çaji* ① *loo*-guh cha-yee
teeth *dhëmbë* ⓜ pl *dhuhm*-buh
telephone *telefon* ⓜ te-le-*fon*
television *televizor* ⓜ te-le-vee-*zor*
temperature (weather) *temperaturë* ①
tem-pe-ra-*too*-ruh
tent *çadër* ① *cha*-duhr
that (one) *atë* a-*tuh*
they *ata* a-*ta*
thirsty *i etur* ee *e*-toor
this (one) *këtë* kuh-*tuh*
throat *grykë* ① *grew*-kuh
ticket *biletë* ① bee-*le*-tuh
time *kohë* ① *ko*-huh
tired *i lodhur* ee lo-*dhoor*
tissues *shami letre* ① sha-*mee* le-tre
today *sot* sot
toilet *banjë* ① *ba*-nyuh
tomorrow *nesër* ne-*suhr*
tonight *sonte* *son*-te
toothbrush *furçë dhëmbësh* ① *foor*-chuh *dhuhm*-buhsh
toothpaste *pastë dhëmbësh* ① *pas*-tuh *dhuhm*-buhsh
torch (flashlight) *elektrik dore* ① e-lek-*treek* do-re
tour *vizitë* ① vee-*zee*-tuh
tourist office *zyrë turistike* ① *zew*-ruh too-rees-*tee*-ke
towel *peshqir* ① pesh-*cheer*
train *tren* ① tren
translate *përkthej* puhr-*kthey*
travel agency *agjenci udhëtimi* ①
a-dyen-*tsee* oo-dhuh-*tee*-mee
travellers cheque *çek udhëtimi* ⓜ
chek oo-dhuh-*tee*-mee
trousers *pantallona* ① pl pan-ta-*llo*-na
twin beds *krevatë dyshë* ⓜ pl kre-va-*tuh* *dew*-shuh
tyre *gomë* ① *go*-muh

U

underwear ① pl *mbathje* mba-*thye*
urgent *urgjent* oor-*dyent*

V

vacant *bosh* bosh
vacation *pushime* ① pl poo-*shee*-me
vegetable *zarzavate* ① zar-za-*va*-te
vegetarian a *vegjetarian* ve-dye-ta-ree-*an*
visa *vizë* ① *vee*-zuh

W

waiter *kamarier* ka-ma-*ree*-er
walk v *eci* e-*tsee*
wallet *kuletë* ① koo-*le*-tuh
warm a *i ngrohtë* ee ngroh-*tuh*
wash (something) *laj* lai
watch *orë dore* ① o-*ruh* do-re
water *ujë* ⓜ *oo*-yuh
we *ne* ne
weekend *fundjavë* ① *foond*-ya-vuh
west *perëndim* pe-ruhn-*deem*
wheelchair *karrocë invalidi* ① ka-*rro*-tsuh een-va-*lee*-dee
when *kur* koor
where *ku* koo
white *i bardhë* ee *bar*-dhuh
who *kush* koosh
why *pse* pse
wife *grua* ① *groo*-a
window *dritare* ① dree-*ta*-re
wine *verë* ① *ve*-ruh
with *me* me
without *pa* pa
woman *grua* ① *groo*-a
write *shkruaj* shkroo-*ai*

Y

yellow *i verdhë* ee *ver*-dhuh
yes *po* po
yesterday *dje* dee-*e*
you sg inf *ti* tee
you sg pol & pl *ju* yoo

Croatian

croatian & serbian alphabets

croatian	serbian	croatian	serbian	croatian	serbian	croatian	serbian
A a a	А а	*E e* e	Е е	*Lj lj* l'	Љ љ	*Š š* sh	Ш ш
B b be	Б б	*F f* ef	Ф ф	*M m* em	М м	*T t* te	Т т
C c tse	Ц ц	*G g* ge	Г г	*N n* en	Н н	*U u* u	У у
Č č tch	Ч ч	*H h* ha	Х х	*Nj nj* n'	Њ њ	*V v* ve	В в
Ć ć ch	Ћ ћ	*I i* i	И и	*O o* o	О о	*Z z* zed	З з
D d de	Д д	*J j* y	Ј ј	*P p* pe	П п	*Ž ž* zh	Ж ж
Dž dž dzh	Џ џ	*K k* ka	К к	*R r* er	Р р		
Đ đ j	Ђ ђ	*L l* el	Л л	*S s* es	С с		

croatian/serbian

HRVATSKI

introduction

Did you know that the words *Dalmatian* and *cravat* come from Croatian (*hrvatski* hr·vat·ski), which is also referred to as Serbo-Croatian? Linguists commonly refer to the varieties spoken in Croatia, Bosnia-Hercegovina, Montenegro and Serbia with the umbrella term 'Serbo-Croatian' while acknowledging dialectical differences between them. Croats, Serbs, Bosnians and Montenegrins themselves generally maintain that they speak different languages, however – a reflection of their desire to retain separate ethnic identities.

As the language of about 5 million people in one of the world's newest countries, Croatian has an intriguing, cosmopolitan and at times fraught history. Its linguistic ancestor was brought to the region in the sixth and seventh centuries AD by the South Slavs, who may have crossed the Danube from the area now known as Poland. This ancestral language split off into two branches: East South Slavic, which later evolved into Bulgarian and Macedonian, and West South Slavic, of which Slovene, Serbian and Croatian are all descendants.

Croatia may be a peaceful country today but the Balkan region to which it belongs has a long history of invasion and conflict. These upheavals have enriched and politicised the language. The invasion by Charlemagne's armies and the conversion of Croats to the Roman Church in AD 803 left its mark on Croatian in the form of words borrowed from Latin and the adoption of the Latin alphabet rather than the Cyrillic alphabet (with which Serbian is written). Subsequent invasions by the Hapsburg, Ottoman and Venetian empires added vibrancy to the language through an influx of German, Turkish and Venetian dialect words. Many words from the standard Italian of Croatia's neighbour Italy have also been absorbed.

The good news is that if you venture into Serbia, Bosnia or Montenegro, you'll be able to enrich your travel experience there by using this chapter. In case of the most common differences between Croatian and Serbian, both translations are given and indicated with ©/Ⓢ. The Cyrillic alphabet (used alternatively with the Latin alphabet in Serbia, Bosnia and Montenegro) is also included on the page opposite. Croatian is a handy lingua franca in any of the other states that made up part of the former Yugoslavia, as it's an official language in Bosnia-Hercegovina as well as Montenegro (along with Serbian and Bosnian) and people in Macedonia and Slovenia, who speak closely related languages, generally understand Croatian. In other words (often heard throughout this region) – *nema problema* ne·ma pro·ble·ma (no problem)!

pronunciation

vowel sounds

In written Croatian, vowels that appear next to each other don't run together as in English. When you see two or more vowels written next to each other in a Croatian word, pronounce them separately.

symbol	english equivalent	croatian example	transliteration
a	father	*zdravo*	zdra·vo
ai	aisle	*ajvar*	ai·var
e	bet	*pet*	pet
i	hit	*sidro*	si·dro
o	pot	*brod*	brod
oy	toy	*tvoj*	tvoy
u	put	*skupo*	sku·po

word stress

As a general rule, in two-syllable words in Croatian stress usually falls on the first syllable. In words of three or more syllables, stress may fall on any syllable except the last. In our pronunciation guides, the stressed syllable is italicised.

Croatian also has what's known as 'pitch accent'. A stressed vowel may have either a rising or a falling pitch and be long or short. The combination of stress, pitch and vowel length in a given syllable occasionally affects the meaning of a word, but you don't need to worry about reproducing this feature of Croatian and we haven't indicated it in this book. In the few cases where it's important, it should be clear from the context what's meant. You may notice though that the speech of native speakers has an appealing musical lilt to it.

consonant sounds

Croatian consonant sounds all have close equivalents in English. The rolled r sound can be pronounced in combination with other consonants as a separate syllable – eg *Hrvat* hr·vat (Croat). If the syllables without vowels look a bit intimidating, try inserting a slight 'uh' sound before the r to help them run off your tongue more easily.

symbol	english equivalent	croatian example	transliteration
b	bed	*glazba*	glaz·ba
ch	cheat	*četiri, ćuk*	che·ti·ri, chuk
d	dog	*doručak*	do·ru·chak
f	fat	*fotograf*	fo·to·graf
g	go	*jagoda*	ya·go·da
h	hat	*hodnik*	hod·nik
j	joke	*džep, đak*	jep, jak
k	kit	*krov*	krov
l	lot	*lutka*	lut·ka
ly	million	*nedjelja*	ned·ye·lya
m	man	*mozak*	mo·zak
n	not	*nafta*	naf·ta
ny	canyon	*kuhinja*	ku·hi·nya
p	pet	*petak*	pe·tak
r	run (rolled)	*radnik*	rad·nik
s	sun	*sastanak*	sas·ta·nak
sh	shot	*košta*	kosh·ta
t	top	*sat*	sat
ts	hats	*prosinac*	pro·si·nats
v	very	*viza*	vi·za
y	yes	*svjetlost*	svyet·lost
z	zero	*zec*	zets
zh	pleasure	*koža*	ko·zha
'	a slight y sound	*kašalj, siječanj*	ka·shal', si·ye·chan'

basics

language difficulties

Do you speak English?
Govorite/Govoriš li engleski? pol/inf — *go*·vo·ri·te/*go*·vo·rish li *en*·gle·ski

Do you understand?
Da li razumijete/razumiješ? pol/inf — da li ra·*zu*·mi·ye·te/ra·*zu*·mi·yesh

I (don't) understand.
Ja (ne) razumijem. — ya (ne) ra·*zu*·mi·yem

What does (dobro) mean?
Što znači (dobro)? — shto *zna*·chi (*do*·bro)

How do you ...?	*Kako se ...?*	*ka*·ko se ...
pronounce this	*ovo izgovara*	*o*·vo iz·*go*·va·ra
write (*dobro*)	*piše (dobro)*	*pi*·she (*do*·bro)

Could you please ...?	*Možete li ...?* pol	*mo*·zhe·te li ...
	Možeš li ...? inf	*mo*·zhesh li ...
repeat that	*to ponoviti*	to po·*no*·vi·ti
speak more slowly	*govoriti sporije*	go·*vo*·ri·ti *spo*·ri·ye
write it down	*to napisati*	to na·*pi*·sa·ti

essentials		
Yes.	*Da.*	da
No.	*Ne.*	ne
Please.	*Molim.*	*mo*·lim
Thank you	*Hvala vam/ti*	*hva*·la vam/ti
(very much).	*(puno).* pol/inf	(*pu*·no)
You're welcome.	*Nema na čemu.*	*ne*·ma na *che*·mu
Excuse me.	*Oprostite.*	o·*pro*·sti·te
Sorry.	*Žao mi je.*	*zha*·o mi ye

numbers

0	*nula*	nu·la	14	*četrnaest*	che·tr·na·est
1	*jedan* m	ye·dan	15	*petnaest*	pet·na·est
	jedna f	yed·na	16	*šesnaest*	shes·na·est
	jedno n	yed·no	17	*sedamnaest*	se·dam·na·est
2	*dva* m&n	dva	18	*osamnaest*	o·sam·na·est
	dvije f	dvi·ye	19	*devetnaest*	de·vet·na·est
3	*tri*	tri	20	*dvadeset*	dva·de·set
4	*četiri*	che·ti·ri	21	*dvadeset jedan*	dva·de·set ye·dan
5	*pet*	pet	30	*trideset*	tri·de·set
6	*šest*	shest	40	*četrdeset*	che·tr·de·set
7	*sedam*	se·dam	50	*pedeset*	pe·de·set
8	*osam*	o·sam	60	*šezdeset*	shez·de·set
9	*devet*	de·vet	70	*sedamdeset*	se·dam·de·set
10	*deset*	de·set	80	*osamdeset*	o·sam·de·set
11	*jedanaest*	ye·da·na·est	90	*devedeset*	de·ve·de·set
12	*dvanaest*	dva·na·est	100	*sto*	sto
13	*trinaest*	tri·na·est	1000	*tisuću/hiljadu* ©/ⓈⒸ	ti·su·chu/hi·lya·du

time & dates

What time is it?	*Koliko je sati?*	ko·*li*·ko ye *sa*·ti
It's one o'clock.	*Jedan je sat.*	ye·dan je *sa*·t
It's (10) o'clock.	*(Deset) je sati.*	(de·set) ye *sa*·ti
Quarter past (10).	*(Deset) i petnaest.*	(de·set) i *pet*·na·est
Half-past (10).	*(Deset) i po.*	(de·set) i *po*
Quarter to (10).	*Petnaest do (deset).*	*pet*·na·est do (de·set)
At what time?	*U koliko sati?*	u ko·*li*·ko *sa*·ti
At ...	*U ...*	u ...
am	*prijepodne*	pri·ye·*pod*·ne
pm	*popodne*	po·*pod*·ne
Monday	*ponedjeljak*	po·*ne*·dye·lyak
Tuesday	*utorak*	u·to·rak
Wednesday	*srijeda*	sri·*ye*·da
Thursday	*četvrtak*	chet·*vr*·tak
Friday	*petak*	*pe*·tak
Saturday	*subota*	su·bo·ta
Sunday	*nedjelja*	ne·*dye*·lya

basics – CROATIAN

55

January	*siječanj*	*si·ye·chan'*
February	*veljača*	*ve·lya·cha*
March	*ožujak*	*o·zhu·yak*
April	*travanj*	*tra·van'*
May	*svibanj*	*svi·ban'*
June	*lipanj*	*li·pan'*
July	*srpanj*	*sr·pan'*
August	*kolovoz*	*ko·lo·voz*
September	*rujan*	*ru·yan*
October	*listopad*	*li·sto·pad*
November	*studeni*	*stu·de·ni*
December	*prosinac*	*pro·si·nats*

What date is it today?	*Koji je danas datum?*	*ko·yi ye da·nas da·tum*
It's (18 October).	*(Osamnaesti listopad).*	*(o·sam·na·e·sti li·sto·pad)*
since (May)	*od (svibnja)*	od (*svib·nya*)
until (June)	*do (lipnja)*	do (*lip·nya*)
last night	*sinoć*	*si·noch*
last week	*prošlog tjedna* ⓒ	*prosh·log tyed·na*
	prošle nedelje ⓢ	*prosh·le ne·de·lye*
last month	*prošlog mjeseca*	*prosh·log mye·se·tsa*
last year	*prošle godine*	*prosh·le go·di·ne*
next week	*iduću tjedna* ⓒ	*i·du·cheg tyed·na*
	iduće nedelje ⓢ	*i·du·che ne·de·lye*
next month	*iduću mjeseca*	*i·du·cheg mye·se·tsa*
next year	*iduće godine*	*i·du·che go·di·ne*
yesterday/	*jučer/*	*yu·cher/*
tomorrow ...	*sutra ...*	*su·tra ...*
morning	*ujutro*	*u·yu·tro*
afternoon	*popodne*	*po·pod·ne*
evening	*uvečer*	*u·ve·cher*

weather

What's the weather like?	Kakvo je vrijeme?	kak·vo ye vri·ye·me
It's ...	... je.	... ye
cloudy	Oblačno	o·blach·no
cold	Hladno	hlad·no
hot	Vruće	vru·che
raining	Kišovito	ki·sho·vi·to
snowing	Snjegovito	snye·go·vi·to
sunny	Sunčano	sun·cha·no
warm	Toplo	to·plo
windy	Vjetrovito	vye·tro·vi·to
spring	proljeće n	pro·lye·che
summer	ljeto n	lye·to
autumn	jesen f	ye·sen
winter	zima f	zi·ma

border crossing

I'm here ...	Ja sam ovdje ...	ya sam ov·dye ...
in transit	u prolazu	u pro·la·zu
on business	poslovno	po·slov·no
on holiday	na odmoru	na od·mo·ru
I'm here for ...	Ostajem ovdje ...	o·sta·yem ov·dye ...
(10) days	(deset) dana	(de·set) da·na
(two) months	(dva) mjeseca	(dva) mye·se·tsa
(three) weeks	(tri) tjedna ©	(tri) tyed·na
	(tri) nedelje ⑤	(tri) ne·de·lye

I'm going to (Zagreb).
Ja idem u (Zagreb).   ya i·dem u (za·greb)

I'm staying at the (Intercontinental).
Odsjesti ću u (Interkontinentalu).   od·sye·sti chu u (in·ter·kon·ti·nen·ta·lu)

I have nothing to declare.
Nemam ništa za prijaviti.   ne·mam nish·ta za pri·ya·vi·ti

I have something to declare.
Imam nešto za prijaviti.   i·mam nesh·to za pri·ya·vi·ti

That's (not) mine.
To (ni)je moje.   to (ni·)ye mo·ye

transport

tickets & luggage

Where can I buy a ticket?
Gdje mogu kupiti kartu?   gdye *mo*·gu *ku*·pi·ti *kar*·tu

Do I need to book a seat?
Trebam li rezervirati mjesto?   *tre*·bam li re·zer·*vi*·ra·ti *myes*·to

One ... ticket	*Jednu ... kartu*	*yed*·nu ... *kar*·tu
(to Split), please.	*(do Splita), molim.*	(do *spli*·ta) *mo*·lim
one-way	*jednosmjernu*	*yed*·no·smyer·nu
return	*povratnu*	*po*·vrat·nu

I'd like to ... my	*Želio/Željela bih ...*	*zhe*·li·o/*zhe*·lye·la bih ...
ticket, please.	*svoju kartu, molim.* m/f	*svoy*·u *kar*·tu *mo*·lim
cancel	*poništiti*	*po*·ni·shti·ti
change	*promijeniti*	*pro*·mi·ye·ni·ti
collect	*uzeti*	*u*·ze·ti
confirm	*potvrditi*	pot·*vr*·di·ti

I'd like a ...	*Želio/Željela bih ...*	*zhe*·li·o/*zhe*·lye·la bih ...
seat, please.	*sjedište, molim.* m/f	*sye*·dish·te *mo*·lim
nonsmoking	*nepušačko*	*ne*·pu·shach·ko
smoking	*pušačko*	*pu*·shach·ko

How much is it?
Koliko stoji?   ko·*li*·ko *stoy*·i

Is there air conditioning?
Imate li klima-uređaj?   *i*·ma·te li *kli*·ma·u·re·jai

Is there a toilet?
Imate li zahod/toalet? ©/®   *i*·ma·te li *za*·hod/to·a·*let*

How long does the trip take?
Koliko traje putovanje?   ko·*li*·ko *trai*·e pu·to·*va*·nye

Is it a direct route?
Je li to direktan pravac?   ye li to di·*rek*·tan *pra*·vats

Where can I find a luggage locker?
Gdje se nalazi pretinac/sanduče   gdye se *na*·la·zi *pre*·ti·nats/*san*·du·che
za odlaganje prtljage? ©/®   za od·*la*·ga·nye prt·*lya*·ge

My luggage has been ...	Moja prtljaga je ...	moy·a prt·lya·ga ye ...
damaged	oštećena	osh·te·che·na
lost	izgubljena	iz·gub·lye·na
stolen	ukradena	u·kra·de·na

getting around

Where does flight (10) arrive?
Gdje stiže let (deset)?
gdye *sti*·zhe let (*de*·set)

Where does flight (10) depart?
Odakle kreće let (deset)?
o·*dak*·le *kre*·che let (*de*·set)

Where's (the) ...?	Gdje se nalazi ...?	gdye se *na*·la·zi ...
arrivals hall	dvorana za dolaske	dvo·*ra*·na za *do*·las·ke
departures hall	dvorana za odlaske	dvo·*ra*·na za *od*·las·ke
duty-free shop	duty-free	*dyu*·ti·fri
	prodavaonica	pro·da·va·o·ni·tsa
gate (12)	izlaz (dvanaest)	*iz*·laz (*dva*·na·est)

Which ... goes	Koji ... ide	*koy*·i ... *i*·de
to (Dubrovnik)?	za (Dubrovnik)?	za (*du*·brov·nik)?
boat	brod	brod
bus	autobus	a·*u·to*·bus
plane	zrakoplov/avion ©/Ⓢ	zra·ko·plov/a·*vi*·on ©/Ⓢ
train	vlak/voz ©/Ⓢ	vlak/voz

What time's the ... bus?	Kada ide ... autobus?	*ka*·da *i*·de ... a·*u·to*·bus
first	prvi	*pr*·vi
last	zadnji	*zad*·nyi
next	slijedeći	sli·*ye*·de·chi

At what time does it arrive/leave?
U koliko sati stiže/kreće?
u ko·*li*·ko *sa*·ti *sti*·zhe/*kre*·che

How long will it be delayed?
Koliko kasni?
ko·*li*·ko *kas*·ni

What station/stop is this?
Koja stanica je ovo?
koy·a *sta*·ni·tsa ye *o*·vo

What's the next station/stop?
Koja je slijedeća stanica?
koy·a ye sli·*ye*·de·cha *sta*·ni·tsa

Does it stop at (Zadar)?
Da li staje u (Zadru)?
da li *sta*·ye u (*zad*·ru)

Please tell me when we get to (Pula).
   Molim vas recite mi   *mo·lim vas re·tsi·te mi*
   kada stignemo u (Pulu).   *ka·da stig·ne·mo u (pu·lu)*

How long do we stop here?
   Koliko dugo ostajemo ovdje?   ko·li·ko du·go o·stai·e·mo ov·dye

Is this seat available?
   Da li je ovo sjedište slobodno?   da li ye o·vo sye·dish·te slo·bod·no

That's my seat.
   Ovo je moje sjedište.   o·vo ye moy·e sye·dish·te

I'd like a taxi ...	*Trebam taksi ...*	*tre·bam tak·si ...*
at (9am)	*u (devet prijepodne)*	u (de·vet pri·ye·pod·ne)
now	*sada*	sa·da
tomorrow	*sutra*	su·tra

Is this taxi available?
   Da li je ovaj taksi slobodan?   da li ye o·vai tak·si slo·bo·dan

How much is it to ...?
   Koliko stoji prijevoz do ...?   ko·li·ko stoy·i pri·ye·voz do ...

Please put the meter on.
   Molim uključite taksimetar.   mo·lim uk·lyu·chi·te tak·si·me·tar

Please take me to (this address).
   Molim da me odvezete   mo·lim da me od·ve·ze·te
   na (ovu adresu).   na (o·vu a·dre·su)

Please ...	*Molim vas ...*	*mo·lim vas ...*
slow down	*usporite*	u·spo·ri·te
stop here	*stanite ovdje*	sta·ni·te ov·dye
wait here	*pričekajte ovdje*	pri·che·kai·te ov·dye

car, motorbike & bicycle hire

I'd like to	*Želio/Željela*	zhe·li·o/zhe·lye·la
hire a ...	*bih iznajmiti ...* m/f	bih iz·nai·mi·ti ...
bicycle	*bicikl*	bi·tsi·kl
car	*automobil*	a·u·to·mo·bil
motorbike	*motocikl*	mo·to·tsi·kl
with ...	*sa ...*	sa ...
a driver	*vozačem*	vo·za·chem
air conditioning	*klima-uređajem*	kli·ma·u·re·jai·em

How much for ... hire?	Koliko stoji najam po ...?	ko·li·ko stoy·i nai·am po ...
hourly	satu	sa·tu
daily	danu	da·nu
weekly	tjednu/nedelji ©/Ⓢ	tyed·nu/ne·de·lyi

air	zrak/vazduh m ©/Ⓢ	zrak/vaz·duh
oil	ulje n	u·lye
petrol	benzin m	ben·zin
tyres	gume f pl	gu·me

I need a mechanic.
Trebam automehaničara. tre·bam a·u·to·me·ha·ni·cha·ra

I've run out of petrol.
Nestalo mi je benzina. ne·sta·lo mi ye ben·zi·na

I have a flat tyre.
Imam probušenu gumu. i·mam pro·bu·she·nu gu·mu

directions

Where's the ...?	Gdje je ...?	gdye ye ...
bank	banka	ban·ka
city centre	gradski centar	grad·ski tsen·tar
hotel	hotel	ho·tel
market	tržnica/pijaca ©/Ⓢ	trzh·ni·tsa/pi·ya·tsa
police station	policijska stanica	po·li·tsiy·ska sta·ni·tsa
post office	poštanski ured	po·shtan·ski u·red
public toilet	javni zahod/toalet ©/Ⓢ	yav·ni za·hod/to·a·let
tourist office	turistička agencija	tu·ris·tich·ka a·gen·tsi·ya

Is this the road to (Pazin)?
Je li ovo cesta/put za (Pazin)? ©/Ⓢ ye li o·vo tse·sta/put za (pa·zin)

Can you show me (on the map)?
Možete li mi to
pokazati (na karti)? mo·zhe·te li mi to
po·ka·za·ti (na kar·ti)

What's the address?
Koja je adresa? koy·a ye a·dre·sa

How far is it?
Koliko je udaljeno? ko·li·ko ye u·da·lye·no

How do I get there?
Kako mogu tamo stići? ka·ko mo·gu ta·mo sti·chi

Turn ...	Skrenite ...	skre·ni·te ...
at the corner	na uglu	na u·glu
at the traffic lights	na semaforu	na se·ma·fo·ru
left/right	lijevo/desno	li·ye·vo/de·sno

It's ...	Nalazi se ...	na·la·zi se ...
behind ...	iza ...	i·za ...
far away	daleko	da·le·ko
here	ovdje	ov·dye
in front of ...	ispred ...	i·spred ...
left	lijevo	li·ye·vo
near ...	blizu ...	bli·zu ...
next to ...	pored ...	po·red ...
on the corner	na uglu	na u·glu
opposite ...	nasuprot ...	na·su·prot ...
right	desno	de·sno
straight ahead	ravno naprijed	rav·no na·pri·yed
there	tamo	ta·mo

by bus	autobusom	a·u·to·bu·som
by taxi	taksijem	tak·si·yem
by train	vlakom/vozom ©/Ⓢ	vla·kom/vo·zom
on foot	pješke	pyesh·ke

north	sjever m	sye·ver
south	jug m	yug
east	istok m	is·tok
west	zapad m	za·pad

signs

Ulaz/Izlaz	u·laz/iz·laz	**Entrance/Exit**
Otvoreno/Zatvoreno	ot·vo·re·no/zat·vo·re·no	**Open/Closed**
Slobodna Mjesta	slo·bod·na mye·sta	**Rooms Available**
Bez Slobodnih Mjesta	bez slo·bod·nih mye·sta	**No Vacancies**
Informacije	in·for·ma·tsi·ye	**Information**
Policijska Stanica	po·li·tsiy·ska sta·ni·tsa	**Police Station**
Zabranjeno	za·bra·nye·no	**Prohibited**
WC	ve·tse	**Toilets**
Muški	mush·ki	**Men**
Ženski	zhen·ski	**Women**
Toplo/Hladno	to·plo/hlad·no	**Hot/Cold**

accommodation

finding accommodation

Where's a ...?	Gdje se nalazi ...?	gdye se na·la·zi ...
camping ground	kamp	kamp
guesthouse	privatni smještaj	pri·vat·ni smyesh·tai
	za najam	za nai·am
hotel	hotel	ho·tel
youth hostel	prenoćište za	pre·no·chish·te za
	mladež	mla·dezh

Can you recommend	Možete li	mo·zhe·te li
somewhere ...?	preporučiti negdje ...?	pre·po·ru·chi·ti neg·dye ...
cheap	jeftino	yef·ti·no
good	dobro	do·bro
nearby	blizu	bli·zu

I'd like to book a room, please.
Želio/Željela bih rezervirati   zhe·li·o/zhe·lye·la bih re·zer·vi·ra·ti
sobu, molim. m/f   so·bu mo·lim

I have a reservation.
Imam rezervaciju.   i·mam re·zer·va·tsi·yu

My name's ...
Moje ime je ...   moy·e i·me ye ...

Do you have a ...	Imate li ...?	i·ma·te li ...
room?		
single	jednokrevetnu sobu	yed·no·kre·vet·nu so·bu
double	sobu sa duplim	so·bu sa dup·lim
	krevetom	kre·ve·tom
twin	dvokrevetnu sobu	dvo·kre·vet·nu so·bu

How much is it per ...?	Koliko stoji po ...?	ko·li·ko sto·yi po ...
night	noći	no·chi
person	osobi	o·so·bi

Can I pay by ...?	Mogu li platiti sa ...?	mo·gu li pla·ti·ti sa ...
credit card	kreditnom	kre·dit·nom
	karticom	kar·ti·tsom
travellers cheque	putničkim čekom	put·nich·kim che·kom

For (three) nights.
Na (tri) noći.
na (tri) no·chi

From (2 July) to (6 July).
Od (drugog srpnja) do (šestog srpnja).
od (dru·gog srp·nya) do (she·stog srp·nya)

Can I see it?
Mogu li je vidjeti?
mo·gu li ye vi·dye·ti

Am I allowed to camp here?
Mogu li ovdje kampirati?
mo·gu li ov·dye kam·pi·ra·ti

Where can I find the nearest camp site?
Gdje se nalazi najbliže mjesto za kampiranje?
gdye se na·la·zi nai·bli·zhe mye·sto za kam·pi·ra·nye

requests & queries

When/Where is breakfast served?
Kada/Gdje služite doručak?
ka·da/gdye slu·zhi·te do·ru·chak

Please wake me at (seven).
Probudite me u (sedam), molim.
pro·bu·di·te me u (se·dam) mo·lim

Could I have my key, please?
Mogu li dobiti moj ključ, molim?
mo·gu li do·bi·ti moy klyuch mo·lim

Could I have another (blanket)?
Mogu li dobiti jednu dodatnu (deku)?
mo·gu li do·bi·ti yed·nu do·dat·nu (de·ku)

Is there a/an ...?	*Imate li ...?*	i·ma·te li ...
elevator	*dizalo/lift* ©/®	di·za·lo/lift
safe	*sef*	sef
The room is too ...	*Suviše je ...*	su·vi·she ye ...
expensive	*skupo*	sku·po
noisy	*bučno*	buch·no
small	*malo*	ma·lo
The ... doesn't work.	*... je neispravan.*	... ye ne·i·spra·van
air conditioning	*Klima-uređaj*	kli·ma·u·re·jai
fan	*Ventilator*	ven·ti·la·tor

This ... isn't clean.	*Ova ... nije čista.*	o·va ... ni·ye chis·ta
blanket	*deka*	de·ka
sheet	*plahta* ⓒ	plah·ta

This ... isn't clean.	*Ovaj ... nije čist.*	o·va ... ni·ye chist
sheet	*čaršav* Ⓢ	char·shav
towel	*ručnik/peškir* ⓒ/Ⓢ	ruch·nik/pesh·kir

checking out

What time is checkout?
U koliko sati treba napustiti sobu? — u ko·li·ko sa·ti tre·ba na·pu·sti·ti so·bu

Can I leave my luggage here?
Mogu li ovdje ostaviti svoje torbe? — mo·gu li ov·dye o·sta·vi·ti svoy·e tor·be

Could I have	*Mogu li dobiti*	mo·gu li do·bi·ti
my ..., please?	*..., molim?*	... mo·lim
deposit	*svoj depozit*	svoy de·po·zit
passport	*svoju putovnicu/*	svoy·u pu·tov·ni·tsu/
	pasoš ⓒ/Ⓢ	pa·sosh
valuables	*svoje dragocjenosti*	svo·ye dra·go·tsye·no·sti

communications & banking

the internet

Where's the local Internet café?
Gdje je mjesni internet kafić? — gdye ye mye·sni in·ter·net ka·fich

How much is it per hour?
Koja je cijena po satu? — koy·a ye tsi·ye·na po sa·tu

I'd like to ...	*Želio/Željela bih ... m/f*	zhe·li·o/zhe·lye·la bih ...
check my email	*provjeriti svoj email*	pro·vye·ri·ti svoy i·meyl
get Internet access	*pristup internetu*	pri·stup in·ter·ne·tu
use a printer	*koristiti pisač/*	ko·ri·sti·ti pi·sach/
	štampač ⓒ/Ⓢ	shtam·pach
use a scanner	*koristiti skener*	ko·ri·sti·ti ske·ner

mobile/cell phone

I'd like a ...	Trebao/Trebala bih ... m/f	tre·ba·o/tre·ba·la bih ...
mobile/cell phone for hire	iznajmiti mobilni telefon	iz·nai·mi·ti mo·bil·ni te·le·fon
SIM card for your network	SIM karticu za vašu mrežu	sim kar·ti·tsu za va·shu mre·zhu

What are the rates?
Koje su cijene telefoniranja? — ko·ye su tsi·ye·ne te·le·fo·ni·ra·nya

telephone

What's your phone number?
Koji je vaš/tvoj broj telefona? pol/inf — koy·i ye vash/tvoy broy te·le·fo·na

The number is ...
Broj je ... — broy ye ...

Where's the nearest public phone?
Gdje je najbliži javni telefon? — gdye ye nai·bli·zhi yav·ni te·le·fon

I'd like to buy a phonecard.
Želim kupiti telefonsku karticu. — zhe·lim ku·pi·ti te·le·fon·sku kar·ti·tsu

I want to ...	Želim ...	zhe·lim ...
call (Singapore)	nazvati (Singapur)	naz·va·ti (sin·ga·pur)
make a (local) call	obaviti (lokalni) poziv	o·ba·vi·ti (lo·kal·ni) po·ziv
reverse the charges	obaviti poziv na račun pozvanog	o·ba·vi·ti po·ziv na ra·chun poz·va·nog

How much does ... cost?	Koliko košta ...?	ko·li·ko kosh·ta ...
a (three)-minute call	poziv od (tri) minute	po·ziv od (tri) mi·nu·te
each extra minute	svaka naknadna minuta	sva·ka nak·nad·na mi·nu·ta

(3 kuna) per (30) seconds.	(3 kune) po (30) sekundi.	(tri ku·ne) po (tri·de·set) se·kun·di

post office

I want to send a ...	Želim poslati ...	zhe·lim po·sla·ti ...
fax	telefaks	te·le·faks
letter	pismo	pi·smo
parcel	paket	pa·ket
postcard	dopisnicu	do·pi·sni·tsu

I want to buy a/an ...	Želim kupiti ...	zhe·lim ku·pi·ti ...
envelope	omotnicu/koverat ©/®	o·mot·ni·tsu/ko·ve·rat
stamp	poštansku marku	posh·tan·sku mar·ku

Please send it	Molim da pošaljete	mo·lim da po·sha·lye·te
by ... to (Australia).	to ... u (Australiju).	to ... u (a·u·stra·li·yu)
airmail	zračnom/vazdušnom poštom ©/®	zrach·nom/vaz·dush·nom posh·tom
express mail	ekspres poštom	eks·pres posh·tom
registered mail	preporučenom poštom	pre·po·ru·che·nom posh·tom
surface mail	običnom poštom	o·bich·nom posh·tom

Is there any mail for me?
Ima li bilo kakve pošte za mene?   i·ma li bi·lo kak·ve posh·te za me·ne

bank

Where's a/an ...?	Gdje se nalazi ...?	gdye se na·la·zi ...
ATM	bankovni automat	ban·kov·ni a·u·to·mat
foreign exchange office	mjenjačnica za strane valute	mye·nyach·ni·tsa za stra·ne va·lu·te

Where can I ...?	Gdje mogu ...?	gdye mo·gu ...
I'd like to ...	Želio/Željela bih ... m/f	zhe·li·o/zhe·lye·la bih ...
arrange a transfer	obaviti prijenos novca	o·ba·vi·ti pri·ye·nos nov·tsa
cash a cheque	unovčiti ček	u·nov·chi·ti chek
change a travellers cheque	zamijeniti putnički ček	za·mi·ye·ni·ti put·nich·ki chek
change money	zamijeniti novac	za·mi·ye·ni·ti no·vats
get a cash advance	uzeti predujam/avans u gotovini ©/®	u·ze·ti pre·du·yam/a·vans u go·to·vi·ni
withdraw money	podignuti novac	po·dig·nu·ti no·vats

What's the ...?	Koji/Kolika je ...? m/f	koy·i/ko·li·ka ye ...
charge for that	pristojba/tarifa	pri·stoy·ba/ta·ri·fa
	za to f ©/⑤	za to
exchange rate	tečaj/kurs	te·chai/kurs
	razmjene m ©/⑤	raz·mye·ne

It's ...	To je ...	to ye ...
(50) kuna	(pedeset) kuna	(pe·de·set) ku·na
free	besplatno	bes·plat·no

What time does the bank open?
U koliko sati se otvara banka? — u ko·li·ko sa·ti se ot·va·ra ban·ka

Has my money arrived yet?
Da li je moj novac stigao? — da li ye moy no·vats sti·ga·o

sightseeing

getting in

What time does it open/close?
U koliko sati se otvara/zatvara? — u ko·li·ko sa·ti se ot·va·ra/zat·va·ra

What's the admission charge?
Koliko stoji ulaznica? — ko·li·ko stoy·i u·laz·ni·tsa

Is there a discount for students/children?
Imate li popust za — i·ma·te li po·pust za
studente/djecu? — stu·den·te/dye·tsu

I'd like a ...	Želio/Željela bih ... m/f	zhe·li·o/zhe·lye·la bih ...
catalogue	katalog	ka·ta·log
guide	turistički vodič	tu·ri·stich·ki vo·dich
local map	kartu mjesta	kar·tu mye·sta

I'd like to see ...
Želio/Željela bih vidjeti ... m/f — zhe·li·o/zhe·lye·la bih vi·dye·ti ...

What's that?
Što je to? — shto ye to

Can I take a photo?
Mogu li slikati? — mo·gu li sli·ka·ti

tours

When's the next ...?	*Kada je idući/ iduća ...?* m/f	*ka·da ye i·du·chi/ i·du·cha ...*
day trip	*dnevni izlet* m	*dnev·ni iz·let*
tour	*turistička ekskurzija* f	*tu·ri·stich·ka ek·skur·zi·ya*

Is ... included?	*Da li je ... uključen/ uključena?* m/f	*da li ye ... uk·lyu·chen/ uk·lyu·che·na*
accommodation	*smještaj* m	*smye·shtai*
the admission charge	*ulaznica* f	*u·laz·ni·tsa*
food	*hrana* f	*hra·na*
transport	*prijevoz* m	*pri·ye·voz*

How long is the tour?
Koliko traje ekskurzija? ko·*li*·ko trai·e ek·*skur*·zi·ya

What time should we be back?
U koje bi se vrijeme trebali vratiti? u *koy*·e bi se vri·*ye*·me *tre*·ba·li *vra*·ti·ti

sightseeing

castle	*dvorac* m	*dwa*·rats
cathedral	*katedrala* f	ka·te·*dra*·la
church	*crkva* f	*tsr*·kva
main square	*glavni trg* m	*glav*·ni trg
monastery	*samostan/manastir* m ©/⑤	sa·mo·stan/*ma*·nas·tir
monument	*spomenik* m	*spo*·me·nik
museum	*muzej* m	*mu*·zey
old city	*stari grad* m	*sta*·ri grad
palace	*palača* f	*pa*·la·cha
ruins	*ruševine* f pl	*ru*·she·vi·ne
stadium	*stadion* m	*sta*·di·on
statue	*kip* m	kip

shopping

enquiries

Where's a ...?	*Gdje je ...?*	gdye ye ...
bank	*banka*	*ban*·ka
bookshop	*knjižara*	*knyi*·zha·ra
camera shop	*prodavaonica*	pro·da·va·o·ni·tsa
	fotoaparata	*fo*·to·a·pa·*ra*·ta
department store	*robna kuća*	*rob*·na *ku*·cha
grocery store	*prodavaonica*	pro·da·va·o·ni·tsa
	namirnica	na·*mir*·ni·tsa
market	*tržnica/pijaca* ©/Ⓢ	*tr*·zhni·tsa/*pi*·ya·tsa
newsagency	*prodavaonica*	pro·da·va·o·ni·tsa
	novina	*no*·vi·na
supermarket	*supermarket*	*su*·per·*mar*·ket

Where can I buy (a padlock)?
Gdje mogu kupiti (lokot)? gdye *mo*·gu *ku*·pi·ti (*lo*·kot)

I'm looking for ...
Tražim ... tra·zhim

Can I look at it?
Mogu li to pogledati? *mo*·gu li to *po*·gle·da·ti

Do you have any others?
Imate li bilo kakve druge? *i*·ma·te li *bi*·lo *kak*·ve *dru*·ge

Does it have a guarantee?
Ima li ovo garanciju? *i*·ma li o·vo ga·*ran*·tsi·yu

Can I have it sent abroad?
Možete li mi to *mo*·zhe·te li mi to
poslati u inozemstvo? po·*sla*·ti u i·no·*zemst*·vo

Can I have my (backpack) repaired?
Mogu li popraviti svoj (ranac)? *mo*·gu li *po*·pra·vi·ti svoy (*ra*·nats)

It's faulty.
Neispravno je. ne·*is*·prav·no ye

I'd like ..., please.	*Želio/Željela bih ...* m/f	zhe·li·o/zhe·lye·la bih ...
a bag	*vrećicu*	*vre*·chi·tsu
a refund	*povrat novca*	*pov*·rat *nov*·tsa
to return this	*ovo vratiti*	o·vo *vra*·ti·ti

paying

How much is it?
 Koliko stoji/košta? ©/⑤   ko·*li*·ko *sto*·yi/*kosh*·ta

Can you write down the price?
 Možete li napisati cijenu?   *mo*·zhe·te li na·*pi*·sa·ti tsi·*ye*·nu

That's too expensive.
 To je preskupo.   to ye *pre*·sku·po

Do you have something cheaper?
 Imate li nešto jeftinije?   i·ma·te li *nesh*·to yef·*ti*·ni·ye

I'll give you (five kuna).
 Dati ću vam (pet kuna).   *da*·ti chu vam (pet *ku*·na)

There's a mistake in the bill.
 Ima jedna greška na računu.   i·ma *yed*·na *gresh*·ka na ra·*chu*·nu

Do you accept ...?	*Da li prihvaćate ...?*	da li *pri*·hva·cha·te ...
credit cards	*kreditne kartice*	*kre*·dit·ne *kar*·ti·tse
debit cards	*debitne kartice*	*de*·bit·ne *kar*·ti·tse
travellers cheques	*putničke čekove*	*put*·nich·ke *che*·ko·ve

I'd like ..., please.	*Želio/Željela bih ...* **m/f**	zhe·li·o/zhe·lye·la bih ...
a receipt	*račun*	*ra*·chun
my change	*moj ostatak novca*	moy o·*sta*·tak *nov*·tsa

clothes & shoes

Can I try it on?	*Mogu li to probati?*	*mo*·gu li to *pro*·ba·ti
My size is (40).	*Moja veličina je (četrdeset).*	*moy*·a ve·li·*chi*·na ye (che·tr·*de*·set)
It doesn't fit.	*Ne odgovara mi to.*	ne od·*go*·va·ra mi to

small	*sitna*	*sit*·na
medium	*srednja*	*sred*·nya
large	*krupna*	*krup*·na

books & music

I'd like (a) ...	Želio/Željela bih ... m/f	zhe·li·o/zhe·lye·la bih ...
newspaper	novine	no·vi·ne
(in English)	(na engleskom)	(na en·gles·kom)
pen	kemijsku	ke·miy·sku

Is there an English-language bookshop?
Postoji li knjižara za   po·stoy·i li knyi·zha·ra za
engleski jezik?   en·gle·ski ye·zik

I'm looking for something by (Oliver Dragojević).
Tražim nešto od   tra·zhim nesh·to od
(Olivera Dragojevića).   (o·li·ve·ra dra·goy·e·vi·cha)

Can I listen to this?
Mogu li ovo poslušati?   mo·gu li o·vo po·slu·sha·ti

photography

Can you ...?	Možete li ...?	mo·zhe·te li ...
develop this film	razviti ovaj film	raz·vi·ti o·vai film
load my film	staviti moj film	sta·vi·ti moy film
	u foto-aparat	u fo·to·a·pa·rat
transfer photos	prebaciti	pre·ba·tsi·ti
from my	fotografije sa	fo·to·gra·fi·ye sa
camera to CD	mog aparata na CD	mog a·pa·ra·ta na tse de

I need a/an ... film	Trebam ... film	tre·bam ... film
for this camera.	za ovaj foto-aparat.	za o·vai fo·to·a·pa·rat
APS	APS	a pe es
B&W	crno-bijeli	tsr·no·bi·ye·li
colour	kolor	ko·lor

I need a ... film	Trebam film ...	tre·bam film ...
for this camera.	za ovaj foto-aparat.	za o·vai fo·to·a·pa·rat
slide	za dijapozitive	za di·ya·po·zi·ti·ve
(200) speed	brzine (dvijesto)	br·zi·ne (dvi·ye·sto)

When will it	Kada će to biti	ka·da che to bi·ti
be ready?	gotovo?	go·to·vo

meeting people

greetings, goodbyes & introductions

Hello.	*Dobar dan.*	*do·bar dan*
Hi.	*Ćao.*	*cha·o*
Good night.	*Laku noć.*	*la·ku noch*
Goodbye.	*Zbogom.*	*zbo·gom*
Bye.	*Ćao.*	*cha·o*
See you later.	*Doviđenja.*	*do·vi·je·nya*
Mr	*Gospodin*	*go·spo·din*
Mrs	*Gospođa*	*go·spo·ja*
Miss	*Gospođica*	*go·spo·ji·tsa*
How are you?	*Kako ste/si?* pol/inf	*ka·ko ste/si*
Fine. And you?	*Dobro. A vi/ti?* pol/inf	*do·bro a vi/ti*
What's your name?	*Kako se zovete/zoveš?* pol/inf	*ka·ko se zo·ve·te/zo·vesh*
My name is …	*Zovem se …*	*zo·vem se …*
I'm pleased to meet you.	*Drago mi je da smo se upoznali.*	*dra·go mi ye da smo se u·poz·na·li*

This is my …	*Ovo je moj/moja …* m/f	*o·vo ye moy/moy·a …*
boyfriend	*dečko*	*dech·ko*
brother	*brat*	*brat*
daughter	*ćerka*	*cher·ka*
father	*otac*	*o·tats*
friend	*prijatelj/prijateljica* m/f	*pri·ya·tel'/pri·ya·te·lyi·tsa*
girlfriend	*cura/devojka* ©/ⓢ	*tsu·ra/de·voy·ka*
husband	*muž*	*muzh*
mother	*majka*	*mai·ka*
partner (intimate)	*suprug/supruga* m/f	*su·prug/su·pru·ga*
sister	*sestra*	*ses·tra*
son	*sin*	*sin*
wife	*žena*	*zhe·na*

Here's my …	*Ovo je moj/moja …* m/f	*o·vo ye moy/moy·a …*
What's your …?	*Koji je tvoj …?* m	*koy·i ye tvoy …*
	Koja je tvoja …? f	*koy·a ye tvoy·a …*
(email) address	*(email) adresa* f	*(i·meyl) a·dre·sa*
fax number	*broj faksa* m	*broy fak·sa*
phone number	*broj telefona* m	*broy te·le·fo·na*

occupations

What's your occupation?	Čime se bavite?	chi·me se ba·vi·te
I'm a/an ...	Ja sam ...	ya sam ...
artist	umjetnik m	um·yet·nik
	umjetnica f	um·yet·ni·tsa
businessperson	poslovna osoba	po·slo·vna o·so·ba
farmer	poljodjelac ©	po·lyo·dye·lats
	zemljoradnik ⑤	zem·lyo·rad·nik
office worker	službenik m	sluzh·be·nik
	službenica f	sluzh·be·ni·tsa
scientist	znanstvenik ©	znans·tve·nik
	naučnik ⑤	na·uch·nik
tradesperson	zanatlija	za·nat·li·ya

background

Where are you from?	Odakle ste?	o·da·kle ste
I'm from ...	Ja sam iz ...	ya sam iz ...
Australia	Australije	a·u·stra·li·ye
Canada	Kanade	ka·na·de
England	Engleske	en·gles·ke
New Zealand	Novog Zelanda	no·vog ze·lan·da
the USA	Amerike	a·me·ri·ke
Are you married?	Jeste li vi vjenčani?	ye·ste li vi vyen·cha·ni
I'm married.	Ja sam u braku.	ya sam u bra·ku
I'm single.	Ja sam neoženjen. m	ya sam ne·o·zhe·nyen
	Ja sam neudata. f	ya sam ne·u·da·ta

age

How old ...?	Koliko ... godina?	ko·li·ko ... go·di·na
are you	imate/imaš pol/inf	i·ma·te/i·mash
is your daughter	vaša kći ima	va·sha k·chi i·ma
is your son	vaš sin ima	vash sin i·ma
I'm ... years old.	Imam ... godina.	i·mam ... go·di·na
He/She is ... years old.	On/Ona ima ... godina.	on/o·na i·ma ... go·di·na

74

feelings

I'm (not) ...	Ja (ni)sam ...	ya (ni-)sam ...
Are you ...?	Jeste li ...?	ye·ste li ...
happy	sretni	sret·ni
hungry	gladni	glad·ni
OK	dobro	dob·ro
sad	tužni	tuzh·ni
thirsty	žedni	zhed·ni
tired	umorni	u·mor·ni

Are you hot/cold?
Je li vam toplo/hladno?   ye li vam to·plo/hlad·no

I'm (not) hot/cold.
Meni (ni)je toplo/hladno.   me·ni (ni·)ye to·plo/hlad·no

entertainment

going out

Where can	Gdje mogu	gdye mo·gu
I find ...?	pronaći ...?	pro·na·chi ...
clubs	noćne klubove	noch·ne klu·bo·ve
gay venues	gay lokale	gey lo·ka·le
pubs	gostionice	go·sti·o·ni·tse
I feel like going to a/the ...	Želim otići ...	zhe·lim o·ti·chi ...
concert	na koncert	na kon·tsert
movies	u kino/bioskop ©/⑤	u ki·no/bi·os·kop
party	na zabavu	na za·ba·vu
restaurant	u restoran	u re·sto·ran
theatre	u kazalište	u ka·za·lish·te

interests

Do you like ...?	Volite li ...?	vo·li·te li ...
I (don't) like ...	Ja (ne) volim ...	ya (ne) vo·lim ...
art	umjetnost	um·yet·nost
cooking	kuhanje	ku·ha·nye
movies	filmove	fil·mo·ve
reading	čitanje	chi·ta·nye
shopping	kupovanje	ku·po·va·nye
sport	sport	sport
travelling	putovanja	pu·to·va·nya
Do you like to ...?	Da li volite da ...?	da li vo·li·te da ...
dance	plešete	ple·she·te
listen to music	slušate glazbu/	slu·sha·te glaz·bu/
	muziku ©/⑤	mu·zi·ku

food & drink

finding a place to eat

Can you recommend a ...?	Možete li preporučiti neki ...?	mo·zhe·te li pre·po·ru·chi·ti ne·ki ...
bar	bar	bar
café	kafić	ka·fich
restaurant	restoran	re·sto·ran
I'd like ...	Želim ...	zhe·lim ...
a table for (five)	stol za (petoro)	stol za (pe·to·ro)
the (non)smoking section	(ne)pušačko mjesto	(ne·)pu·shach·ko mye·sto

ordering food

breakfast	doručak m	do·ru·chak
lunch	ručak m	ru·chak
dinner	večera f	ve·che·ra
snack	užina f	u·zhi·na
today's special	specijalitet dana m	spe·tsi·ya·li·tet da·na

What would you recommend?	Što biste nam preporučili?	shto *bi*·ste nam pre·po·*ru*·chi·li
I'd like (the) ..., please.	Mogu li dobiti ..., molim?	*mo*·gu li *do*·bi·ti ... *mo*·lim
bill	račun	ra·chun
drink list	cjenik pića	tsye·nik *pi*·cha
menu	jelovnik	ye·*lov*·nik
that dish	ono jelo	o·no ye·lo

drinks

coffee/tea ...	kava/čaj ...	*ka*·va/chai ...
with milk	sa mlijekom	sa mli·*ye*·kom
without sugar	bez šećera	bez she·che·ra
(orange) juice	sok (od naranče) m	sok (od *na*·ran·che)
mineral water	mineralna voda f	*mi*·ne·ral·na vo·da
soft drink	bezalkoholno piće m	be·zal·ko·hol·no *pi*·che
(hot) water	(topla) voda f	(*to*·pla) vo·da

in the bar

I'll have ...	Želim naručiti ...	*zhe*·lim na·*ru*·chi·ti ...
I'll buy you a drink.	Častim vas/te pićem. pol/inf	*cha*·stim vas/te *pi*·chem
What would you like?	Što želite/želiš? pol/inf	shto *zhe*·li·te/*zhe*·lish
Cheers!	Živjeli!	*zhi*·vye·li
brandy	rakija f	*ra*·ki·ya
champagne	šampanjac m	sham·*pa*·nyats
cocktail	koktel m	kok·*tel*
plum brandy	šljivovica f	*shlyi*·vo·vi·tsa
a bottle/glass of beer	boca/čaša piva	*bo*·tsa/*cha*·sha *pi*·va
a shot of (whiskey)	jedna čašica (viskija)	*yed*·na *cha*·shi·tsa (*vi*·ski·ya)
a bottle/glass of ... wine	boca/čaša ... vina	*bo*·tsa/*cha*·sha ... *vi*·na
red	crnog	tsr·nog
sparkling	pjenušavog	pye·*nu*·sha·vog
white	bijelog	bi·*ye*·log

self-catering

What's the local speciality?

Što je ovdje područni/lokalni   shto ye ov·dye po·druch·ni/lo·kal·ni
specijalitet? ⓒ/ⓢ   spe·tsi·ya·li·tet

What's that?

Što je to?   shto ye to

How much is (a kilo of cheese)?

Koliko stoji/košta (kila sira)? ⓒ/ⓢ   ko·li·ko sto·yi/kosh·ta (ki·la si·ra)

I'd like ...   Želim ...   zhe·lim ...
  (200) grams   (dvijesto) grama   (dvi·ye·sto) gra·ma
  (two) kilos   (dvije) kile   (dvi·ye) ki·le
  (three) pieces   (tri) komada   (tri) ko·ma·da
  (six) slices   (šest) krišaka   (shest) kri·sha·ka

Less.   Manje.   ma·nye
Enough.   Dosta.   do·sta
More.   Više.   vi·she

special diets & allergies

Is there a vegetarian restaurant near here?

Da li znate za vegetarijanski   da li zna·te za ve·ge·ta·ri·yan·ski
restoran ovdje blizu?   re·sto·ran ov·dye bli·zu

Do you have vegetarian food?

Da li imate vegetarijanski obrok? da li i·ma·te ve·ge·ta·ri·yan·ski o·brok

Could you prepare a   Možete li prirediti   mo·zhe·te li pri·re·di·ti
meal without ...?   obrok koji ne sadrži ...? o·brok koy·i ne sa·dr·zhi ...
  butter   maslac   ma·slats
  eggs   jaja   yai·a
  meat stock   mesni bujon   mes·ni bu·yon

I'm allergic   Ja sam alergičan/   ya sam a·ler·gi·chan/
to ...   alergična na ... m/f   a·ler·gich·na na ...
  dairy produce   mliječne proizvode   mli·yech·ne pro·iz·vo·de
  gluten   gluten   glu·ten
  MSG   glutaminat   glu·ta·mi·nat
  nuts   razne orahe   raz·ne o·ra·he
  seafood   morske plodove   mor·ske plo·do·ve

menu decoder

baklava f	ba-*kla*-va	pastry with layers of nuts, sugar & cinnamon, soaked in syrup
bečki odrezak m	*bech*-ki o-dre-zak	Wiener schnitzel
burek m	*bu*-rek	flaky pastry stuffed with cheese or meat
čevapčići m pl	che-*vap*-chi-chi	skinless minced beef & lamb sausages
džuveč m	*ju*-vech	tomatoey casserole made from mixed vegetables, pork cutlets & rice
gulaš od divljači m	*gu*-lash od *div*-lya-chi	game goulash
hladetina f	*hla*-de-ti-na	pork brawn with vegetables, boiled eggs, garlic, parsley & paprika
hladni pladanj m	*hlad*-ni *pla*-dan'	cold cuts
janjeća čorba f	*ya*-nye-cha *chor*-ba	lamb stew
janjetina na ražnju f	*ya*-nye-ti-na na *razh*-nyu	lamb cooked on a spit
japraci m pl	ya-*pra*-tsi	mincemeat parcels rolled in vine or silver beet leaves (also called **arambašiči** a-ram-*ba*-shi-chi)
juha od graha f	*yu*-ha od *gra*-ha	soup made from dried kidney or borlotti beans, smoked bacon bones (or smoked pork hock), onion, carrot, bay leaf & garlic
kiseli kupus m	*ki*-se-li *ku*-pus	sauerkraut – prepared from whole cored cabbage heads layered with horseradish, bay leaves, garlic, dried red pepper & salt
kobasica f	ko-*ba*-si-tsa	sausage
kotlovina f	*kot*-lo-vi-na	fried pork chops simmered in a piquant sauce

ledene kocke f pl	le·de·ne kots·ke	coffee- or chocolate-flavoured sponge cake layered with chocolate cream
lička kisela čorba f	lich·ka ki·se·la chor·ba	stew prepared with cubed meat, mixed vegetables & cabbage
mađarica f	ma·ja·ri·tsa	layers of a rich sweet baked dough interspersed with a chocolate cream filling & topped with melted chocolate
miješano meso n	mi·ye·sha·no me·so	mixed grill
musaka f	mu·sa·ka	layered lasagne-style dish containing meat & vegetables
odojak na ražnju m	o·doy·ak na razh·nyu	suckling pig roasted on a spit
paprikaš m	pa·pri·kash	beef or fish stew flavoured with paprika
pastičada f	pa·sti·cha·da	beef rounds larded with smoked bacon & stewed with fried vegetables – served with a white wine sauce
pastirska juha f	pa·stir·ska yu·ha	soup made from cubed lamb, veal chops & pork neck
pita sa špinatom f	pi·ta sa shpi·na·tom	spinach pie & cottage cheese pie
pršut m	pr·shut	smoke-dried ham
punjene paprike f pl	pu·nye·ne pa·pri·ke	capsicums stuffed with rice, tomato paste, parsley, onion & mincemeat then oven baked
ražnjići m pl	razh·nyi·chi	shish kebabs
riblja juha f	rib·lya yu·ha	fish chowder made of freshwater fish
sarma f	sar·ma	sour cabbage leaves stuffed with a mixture of ground meat, rice & garlic
štrudla f	shtru·dla	strudel with a sweet or savoury filling
tartuf m	tar·tuf	truffle – sometimes served shaved over scrambled eggs or risotto

emergencies

basics

Help!	Upomoć!	u·po·moch
Stop!	Stanite!	sta·ni·te
Go away!	Maknite se!	mak·ni·te se
Thief!	Lopov!	lo·pov
Fire!	Požar!	po·zhar
Watch out!	Pazite!	pa·zi·te

Call ...!	Zovite ...!	zo·vi·te ...
a doctor	liječnika/lekara ©/⑤	li·yech·ni·ka/le·ka·ra
an ambulance	hitnu pomoć	hit·nu po·moch
the police	policiju	po·li·tsi·yu

It's an emergency!
Imamo hitan slučaj.   i·ma·mo hi·tan slu·chai

Could you help me, please?
Molim vas, možete li mi pomoći?   mo·lim vas mo·zhe·te li mi po·mo·chi

Can I use your phone?
Mogu li koristiti vaš telefon?   mo·gu li ko·ri·sti·ti vash te·le·fon

I'm lost.
Izgubio/Izgubila sam se. m/f   iz·gu·bi·o/iz·gu·bi·la sam se

Where are the toilets?
Gdje se nalaze zahodi/toaleti? ©/⑤   gdye se na·la·ze za·ho·di/to·a·le·ti

police

Where's the police station?
Gdje se nalazi policijska stanica?   gdye se na·la·zi po·li·tsiy·ska sta·ni·tsa

I want to report an offence.
Želim prijaviti prekršaj.   zhe·lim pri·ya·vi·ti pre·kr·shai

I have insurance.
Imam osiguranje.   i·mam o·si·gu·ra·nye

I've been ...	Ja sam bio/bila ... m/f	ya sam bi·o/bi·la ...
assaulted	napadnut/napadnuta m/f	na·pad·nut/na·pad·nu·ta
raped	silovan/silovana m/f	si·lo·van/si·lo·va·na
robbed	opljačkan m	op·lyach·kan
	opljačkana f	op·lyach·ka·na

My ... was/were stolen.	Ukrali su mi ...	u·kra·li su mi ...
I've lost my ...	Izgubio/Izgubila	iz·gu·bi·o/iz·gu·bi·la
	sam ... m/f	sam ...
backpack	svoj ranac	svoy ra·nats
bags	svoje torbe	svoy·e tor·be
credit card	svoju kreditnu	svoy·oo kre·dit·nu
	karticu	kar·ti·tsu
jewellery	svoj nakit	svoy na·kit
money	svoj novac	svoy no·vats
passport	svoju putovnicu ©	svoy·oo pu·tov·ni·tsu
	svoj pasoš ⑤	svoy pa·sosh
travellers cheques	svoje putničke	svoy·e put·nich·ke
	čekove	che·ko·ve
I want to contact	Želim stupiti u	zhe·lim stu·pi·ti u
my ...	kontakt sa ...	kon·takt sa ...
consulate	svojom ambasadom	svoy·om am·ba·sa·dom
embassy	svojim konzulatom	svoy·im kon·zu·la·tom

health

medical needs

Where's the	Gdje je najbliži/	gdye ye nai·bli·zhi/
nearest ...?	najbliža ...? m/f	nai·bli·zha ...
dentist	zubar m	zu·bar
doctor	liječnik/lekar m ©/⑤	li·yech·nik/le·kar
hospital	bolnica f	bol·ni·tsa
(night) pharmacist	(noćna) ljekarna/	(noch·na) lye·kar·na
	apoteka f ©/⑤	a·po·te·ka

I need a doctor (who speaks English).
Trebam liječnika/lekara   tre·bam li·yech·ni·ka/le·ka·ra
(koji govori engleski). ©/⑤   (koy·i go·vo·ri en·gle·ski)

Could I see a female doctor?
Mogu li dobiti ženskog   mo·gu li do·bi·ti zhen·skog
liječnika/lekara? ©/⑤   li·yech·ni·ka/le·ka·ra

I've run out of my medication.
Nestalo mi je lijekova.   ne·sta·lo mi ye li·ye·ko·va

symptoms, conditions & allergies

I'm sick.	Ja sam bolestan/	ya sam *bo*·le·stan/
	bolesna. m/f	*bo*·le·sna
It hurts here.	Boli me ovdje.	*bo*·li me *ov*·dye
I have ...	Imam ...	*i*·mam ...

asthma	astma f	*ast*·ma
bronchitis	bronhitis m	bron·*hi*·tis
constipation	zatvorenje n	zat·vo·*re*·nye
cough	kašalj m	*ka*·shal′
diarrhoea	proljev m	*pro*·lyev
fever	groznica f	*gro*·zni·tsa
headache	glavobolja f	gla·*vo*·bo·lya
heart condition	poremećaj srca m	*po*·re·me·chai *sr*·tsa
nausea	mučnina f	much·*ni*·na
pain	bol m	bol
sore throat	grlobolja f	gr·*lo*·bo·lya
toothache	zubobolja f	zu·*bo*·bo·lya

| I'm allergic to ... | Ja sam alergičan/ | ya sam a·*ler*·gi·chan/ |
| | alergična na ... m/f | a·*ler*·gich·na na ... |

antibiotics	antibiotike	*an*·ti·bi·o·ti·ke
anti-inflammatories	lijekove protiv upale	li·*ye*·ko·ve *pro*·tiv *u*·pa·le
aspirin	aspirin	a·*spi*·rin
bees	pčele	*pche*·le
codeine	kodein	ko·*de*·in
penicillin	penicilin	pe·ni·*tsi*·lin

antiseptic	antiseptik m	an·ti·*sep*·tik
bandage	zavoj m	*za*·voy
contraceptives	sredstva za	*sreds*·tva za
	sprječavanje	spri·ye·*cha*·va·nye
	trudnoće n pl	trud·*no*·che
diarrhoea medicine	lijekovi protiv	li·*ye*·ko·vi *pro*·tiv
	proljeva m pl	*pro*·lye·va
insect repellent	sredstvo za odbijanje	*sreds*·tvo za od·*bi*·ya·nye
	insekata n	in·se·ka·ta
laxatives	laksativi m pl	*lak*·sa·ti·vi
painkillers	tablete protiv bolova f pl	*ta*·ble·te *pro*·tiv bo·lo·va
rehydration salts	soli za rehidrataciju f	*so*·li za *re*·hi·dra·ta·tsi·yu
sleeping tablets	tablete za spavanje f pl	*ta*·ble·te za *spa*·va·nye

english–croatian dictionary

Croatian nouns in this dictionary have their gender indicated by ⓜ (masculine), ⓕ (feminine) or ⓝ (neuter). If it's a plural noun, you'll also see pl. Adjectives are given in the masculine form only. Words are also marked as a (adjective), v (verb), sg (singular), pl (plural), inf (informal), pol (polite), ⓒ (Croatian) or ⓢ (Serbian) where necessary.

A

accident *nezgoda* ⓕ *nez-go-da*
accommodation *smještaj* ⓜ *smye-shtai*
adaptor *konverter* ⓜ *kon-ver-ter*
address *adresa* ⓕ *a-dre-sa*
after *poslije* *po-sli-ye*
air-conditioned *klimatiziran* kli-ma-ti-zi-ran
airplane *zrakoplov/avion* ⓜ
  zra-ko-plov/a-vi-on ⓒ/ⓢ
airport *zračna luka* ⓕ */aerodrom* ⓜ
  zrach-na lu-ka/a-e-ro-drom ⓒ/ⓢ
alcohol *alkohol* ⓜ *al-ko-hol*
all *sve* sve
allergy *alergija* ⓕ *a-ler-gi-ya*
ambulance *hitna pomoć* ⓕ *hit-na po-moch*
and *i* i
ankle *gležanj/članak* ⓜ *gle-zhan'/chla-nak* ⓒ/ⓢ
arm *ruka* ⓕ *ru-ka*
ashtray *pepeljara* ⓕ *pe-pe-lya-ra*
ATM *bankovni automat* ⓜ *ban-kov-ni a-u-to-mat*

B

baby *beba* ⓕ *be-ba*
back (body) *leđa* ⓝ pl *le-ja*
backpack *ranac* ⓜ *ra-nats*
bad *loš* losh
bag *torba* ⓕ *tor-ba*
baggage claim *šalter za podizanje prtljage* ⓜ
  shal-ter za po-di-za-nye prt-lya-ge
bank *banka* ⓕ *ban-ka*
bar *bar* ⓜ bar
bathroom *kupaonica* ⓕ *ku-pa-o-ni-tsa*
battery (car) *akumulator* ⓜ *a-ku-mu-la-tor*
battery (general) *baterija* ⓕ *ba-te-ri-ya*
beautiful *lijep* li-yep
bed *krevet* ⓜ *kre-vet*
beer *pivo* ⓝ *pi-vo*
before *prije* *pri-ye*
behind *iza* *i-za*
bicycle *bicikl* ⓜ *bi-tsi-kl*
big *velik* *ve-lik*
bill *račun* ⓜ *ra-chun*

black *crn* tsrn
blanket *deka* ⓕ *de-ka*
blood group *krvna grupa* ⓕ *krv-na gru-pa*
blue *plav* plav
boat (ship) *brod* ⓜ brod
boat (smaller/private) *čamac* ⓜ *cha-mats*
book (make a reservation) v *rezervirati* re-zer-vi-ra-ti
Bosnia-Hercegovina *Bosna i Hercegovina* ⓕ
  bos-na i her-tse-go-vi-na
Bosnian (language) *bosanski jezik* ⓜ *bo-san-ski ye-zik*
bottle *boca* ⓕ *bo-tsa*
bottle opener *otvarač za boce* ⓜ *ot-va-rach za bo-tse*
boy *dječak* ⓜ *dye-chak*
brakes (car) *kočnice* ⓕ pl *koch-ni-tse*
breakfast *doručak* ⓜ *do-ru-chak*
broken (faulty) *pokvaren* *po-kva-ren*
bus *autobus* ⓜ *a-u-to-bus*
business *biznis* ⓜ *biz-nis*
buy *kupiti* *ku-pi-ti*

C

café *kafić/kavana* ⓜ/ⓕ *ka-fich/ka-va-na*
camera *foto-aparat* ⓜ *fo-to-a-pa-rat*
camp site *mjesto za kampiranje* ⓝ
  mye-sto za kam-pi-ra-nye
cancel *poništiti* *po-ni-shti-ti*
can opener *otvarač za limenke/konzerve* ⓜ
  ot-va-rach za li-men-ke/kon-zer-ve ⓒ/ⓢ
car *automobil* ⓜ *a-u-to-mo-bil*
cash *gotovina* ⓕ *go-to-vi-na*
cash (a cheque) v *unovčiti* u-nov-chi-ti
cell phone *mobilni telefon* ⓜ *mo-bil-ni te-le-fon*
centre *centar* ⓜ *tsen-tar*
change (money) v *zamijeniti* za-mi-ye-ni-ti
cheap *jeftin* *yef-tin*
check (bill) *račun* ⓜ *ra-chun*
check-in *prijemni šalter* ⓜ *pri-yem-ni shal-ter*
chest *prsa/grudi* ⓝ pl *pr-sa/gru-di* ⓒ/ⓢ
child *dijete* ⓝ *di-ye-te*
cigarette *cigareta* ⓕ *tsi-ga-re-ta*
city *grad* ⓜ grad
clean a *čist* chist
closed *zatvoren* *zat-vo-ren*
coffee *kava* ⓕ *ka-va*

A

DICTIONARY

coins novčići ⓜ pl *nov-chi-chi*
cold a hladan *hla-dan*
collect call poziv na račun nazvane osobe ⓜ
  po-ziv na ra-chun naz-va-ne o-so-be
come doći *do-chi*
computer računalo ⓝ/kompjuter ⓜ
  ra-chu-na-lo/komp-yu-ter ©/⑤
condom prezervativ ⓜ *pre-zer-va-tiv*
contact lenses kontakt leće ① pl/kontaktna sočiva
  ⓝ pl *kon-takt le-che/kon-takt-na so-chi-va* ©/⑤
cook v kuhati *ku-ha-ti*
cost cijena ① *tsi-ye-na*
credit card kreditna kartica ① *kre-dit-na kar-ti-tsa*
Croatia Hrvatska ① *hr-vat-ska*
Croatian (language) hrvatski ⓜ *hr-vat-ski*
Croatian a hrvatski *hr-vat-ski*
cup šalica/šoljica ① *sha-li-tsa/sho-l'i-tsa* ©/⑤
currency exchange tečaj/kurs stranih valuta ⓜ
  te-chai/kurs stra-nih va-lu-ta ©/⑤
customs (immigration) carinarnica ① *tsa-ri-nar-ni-tsa*

D

dangerous opasan *o-pa-san*
date (time) datum ⓜ *da-tum*
day dan *dan*
delay zakašnjenje ⓝ *za-kash-nye-nye*
dentist zubar ⓜ *zu-bar*
depart otići *o-ti-chi*
diaper pelene ① pl *pe-le-ne*
dictionary rječnik ⓜ *ryech-nik*
dinner večera ① *ve-che-ra*
direct direktan *di-rek-tan*
dirty prljav *pr-lyav*
disabled onesposobljen *o-ne-spo-sob-lyen*
discount popust ⓜ *po-pust*
doctor liječnik/lekar ⓜ *li-yech-nik/le-kar* ©/⑤
double bed dupli krevet ⓜ *du-pli kre-vet*
double room dvokrevetna soba ① *dvo-kre-vet-na so-ba*
drink piće ⓝ *pi-che*
drive v voziti *vo-zi-ti*
drivers licence vozačka dozvola ① *vo-zach-ka doz-vo-la*
drug (illicit) droga ① *dro-ga*
dummy (pacifier) duda/cucla ① *du-da/tsu-tsla* ©/⑤

E

ear uho ⓝ *u-ho*
east istok ⓜ *i-stok*
eat jesti *ye-sti*
economy class drugi razred ⓜ *dru-gi raz-red*
electricity struja ① *stru-ya*
elevator dizalo ⓝ/lift ⓜ *di-za-lo/lift* ©/⑤

email e-mail ⓜ *i-me-il*
embassy ambasada ① *am-ba-sa-da*
emergency hitan slučaj ⓜ *hi-tan slu-chai*
English (language) engleski ⓜ *en-gle-ski*
entrance ulaz ⓜ *u-laz*
evening večer ① *ve-cher*
exchange rate tečaj/kurs razmjene ⓜ
  te-chai/kurs raz-mye-ne ©/⑤
exit izlaz ⓜ *iz-laz*
expensive skup *skup*
express mail ekspres pošta ① *eks-pres posh-ta*
eye oko ⓝ *o-ko*

F

far daleko *da-le-ko*
fast brz *brz*
father otac ⓜ *o-tats*
film (camera) film ⓜ *film*
finger prst ⓜ *prst*
first-aid kit pribor za prvu pomoć ⓜ
  pri-bor za pr-vu po-moch
first class prvi razred ⓜ *pr-vi raz-red*
fish riba ① *ri-ba*
food hrana ① *hra-na*
foot stopalo ⓝ *sto-pa-lo*
fork viljuška ① *vi-lyush-ka*
free (of charge) besplatan *be-spla-tan*
friend prijatelj/prijateljica ⓜ/①
  pri-ya-tel'/pri-ya-te-lyi-tsa
fruit voće ⓝ *vo-che*
full pun *pun*
funny smješan *smye-shan*

G

gift dar/poklon ⓜ *dar/pok-lon* ©/⑤
girl djevojčica ① *dye-voy-chi-tsa*
glass (drinking) čaša ① *cha-sha*
glasses naočale ① pl *na-o-cha-le*
go ići *i-chi*
good dobar *do-bar*
green zelen *ze-len*
guide vodič ⓜ *vo-dich*

H

half polovina ① *po-lo-vi-na*
hand ruka ① *ru-ka*
handbag ručna torbica ① *ruch-na tor-bi-tsa*
happy sretan *sre-tan*
have imati *i-ma-ti*
he on *on*

head *glava* ⓕ *gla*-va
heart *srce* ⓝ *sr*-tse
heat *vrućina* ⓕ *vru-chi*-na
heavy *težak* *te-zhak*
help v *pomoći* *po-mo-chi*
here *ovdje* *ov*-dye
high *visok* *vi*-sok
highway *autoput* ⓜ *a*-u-to-put
hike v *pješačiti* *pye-sha-chi*-ti
holidays *praznici* ⓜ pl *praz*-ni-tsi
homosexual *homoseksualac/homoseksualka* ⓜ/ⓕ *ho-mo-sek-su-a-*lats/ho-mo-sek-su-*al*-ka
hospital *bolnica* ⓕ *bol*-ni-tsa
hot *vruć* vruch
hotel *hotel* ⓜ *ho-tel*
hungry *gladan/gladna* ⓜ/ⓕ *gla-*dan/*gla*-dna
husband *muž* ⓜ muzh

I

I *ja* ya
identification (card) *osobna iskaznica/lična karta* ⓕ *o-sob-*na i-*skaz-*ni-tsa/*lich-*na *kar*-ta ©/Ⓢ
ill *bolestan* *bo-le-*stan
important *važan* *va-*zhan
included *uključen* *uk-lyu-*chen
injury *povreda* ⓕ *po-vre-*da
insurance *osiguranje* ⓝ *o-si-gu-ra-*nye
Internet *internet* ⓜ *in-*ter-net
interpreter *tumač* ⓜ *tu-*mach

J

jewellery *nakit* ⓜ *na-*kit
job *posao* ⓜ *po-*sa-o

K

key *ključ* ⓜ klyuch
kilogram *kilogram* ⓜ *ki-*lo-*gram*
kitchen *kuhinja* ⓕ *ku-hi-*nya
knife *nož* ⓜ nozh

L

laundry (place) *praonica* ⓕ pra-*o*-ni-tsa
lawyer *pravnik* ⓜ *prav-*nik
left (direction) *lijevi* li-*ye*-vi
left-luggage office *ured za odlaganje prtljage* ⓝ u-red za *od-*la-ga-nye prt-*lya-*ge
leg *noga* ⓕ *no-*ga
lesbian *lezbijka* ⓕ *lez-*biy-ka
less *manje* *ma-*nye

letter (mail) *pismo* ⓝ *pi-*smo
lift (elevator) *dizalo* ⓕ/*lift* ⓜ *di-*za-lo/lift ©/Ⓢ
light *svjetlost* ⓕ *svyet-*lost
like v *dopadati se* *do-*pa-da-ti se
lock *brava* ⓕ *bra-*va
long *dugačak* *du-*ga-chak
lost *izgubljen* *iz-gub-*lyen
lost-property office *ured za izgubljene stvari* u-red za *iz-*gub-lye-ne *stva-*ri
love v *voljeti* *vo-*lye-ti
luggage *prtljaga* ⓕ *prt-*lya-ga
lunch *ručak* ⓜ *ru-*chak

M

mail *pošta* ⓕ *posh-*ta
man *čovjek* ⓜ *cho-*vyek
map (of country) *karta* ⓕ *kar-*ta
map (of town) *plan grada* ⓜ plan *gra-*da
market *tržnica/pijaca* ⓕ *trzh-*ni-tsa ©/Ⓢ
matches *šibice* ⓕ pl *shi-*bi-tse
meat *meso* ⓝ *me-*so
medicine *lijekovi* ⓜ pl li-*ye-*ko-vi
menu *jelovnik* ⓜ *ye-lov-*nik
message *poruka* ⓕ *po-ru-*ka
milk *mlijeko* ⓝ mli-*ye*-ko
minute *minuta* ⓕ *mi-nu-*ta
mobile phone *mobilni telefon* ⓜ *mo-*bil-ni te-*le*-fon
money *novac* ⓜ *no-*vats
Montenegro *Crna Gora* ⓕ *tsr-*na *go-*ra
month *mjesec* ⓜ *mye-*sets
morning *jutro* ⓝ *yu-*tro
mother *majka* ⓕ *mai-*ka
motorcycle *motocikl* ⓜ *mo-to-*tsi-kl
motorway *autoput* ⓜ *a-*u-to-put
mouth *usta* ⓝ pl *u-*sta
music *glazba* ⓕ *glaz-*ba

N

name *ime* ⓝ *i-*me
napkin *salveta* ⓕ *sal-ve-*ta
nappy *pelene* ⓕ pl *pe-*le-ne
near *blizu* *bli-*zu
neck *vrat* ⓜ vrat
new *nov* nov
news *vijesti* ⓕ pl *vi-*ye-sti
newspaper *novine* ⓕ pl *no-*vi-ne
night *noć* ⓕ noch
no *ne* ne
noisy *bučan* *bu-*chan
nonsmoking *nepušački* *ne-*pu-shach-ki
north *sjever* ⓜ *sye-*ver

nose *nos* ⓜ nos
now *sada* sa-da
number *broj* ⓜ broy

O

oil (engine) *ulje* ⓝ u-lye
old *star* star
one-way ticket *jednosmjerna karta* ⓕ
yed-no-smyer-na kar-ta
open a *otvoren* ot-vo-ren
outside *vani/napolju* va-ni/na-po-l'u ©/Ⓢ

P

package *paket* ⓜ pa-ket
paper *papir* ⓜ pa-pir
park (car) v *parkirati* par-ki-ra-ti
passport *putovnica* ⓕ/*pasoš* ⓜ
pu-tov-ni-tsa/pa-sosh ©/Ⓢ
pay *platiti* pla-ti-ti
pen *kemijska* ⓕ ke-miy-ska
petrol *benzin* ⓜ ben-zin
pharmacy *ljekarna/apoteka* ⓕ
lye-kar-na/a-po-te-ka ©/Ⓢ
phonecard *telefonska kartica* ⓕ
te-le-fon-ska kar-ti-tsa
photo *fotografija* ⓕ fo-to-gra-fi-ya
plate *tanjur* ⓜ ta-nyur
police *policija* ⓕ po-li-tsi-ya
postcard *dopisnica* ⓕ do-pi-sni-tsa
post office *poštanski ured* ⓜ posh-tan-ski u-red
pregnant *trudna* trud-na
price *cijena* ⓕ tsi-ye-na

Q

quiet *tih* tih

R

rain *kiša* ⓕ ki-sha
razor *brijač* ⓜ bri-yach
receipt *račun* ⓜ ra-chun
red *crven* tsr-ven
refund *povrat novca* ⓜ pov-rat nov-tsa
registered mail *preporučena pošta* ⓕ
pre-po-ru-che-na posh-ta
rent v *iznajmiti* iz-nai-mi-ti
repair v *popraviti* po-pra-vi-ti
reservation *rezervacija* ⓕ re-zer-va-tsi-ya
restaurant *restoran* ⓜ re-sto-ran
return v *vratiti se* vra-ti-ti se

return ticket *povratna karta* ⓕ po-vra-tna kar-ta
right (direction) *desno* de-sno
road *cesta* ⓕ/*put* ⓜ tse-sta/put ©/Ⓢ
room *soba* ⓕ so-ba

S

safe a *siguran* si-gu-ran
sanitary napkin *higijenski uložak* ⓜ
hi-gi-yen-ski u-lo-zhak
seat *sjedište* ⓝ sye-dish-te
send *poslati* po-sla-ti
Serbia *Srbija* ⓕ sr-bi-ya
Serbian (language) *srpski jezik* ⓜ srp-ski ye-zik
service station *benzinska stanica* ⓕ
ben-zin-ska sta-ni-tsa
sex *seks* ⓜ seks
shampoo *šampon* ⓜ sham-pon
share (a dorm) *dijeliti* di-ye-li-ti
shaving cream *pjena za brijanje* ⓕ
pye-na za bri-ya-nye
she *ona* o-na
sheet (bed) *plahta* ⓕ/*čaršav* ⓜ
pla-hta/char-shav ©/Ⓢ
shirt *košulja* ⓕ ko-shu-lya
shoes *cipele* ⓕ pl tsi-pe-le
shop *prodavaonica* ⓕ pro-da-va-o-ni-tsa
short *kratak* kra-tak
shower *tuš* ⓜ tush
single room *jednokrevetna soba* ⓕ
yed-no-kre-vet-na so-ba
skin *koža* ⓕ ko-zha
skirt *suknja* ⓕ suk-nya
sleep v *spavati* spa-va-ti
slowly *sporo* spo-ro
small *mali* ma-li
smoke (cigarettes) v *pušiti* pu-shi-ti
soap *sapun* ⓜ sa-pun
some *malo* ma-lo
soon *uskoro* u-sko-ro
south *jug* ⓜ yug
souvenir shop *prodavaonica suvenira* ⓕ
pro-da-va-o-ni-tsa su-ve-ni-ra
speak *govoriti* go-vo-ri-ti
spoon *žlica/kašika* ⓕ zhli-tsa/ka-shi-ka ©/Ⓢ
stamp *poštanska marka* ⓕ posh-tan-ska mar-ka
stand-by ticket *uvjetna/uslovna karta* ⓕ
uv-yet-na/us-lov-na kar-ta ©/Ⓢ
station (train) *stanica* ⓕ sta-ni-tsa
stomach *želudac* ⓜ zhe-lu-dats
stop v *zaustaviti* za-u-sta-vi-ti
stop (bus) *stanica* ⓕ sta-ni-tsa
street *ulica* ⓕ u-li-tsa

student *student* ⓜ & ⓕ *stu*-dent
sun *sunce* ⓕ *sun*-tse
sunscreen *losion za zaštitu od sunca* ⓜ
  lo-si-on za *zash*-ti-tu od *sun*-tsa
swim v *plivati pli*-va-ti

T

tampon *tampon* ⓜ *tam*-pon
taxi *taksi* ⓜ *tak*-si
teaspoon *žličica/kašičica* ⓕ
  zhli-chi-tsa/ka-*shi*-chi-tsa ©/Ⓢ
teeth *zubi* ⓜ pl *zu*-bi
telephone *telefon* ⓜ te-*le*-fon
television *televizija* ⓕ te-le-*vi*-zi-ya
temperature (weather) *temperatura* ⓕ tem-pe-ra-*tu*-ra
tent *šator* ⓜ *sha*-tor
that (one) *ono* o-no
they *oni/one/ona* ⓜ/ⓕ/ⓝ o-ni/o-ne/o-na
thirsty *žedan* zhe-dan
this (one) *ovo* o-vo
throat *grlo* ⓝ *gr*-lo
ticket *karta* ⓕ *kar*-ta
time *vrijeme* ⓝ vri-*ye*-me
tired *umoran* u-mo-ran
tissues *papirnati rupčići* ⓜ pl pa-*pir*-na-ti *rup*-chi-chi
  papirne maramice ⓕ pl pa-*pir*-ne ma-ra-mi-tse Ⓢ
today *danas* da-nas
toilet *zahod/toalet* ⓜ za-*hod*/to-a-*let* ©/Ⓢ
tomorrow *sutra* su-tra
tonight *večeras* ve-*che*-ras
toothbrush *četkica za zube* ⓕ *chet*-ki-tsa za *zu*-be
toothpaste *pasta za zube* ⓕ *pa*-sta za *zu*-be
torch (flashlight) *ručna svjetiljka* ⓕ *ruch*-na svye-*til'*-ka
tour *ekskurzija* ⓕ ek-*skur*-zi-ya
tourist office *turistička agencija* ⓕ
  tu-*ri*-stich-ka a-*gen*-tsi-ya
towel *ručnik/peškir* ⓜ *ruch*-nik/*pesh*-kir ©/Ⓢ
train *vlak/voz* ⓜ vlak/voz ©/Ⓢ
translate *prevesti* pre-ve-sti
travel agency *putna agencija* ⓕ *put*-na a-*gen*-tsi-ya
travellers cheque *putnički ček* ⓜ *put*-nich-ki chek
trousers *hlače/pantalone* ⓕ pl
  hla-che/pan-ta-*lo*-ne ©/Ⓢ
twin beds *dva kreveta* ⓜ pl dva *kre*-ve-ta
tyre *guma* ⓕ *gu*-ma

U

underwear *donje rublje* ⓝ *do*-nye *rub*-lye
urgent *hitan hi*-tan

V

vacant *prazan pra*-zan
vacation *praznici* ⓜ pl *praz*-ni-tsi
vegetable *povrće* ⓝ *po*-vr-che
vegetarian a *vegetarijanski* ve-ge-ta-*ri*-yan-ski
visa *viza* ⓕ *vi*-za

W

waiter *konobar* ⓜ *ko*-no-bar
walk v *hodati* ho-da-ti
wallet *novčanik* ⓜ *nov*-cha-nik
warm *topao* to-pa-o
wash (something) *oprati* o-pra-ti
watch *sat* ⓜ sat
water *voda* ⓕ *vo*-da
we *mi* mi
weekend *vikend* ⓜ *vi*-kend
west *zapad* ⓜ *za*-pad
wheelchair *invalidska kolica* ⓕ pl in-*va*-lid-ska ko-*li*-tsa
when *kada* ka-da
where *gdje* gdye
white *bijel* bi-*yel*
who *tko* tko
why *zašto zash*-to
wife *žena* ⓕ *zhe*-na
window *prozor* ⓜ *pro*-zor
wine *vino* ⓝ *vi*-no
with *sa* sa
without *bez* bez
woman *žena* ⓕ *zhe*-na
write *napisati* na-*pi*-sa-ti

Y

yellow *žut* zhut
yes *da* da
yesterday *jučer yu*-cher
you sg inf *ti* ti
you sg pol & pl *vi* vi

French

french alphabet

A a a	*B b* be	*C c* se	*D d* de	*E e* eu
F f ef	*G g* zhe	*H h* ash	*I i* i	*J j* zhi
K k ka	*L l* el	*M m* em	*N n* en	*O o* o
P p pe	*Q q* kew	*R r* er	*S s* es	*T t* te
U u ew	*V v* ve	*W w* dubl ve	*X x* iks	*Y y* i grek
Z z zed				

■ french

FRANÇAIS

FRENCH
français

introduction

What do you think of when the word 'French' comes up? A *bon vivant*, drinking an *apéritif tête-à-tête* with a friend at a *café*, while studying the *à la carte* menu and making some witty *double entendres*? Are you getting *déjà vu* yet? Chances are you already know a few fragments of French (*français* fron-sey) – *bonjour, oui, au revoir, bon voyage* and so on. Even if you missed out on French lessons, though, that first sentence (forgive the stereotyping) is evidence that you probably know quite a few French words without realising it. And thanks to the Norman invasion of England in the 11th century, many common English words have a French origin – some estimate, in fact, that three-fifths of everyday English vocabulary arrived via French.

So, after centuries of contact with English, French offers English speakers a relatively smooth path to communicating in another language. The structure of a French sentence won't come as a surprise and the sounds of the language are generally common to English as well. The few sounds that do differ will be familiar to most through television and film examples of French speakers – the silent 'h' and the throaty 'r', for example. French is a distant cousin of English, but is most closely related to its Romance siblings, Italian and Spanish. These languages developed from the Latin spoken by the Romans during their conquests of the 1st century BC.

Almost 30 countries cite French as an official language (not always the only language, of course), in many cases due to France's colonisation of various countries in Africa, the Pacific and the Caribbean. It's the mother tongue of around 80 million people in places like Belgium, Switzerland, Luxembourg, Monaco, Canada and Senegal as well as France, and another 50 million speak it as a second language. French was the language of international diplomacy until the early 20th century, and is still an official language of a number of international organisations, including the Red Cross, the United Nations and the International Olympic Committee.

As well as the advantage of learning a language that's spoken all around the world, there are more subtle benefits to French. Being told of a wonderful vineyard off the tourist track, for example, or discovering that there's little truth in the cliché that the French are rude. And *regardez* the significant body of literature (the Nobel Prize for Literature has gone to French authors a dozen times), film and music ... You'll find the reasons to speak French just keep growing.

introduction – FRENCH

91

pronunciation

vowel sounds

Generally, French vowel sounds are short and don't glide into other vowels. Note that the ey in *café* is close to the English sound, but it's shorter and sharper.

symbol	english equivalent	french example	transliteration
a	run	*tasse*	tas
ai	aisle	*travail*	tra-vai
air	fair	*faire*	fair
e	bet	*fesses*	fes
ee	see	*lit*	lee
eu	nurse	*deux*	deu
ew	ee pronounced with rounded lips	*tu*	tew
ey	as in 'bet', but longer	*musée*	moo-zey
o	pot	*pomme*	pom
oo	moon	*chou*	shoo

There are also four nasal vowels in French. They're pronounced as if you're trying to force the sound out of your nose rather than your mouth. In French, nasal vowels cause the following nasal consonant sound to be omitted, but a 'hint' of what the implied consonant is can sometimes be heard. We've used nasal consonant sounds (m, n, ng) with the nasal vowel to help you produce the sound with more confidence. Since the four nasal sounds can be quite close, we've simplified it this way:

symbol	english equivalent	french example	transliteration
om/on/ong	like the 'o' in 'pot', plus nasal consonant sound	*mouton*	moo-ton
um/un/ung	similar to the 'a' in 'bat', plus nasal consonant sound	*magasin*	ma-ga-zun

consonant sounds

symbol	english equivalent	french example	transliteration
b	bed	*billet*	bee-yey
d	dog	*date*	dat
f	fat	*femme*	fam
g	go	*grand*	gron
k	kit	*carte*	kart
l	lot	*livre*	leev-re
m	man	*merci*	mair-see
n	not	*non*	non
ny	canyon	*signe*	see-nye
ng	ring	*cinquante*	sung-kont
p	pet	*parc*	park
r	run (throaty)	*rue*	rew
s	sun	*si*	see
sh	shot	*changer*	shon-zhey
t	top	*tout*	too
v	very	*verre*	vair
w	win	*oui*	wee
y	yes	*payer*	pe-yey
z	zero	*vous avez*	voo-za-vey
zh	pleasure	*je*	zhe

word stress

Syllables in French words are, for the most part, equally stressed. English speakers tend to stress the first syllable, so try adding a light stress on the final syllable to compensate. The rhythm of a French sentence is based on breaking the phrase into meaningful sections, then stressing the final syllable pronounced in each section. The stress at these points is characterised by a slight rise in intonation.

basics

language difficulties

Do you speak English?
Parlez-vous anglais? — par-ley-voo ong-gley

Do you understand?
Comprenez-vous? — kom-pre-ney-voo

I understand.
Je comprends. — zhe kom-pron

I don't understand.
Je ne comprends pas. — zhe ne kom-pron pa

What does (*beaucoup*) mean?
Que veut dire (beaucoup)? — ke veu deer (bo-koo)

How do you ...?	Comment ...?	ko-mon ...
pronounce this	le prononcez-vous	le pro-non-sey voo
write (*bonjour*)	est-ce qu'on écrit (*bonjour*)	es kon ey-kree (bon-zhoor)

Could you please ...?	Pourriez-vous ..., s'il vous plaît?	poo-ree-yey voo ... seel voo pley
repeat that	répéter	rey-pey-tey
speak more slowly	parler plus lentement	par-ley plew lon-te-mon
write it down	l'écrire	ley-kreer

essentials

Yes.	*Oui.*	wee
No.	*Non.*	non
Please.	*S'il vous plaît.*	seel voo pley
Thank you (very much).	*Merci (beaucoup).*	mair-see (bo-koo)
You're welcome.	*Je vous en prie.*	zhe voo zon-pree
Excuse me.	*Excusez-moi.*	ek-skew-zey-mwa
Sorry.	*Pardon.*	par-don

numbers

0	*zéro*	zey-ro	16	*seize*	sez
1	*un*	un	17	*dix-sept*	dee-set
2	*deux*	deu	18	*dix-huit*	dee-zweet
3	*trois*	trwa	19	*dix-neuf*	deez-neuf
4	*quatre*	ka-tre	20	*vingt*	vung
5	*cinq*	sungk	21	*vingt et un*	vung tey un
6	*six*	sees	22	*vingt-deux*	vung-deu
7	*sept*	set	30	*trente*	tront
8	*huit*	weet	40	*quarante*	ka-ront
9	*neuf*	neuf	50	*cinquante*	sung-kont
10	*dix*	dees	60	*soixante*	swa-sont
11	*onze*	onz	70	*soixante-dix*	swa-son-dees
12	*douze*	dooz	80	*quatre-vingts*	ka-tre-vung
13	*treize*	trez	90	*quatre-vingt-dix*	ka-tre-vung-dees
14	*quatorze*	ka-torz	100	*cent*	son
15	*quinze*	kunz	1000	*mille*	meel

time & dates

What time is it?	*Quelle heure est-il?*	kel eur ey-teel
It's one o'clock.	*Il est une heure.*	ee-ley ewn eu
It's (10) o'clock.	*Il est (dix) heures.*	ee-ley (deez) eu
Quarter past (one).	*Il est (une) heure et quart.*	ee-ley (ewn) eu ey kar
Half past (one).	*Il est (une) heure et demie.*	ee-ley (ewn) eu ey de-mee
Quarter to (one).	*Il est (une) heure*	ee-ley (ewn) eu
	moins le quart.	mwun le kar
At what time ...?	*À quelle heure ...?*	a kel eu ...
At ...	*À ...*	a ...
in the morning	*du matin*	dew ma-tun
in the afternoon	*de l'après-midi*	de la-prey-mee-dee
in the evening	*du soir*	dew swar
Monday	*lundi*	lun-dee
Tuesday	*mardi*	mar-dee
Wednesday	*mercredi*	mair-kre-dee
Thursday	*jeudi*	zheu-dee
Friday	*vendredi*	von-dre-dee
Saturday	*samedi*	sam-dee
Sunday	*dimanche*	dee-monsh

January	*janvier*	zhon-vyey
February	*février*	feyv-ryey
March	*mars*	mars
April	*avril*	a-vreel
May	*mai*	mey
June	*juin*	zhwun
July	*juillet*	zhwee-yey
August	*août*	oot
September	*septembre*	sep-tom-bre
October	*octobre*	ok-to-bre
November	*novembre*	no-vom-bre
December	*décembre*	dey-som-bre

What date is it today?
   C'est quel jour aujourd'hui?   sey kel zhoor o-zhoor-dwee

It's (18 October).
   C'est le (dix-huit octobre).   sey le (dee-zwee tok-to-bre)

since (May)	*depuis (mai)*	de-pwee (mey)
until (June)	*jusqu'à (juin)*	zhoos-ka (zhwun)
today	*aujourd'hui*	o-zhoor-dwee
tonight	*ce soir*	se swar

last ...
night	*hier soir*	ee-yair swar
week	*la semaine dernière*	la se-men dair-nyair
month	*le mois dernier*	le mwa dair-nyey
year	*l'année dernière*	la-ney dair-nyair

next ...
week	*la semaine prochaine*	la se-men pro-shen
month	*le mois prochain*	le mwa pro-shen
year	*l'année prochaine*	la-ney pro-shen

yesterday/tomorrow ...   *hier/demain ...*   ee-yair/de-mun ...
morning	*matin*	ma-tun
afternoon	*après-midi*	a-pre-mee-dee
evening	*soir*	swar

weather

What's the weather like?	*Quel temps fait-il?*	kel tom fey·teel
It's ...		
cloudy	*Le temps est couvert.*	le tom ey koo·vair
cold	*Il fait froid.*	eel fey frwa
hot	*Il fait chaud.*	eel fey sho
raining	*Il pleut.*	eel pleu
snowing	*Il neige.*	eel nezh
sunny	*Il fait beau.*	eel fey bo
warm	*Il fait chaud.*	eel fey sho
windy	*Il fait du vent.*	eel fey dew von
spring	*printemps* m	prun·tom
summer	*été* m	ey·tey
autumn	*automne* m	o·ton
winter	*hiver* m	ee·vair

border crossing

I'm here ...	*Je suis ici ...*	zhe swee zee·see ...
in transit	*de passage*	de pa·sazh
on business	*pour le travail*	poor le tra·vai
on holiday	*pour les vacances*	poor ley va·kons
I'm here for ...	*Je suis ici pour ...*	zhe swee zee·see poor ...
(10) days	*(dix) jours*	(dees) zhoor
(three) weeks	*(trois) semaines*	(trwa) se·men
(two) months	*(deux) mois*	(deu) mwa

I'm going to (Paris).
Je vais à (Paris). — zhe vey a (pa·ree)

I'm staying at the (Hotel Grand).
Je loge à (l'hotel Grand). — zhe lozh a (lo·tel gron)

I have nothing to declare.
Je n'ai rien à déclarer. — zhe ney ryun a dey·kla·rey

I have something to declare.
J'ai quelque chose à déclarer. — zhey kel·ke·shoz a dey·kla·rey

That's not mine.
Ce n'est pas à moi. — se ney pa a mwa

transport

tickets & luggage

Where can I buy a ticket?
Où peut-on acheter un billet? oo pe·ton ash·tey um bee·yey

Do I need to book a seat?
Est-ce qu'il faut réserver une place? es·keel fo rey·zer·vey ewn plas

One ... ticket	*Un billet ... (pour*	um bee·yey ... (poor
(to Bordeaux), please.	*Bordeaux), s'il vous plaît.*	bor·do) seel voo pley
one-way	*simple*	sum·ple
return	*aller et retour*	a·ley ey re·toor

I'd like to ... my	*Je voudrais ... mon*	zhe voo·drey ... mom
ticket, please.	*billet, s'il vous plaît.*	bee·yey seel voo pley
cancel	*annuler*	a·new·ley
change	*changer*	shon·zhey
collect	*retirer*	re·tee·rey
confirm	*confirmer*	kon·feer·mey

I'd like a ... seat,	*Je voudrais une place*	zhe voo·drey ewn plas
please.	*..., s'il vous plaît.*	... seel voo pley
(non)smoking	*non-fumeur*	non few·me
smoking	*fumeur*	few·me

How much is it?
C'est combien? sey kom·byun

Is there air conditioning?
Est-qu'il y a la climatisation? es·keel ya la klee·ma·tee·za·syon

Is there a toilet?
Est-qu'il y a des toilettes? es·keel ya dey twa·let

How long does the trip take?
Le trajet dure combien de temps? le tra·zhey dewr kom·byun de tom

Is it a direct route?
Est-ce que c'est direct? es·ke sey dee·rekt

I'd like a luggage locker.
Je voudrais une zhe voo·drey ewn
consigne automatique. kon·see·nye o·to·ma·teek

My luggage	Mes bagages	mey ba·gazh
has been ...	ont été ...	on tey·tey ...
damaged	endommagés	on·do·ma·zhey
lost	perdus	per·dew
stolen	volés	vo·ley

getting around

Where does flight (008) arrive?
Où atteri le vol (008)?   oo a·te·ree le vol (zey·ro zey·ro weet)

Where does flight (008) depart?
D'où décolle le vol (008)?   doo dey·kol le vol (zey·ro zey·ro weet)

Where's (the) ...?	Où se trouve ...?	oo se troo·ve ...
arrivals hall	le hall d'arrivée	le hol da·ree·vey
departures hall	le hall des departs	le hol dey dey·par
duty-free shop	le magasin duty-free	le ma·ga·zun dyoo·tee free
gate (12)	porte (douze)	port (dooz)

Is this the ... to (Nice)?	Est ce ... pour (Nice)?	es se ... poor (nees)
boat	le bateau	le ba·to
bus	le bus	le bews
plane	l'avion	la·vyon
train	le train	le trun

What time's	Le ... bus passe	le ... bews pas
the ... bus?	à quelle heure?	a kel e
first	premier	pre·myey
last	dernier	dair·nyey
next	prochain	pro·shun

At what time does it arrive/leave?
A quelle heure est ce qu'il arrive/part?   a kel eur es se keel a·ree·ve/par

How long will it be delayed?
De combien de temps est-il retardé?   de kom·byun de tom es·teel re·tar·dey

What station is this?
C'est quelle gare?   sey kel gar

What's the next station?
Quelle est la prochaine gare?   kel ey la pro·shen gar

Does it stop at (Amboise)?
Est-ce qu'il s'arrête à (Amboise)?   es·kil sa·ret a (om·bwaz)

Please tell me when we get to (Nantes).
Pouvez-vous me dire quand
nous arrivons à (Nantes)?
poo·vey·voo me deer kon
noo za·ree·von a (nont)

How long do we stop here?
Combien de temps on s'arrête ici?
kom·byun de tom on sa·ret ee·see

Is this seat available?
Est-ce que cette place est libre?
es·ke set plas ey lee·bre

That's my seat.
C'est ma place.
sey ma plas

I'd like a taxi ... | *Je voudrais un taxi ...* | zhe voo·drey un tak·see ...
at (9am) | *à (neuf heures* | a (neu veur
 | *du matin)* | dew ma·tun)
now | *maintenant* | mun·te·non
tomorrow | *demain* | de·mun

Is this taxi available?
Vous êtes libre?
voo·zet lee·bre

How much is it to ...?
C'est combien pour aller à ...?
sey kom·byun poor a·ley a ...

Please put the meter on.
Mettez le compteur, s'il vous plaît.
me·tey le kon·teseel voo pley

Please take me to (this address).
Conduisez-moi à (cette adresse),
s'il vous plaît.
kon·dwee·zey mwa a (set a·dres)
seel voo pley

Please ... | *..., s'il vous plaît.* | ... seel voo pley
slow down | *Roulez plus lentement* | roo·ley plew lont·mon
stop here | *Arrêtez-vous ici* | a·rey·tey voo ee·see
wait here | *Attendez ici* | a·ton·dey ee·see

car, motorbike & bicycle hire

I'd like to hire a ... | *Je voudrais louer ...* | zhe voo·drey loo·wey ...
bicycle | *un vélo* | un vey·lo
car | *une voiture* | ewn vwa·tewr
motorbike | *une moto* | ewn mo·to

with ... | *avec ...* | a·vek ...
a driver | *un chauffeur* | un sho·feur
air conditioning | *climatisation* | klee·ma·tee·za·syon

How much for ... hire?	Quel est le tarif par ...?	kel ey le ta·reef par ...
hourly	heure	eur
daily	jour	zhoor
weekly	semaine	se·men

air	air m	air
oil	huile f	weel
petrol	essence f	es·sons
tyres	pneus f pl	pneu

I need a mechanic.
 J'ai besoin d'un mécanicien.   zhey be·zwun dun mey·ka·nee·syun

I've run out of petrol.
 Je suis en panne d'essence.   zhe swee zon pan de·sons

I have a flat tyre.
 Mon pneu est à plat.   mom pneu ey ta pla

directions

Where's the ...?	Où est-ce qu'il y a ...?	oo es·keel ya ...
bank	la banque	la bongk
city centre	le centre-ville	ler son·tre·veel
hotel	l'hôtel	lo·tel
market	le marché	le mar·shey
police station	le commissariat	le kom·mee·sar·ya
	de police	de po·lees
post office	le bureau de poste	le bew·ro de post
public toilet	des toilettes	dey twa·let
tourist office	l'office de tourisme	lo·fees de too·rees·me

Is this the road to (Toulouse)?
 C'est la route pour (Toulouse)?   sey la root poor (too·looz)

Can you show me (on the map)?
 Pouvez-vous m'indiquer (sur la carte)?   poo·vey·voo mun·dee·key (sewr la kart)

What's the address?
 Quelle est l'adresse?   kel ey la·dres

How far is it?
 C'est loin?   sey lwun

How do I get there?
 Comment faire pour y aller?   ko·mon fair poor ee a·ley

Turn ...	Tournez ...	toor·ney ...
at the corner	au coin	o kwun
at the traffic lights	aux feux	o feu
left/right	à gauche/droite	a gosh/drwat

It's ...	C'est ...	sey ...
behind ...	derrière ...	dair·yair ...
far away	loin d'ici	lwun dee·see
here	ici	ee·see
in front of ...	devant ...	de·von ...
left	à gauche	a gosh
near (to ...)	près (de ...)	prey (de ...)
next to ...	à côté de ...	a ko·tey de ...
opposite ...	en face de ...	on fas de ...
right	à droite	a drwat
straight ahead	tout droit	too drwa
there	là	la

north	nord m	nor
south	sud m	sewd
east	est m	est
west	ouest m	west

by bus	en bus	om bews
by taxi	en taxi	on tak·see
by train	en train	on trun
on foot	à pied	a pyey

signs

Entrée/Sortie	on·trey/sor·tee	Entrance/Exit
Ouvert/Fermé	oo·vair/fair·mey	Open/Closed
Chambre Libre	shom·bre lee·bre	Rooms Available
Complet	kom·pley	No Vacancies
Renseignements	ron·sen·ye·mon	Information
Commissariat De Police	ko·mee·sar·ya de po·lees	Police Station
Interdit	in·teyr·dee	Prohibited
Toilettes	twa·let	Toilets
Hommes	om	Men
Femmes	fam	Women
Chaude/Froide	shod/frwad	Hot/Cold

accommodation

finding accommodation

Where's a ...?	*Où est-ce qu'on peut trouver ...?*	oo es·kon peu troo·vey ...
camping ground	*un terrain de camping*	un tey·run de kom·peeng
guesthouse	*une pension*	ewn pon·see·on
hotel	*un hôtel*	un o·tel
youth hostel	*une auberge de jeunesse*	ewn o·bairzh de zhe·nes

Can you recommend somewhere ...?	*Est-ce que vous pouvez recommander un logement ...?*	es·ke voo poo·vey re·ko·mon·dey un lozh·mon ...
cheap	*pas cher*	pa shair
good	*de bonne qualité*	de bon ka·lee·tey
nearby	*près d'ici*	prey dee·see

I'd like to book a room, please.
Je voudrais réserver une chambre, s'il vous plaît.
zhe voo·drey rey·zair·vey ewn shom·bre seel voo pley

I have a reservation.
J'ai une réservation.
zhey ewn rey·zair·va·syon

My name is ...
Mon nom est ...
mon nom ey ...

Do you have a ... room?	*Avez-vous une chambre ...?*	a·vey·voo ewn shom·bre ...
single	*à un lit*	a un lee
double	*avec un grand lit*	a·vek ung gron lee
twin	*avec des lits jumeaux*	a·vek dey lee zhew·mo

Can I pay by ...?	*Est-ce qu'on peut payer avec ...?*	es·kom peu pey·yey a·vek ...
credit card	*une carte de crédit*	ewn kart de krey·dee
travellers cheque	*des chèques de voyage*	dey shek de vwa·yazh

How much is it per ...?	*Quel est le prix par ...?*	kel ey le pree par ...
night	*nuit*	nwee
person	*personne*	pair·son

I'd like to stay for (two) nights.
Je voudrais rester pour (deux) nuits.
zhe voo·drey res·tey poor (der) nwee

From (July 2) to (July 6).
Du (deux juillet) au (six juillet).
dew (de zhwee·yey) o (see zhwee·yey)

Can I see it?
Est-ce que je peux la voir?
es·ke zhe peu la vwar

Am I allowed to camp here?
Est-ce que je peux camper ici?
es·ke zhe peu kom·pey ee·see

Where's the nearest camp site?
Où est le terrain de camping
le plus proche?
oo ey ler tey·run de kom·peeng
le plew prosh

requests & queries

When/Where is breakfast served?
Quand/Où le petit
déjeuner est-il servi?
kon/oo le pe·tee
dey·zhe·ney ey·teel sair·vee

Please wake me at (seven).
Réveillez-moi à (sept)
heures, s'il vous plaît.
rey·vey·yey·mwa a (set)
eur seel voo pley

Could I have my key, please?
Est-ce que je pourrais avoir
la clé, s'il vous plaît?
es·ke zhe poo·rey a·vwar
la kley seel voo pley

Can I get another (blanket)?
Est-ce que je peux avoir
une autre (couverture)?
es·ke zhe pe a·vwar
ewn o·tre (koo·vair·tewr)

Is there a/an ...?	*Avez-vous un ...?*	a·vey·voo un ...
elevator	*ascenseur*	a·son·seur
safe	*coffre-fort*	ko·fre·for

The room is too ...	*C'est trop ...*	sey tro ...
expensive	*cher*	shair
noisy	*bruyant*	brew·yon
small	*petit*	pe·tee

The ... doesn't work.	... ne fonctionne pas.	... ne fong·syon pa
air conditioning	La climatisation	klee·ma·tee·za·syon
fan	Le ventilateur	le von·tee·la·teur
toilet	Les toilettes	le twa·let

This ... isn't clean.	... n'est pas propre.	... ney pa pro·pre
pillow	Cet oreiller	set o·rey·yey
sheet	Ce drap	se drap
towel	Cette serviette	set sair·vee·et

checking out

What time is checkout?
Quand faut-il régler? — kon fo·teel rey·gley

Can I leave my luggage here?
Puis-je laisser mes bagages? — pweezh ley·sey mey ba·gazh

Could I have my ..., please?	Est-ce que je pourrais avoir ..., s'il vous plaît?	es·ke zhe poo·rey a·vwar ... seel voo pley
deposit	ma caution	ma ko·syon
passport	mon passeport	mon pas·por
valuables	mes biens précieux	mey byun prey·syeu

communications & banking

the internet

Where's the local Internet café?
Où est le cybercafé du coin? — oo ey le see·bair·ka·fey dew kwun

How much is it per hour?
C'est combien l'heure? — sey kom·byun leur

I'd like to ...	Je voudrais ...	zhe voo·drey ...
check my email	consulter mon courrier électronique	kon·sewl·tey mong koor·yey ey·lek·tro·neek
get Internet access	me connecter à l'internet	me ko·nek·tey a lun·tair·net
use a printer	utiliser une imprimante	ew·tee·lee·zey ewn um·pree·mont
use a scanner	utiliser un scanner	ew·tee·lee·zey un ska·nair

mobile/cell phone

I'd like a ...	Je voudrais ...	zhe voo·drey ...
mobile/cell phone for hire	louer un portable	loo·ey um por·ta·ble
SIM card for your network	une carte SIM pour le réseau	ewn kart seem poor le rey·zo

What are the rates?	Quels sont les tarifs?	kel son ley ta·reef

telephone

What's your phone number?
Quel est votre numéro de téléphone?   kel ey vo·tre new·mey·ro de tey·ley·fon

The number is ...
Le numéro est ...   le new·mey·ro ey ...

Where's the nearest public phone?
Où est le téléphone   oo ey le tey·ley·fon
public le plus proche?   pewb·leek le plew prosh

I'd like to buy a phone card.
Je voudrais acheter   zhe voo·drey ash·tey
une carte téléphonique.   ewn kart tey·ley·fo·neek

I want to ...	Je veux ...	zhe ve ...
call (Singapore)	téléphoner avec préavis (à Singapour)	tey·ley·fo·ney a·vek prey·a·vee (a sung·ga·poor)
make a local call	faire un appel local	fair un a·pel lo·kal
reverse the charges	téléphoner en PCV	tey·ley·fo·ney om pey·sey·vey

How much does ... cost?	Quel est le prix ...?	kel ey le pree ...
a (three)-minute call	d'une communication de (trois) minutes	dewn ko·mew·nee·ka·syon de (trwa) mee·newt
each extra minute	de chaque minute supplémentaire	de shak mee·newt sew·pley·mon·tair

It's (one euro) per (minute).
(Un euro) pour (une minute).   (un eu·ro) poor (ewn mee·newt)

post office

I want to send a ...	*Je voudrais envoyer ...*	zhe voo·drey on·vwa·yey ...
fax	*un fax*	un faks
letter	*une lettre*	ewn le·tre
parcel	*un colis*	ung ko·lee
postcard	*une carte postale*	ewn kart pos·tal
I want to buy a/an ...	*Je voudrais acheter ...*	zhe voo·drey ash·tey ...
envelope	*une enveloppe*	ewn on·vlop
stamp	*un timbre*	un tum·bre
Please send it	*Envoyez-le (en Australie)*	on·vwa·yey·le (on os·tra·lee)
(to Australia) by ...	*..., s'il vous plaît.*	... seel voo pley
airmail	*par avion*	par a·vyon
express mail	*en exprès*	on neks·pres
registered mail	*en recommandé*	on re·ko·mon·dey
surface mail	*par voie de terre*	par vwa de tair

Is there any mail for me?
Y a-t-il du courrier pour moi? — ya·teel dew koor·yey poor mwa

bank

Where's a/an ...?	*Où est ...?*	oo ey ...
ATM	*le guichet automatique*	le gee·shey o·to·ma·teek
foreign exchange office	*le bureau de change*	le bew·ro de shonzh
I'd like to ...	*Je voudrais ...*	zhe voo·drey ...
arrange a transfer	*faire un virement*	fair un veer·mon
cash a cheque	*encaisser un chèque*	ong·key·sey un shek
change a travellers cheque	*changer des chèques de voyage*	shon·zhey dey shek de vwa·yazh
change money	*changer de l'argent*	shon·zhey de lar·zhon
get a cash advance	*une avance de crédit*	ewn a·vons de krey·dee
withdraw money	*retirer de l'argent*	re·tee·rey de lar·zhon
What's the ...?	*Quel est ...?*	kel ey ...
charge for that	*le tarif*	le ta·reef
exchange rate	*le taux de change*	le to de shonzh

It's ...	C'est ...	sey ...
(12) euros	(douze) euros	(dooz) eu·ro
free	gratuit	gra·twee

What time does the bank open?
À quelle heure ouvre la banque?   a kel eur oo·vre la bongk

Has my money arrived yet?
Mon argent est-il arrivé?   mon ar·zhon ey·teel a·ree·vey

sightseeing

getting in

What time does it ...?	Quelle est l'heure ...?	kel ey leur ...
close	de fermeture	de fer·me·tewr
open	d'ouverture	doo·vair·tewr

What's the admission charge?
Quel est le prix d'admission?   kel ey le pree dad·mee·syon

Is there a discount for children/students?
Il y a une réduction pour les   eel ya ewn rey·dewk·syon poor ley
enfants/étudiants?   zon·fon/zey·tew·dyon

I'd like a ...	Je voudrais ...	zhe voo·drey ...
catalogue	un catalogue	ung ka·ta·log
guide	un guide	ung geed
local map	une carte de la région	ewn kart de la rey·zhyon

I'd like to see ...	J'aimerais voir ...	zhem·rey vwar ...
What's that?	Qu'est-ce que c'est?	kes·ke sey
Can I take photos?	Je peux prendre des photos?	zhe peu pron·dre dey fo·to

tours

When's the next ...?	C'est quand la prochaine ...?	sey kon la pro·shen ...
day trip	excursion d'une journée	eks·kewr·syon dewn zhoor·ney
tour	excursion	eks·kewr·syon

Is ... included?	Est-ce que ... est inclus/incluse? m/f	es·ke ... ey tung·klew/tung·klewz
accommodation	le logement m	le lozh·mon
the admission charge	l'admission f	lad·mee·syon
food	la nourriture f	la noo·ree·tewr
transport	le transport m	le trons·por

How long is the tour?
L'excursion dure combien de temps?   leks·kewr·syon dewr kom·byun de tom

What time should we be back?
On doit rentrer pour quelle heure?   on dwa ron·trey poor kel eur

sightseeing

castle	château m	sha·to
cathedral	cathédrale f	ka·tey·dral
church	église f	ey·gleez
main square	place centrale f	plas son·tral
monastery	monastère m	mo·na·stair
monument	monument m	mo·new·mon
museum	musée m	mew·zey
old city	vieille ville f	vyey veel
palace	palais m	pa·ley
ruins	ruines f pl	rween
stadium	stade m	stad
statues	statues f pl	sta·tew

shopping

enquiries

Where's a ...?	Où est ...?	oo es ...
bank	la banque	la bongk
bookshop	la librairie	la lee·brey·ree
camera shop	le magasin photo	le ma·ga·zun fo·to
department store	le grand magasin	le gron ma·ga·zun
grocery store	l'épicerie	ley·pee·sree
market	le marché	le mar·shey
newsagency	le marchand de journaux	le mar·shon de zhoor·no
supermarket	le supermarché	le sew·pair·mar·shey

Where can I buy (a padlock)?
Où puis-je acheter (un cadenas)?
oo pweezh ash·tey (un kad·na)

I'm looking for . . .
Je cherche . . .
zhe shairsh . . .

Can I look at it?
Est-ce que je peux le voir?
es·ke zhe peu le vwar

Do you have any others?
Vous en avez d'autres?
voo zon a·vey do·tre

Does it have a guarantee?
Est-ce qu'il y a une garantie?
es keel ya ewn ga·ron·tee

Can I have it sent overseas?
Pouvez-vous me l'envoyer à l'étranger?
poo·vey·voo me lon·vwa·yey a ley·tron·zhey

Can I have my . . . repaired?
Puis-je faire réparer . . .?
pwee·zhe fair rey·pa·rey . . .

It's faulty.
C'est défectueux.
sey dey·fek·tweu

I'd like . . ., please.
Je voudrais . . ., s'il vous plaît.
zhe voo·drey . . . seel voo pley

    a bag
    un sac
    un sak

    a refund
    un remboursement
    un rom·boors·mon

    to return this
    rapporter ceci
    ra·por·tey se·see

paying

How much is it?
C'est combien?
sey kom·byun

Can you write down the price?
Pouvez-vous écrire le prix?
poo·vey·voo ey·kreer le pree

That's too expensive.
C'est trop cher.
sey tro shair

Can you lower the price?
Vous pouvez baisser le prix?
voo poo·vey bey·sey le pree

I'll give you (five) euros.
Je vous donnerai (cinq) euros.
zhe voo don·rey (sungk) eu·ro

There's a mistake in the bill.
Il y a une erreur dans la note.
eel ya ewn ey·reur don la not

Do you accept ...?	Est-ce que je peux payer avec ...?	es·ke zhe pe pey·yey a·vek ...
credit cards	une carte de crédit	ewn kart de krey·dee
debit cards	une carte de débit	ewn kart de dey·bee
travellers cheques	des chèques de voyages	dey shek de vwa·yazh

I'd like ..., please.	Je voudrais ..., s'il vous plaît.	zhe voo·drey ... seel voo pley
a receipt	un reçu	un re·sew
my change	ma monnaie	ma mo·ney

clothes & shoes

Can I try it on?	Puis-je l'essayer?	pwee·zhe ley·sey·yey
My size is (42).	Je fais du (quarante-deux).	zhe fey dew (ka·ront·deu)
It doesn't fit.	Ce n'est pas la bonne taille.	se ney pa la bon tai

small	petit	pe·tee
medium	moyen	mwa·yen
large	grand	gron

books & music

I'd like a ...	Je voudrais ...	zhe voo·drey ...
newspaper	un journal	un zhoor·nal
(in English)	(en anglais)	(on ong·gley)
pen	un stylo	un stee·lo

Is there an English-language bookshop?
Y a-t-il une librairie anglaise? — ya·teel ewn lee·brey·ree ong·gleyz

I'm looking for something by (Camus).
Je cherche quelque chose de (Camus). — zhe shairsh kel·ke shoz de (ka·mew)

Can I listen to this?
Je peux l'écouter ici? — zhe peu ley·koo·tey ee·see

photography

Can you ...?	Pouvez-vous ...?	poo·vey·voo ...
burn a CD from my memory card	copier un CD de ma carte memoire	ko·pyey un se·de de ma kart mey·mwar
develop this film	développer cette pellicule	dey·vlo·pey set pey·lee·kewl
load my film	charger ma pellicule	shar·zhey ma pey·lee·kewl
I need a/an ...	J'ai besoin d'une	zhey be·zwun dewn
film for this camera.	pellicule ... pour cet appareil.	pey·lee·kewl ... poor sey·ta·pa·rey
APS	APS	a·pey·es
B&W	en noir et blanc	on nwar ey·blong
colour	couleur	koo·leur
slide	diapositive	dya·po·zee·teev
(200) speed	rapidité (deux cent)	ra·pee·dee·tey (deu son)

When will it be ready?
Quand est-ce que cela sera prêt? kon tes·ke se·la se·ra prey

meeting people

greetings, goodbyes & introductions

Hello.	Bonjour.	bon·zhoor
Hi.	Salut.	sa·lew
Good night.	Bonsoir.	bon·swar
Goodbye.	Au revoir.	o re·vwar
See you later.	À bientôt.	a byun·to
Mr	Monsieur	me·syeu
Mrs	Madame	ma·dam
Miss	Mademoiselle	mad·mwa·zel
How are you?	Comment allez-vous?	ko·mon ta·ley·voo
Fine, thanks. And you?	Bien, merci. Et vous?	byun mair·see ey voo
What's your name?	Comment vous appelez-vous?	ko·mon voo za·pley·voo
My name is ...	Je m'appelle ...	zhe ma·pel ...
I'm pleased to meet you.	Enchanté/Enchantée. m/f	on·shon·tey

This is my ...	Voici mon/ma ... m/f	vwa·see mon/ma ...
boyfriend	petit ami	pe·tee ta·mee
brother	frère	frair
daughter	fille	fee·ye
father	père	pair
friend	ami/amie m/f	a·mee
girlfriend	petite amie	pe·teet a·mee
husband	mari	ma·ree
mother	mère	mair
partner (intimate)	partenaire	par·te·nair
sister	sœur	seur
son	fils	fees
wife	femme	fam

Here's my ...	Voici mon ...	vwa·see mon ...
What's your ...?	Quel est votre ...? pol	kel ey vo·tre ...
	Quel est ton ...? inf	kel ey ton ...
address	adresse	a·dress
email address	e-mail	ey·mel
fax number	numéro de fax	new·mey·ro de faks
phone number	numéro de téléphone	new·mey·ro de tey·ley·fon

occupations

What's your occupation?

Vous faites quoi comme métier? pol		voo fet kwa kom mey·tyey
Tu fais quoi comme métier? inf		tew fey kwa kom mey·tyey

I'm a/an ...	Je suis un/une ... m/f	zhe swee zun/zewn ...
artist	artiste m&f	ar·teest
businessperson	homme/femme d'affaires m/f	om/fem da·fair
farmer	agriculteur m	a·gree·kewl·teur
	agricultrice f	a·gree·kewl·trees
manual worker	ouvrier/ouvrière m/f	oo·vree·yey/oo·vree·yair
office worker	employé/employée de bureau m/f	om·plwa·yey de bew·ro
scientist	scientifique m&f	syon·tee·feek
student	étudiant/étudiante m/f	ey·tew·dyon/ey·tew·dyont
tradesperson	ouvrier qualifié m&f	oo·vree·yey ka·lee·fyey

background

Where are you from?	*Vous venez d'où?* pol	voo ve·ney doo
	Tu viens d'où? inf	tew vyun doo
I'm from ...	*Je viens ...*	zhe vyun ...
Australia	*d'Australie*	dos·tra·lee
Canada	*du Canada*	dew ka·na·da
England	*d'Angleterre*	dong·gle·tair
New Zealand	*de la Nouvelle-Zélande*	de la noo·vel·zey·lond
the USA	*des USA*	dey zew·es·a

Are you married?
Est-ce que vous êtes marié(e)? m/f pol	es·ke voo zet mar·yey
Est-ce que tu es marié(e)? m/f inf	es·ke tew ey mar·yey

I'm married.
Je suis marié/mariée. m/f	zhe swee mar·yey

I'm single.
Je suis célibataire. m&f	zhe swee sey·lee·ba·tair

age

How old ...?	*Quel âge ...?*	kel azh ...
are you	*avez-vous* pol	a·vey·voo
	as-tu inf	a·tew
is your daughter	*a votre fille* pol	a vo·tre fee·ye
is your son	*a votre fils* pol	a vo·tre fees
I'm ... years old.	*J'ai ... ans.*	zhey ... on
He/She is ... years old.	*Il/Elle a ... ans.*	eel/el a ... on

feelings

I'm (not) ...	*Je (ne) suis (pas)...*	zhe (ne) swee (pa) ...
Are you ...?	*Êtes-vous ...?* pol	et voo ...
	Es-tu ...? inf	ey·tew ...
happy	*heureux/heureuse* m/f	er·reu/er·reuz
sad	*triste* m&f	treest

114

I'm ...	J'ai ...	zhey ...
I'm not ...	Je n'ai pas ...	zhe ney pa ...
Are you ...?	Avez-vous ...? pol	a-vey voo ...
	As-tu ...? inf	a-tew ...
cold	froid/froide m/f	frwa/frwad
hot	chaud/chaude m/f	sho/shod
hungry	faim m&f	fum
thirsty	soif m&f	swaf

entertainment

going out

Where can I find ...?	Où sont les ...?	oo son ley ...
clubs	clubs	kleub
gay venues	boîtes gaies	bwat gey
pubs	pubs	peub
I feel like going to a/the ...	Je voudrais aller ...	zhe voo-drey a-ley ...
concert	à un concert	a ung kon-sair
movies	au cinéma	o see-ney-ma
party	à la fête	a la feyt
restaurant	au restaurant	o res-to-ron
theatre	au théâtre	o tey-a-tre

interests

Do you like ...?	Aimes-tu ...? inf	em-tew ...
I like ...	J'aime ...	zhem ...
I don't like ...	Je n'aime pas ...	zhe nem pa ...
art	l'art	lar
cooking	cuisiner	kwee-zee-ney
movies	le cinéma	le see-ney-ma
nightclubs	les boîtes	ley bwat
reading	lire	leer
shopping	faire des courses	fair dey koors
sport	le sport	le spor
travelling	voyager	vwa-ya-zhey

Do you like to ...?	Aimes-tu ...? inf	em-tew ...
dance	danser	don-sey
go to concerts	aller aux concerts	a-ley o kon-sair
listen to music	écouter de	ey-koo-tey de la
	la musique	mew-zeek

food & drink

finding a place to eat

Can you	Est-ce que vous pouvez	es-ke voo poo-vey
recommend a ...?	me conseiller ...?	me kon-sey-yey ...
bar	un bar	um bar
café	un café	ung ka-fey
restaurant	un restaurant	un res-to-ron
I'd like ..., please.	Je voudrais ...,	zhe voo-drey ...
	s'il vous plaît.	seel voo pley
a table for (five)	une table pour	ewn ta-ble poor
	(cinq) personnes	(sungk) pair-son
the (non)smoking	un endroit pour	un on-drwa poor
section	(non-)fumeurs	non-few-me

ordering food

breakfast	petit déjeuner m	pe-tee dey-zhe-ney
lunch	déjeuner m	dey-zhe-ney
dinner	dîner m	dee-ney
snack	casse-croûte m	kas-kroot

What would you recommend?
Qu'est-ce que vous conseillez?   kes-ke voo kon-sey-yey

I'd like (the) ...,	Je voudrais ...,	zhe voo-drey ...
please.	s'il vous plaît.	seel voo pley
bill	l'addition	la-dee-syon
drink list	la carte des boissons	la kart dey bwa-son
menu	la carte	la kart
that dish	ce plat	ser pla
wine list	la carte des vins	la kart dey vun

drinks

(cup of) coffee ...	*(un) café ...*	(ung) ka·fey ...
(cup of) tea ...	*(un) thé ...*	(un) tey ...
with milk	*au lait*	o ley
without sugar	*sans sucre*	son sew·kre
(orange) juice	*jus (d'orange)* m	zhew (do·ronzh)
soft drink	*boisson non-alcoolisée* f	bwa·son non·al·ko·lee·zey
... water	*eau ...*	o ...
hot	*chaude*	shod
sparkling mineral	*minérale gazeuse*	mee·ney·ral ga·zeuz
still mineral	*minérale non-gazeuse*	mee·ney·ral nong·ga·zeuz

in the bar

I'll have ...	*Je prends ...*	zhe pron ...
I'll buy you a drink.	*Je vous offre un verre.*	zhe voo zo·fre un vair
What would you like?	*Qu'est-ce que vous voulez?*	kes·ke voo voo·ley
Cheers!	*Santé!*	son·tey
brandy	*cognac* m	ko·nyak
champagne	*champagne* m	shom·pan·ye
cocktail	*cocktail* m	kok·tel
a shot of (whisky)	*un petit verre de (whisky)*	um pe·tee vair de (wees·kee)
a bottle of ... wine	*une bouteille de vin ...*	ewn boo·tey de vun ...
a glass of ... wine	*un verre de vin ...*	un vair de vun ...
red	*rouge*	roozh
sparkling	*mousseux*	moo·seu
white	*blanc*	blong
a ... of beer	*... de bière*	... de byair
glass	*un verre*	un vair
bottle	*une bouteille*	ewn boo·tey

self-catering

What's the local speciality?
Quelle est la spécialité locale? kel ey la spey·sya·lee·tey lo·kal

What's that?
Qu'est-ce que c'est, ça? kes·ke sey sa

How much is (a kilo of cheese)?
C'est combien (le kilo de fromage)? sey kom·byun (le kee·lo de fro·mazh)

I'd like ...	*Je voudrais ...*	zhe voo·drey ...
(200) grams	*(deux cents) grammes*	(deu son) gram
(two) kilos	*(deux) kilos*	(deu) kee·lo
(three) pieces	*(trois) morceaux*	(trwa) mor·so
(six) slices	*(six) tranches*	(sees) tronsh

Less.	*Moins.*	mwun
Enough.	*Assez.*	a·sey
More.	*Plus.*	plew

special diets & allergies

Is there a vegetarian restaurant near here?
Y a-t-il un restaurant ya·teel un res·to·ron
végétarien par ici? vey·zhey·ta·ryun par ee·see

Do you have vegetarian food?
Vous faites les repas végétarien? voo fet ley re·pa vey·zhey·ta·ryun

Could you prepare	*Pouvez-vous préparer*	poo·vey·voo prey·pa·rey
a meal without ...?	*un repas sans ...?*	un re·pa son ...
butter	*beurre*	beur
eggs	*œufs*	zeu
meat stock	*bouillon gras*	boo·yon gra

I'm allergic to ...	*Je suis allergique ...*	zhe swee za·lair·zheek ...
dairy produce	*aux produits laitiers*	o pro·dwee ley·tyey
gluten	*au gluten*	o glew·ten
MSG	*au glutamate*	o glew·ta·mat
	de sodium	de so·dyom
nuts	*au noix*	no nwa
seafood	*aux fruits de mer*	o frwe de mair

menu decoder

baba au rhum m	ba·ba o rom	small sponge cake, often with raisins, soaked in a rum-flavoured syrup
béarnaise f	bey·ar·neyz	white sauce of wine or vinegar beaten with egg yolks & flavoured with herbs
blanquette de veau f	blong·ket de vo	veal stew in white sauce with cream
bombe glacée f	bom·be gla·sey	ice cream with candied fruits, glazed chestnuts & cream
bouillabaisse f	bwee·ya·bes	fish soup stewed in a broth with garlic, orange peel, fennel, tomatoes & saffron
brioche f	bree·yosh	small roll or cake sometimes flavoured with nuts, currants or candied fruits
brochette f	bro·shet	grilled skewer of meat or vegetables
consommé m	kon·so·mey	clarified meat or fish-based broth
contre-filet m	kon·tre·fee·ley	beef sirloin roast
coulis m	koo·lee	fruit or vegetable purée, used as a sauce
croque-madame m	krok·ma·dam	grilled or fried ham & cheese sandwich, topped with a fried egg
croquembouche m	kro·kom·boosh	cream puffs dipped in caramel
croque-monsieur m	krok·mes·yeu	grilled or fried ham & cheese sandwich
croustade f	kroo·stad	puff pastry filled with fish, seafood, meat, mushrooms or vegetables
dijonnaise	dee·zho·nez	dishes with a mustard-based sauce
estouffade f	es·too·fad	meat stewed in wine with carrots & herbs
friand m	free·yon	pastry stuffed with minced sausage meat, ham & cheese, or almond cream
fricandeau m	free·kon·do	veal fillet simmered in white wine, vegetables herbs & spices • a pork pâté

fricassée f	free·ka·sey	lamb, veal or poultry in a thick creamy sauce with mushrooms & onions
grenadin m	gre·na·dun	veal (or sometimes poultry) fillet, wrapped in a thin slice of bacon
michette f	mee·shet	savoury bread stuffed with cheese, olives, onions & anchovies
pan-bagnat m	pun ban·ya	small round bread loaves, filled with onions, vegetables, anchovies & olives
plateau de fromage m	pla·to de fro·mazh	cheese board or platter
pomme duchesse f	pom dew·shes	fritter of mashed potato, butter & egg yolk
pot-au-feu m	po·to·fe	beef, root vegetable & herb stockpot
potée f	po·tey	meat & vegetables cooked in a pot
profiterole m	pro·fee·trol	small pastry with savoury or sweet fillings
puits d'amour m	pwee da·moor	puff pastry filled with custard or jam
quenelle f	ke·nel	fish or meat dumpling, often poached
quiche f	keesh	tart with meat, fish or vegetable filling
raclette f	ra·klet	hot melted cheese, served with potatoes & gherkins
ragoût m	ra·goo	stew of meat, fish and/or vegetables
ratatouille f	ra·ta·too·ye	vegetable stew
roulade f	roo·lad	slice of meat or fish rolled around stuffing
savarin m	sa·va·run	sponge cake soaked with a rum syrup & filled with custard, cream & fruits
savoie f	sav·wa	light cake made with beaten egg whites
tartiflette f	tar·tee·flet	dish of potatoes, cheese & bacon
velouté m	ver·loo·tey	rich, creamy soup, usually prepared with vegetables, shellfish or fish purée
vol-au-vent m	vo·lo·von	puff pastry filled with a mixture of sauce & meat, seafood or vegetables

emergencies

basics

Help!	Au secours!	o skoor
Stop!	Arrêtez!	a·rey·tey
Go away!	Allez-vous-en!	a·ley·voo·zon
Thief!	Au voleur!	o vo·leur
Fire!	Au feu!	o feu
Watch out!	Faites attention!	fet a·ton·syon
Call ...!	Appelez ...!	a·pley ...
a doctor	un médecin	un meyd·sun
an ambulance	une ambulance	ewn om·bew·lons
the police	la police	la po·lees

It's an emergency!
C'est urgent!
sey tewr·zhon

Could you help me, please?
Est-ce que vous pourriez
m'aider, s'il vous plaît?
es·ke voo poo·ryey
mey·dey seel voo pley

Could I use the telephone?
Est-ce que je pourrais utiliser
le téléphone?
es·ke zhe poo·rey ew·tee·lee·zey
le tey·ley·fon

I'm lost.
Je suis perdu/perdue. m/f
zhe swee pair·dew

Where are the toilets?
Où sont les toilettes?
oo son ley twa·let

police

Where's the police station?
Où est le commissariat de police?
oo ey le ko·mee·sar·ya de po·lees

I want to report an offence.
Je veux signaler un délit.
zhe veu see·nya·ley un dey·lee

I have insurance.
J'ai une assurance.
zhey ewn a·sew·rons

I've been assaulted.
J'ai été attaqué/attaquée. m/f
zhey ey·tey a·ta·key

I've been raped.		
J'ai été violé/violée. m/f		zhey ey·tey vyo·ley
I've been robbed.		
On m'a volé.		on ma vo·ley
I've lost my ...	*J'ai perdu ...*	zhey pair·dew ...
My ... was/were stolen.	*On m'a volé ...*	on ma vo·ley ...
backpack	*mon sac à dos*	mon sak a do
bags	*mes valises*	mey va·leez
credit card	*ma carte de crédit*	ma kart de krey·dee
handbag	*mon sac à main*	mon sak a mun
jewellery	*mes bijoux*	mey bee·zhoo
money	*mon argent*	mon ar·zhon
passport	*mon passeport*	mom pas·por
travellers cheques	*mes chèques de voyage*	mey shek de vwa·yazh
wallet	*mon portefeuille*	mom por·te·feu·ye
I want to contact my ...	*Je veux contacter mon ...*	zher veu kon·tak·tey mon ...
consulate	*consulat*	kon·sew·la
embassy	*ambassade*	om·ba·sad

health

medical needs

Where's the nearest ...?	*Où y a t-il ... par ici?*	oo ee a teel ... par ee·see
dentist	*un dentiste*	un don·teest
doctor	*un médecin*	un meyd·sun
hospital	*un hôpital*	u·no·pee·tal
(night) pharmacist	*une pharmacie (de nuit)*	ewn far·ma·see (de nwee)

I need a doctor (who speaks English).
J'ai besoin d'un médecin (qui parle anglais).
zhey be·zwun dun meyd·sun (kee parl ong·gley)

Could I see a female doctor?
Est-ce que je peux voir une femme médecin?
es·ke zhe peu vwar ewn fam meyd·sun

I've run out of my medication.
Je n'ai plus de médicaments.
zhe ney plew de mey·dee·ka·mon

122

symptoms, conditions & allergies

I'm sick.	*Je suis malade.*	zhe swee ma·lad
It hurts here.	*J'ai une douleur ici.*	zhey ewn doo·leur ee·see

I have (a) ...	*J'ai ...*	zhey ...
asthma	*de l'asthme*	de las·me
bronchitis	*la bronchite*	la bron·sheet
constipation	*la constipation*	la kon·stee·pa·syon
cough	*la toux*	la too
diarrhoea	*la diarrhée*	la dya·rey
fever	*la fièvre*	la fyev·re
headache	*mal à la tête*	mal a la tet
heart condition	*maladie de cœur*	ma·la·dee de keur
nausea	*la nausée*	la no·zey
pain	*une douleur*	ewn doo·leur
sore throat	*mal à la gorge*	mal a la gorzh
toothache	*mal aux dents*	mal o don

I'm allergic to ...	*Je suis allergique ...*	zhe swee za·lair·zheek ...
antibiotics	*aux antibiotiques*	o zon·tee·byo·teek
anti-inflammatories	*aux antiinflammatoires*	o zun·tee·un·fla·ma·twar
aspirin	*à l'aspirine*	a las·pee·reen
bees	*aux abeilles*	o za·bey·ye
codeine	*à la codéine*	a la ko·dey·een
penicillin	*à la pénicilline*	a la pey·nee·see·leen

antiseptic	*antiseptique* m	on·tee·sep·teek
bandage	*pansement* m	pons·mon
condoms	*préservatifs* m pl	prey·zair·va·teef
contraceptives	*contraceptifs* m pl	kon·tre·sep·teef
diarrhoea medicine	*médecine pour la diarrhée* f	med·seen poor la dya·ey
insect repellent	*repulsif anti-insectes* m	rey·pewl·seef on·tee·un·sekt
laxatives	*laxatifs* m pl	lak·sa·teef
painkillers	*analgésiques* m pl	a·nal·zhey·zeek
rehydration salts	*sels de réhydratation* m pl	seyl de rey·ee·dra·ta·syon
sleeping tablets	*somnifères* m pl	som·nee·fair

english–french dictionary

French nouns and adjectives in this dictionary have their gender indicated by ⓜ (masculine) or ⓕ (feminine). If it's a plural noun, you'll also see pl. Words are also marked as n (noun), a (adjective), v (verb), sg (singular), pl (plural), inf (informal) and pol (polite) where necessary.

A

accident *accident* ⓜ ak-see-don
accommodation *logement* ⓜ lozh-mon
adaptor *adaptateur* ⓜ a-dap-ta-teur
address *adresse* ⓕ a-dres
after *après* a-prey
air-conditioned *climatisé* kee-ma-tee-zey
airplane *avion* ⓜ a-vyon
airport *aéroport* ⓜ a-ey-ro-por
alcohol *alcool* ⓜ al-kol
all *tout/toute* ⓜ/ⓕ too/toot
allergy *allergie* ⓕ a-lair-zhee
ambulance *ambulance* ⓕ om-bew-lons
and *et* ey
ankle *cheville* ⓕ she-vee-ye
arm *bras* ⓜ bra
ashtray *cendrier* ⓜ son-dree-yey
ATM *guichet automatique de banque* ⓜ
  gee-shey o-to-ma-teek de bonk

B

baby *bébé* ⓜ bey-bey
back (body) *dos* ⓜ do
backpack *sac à dos* ⓜ sak a do
bad *mauvais/mauvaise* ⓜ/ⓕ mo-vey/mo-veyz
bag *sac* ⓜ sak
baggage claim *retrait des bagages* ⓜ
  re-trey dey ba-gazh
bank *banque* ⓕ bonk
bar *bar* ⓜ bar
bathroom *salle de bain* ⓕ sal de bun
battery (car) *batterie* ⓕ bat-ree
battery (general) *pile* ⓕ peel
beautiful *beau/belle* ⓜ/ⓕ bo/bel
bed *lit* ⓜ lee
beer *bière* ⓕ byair
before *avant* a-von
behind *derrière* dair-yair
Belgium *Belgique* ⓕ bel-zheek
bicycle *vélo* ⓜ vey-lo

big *grand/grande* ⓜ/ⓕ gron/grond
bill *addition* ⓕ a-dee-syon
black *noir/noire* ⓜ/ⓕ nwar
blanket *couverture* ⓕ koo-vair-tewr
blood group *groupe sanguin* ⓜ groop song-gun
blue *bleu/bleue* ⓜ/ⓕ bler
book (make a reservation) v *réserver* rey-zair-vey
bottle *bouteille* ⓕ boo-tey
bottle opener *ouvre-bouteille* ⓜ oo-vre-boo-tey
boy *garçon* ⓜ gar-son
brakes (car) *freins* ⓜ frun
breakfast *petit déjeuner* ⓜ pe-tee dey-zheu-ney
broken (faulty) *défectueux/défectueuse* ⓜ/ⓕ
  dey-fek-tweu/dey-fek-tweuz
bus (auto)bus ⓜ (o-to)bews
business *affaires* ⓕ a-fair
buy *acheter* ash-tey

C

café *café* ⓜ ka-fey
camera *appareil photo* ⓜ a-pa-rey fo-to
camp site *terrain de camping* ⓜ tey-run de kom-peeng
can opener *ouvre-boîte* ⓜ oo-vre-bwat
cancel *annuler* a-new-ley
car *voiture* ⓕ vwa-tewr
cash *argent* ⓜ ar-zhon
cash (a cheque) v *encaisser* ong-key-sey
cell phone *téléphone portable* ⓜ tey-ley-fon por-ta-ble
centre *centre* ⓜ son-tre
change (money) v *échanger* ey-shon-zhey
cheap *bon marché* ⓜ & ⓕ bon mar-shey
check (bill) *addition* ⓕ la-dee-syon
check-in n *enregistrement* ⓜ on-re-zhee-stre-mon
chest *poitrine* ⓕ pwa-treen
child *enfant* ⓜ & ⓕ on-fon
cigarette *cigarette* ⓕ see-ga-ret
city *ville* ⓕ veel
clean a *propre* ⓜ & ⓕ pro-pre
closed *fermé/fermée* ⓜ/ⓕ fair-mey
coffee *café* ⓜ ka-fey
coins *pièces* ⓕ pyes
cold a *froid/froide* ⓜ/ⓕ frwa/frwad

collect call *appel en PCV* ⓜ a·pel on pey·sey·vey
come *venir* ve·neer
computer *ordinateur* ⓜ or·dee·na·teur
condom *préservatif* ⓜ prey·zair·va·teef
contact lenses *verres de contact* ⓜ vair de kon·takt
cook v *cuire* kweer
cost *coût* ⓜ koo
credit card *carte de crédit* ⓕ kart de krey·dee
cup *tasse* ⓕ tas
currency exchange *taux de change* ⓜ to de shonzh
customs (immigration) *douane* ⓕ dwan

D

dangerous *dangereux/dangereuse* ⓜ/ⓕ don·zhreu/don·zhreuz
date (time) *date* ⓕ dat
day *date de naissance* ⓕ dat de ney·sons
delay *retard* ⓜ re·tard
dentist *dentiste* ⓜ don·teest
depart *partir* par·teer
diaper *couche* ⓕ koosh
dictionary *dictionnaire* ⓜ deek·syo·nair
dinner *dîner* ⓜ dee·ney
direct *direct/directe* ⓜ/ⓕ dee·rekt
dirty *sale* ⓜ&ⓕ sal
disabled *handicapé/handicapée* ⓜ/ⓕ on·dee·ka·pey
discount *remise* ⓕ re·meez
doctor *médecin* ⓜ meyd·sun
double bed *grand lit* ⓜ gron lee
double room *chambre pour deux personnes* ⓕ shom·bre poor de pair·son
drink *boisson* ⓕ bwa·son
drive v *conduire* kon·dweer
drivers licence *permis de conduire* ⓜ pair·mee de kon·dweer
drugs (illicit) *drogue* ⓕ drog
dummy (pacifier) *tétine* ⓕ tey·teen

E

ear *oreille* ⓕ o·rey
east *est* ⓜ est
eat *manger* mon·zhey
economy class *classe touriste* ⓕ klas too·reest
electricity *électricité* ⓕ ey·lek·tree·see·tey
elevator *ascenseur* ⓜ a·son·seur
email *e-mail* ⓜ ey·mel
embassy *ambassade* ⓕ om·ba·sad
emergency *cas urgent* ⓜ ka ewr·zhon
English (language) *anglais/anglaise* ⓜ/ⓕ ong·gley/ong·gleyz
entrance *entrée* ⓕ on·trey
evening *soir* ⓜ swar
exchange rate *taux de change* ⓜ to de shonzh
exit *sortie* ⓕ sor·tee
expensive *cher/chère* ⓜ/ⓕ shair
express mail *exprès* eks·pres
eye *œil* ⓜ eu·yee

F

far *lointain/lointaine* ⓜ/ⓕ lwun·tun/lwun·ten
fast *rapide* ⓜ&ⓕ ra·peed
father *père* ⓜ pair
film (camera) *pellicule* ⓕ pey·lee·kewl
finger *doigt* ⓜ dwa
first-aid kit *trousse à pharmacie* ⓕ troos a far·ma·see
first class *première classe* ⓕ pre·myair klas
fish *poisson* ⓜ pwa·son
food *nourriture* ⓕ noo·ree·tewr
foot *pied* ⓜ pyey
fork *fourchette* ⓕ foor·shet
France *France* frons
free (of charge) *gratuit/gratuite* ⓜ/ⓕ gra·twee/gra·tweet
French (language) *Français* fron·sey
friend *ami/amie* ⓜ/ⓕ a·mee
fruit *fruit* ⓜ frwee
full *plein/pleine* ⓜ/ⓕ plun/plen
funny *drôle* ⓜ&ⓕ drol

G

gift *cadeau* ⓜ ka·do
girl *fille* ⓕ fee·ye
glass (drinking) *verre* ⓜ vair
glasses *lunettes* ⓕ pl lew·net
go *aller* a·ley
good *bon/bonne* ⓜ/ⓕ bon
green *vert/verte* ⓜ/ⓕ vair
guide n *guide* ⓜ geed

H

half *moitié* ⓕ mwa·tyey
hand *main* ⓕ mun
handbag *sac à main* ⓜ sak a mun
happy *heureux/heureuse* ⓜ/ⓕ eu·reu/eu·reuz
have *avoir* a·vwar

he *il* eel
head *tête* ① tet
heart *cœur* ⓜ keur
heat *chaleur* ① sha-leur
heavy *lourd/lourde* ⓜ/① loor/loord
help v *aider* ey-dey
here *ici* ee-see
high *haut/haute* ⓜ/① o/ot
highway *autoroute* ① o-to-root
hike v *faire la randonnée* fair la ron-do-ney
holiday *vacances* ① pl va-kons
homosexual n *homosexuel/homosexuelle* ⓜ/①
    o-mo-sek-swel
hospital *hôpital* ⓜ o-pee-tal
hot *chaud/chaude* ⓜ/① sho/shod
hotel *hôtel* ⓜ o-tel
(be) hungry *avoir faim* a-vwar fum
husband *mari* ⓜ ma-ree

I

I *je* zhe
identification (card) *carte d'identité* ①
    kart dee-don-tee-tey
ill *malade* ⓜ&① ma-lad
important *important/importante* ⓜ/①
    um-por-ton/um-por-tont
included *compris/comprise* ⓜ/①
    kom-pree/kom-preez
injury *blessure* ① bley-sewr
insurance *assurance* ① a-sew-rons
Internet *Internet* un-tair-net
interpreter *interprète* ⓜ&① un-tair-pret

J

jewellery *bijoux* ⓜ pl bee-zhoo
job *travail* ⓜ tra-vai

K

key *clé* ① kley
kilogram *kilogramme* ① kee-lo-gram
kitchen *cuisine* ① kwee-zeen
knife *couteau* ⓜ koo-to

L

laundry (place) *blanchisserie* ① blon-shees-ree
lawyer *avocat/avocate* ⓜ/① a-vo-ka/a-vo-kat

left (direction) *à gauche* a gosh
left-luggage office *consigne* ① kon-see-nye
leg *jambe* ① zhomb
lesbian n *lesbienne* ① les-byen
less *moins* mwun
letter (mail) *lettre* ① ley-trer
lift (elevator) *ascenseur* ① a-son-seur
light *lumière* ① lew-myair
like v *aimer* ey-mey
lock *serrure* ① sey-rewr
long *long/longue* ⓜ/① long(k)
lost *perdu/perdue* ⓜ/① pair-dew
lost-property office *bureau des objets trouvés* ①
    bew-ro dey zob-zhey troo-vey
love v *aimer* ey-mey
luggage *bagages* ⓜ pl ba-gazh
lunch *déjeuner* ① dey-zheu-ney

M

mail *courrier* ⓜ koo-ryey
man *homme* ⓜ om
map *carte* ① kart
market *marché* ⓜ mar-shey
matches *allumettes* ① pl a-lew-met
meat *viande* ① vyond
medicine *médecine* ① med-seen
menu *carte* kart
message *message* ⓜ mey-sazh
milk *lait* ⓜ ley
minute *minute* ① mee-newt
mobile phone *téléphone portable* ⓜ
    tey-ley-fon por-ta-ble
money *argent* ⓜ ar-zhon
month *mois* ⓜ mwa
morning *matin* ⓜ ma-tun
mother *mère* ① mair
motorcycle *moto* ⓜ mo-to
motorway *autoroute* ① o-to-root
mouth *bouche* ① boosh
music *musique* ① mew-zeek

N

name *nom* ⓜ nom
napkin *serviette* ① sair-vyet
nappy *couche* ① koosh
near *près de* prey de
neck *cou* ⓜ koo
new *nouveau/nouvelle* ⓜ/① noo-vo/noo-vel

news *les nouvelles* ley noo-vel
newspaper *journal* ⓜ zhoor-nal
night *nuit* ① nwee
no *non* non
noisy *bruyant/bruyante* ⓜ/① brew/yon/brew-yont
nonsmoking *non-fumeur* non-few-meur
north *nord* ⓜ nor
nose *nez* ⓜ ney
now *maintenant* mun-te-non
number *numéro* ⓜ new-mey-ro

O

oil (engine) *huile* ① weel
old *vieux/vieille* ⓜ/① vyeu/vyey
one-way ticket *billet simple* ① bee-yey sum-ple
open a *ouvert/ouverte* ⓜ/① oo-vair/oo-vairt
outside *dehors* de-or

P

package *paquet* ⓜ pa-key
paper *papier* ⓜ pa-pyey
park (car) ∨ *garer (une voiture)* ga-rey (ewn vwa-tewr)
passport *passeport* ⓜ pas-por
pay *payer* pey-yey
pen *stylo* ⓜ stee-lo
petrol *essence* ① ey-sons
pharmacy *pharmacie* ① far-ma-see
phonecard *télécarte* ① tey-ley-kart
photo *photo* ① fo-to
plate *assiette* ① a-syet
police *police* ① po-lees
postcard *carte postale* ① kart pos-tal
post office *bureau de poste* ⓜ bew-ro de post
pregnant *enceinte* on-sunt
price *prix* ⓜ pree

Q

quiet *tranquille* ⓜ & ① trong-keel

R

rain n *pluie* ① plwee
razor *rasoir* ⓜ ra-zwar
receipt *reçu* ⓜ re-sew
red *rouge* roozh
refund *remboursement* ⓜ rom-boor-se-mon
registered mail *en recommandé* on re-ko-mon-dey

rent ∨ *louer* loo-ey
repair ∨ *réparer* rey-pa-rey
reservation *réservation* ① rey-zair-va-syon
restaurant *restaurant* ⓜ res-to-ron
return ∨ *revenir* rev-neer
return ticket *aller retour* ⓜ a-ley re-toor
right (direction) *à droite* a drwat
road *route* ① root
room *chambre* ① shom-bre

S

safe a *sans danger* ⓜ & ① son don-zhey
sanitary napkin *serviette hygiénique* ①
    sair-vyet ee-zhyey-neek
seat *place* ① plas
send *envoyer* on-vwa-yey
service station *station-service* ① sta-syon-sair-vees
sex *sexe* ⓜ seks
shampoo *shampooing* ⓜ shom-pwung
share (a dorm) *partager* par-ta-zhey
shaving cream *mousse à raser* ① moos a ra-zey
she *elle* el
sheet (bed) *drap* ⓜ dra
shirt *chemise* ① she-meez
shoes *chaussures* ① pl sho-sewr
shop *magasin* ⓜ ma-ga-zun
short *court/courte* ⓜ/① koor/koort
shower *douche* ① doosh
single room *chambre pour une personne* ①
    shom-bre poor ewn pair-son
skin *peau* ① po
skirt *jupe* ① zhewp
sleep ∨ *dormir* dor-meer
slowly *lentement* lon-te-mon
small *petit/petite* ⓜ/① pe-tee/pe-teet
smoke (cigarettes) ∨ *fumer* few-mey
soap *savon* ⓜ sa-von
some *quelques* kel-ke
soon *bientôt* byun-to
south *sud* ⓜ sewd
souvenir shop *magasin de souvenirs* ⓜ
    ma-ga-zun de soov-neer
speak *parler* par-ley
spoon *cuillère* ① kwee-yair
stamp *timbre* ⓜ tum-bre
stand-by ticket *billet stand-by* ⓜ bee-yey stond-bai
station (train) *gare* ① gar
stomach *estomac* ⓜ es-to-ma
stop ∨ *arrêter* a-rey-tey

127

stop (bus) *arrêt* m a-rey
street *rue* f rew
student *étudiant/étudiante* m/f
  ey-tew-dyon/ey-tew-dyont
sun *soleil* m so-ley
sunscreen *écran solaire* m ey-kron so-lair
swim v *nager* na-zhey
Switzerland *Suisse* swees

T

tampons *tampons* m pl tom-pon
taxi *taxi* m tak-see
teaspoon *petite cuillère* f pe-teet kwee-yair
teeth *dents* f don
telephone n *téléphone* m tey-ley-fon
television *télé(vision)* f tey-ley(vee-zyon)
temperature (weather) *température* f
  tom-pey-ra-tewr
tent *tente* f tont
that (one) *cela* se-la
they *ils/elles* m/f eel/el
(be) thirsty *avoir soif* a-vwar swaf
this (one) *ceci* se-see
throat *gorge* f gorzh
ticket *billet* m bee-yey
time *temps* m tom
tired *fatigué/fatiguée* m/f fa-tee-gey
tissues *mouchoirs en papier* m pl
  moo-shwar om pa-pyey
today *aujourd'hui* o-zhoor-dwee
toilet *toilettes* f pl twa-let
tomorrow *demain* de-mun
tonight *ce soir* se swar
toothbrush *brosse à dents* f bros a don
toothpaste *dentifrice* m don-tee-frees
torch (flashlight) *lampe de poche* f lomp de posh
tour *voyage* m vwa-yazh
tourist office *office de tourisme* m
  o-fees-de too-rees-me
towel *serviette* f sair-vyet
train *train* m trun
translate *traduire* tra-dweer
travel agency *agence de voyage* f
  a-zhons de vwa-yazh
travellers cheque *chèque de voyage* m
  shek de vwa-yazh
trousers *pantalon* m pon-ta-lon

twin beds *lits jumeaux* m pl dey lee zhew-mo
tyre *pneu* m pneu

U

underwear *sous-vêtements* m soo-vet-mon
urgent *urgent/urgente* m/f ewr-zhon/ewr-zhont

V

vacant *libre* m & f lee-bre
vacation *vacances* f pl va-kons
vegetable n *légume* m ley-gewm
vegetarian a *végétarien/végétarienne* m/f
  vey-zhey-ta-ryun/vey-zhey-ta-ryen
visa *visa* m vee-za

W

waiter *serveur/serveuse* m/f sair-veur/sair-veurz
walk v *marcher* mar-shey
wallet *portefeuille* m por-te-feu-ye
warm a *chaud/chaude* m/f sho/shod
wash (something) *laver* la-vey
watch *montre* f mon-tre
water *eau* f o
we *nous* noo
weekend *week-end* m week-end
west *ouest* m west
wheelchair *fauteuil roulant* m fo-teu-ye roo-lon
when *quand* kon
where *où* oo
white *blanc/blanche* m/f blong/blonsh
who *qui* kee
why *pourquoi* poor-kwa
wife *femme* f fam
window *fenêtre* f fe-ney-tre
wine *vin* m vun
with *avec* a-vek
without *sans* son
woman *femme* f fam
write *écrire* ey-kreer

Y

yellow *jaune* zhon
yes *oui* wee
yesterday *hier* hee-yair
you sg inf *tu* tew
you sg pol *vous* voo
you pl *vous* voo

Greek

greek alphabet

A α *al*-pha	B β *vi*-ta	Γ γ *gha*-ma	Δ δ *dhel*-ta	E ε *ep*-si-lon
Z ζ *zi*-ta	H η *i*-ta	Θ θ *thi*-ta	I ι *yio*-ta	K κ *ka*-pa
Λ λ *lam*-dha	M μ mi	N ν ni	Ξ ξ ksi	O o *o*-mi-kron
Π π pi	P ρ ro	Σ σ/ς* *sigh*-ma	T τ taf	Y υ *ip*-si-lon
Φ φ fi	X χ hi	Ψ ψ psi	Ω ω *o-me*-gha	

* The letter Σ has two forms for the lower case – σ and ς. The second one is used at the end of words.

ΕΛΛΗΝΙΚΑ

introduction

Aristotle, Plato, Homer, Sappho and Herodotus can't all be wrong in their choice of language – if you've ever come across arcane concepts such as 'democracy', exotic disciplines like 'trigonometry' or a little-known neurosis termed 'the Oedipus complex', then you'll have some inkling of the widespread influence of Greek (Ελληνικά e-li-ni-ka). With just a little Modern Greek under your belt, you'll have a richer understanding of this language's impact on contemporary Western culture.

Modern Greek is a separate branch of the Indo-European language family, with Ancient Greek its only (extinct) relative. The first records of written Ancient Greek date from the 14th to the 12th centuries BC. By the 9th century BC, the Greeks had adapted the Phoenician alphabet to include vowels – the first alphabet to do so – and the script in use today came to its final form some time in the 5th century BC. The Greek script was the foundation for both the Cyrillic and the Latin alphabet.

Although written Greek has been remarkably stable over the millennia, the spoken language has evolved considerably. In the 5th century, the dialect spoken around Athens (known as 'Attic') became the dominant speech as a result of the city-state's cultural and political prestige. Attic gained even greater influence as the medium of administration for the vast empire of Alexander the Great, and remained the official language of the Eastern Roman Empire and the Orthodox Church after the demise of the Hellenistic world. Once the Ottoman Turks took Constantinople in 1453, the Attic dialect lost its official function. In the meantime, the common language, known as Koine (Κοινή ki-ni), continued to evolve, absorbing vocabulary from Turkish, Italian, Albanian and other Balkan languages.

When an independent Greece returned to the world stage in 1832, it needed to choose a national language. Purists advocated a slightly modernised version of Attic known as Καθαρεύουσα ka-tha-re-vu-sa (from the Greek word for 'clean'), which no longer resembled the spoken language. However, Koine had strong support as it was spoken and understood by the majority of Greeks, and in the end it gained official recognition, although it was banned during the military dictatorship (1967–74). Today, Greek is the official language of Greece and a co-official language of Cyprus, and has over 13 million speakers worldwide. Start your Greek adventure with this chapter – and if you're having one of those days when you're dying to say 'It's all Greek to me!', remember that in your shoes, a Greek speaker would say: Αυτά για μένα είναι Κινέζικα af-ta yia me-na i-ne ki-ne-zi-ka (This is Chinese to me)!

pronunciation

vowel sounds

Greek vowels are pronounced separately even when they're written in sequence, eg ζώο *zo·o* (animal). You'll see though, in the table below, that some letter combinations correspond to a single sound – ουρά (queue) is pronounced u·*ra* . When a word ending in a vowel is followed by another word that starts with the same or a similar vowel sound, one vowel is usually omitted and the two words are pronounced as if they were one – Σε ευχαριστώ se ef·kha·ris·*to* becomes Σ' ευχαριστώ sef·kha·ris·*to* (Thank you). Note that the apostrophe (') is used in written Greek to show that two words are joined together.

symbol	english equivalent	greek example	transliteration
a	father	αλλά	a·*la*
e	bet	πλένομαι	ple·no·me
i	hit	πίσω, πόλη, υποφέρω, είδος, οικογένεια, υιός	*pi*·so, po·li, i·po·*fe*·ro, i·dhos, i·ko·ye·ni·a, i·os
ia	nostalgia	ζητιάνος	zi·*tia*·nos
io	ratio	πιο	pio
o	pot	πόνος, πίσω	po·nos, *pi*·so
u	put	ουρά	u·*ra*

word stress

Stress can fall on any of the last three syllables. In our pronunciation guides, the stressed syllable is always in italics, but in written Greek, the stressed syllable is always indicated by an accent over the vowel, eg καλά ka·*la* (good). If a vowel is represented by two letters, it's written on the second letter, eg ζητιάνος zi·*tia*·nos (beggar). If the accent is marked on the first of these two letters, they should be read separately, eg Μάιος *ma*·i·os (May). Where two vowels occur together but are not stressed, a diaeresis (¨) is used to indicate that they should be pronounced separately, eg λαϊκός la·i·*kos* (popular).

consonant sounds

Most Greek consonant sounds are also found in English – only the guttural gh and kh might need a bit of practice. Double consonants are only pronounced once – άλλος a·los (other). However, you'll notice that sometimes two Greek letters in combination form one single consonant sound – the combination of the letters μ and π makes the sound b, and the combination of the letters ν and τ makes the sound d.

symbol	english equivalent	greek example	transliteration
b	**b**ed	μπαρ	**b**ar
d	**d**og	ντομάτα	**d**o·*ma*·ta
dh	**th**at	δεν	**dh**en
dz	a**dds**	τζάμι	**dz**a·*mi*
f	**f**at	φως, αυτή	**f**os, a**f**·*ti*
g	**g**o	γκαρσόν	**g**ar·*son*
gh	guttural sound, between 'goat' and 'loch'	γάτα	*gha*·ta
h	**h**at	χέρι	**h**e·ri
k	**k**it	καλά	ka·*la*
kh	lo**ch** (guttural sound)	χαλί	**kh**a·*li*
l	**l**et	λάδι	*la*·dhi
m	**m**an	μαζί	ma·*zi*
n	**n**ot	ναός	na·*os*
ng	ri**ng**	ελέγχω	e·*le***ng**·kho
p	**p**et	πάνω	*pa*·no
r	**r**ed (trilled)	ράβω	*ra*·vo
s	**s**un	στυλό	sti·*lo*
t	**t**op	τι	ti
th	**th**in	θέα	*the*·a
ts	ha**ts**	τσέπη	**ts**e·pi
v	**v**ery	βίζα, αύριο	*vi*·za, *av*·ri·o
y	**y**es	γέρος	*ye*·ros
z	**z**ero	ζέστη	*ze*·sti

basics

language difficulties

Do you speak English?
Μιλάς Αγγλικά;   mi-*las* ang-gli-*ka*

Do you understand?
Καταλαβαίνεις;   ka-ta-la-*ve*-nis

I understand.
Καταλαβαίνω.   ka-ta-la-*ve*-no

I don't understand.
Δεν καταλαβαίνω.   dhen ka-ta-la-*ve*-no

What does (μώλος) mean?
Τι σημαίνει (μώλος);   ti si-*me*-ni (*mo*-los)

How do you ...?	Πως ...;	pos ...
pronounce this	προφέρεις αυτό	pro-*fe*-ris af-*to*
write (Madhuri)	γράφουν (Μαδουρή)	*ghra*-foun (ma-dhu-*ri*)

Could you	Θα μπορούσες	tha bo-*ru*-ses
please ...?	παρακαλώ να ...;	pa-ra-ka-*lo* na ...
repeat that	το επαναλάβεις	to e-pa-na-*la*-vis
speak more slowly	μιλάς πιο σιγά	mi-*las* pio si-*gha*
write it down	το γράφεις	to *ghrap*-sis

essentials

Yes.	Ναι.	ne
No.	Οχι.	*o*-hi
Please.	Παρακαλώ.	pa-ra-ka-*lo*
Thank you (very much).	Ευχαριστώ (πολύ).	ef-kha-ri-*sto* (po-*li*)
You're welcome.	Παρακαλώ.	pa-ra-ka-*lo*
Excuse me.	Με συγχωρείτε.	me sing-kho-*ri*-te
Sorry.	Συγνώμη.	si-*ghno*-mi

0	μηδέν	mi·*dhen*	15	δεκαπέντε	dhe·ka·*pe*·de
1	ένας/μία/ένα m/f/n	*e*·nas/*mi*·a/*e*·na	16	δεκαέξι	dhe·ka·*ek*·si
2	δύο	*dhi*·o	17	δεκαεφτά	dhe·ka·ef·*ta*
3	τρεις m&f	tris	18	δεκαοχτώ	dhe·ka·okh·*to*
	τρία n	*tri*·a	19	δεκαεννέα	dhe·ka·e·*ne*·a
4	τέσσερις m&f	*te*·se·ris	20	είκοσι	*i*·ko·si
	τέσσερα n	*te*·se·ra	21	είκοσι	*i*·ko·si
5	πέντε	*pe*·de		ένας/μία/	*e*·nas/*mi*·a/
6	έξι	*ek*·si		ένα m/f/n	*e*·na
7	εφτά	ef·*ta*	22	είκοσι δύο	*i*·ko·si *dhi*·o
8	οχτώ	okh·*to*	30	τριάντα	tri·*a*·da
9	εννέα	e·*ne*·a	40	σαράντα	sa·*ra*·da
10	δέκα	*dhe*·ka	50	πενήντα	pe·*ni*·da
11	έντεκα	*e*·de·ka	60	εξήντα	ek·*si*·da
12	δώδεκα	*dho*·dhe·ka	70	εβδομήντα	ev·dho·*mi*·da
13	δεκατρείς m&f	dhe·ka·*tris*	80	ογδόντα	ogh·*dho*·da
	δεκατρία n	dhe·ka·*tri*·a	90	ενενήντα	e·ne·*ni*·da
14	δεκατέσσερις m&f	dhe·ka·*te*·se·ris	100	εκατό	e·ka·*to*
	δεκατέσσερα n	dhe·ka·*te*·se·ra	1000	χίλια	*hi*·lia

time & dates

What time is it?	Τι ώρα είναι;	ti *o*·ra *i*·ne
It's one o'clock.	Είναι (μία) η ώρα.	*i*·ne (*mi*·a) i *o*·ra
It's (10) o'clock.	Είναι (δέκα) η ώρα.	*i*·ne (*dhe*·ka) i *o*·ra
Quarter past (10).	(Δέκα) και τέταρτο.	(*dhe*·ka) ke *te*·tar·to
Half past (10).	(Δέκα) και μισή.	(*dhe*·ka) ke mi·*si*
Quarter to (10).	(Δέκα) παρά τέταρτο.	(*dhe*·ka) pa·*ra* te·*tar*·to
At what time ...?	Τι ώρα ...;	ti *o*·ra ...
At ...	Στις ...	stis ...
Monday	Δευτέρα	dhef·*te*·ra
Tuesday	Τρίτη	*tri*·ti
Wednesday	Τετάρτη	te·*tar*·ti
Thursday	Πέμπτη	*pem*·ti
Friday	Παρασκευή	pa·ra·ske·*vi*
Saturday	Σάββατο	*sa*·va·to
Sunday	Κυριακή	ki·ria·*ki*

basics – GREEK

135

January	Ιανουάριος	i·a·nu·*a*·ri·os
February	Φεβρουάριος	fev·ru·*a*·ri·os
March	Μάρτιος	*mar*·ti·os
April	Απρίλιος	a·*pri*·li·os
May	Μάιος	*ma*·i·os
June	Ιούνιος	i·*u*·ni·os
July	Ιούλιος	i·*u*·li·os
August	Αύγουστος	*av*·ghu·stos
September	Σεπτέμβριος	sep·*tem*·vri·os
October	Οκτώβριος	ok·*tov*·ri·os
November	Νοέμβριος	no·*em*·vri·os
December	Δεκέμβριος	dhe·*kem*·vri·os

What date is it today?

Τι ημερομηνία είναι σήμερα;   ti i·me·ro·mi·*ni*·a *i*·ne *si*·me·ra

It's (18 October).

Είναι (δεκαοχτώ Οκτωβρίου).   *i*·ne (dhe·ka·okh·*to* ok·tov·*ri*·u)

| since (May) | από (το Μάιο) | a·*po* (to *ma*·i·o) |
| until (June) | μέχρι (τον Ιούνιο) | *meh*·ri (ton i·*u*·ni·o) |

yesterday	χτες	khtes
today	σήμερα	*si*·me·ra
tonight	απόψε	a·*pop*·se
tomorrow	αύριο	*av*·ri·o

last ...

night	την περασμένη νύχτα	tin pe·raz·*me*·ni *nikh*·ta
week	την περασμένη εβδομάδα	tin pe·raz·*me*·ni ev·dho·*ma*·dha
month	τον περασμένο μήνα	ton pe·raz·*me*·no *mi*·na
year	τον περασμένο χρόνο	ton pe·raz·*me*·no *khro*·no

next ...

week	την επόμενη εβδομάδα	tin e·*po*·me·ni ev·dho·*ma*·dha
month	τον επόμενο μήνα	ton e·*po*·me·no *mi*·na
year	τον επόμενο χρόνο	ton e·*po*·me·no *khro*·no

yesterday/	χτες/	khtes/
tomorrow ...	αύριο το ...	*av*·ri·o to ...
morning	πρωί	pro·*i*
afternoon	απόγευμα	a·*po*·yev·ma
evening	βράδι	*vra*·dhi

weather

What's the weather like?	Πως είναι ο καιρός;	pos *i*·ne o ke·*ros*
It's ...		
cloudy	Είναι συννεφιά.	*i*·ne si·ne·*fia*
cold	Κάνει κρύο.	*ka*·ni *kri*·o
hot	Κάνει πολλή ζέστη.	*ka*·ni po·*li* ze·sti
raining	Βρέχει.	*vre*·hi
snowing	Χιονίζει.	hio·*ni*·zi
sunny	Είναι λιακάδα.	*i*·ne lia·*ka*·dha
warm	Κάνει ζέστη.	*ka*·ni ze·sti
windy	Φυσάει.	fi·*sa*·i
spring	άνοιξη f	*a*·nik·si
summer	καλοκαίρι n	ka·lo·*ke*·ri
autumn	φθινόπωρο n	fthi·*no*·po·ro
winter	χειμώνας m	hi·*mo*·nas

border crossing

I'm here ...	Είμαι εδώ...	*i*·me e·*dho*...
in transit	τράνζιτ	*tran*·zit
on business	για δουλειά	yia dhu·*lia*
on holiday	σε διακοπές	se dhia·ko·*pes*
I'm here for (three) ...	Είμαι εδώ για (τρεις) ...	*i*·me e·*dho* yia (tris) ...
days	μέρες	*me*·res
weeks	εβδομάδες	ev·dho·*ma*·dhes
months	μήνες	*mi*·nes

I'm going to (Limassol).
Πηγαίνω στη (Λεμεσό). pi·*ye*·no sti (le·me·*so*)

I'm staying at the (Xenia).
Μένω στο (Ξενία). *me*·no sto (kse·*ni*·a)

I have nothing to declare.
Δεν έχω τίποτε να δηλώσω. dhen *e*·kho *ti*·po·te na dhi·*lo*·so

I have something to declare.
Εχω κάτι να δηλώσω. *e*·kho *ka*·ti na dhi·*lo*·so

That's (not) mine.
Αυτό (δεν) είναι δικό μου. af·*to* (dhen) *i*·ne dhi·*ko* mu

transport

tickets & luggage

Where can I buy a ticket?	Που αγοράζω εισιτήριο;	pu a·gho·*ra*·zo i·si·*ti*·ri·o
Do I need to book a seat?	Χρειάζεται να κλείσω θέση;	khri·*a*·ze·te na *kli*·so the·si
One ... ticket	Ένα εισιτήριο ...	*e*·na i·si·*ti*·ri·o ...
to (Patras), please.	για την (Πάτρα), παρακαλώ.	yia tin (*pa*·tra) pa·ra·ka·*lo*
one-way	απλό	a·*plo*
return	με επιστροφή	me e·pi·stro·*fi*
I'd like to ... my	Θα ήθελα να ... το	tha *i*·the·la na ... to
ticket, please.	εισιτήριό μου, παρακαλώ.	i·si·*ti*·ri·o mu pa·ra·ka·*lo*
cancel	ακυρώσω	a·ki·*ro*·so
change	αλλάξω	a·*lak*·so
confirm	επικυρώσω	e·pi·ki·*ro*·so
I'd like a ... seat.	Θα ήθελα μια θέση ...	tha *i*·the·la mia *the*·si ...
nonsmoking	στους μη καπνίζοντες	stus mi kap·*ni*·zo·des
smoking	στους καπνίζοντες	stus kap·*ni*·zo·des

How much is it?
Πόσο κάνει; · *po*·so *ka*·ni

Is there air conditioning?
Υπάρχει έρκοντίσιον; · · · · · · · · · · · · · · i·*par*·hi e·kon·*di*·si·on

Is there a toilet?
Υπάρχει τουαλέτα; · · · · · · · · · · · · · · · · i·*par*·hi tu·a·*le*·ta

How long does the trip take?
Πόσο διαρκεί το ταξίδι; · · · · · · · · · · · · *po*·so dhi·ar·*ki* to tak·*si*·dhi

Is it a direct route?
Πηγαίνει κατ'ευθείαν; · · · · · · · · · · · · · pi·*ye*·ni ka·tef·*thi*·an

Where can I find a luggage locker?
Που μπορώ να βρω τη φύλαξη · · · · · · · pu bo·*ro* na vro ti *fi*·lak·si
αντικειμένων; · · · · · · · · · · · · · · · · · · · a·di·ki·*me*·non

My luggage has	Οι αποσκευές	i a·pos·ke·*ves*
been ...	μου έχουν ...	mu e·khun ...
damaged	πάθει ζημιά	*pa*·thi zi·*mia*
lost	χαθεί	kha·*thi*
stolen	κλαπεί	kla·*pi*

getting around

Where does flight (10) arrive/depart?

Που προσγειώνεται/   pu pros·yi·o·ne·te/
απογειώνεται η πτήση (δέκα);   a·po·yi·o·ne·te i pti·si (*dhe*·ka)

Where's (the) ...?	Που είναι ...;	pu i·ne ...
arrivals hall	η αίθουσα των αφίξεων	i *e*·thu·sa tona·*fik*·se·on
departures hall	η αίθουσα των	i *e*·thu·sa ton
	ανα χωρήσεων	*a*·na kho·*ri*·se·on
duty-free shop	τα αφορολόγητα	ta a·fo·ro·*lo*·yi·ta
gate (nine)	η θύρα (εννέα)	i *thi*·ra (e·*ne*·a)

Is this the ...	Είναι αυτό το ...	i·ne af·*to* to ...
to (Athens)?	για την (Αθήνα);	yia tin (a·*thi*·na)
boat	πλοίο	*pli*·o
bus	λεωφορείο	le·o·fo·*ri*·o
ferry	φέρυ	*fe*·ri
plane	αεροπλάνο	a·e·ro·*pla*·no
train	τρένο	*tre*·no

What time's the	Πότε είναι το ...	*po*·te i·ne to ...
... (bus)?	(λεωφορείο);	(le·o·fo·*ri*·o)
first	πρώτο	*pro*·to
last	τελευταίο	te·lef·*te*·o
next	επόμενο	e·*po*·me·no

At what time does it arrive/depart?

Τι ώρα φτάνει/φεύγει;   ti *o*·ra *fta*·ni/*fev*·yi

What time does it get to (Thessaloniki)?

Τι ώρα φτάνει στη (Θεσσαλονίκη);   ti *o*·ra *fta*·ni sti (the·sa·lo·*ni*·ki)

How long will it be delayed?

Πόση ώρα θα καθυστερήσει;   *po*·si *o*·ra tha ka·thi·ste·*ri*·si

What station is this?

Ποιος σταθμός είναι αυτός;   pios stath·*mos* i·ne af·*tos*

What stop is this?

Ποια στάση είναι αυτή;   pia *sta*·si i·ne af·*ti*

What's the next station?

Ποιος είναι ο επόμενος σταθμός;   pios i·ne o e·*po*·me·nos stath·*mos*

What's the next stop?

Ποια είναι η επόμενη στάση;   pia i·ne i e·*po*·me·ni *sta*·si

Does it stop at (Iraklio)?
Σταματάει στο (Ηράκλειο);　　　　　sta·ma·*ta*·i sto (i·*ra*·kli·o)

Please tell me when we get to (Thessaloniki).
Παρακαλώ πέστε μου όταν　　　　　pa·ra·ka·*lo* pe·ste mu *o*·tan
φτάσουμε στη (Θεσσαλονίκη).　　　　*fta*·su·me sti (the·sa·lo·*ni*·ki)

How long do we stop here?
Πόση ώρα θα σταματήσουμε εδώ;　　po·si *o*·ra tha sta·ma·*ti*·su·me e·*dho*

Is this seat available?
Είναι αυτή η θέση ελεύθερη;　　　　*i*·ne af·*ti* i *the*·si e·*lef*·the·ri

That's my seat.
Αυτή η θέση είναι δική μου.　　　　af·*ti* i *the*·si *i*·ne dhi·*ki* mu

I'd like a taxi ...　　Θα ήθελα ένα ταξί ...　　　tha *i*·the·la *e*·na tak·*si* ...
　at (9am)　　στις (εννέα　　　　　stis (e·*ne*·a
　　　　　　　πριν το μεσημέρι)　　　prin to me·si·*me*·ri)
　now　　　τώρα　　　　　　　*to*·ra
　tomorrow　αύριο　　　　　　　*av*·ri·o

Is this taxi available?
Είναι αυτό το ταξί ελεύθερο;　　　　*i*·ne af·*to* to tak·*si* e·*lef*·the·ro

How much is it to ...?
Πόσο κάνει για ...;　　　　　　　*po*·so *ka*·ni yia ...

Please put the meter on.
Παρακαλώ βάλε το ταξίμετρο.　　　pa·ra·ka·*lo va*·le to tak·*si*·me·tro

Please take me to (this address).
Παρακαλώ πάρε με σε　　　　　　pa·ra·ka·*lo pa*·re me se
(αυτή τη διεύθυνση).　　　　　　(af·*ti* ti dhi·*ef*·thin·si)

Please ...　　Παρακαλώ ...　　　　pa·ra·ka·*lo* ...
　slow down　πήγαινε πιο σιγά　　*pi*·ye·ne pio si·*gha*
　stop here　σταμάτα εδώ　　　　sta·*ma*·ta e·*dho*
　wait here　περίμενε εδώ　　　　pe·*ri*·me·ne e·*dho*

car, motorbike & bicycle hire

I'd like to　　Θα ήθελα να　　　tha *i*·the·la na
hire a ...　　ενοικιάσω ένα ...　　e·ni·ki·*a*·so *e*·na ...
　bicycle　　ποδήλατο　　　　po·*dhi*·la·to
　car　　　αυτοκίνητο　　　af·to·*ki*·ni·to
　motorbike　μοτοσικλέτα　　　mo·to·si·*kle*·ta

with ...	με ...	me ...
a driver	οδηγό	o·dhi·gho
air conditioning	έρκοντίσιον	e·kon·di·si·on
How much for ... hire?	Πόσο νοικάζεται την ...;	po·so ni·kia·ze·te tin ...
hourly	ώρα	o·ra
daily	ημέρα	i·me·ra
weekly	εβδομάδα	ev·dho·ma·dha
air	αέρας m	a·e·ras
oil	λάδι αυτοκινήτου n	la·dhi af·to·ki·ni·tu
petrol	βενζίνα f	ven·zi·na
tyres	λάστιχα n	la·sti·kha

I need a mechanic.	Χρειάζομαι μηχανικό.	khri·a·zo·me mi·kha·ni·ko
I've run out of petrol.	Μου τελείωσε η βενζίνα.	mu te·li·o·se i ven·zi·na
I have a flat tyre.	Μ'έπιασε λάστιχο.	me·pia·se la·sti·kho

directions

Where's the ...?	Που είναι ...?	pu i·ne ...
bank	η τράπεζα	i tra·pe·za
city centre	το κέντρο της πόλης	to ke·dro tis po·lis
hotel	το ξενοδοχείο	to kse·no·dho·hi·o
market	η αγορά	i a·gho·ra
police station	ο αστυνομικός σταθμός	o a·sti·no·mi·kos stath·mos
post office	το ταχυδρομείο	to ta·hi·dhro·mi·o
public toilet	τα δημόσια αποχωρητήρια	ta dhi·mo·si·a a·po·kho·ri·ti·ria
tourist office	το τουριστικό γραφείο	to tu·ri·sti·ko ghra·fi·o

Is this the road to (Lamia)?		
Είναι αυτός ο δρόμος για (τη Λαμία);		i·ne af·tos o dhro·mos yia (ti la·mi·a)

Can you show me (on the map)?		
Μπορείς να μου δείξεις (στο χάρτη);		bo·ris na mu dhik·sis (sto khar·ti)

What's the address?		
Ποια είναι η διεύθυνση;		pia i·ne i dhi·ef·thin·si

How far is it?		
Πόσο μακριά είναι;		po·so ma·kri·a i·ne

How do I get there?		
Πως πηγαίνω εκεί;		pos pi·ye·no e·ki

Turn ...	Στρίψε ...	*strip*·se ...
at the corner	στη γωνία	sti gho·*ni*·a
at the traffic lights	στα φανάρια	sta fa·*na*·ria
left/right	αριστερά/δεξιά	a·ris·te·*ra*/dhek·si·*a*

It's ...	Είναι ...	*i*·ne ...
behind ...	πίσω ...	*pi*·so ...
far away	μακριά	ma·kri·*a*
here	εδώ	e·*dho*
in front of ...	μπροστά από ...	bros·*ta* a·*po* ...
near ...	κοντά ...	ko·*da* ...
next to ...	δίπλα από ...	*dhip*·la a·*po* ...
on the corner	στη γωνία	sti gho·*ni*·a
opposite ...	απέναντι ...	a·*pe*·na·di ...
straight ahead	κατ'ευθείαν	ka·tef·*thi*·an
there	εκεί	e·*ki*

by bus	με λεωφορείο	me le·o·fo·*ri*·o
by boat	με πλοίο	me *pli*·o
by taxi	με ταξί	me tak·*si*
by train	με τρένο	me *tre*·no
on foot	με πόδια	me *po*·dhia

north	βόρια	*vo*·ri·a
south	νότια	*no*·ti·a
east	ανατολικά	a·na·to·li·*ka*
west	δυτικά	dhi·ti·*ka*

signs

Είσοδος/Έξοδος	*i*·so·dhos/*ek*·so·dhos	**Entrance/Exit**
Ανοικτός/Κλειστός	a·nik·*tos*/kli·*stos*	**Open/Closed**
Ελεύθερα Δωμάτια	e·*lef*·the·ra dho·*ma*·ti·a	**Rooms Available**
Πλήρες	*pli*·res	**No Vacancies**
Πληροφορίες	pli·ro·fo·*ri*·es	**Information**
Αστυνομικός Σταθμός	a·sti·no·mi·*kos* stath·*mos*	**Police Station**
Απαγορεύεται	a·pa·gho·*re*·ve·te	**Prohibited**
Τουαλέτες	tu·a·*le*·tes	**Toilets**
Ανδρών	an·*dhron*	**Men**
Γυναικών	yi·ne·*kon*	**Women**
Ζεστό/Κρύο	zes·*to*/khri·o	**Hot/Cold**

accommodation

finding accommodation

Where's a ...?	Που είναι ...;	pu *i*·ne ...
camping ground	χώρος για κάμπινγκ	*kho*·ros yia *kam*·ping
guesthouse	ξενώνας	kse·*no*·nas
hotel	ξενοδοχείο	kse·no·dho·*hi*·o
youth hostel	γιουθ χόστελ	yiuth *kho*·stel

Can you recommend somewhere ...?	Μπορείτε να συστήσετε κάπου ...;	bo·*ri*·te na si·*sti*·se·te *ka*·pu ...
cheap	φτηνό	fti·*no*
good	καλό	ka·*lo*
nearby	κοντινό	ko·di·*no*

I'd like to book a room, please.
Θα ήθελα να κλείσω ένα
δωμάτιο, παρακαλώ.
tha *i*·the·la na *kli*·so *e*·na
dho·*ma*·ti·o pa·ra·ka·*lo*

I have a reservation.
Εχω κάνει κάποια κράτηση.
e·kho *ka*·ni *ka*·pia *kra*·ti·si

My name's ...
Με λένε ...
me *le*·ne ...

Do you have a ... room?	Εχετε ένα ... δωμάτιο;	*e*·he·te *e*·na ... dho·*ma*·ti·o
single	μονό	mo·*no*
double	διπλό	dhi·*plo*
twin	δίκλινο	*dhi*·kli·no

How much is it per ...?	Πόσο είναι για κάθε ...;	*po*·so *i*·ne yia *ka*·the ...
night	νύχτα	*nikh*·ta
person	άτομο	*a*·to·mo

Can I pay ...?	Μπορώ να πληρώσω με ...;	bo·*ro* na pli·*ro*·so me ...
by credit card	πιστωτική κάρτα	pi·sto·ti·*ki kar*·ta
with a travellers cheque	ταξιδιωτική επιταγή	tak·si·dhio·ti·*ki* e·pi·ta·*yi*

accommodation – GREEK

For (three) nights/weeks.
Για (τρεις) νύχτες/εβδομάδες.
yia (tris) *nikh*·tes/ev·dho·*ma*·dhes

From (2 July) to (6 July).
Από (τις δύο Ιουλίου)
a·*po* (tis *dhi*·o i·u·*li*·u)
μέχρι (τις έξι Ιουλίου).
me·khri (tis *ek*·si i·u·*li*·u)

Can I see it?
Μπορώ να το δω;
bo·*ro* na to dho

Am I allowed to camp here?
Μπορώ να κατασκηνώσω εδώ;
bo·*ro* na ka·ta·ski·*no*·so e·*dho*

Where can I find a camp site?
Που μπορώ να βρω το
pu bo·*ro* na vro to
χώρο του κάμπινγκ;
kho·ro tu *kam*·ping

requests & queries

When/Where is breakfast served?
Πότε/Που σερβίρεται το πρόγευμα;
po·te/pu ser·*vi*·re·te to *pro*·yev·ma

Please wake me at (seven).
Παρακαλώ ξύπνησέ με στις (εφτά).
pa·ra·ka·*lo* ksip·ni·*se* me stis (ef·*ta*)

Could I have my key, please?
Μπορώ να έχω το κλειδί μου
bo·*ro* na *e*·kho to kli·*dhi* mu
παρακαλώ;
pa·ra·ka·*lo*

Can I get another (blanket)?
Μπορώ να έχω και άλλη (κουβέρτα);
bo·*ro* na *e*·kho ke *a*·li (ku·*ver*·ta)

This (towel) isn't clean.
Αυτή (η πετσέτα) δεν είναι καθαρό.
af·*ti* (i pet·*se*·ta) dhen *i*·ne ka·tha·*ri*

Is there a/an ...?	Εχετε ...;	*e*·he·te ...
elevator	ασανσέρ	a·san·*ser*
safe	χρηματοκιβώτιο	khri·ma·to·ki·*vo*·ti·o

The room is too ...	Είναι πάρα πολύ ...	*i*·ne *pa*·ra po·*li* ...
expensive	ακριβό	a·kri·*vo*
noisy	θορυβώδες	tho·ri·*vo*·dhes
small	μικρό	mi·*kro*

The ... doesn't work.	... δεν λειτουργεί.	... dhen li·tur·*ghi*
air conditioning	Το έρκοντίσιον	to er·kon·*di*·si·on
fan	Ο ανεμιστήρας	o a·ne·mi·*sti*·ras
toilet	Η τουαλέτα	i tu·a·*le*·ta

checking out

What time is checkout?

Τι ώρα είναι η αναχώρηση;
ti *o*·ra *i*·ne i a·na·*kho*·ri·si

Can I leave my luggage here?

Μπορώ να αφήσω τις βαλίτσες μου εδώ;
bo·*ro* na a·*fi*·so tis va·*lit*·ses mu e·*dho*

Could I have my ..., please?	Μπορώ να έχω ... μου παρακαλώ;	bo·*ro* na *e*·kho ... mu pa·ra·ka·*lo*
deposit	την προκαταβολή	tin pro·ka·ta·vo·*li*
passport	το διαβατήριό	to dhia·va·*ti*·rio
valuables	τα κοσμήματά	ta koz·*mi*·ma·ta

communications & banking

the internet

Where's the local Internet cafe?

Που είναι το τοπικό
καφενείο με διαδίκτυο;
pu *i*·ne to to·pi·*ko*
ka·fe·*ni*·o me dhi·a·*dhik*·ti·o

How much is it per hour?

Πόσο κοστίζει κάθε ώρα;
po·so ko·*sti*·zi *ka*·the *o*·ra

I'd like to ...	Θα ήθελα να ...	tha *i*·the·la na ...
check my email	ελέγχω την ηλεκτρονική αλληλογραφία μου	e·*leng*·so tin i·lek·tro·ni·*ki* a·li·lo·ghra·*fi*·a mu
get Internet access	έχω πρόσβαση στο διαδίκτυο	*e*·kho *pros*·va·si sto dhi·a·*dhik*·ti·o
use a printer	χρησιμοποιήσω έναν εκτυπωτή	khri·si·mo·pi·*i*·so *e*·nan ek·ti·po·*ti*
use a scanner	χρησιμοποιήσω ένα σκάνερ	khri·si·mo·pi·*i*·so *e*·na *ska*·ner

145

mobile/cell phone

I'd like a ...	θα ήθελα ...	tha i·the·la ...
mobile/cell phone for hire	να νοικιάσω ένα κινητό τηλέφωνο	na ni·kia·so e·na ki·ni·to ti·le·fo·no
SIM card for your network	μια κάρτα SIM για το δίκτυό σας	mia kar·ta sim yia to dhik·tio sas
What are the rates?	Ποιες είναι οι τιμές;	pies i·ne i ti·mes

telephone

What's your phone number?
Τι αριθμό τηλεφώνου έχεις;
ti a·rith·mo ti·le·fo·nu e·his

The number is ...
Ο αριθμός είναι ...
o a·rith·mos i·ne ...

Where's the nearest public phone?
Που είναι το πιο κοντινό δημόσιο τηλέφωνο;
pu i·ne to pio ko·di·no dhi·mo·si·o ti·le·fo·no

I'd like to buy a phonecard.
Θέλω να αγοράσω μια τηλεφωνική κάρτα.
the·lo na a·gho·ra·so mia ti·le·fo·ni·ki kar·ta

I want to ...	θέλω να ...	the·lo na ...
call (Singapore)	τηλεφωνήσω (στη Σιγγαπούρη)	ti·le·fo·ni·so (sti sing·ga·pu·ri)
make a local call	κάνω ένα τοπικό τηλέφωνο	ka·no e·na to·pi·ko ti·le·fo·no
reverse the charges	αντιστρέψω τα έξοδα	a·di·strep·so ta ek·so·dha

How much does ... cost?	Πόσο κοστίζει ...;	po·so ko·sti·zi ...
a (three)- minute call	ένα τηλεφώνημα (τριών) λεπτών	e·na ti·le·fo·ni·ma (tri·on) lep·ton
each extra minute	κάθε έξτρα λεπτό	ka·the eks·tra lep·to

It's (40c) per (30) seconds.
(Σαράντα λεπτά) για (τριάντα) δευτερόλεπτα.
(sa·ra·da lep·ta) yia (tri·a·da) dhef·te·ro·lep·ta

post office

I want to send a ...	θέλω να στείλω ...	the·lo na sti·lo ...
fax	ένα φαξ	e·na faks
letter	ένα γράμμα	e·na ghra·ma
parcel	ένα δέμα	e·na dhe·ma
postcard	μια κάρτα	mia kar·ta

I want to buy a/an ...	Θέλω να αγοράσω ένα ...	the·lo na a·gho·ra·so e·na ...
envelope	φάκελο	fa·ke·lo
stamp	γραμματόσημο	ghra·ma·to·si·mo

Please send it (to Australia) by ...	Παρακαλώ στείλτε το ... (στην Αυστραλία).	pa·ra·ka·lo stil·te to ... (stin af·stra·li·a)
airmail	αεροπορικώς	a·e·ro·po·ri·kos
express mail	εξπρές	eks·pres
registered mail	συστημένο	si·sti·me·no
surface mail	δια ξηράς	dhia ksi·ras

Is there any mail for me?
Υπάρχουν γράμματα για μένα;   i·par·khun ghra·ma·ta yia me·na

bank

Where's a/an ...?	Που είναι ...;	pu i·ne ...
ATM	μια αυτόματη μηχανή χρημάτων	mia af·to·ma·ti mi·kha·ni khri·ma·ton
foreign exchange office	ένα γραφείο αλλαγής χρημάτων	e·na ghra·fi·o a·la·yis khri·ma·ton

I'd like to ...	Θα ήθελα να ...	tha i·the·la na ...
Where can I ...?	Που μπορώ να ...;	pu bo·ro na ...
arrange a transfer	τακτοποιήσω μια μεταβίβαση	tak·to·pi·i·so mia me·ta·vi·va·si
cash a cheque	εξαργυρώσω μια επιταγή	ek·sar·yi·ro·so mia e·pi·ta·yi
change a travellers cheque	αλλάξω μια ταξιδιωτική επιταγή	a·lak·so mia tak·si·dhio·ti·ki e·pi·ta·yi
change money	αλλάξω χρήματα	a·lak·so khri·ma·ta
get a cash advance	κάνω μια ανάληψη σε μετρητά	ka·no mia a·na·lip·si se me·tri·ta
withdraw money	αποσύρω χρήματα	a·po·si·ro khri·ma·ta

What's the ...?	Ποια είναι ... ;	pia *i*-ne ...
charge for that	η χρέωση για αυτό	i *khre*-o-si yia af-*to*
exchange rate	η τιμή συναλλάγματος	i ti-*mi* si-na-*lagh*-ma-tos

| It's (12) ... | Κάνει (δώδεκα) ... | *ka*-ni (*dho*-dhe-ka) ... |
| euros | ευρώ | ev-*ro* |

It's free.
Είναι δωρεάν.   *i*-ne dho-re-*an*

What time does the bank open?
Τι ώρα ανοίγει η τράπεζα;   ti *o*-ra a-*ni*-yi i *tra*-pe-za

Has my money arrived yet?
Έχουν φτάσει τα χρήματά μου;   e-khun *fta*-si ta *khri*-ma-*ta* mu

sightseeing

getting in

What time does it open/close?
Τι ώρα ανοίγει/κλείνει;   ti *o*-ra a-*ni*-yi/*kli*-ni

What's the admission charge?
Πόσο κοστίζει η είσοδος;   *po*-so ko-*sti*-zi i *i*-so-dhos

Is there a discount for students/children?
Υπάρχει έκπτωση για   i-*par*-hi ek-*pto*-si yia
σπουδαστές/παιδιά;   spu-dha-*stes*/pe-*dhia*

I'd like a ...	Θα ήθελα ...	tha *i*-the-la ...
catalogue	ένα κατάλογο	e-na ka-*ta*-lo-gho
guide	έναν οδηγό	e-nan o-dhi-*gho*
local map	ένα τοπικό χάρτη	e-na to-pi-*ko* *khar*-ti

I'd like to see ...	Θα ήθελα να δω ...	tha *i*-the-la na dho ...
What's that?	Τι είναι εκείνο;	ti *i*-ne e-*ki*-no
Can I take a photo?	Μπορώ να πάρω μια	bo-*ro* na *pa*-ro mia
	φωτογραφία;	fo-to-ghra-*fi*-a

tours

When's the next tour?

Πότε είναι η επόμενη περιήγηση;   *po·te i·ne i e·po·me·ni pe·ri·i·yi·si*

When's the next ...?	Πότε είναι το επόμενο ...;	*po·te i·ne to e·po·me·no ...*
boat trip	ταξίδι με τη βάρκα	*tak·si·dhi me ti var·ka*
day trip	ημερήσιο ταξίδι	*i·me·ri·si·o tak·si·dhi*

Is ... included?	Συμπεριλαμβάνεται ...;	*si·be·ri·lam·va·ne·te ...*
accommodation	κατάλυμα	*ka·ta·li·ma*
the admission charge	τιμή εισόδου	*ti·mi i·so·dhu*
food	φαγητό	*fa·yi·to*
transport	μεταφορά	*me·ta·fo·ra*

How long is the tour?

Πόση ώρα διαρκεί η περιήγηση;   *po·si o·ra dhi·ar·ki i pe·ri·i·yi·si*

What time should we be back?

Τι ώρα πρέπει να επιστρέψουμε;   *ti o·ra pre·pi na e·pi·strep·su·me*

sightseeing

amphitheatre	αμφιθέατρο n	*am·fi·the·a·tro*
castle	κάστρο n	*ka·stro*
cathedral	μητρόπολη f	*mi·tro·po·li*
church	εκκλησία f	*e·kli·si·a*
fresco	φρέσκο n	*fres·ko*
labyrinth	λαβύρινθος m	*la·vi·rin·thos*
main square	κεντρική πλατεία f	*ken·dhri·ki pla·ti·a*
monastery	μοναστήρι n	*mo·na·sti·ri*
monument	μνημείο n	*mni·mi·o*
mosaic	μωσαϊκό n	*mo·sa·i·ko*
museum	μουσείο n	*mu·si·o*
old city	αρχαία πόλη	*ar·khe·a po·li*
palace	παλάτι n	*pa·la·ti*
ruins	ερρίπια n pl	*e·ri·pi·a*
sculpture	γλυπτική f	*ghlip·ti·ki*
stadium	στάδιο n	*sta·dhi·o*
statue	άγαλμα n	*a·ghal·ma*
temple	ναός m	*na·os*

149

shopping

enquiries

Where's a ...?	Που είναι ...;	pu *i*·ne ...
bank	μια τράπεζα	mia *tra*·pe·za
bookshop	ένα βιβλιοπωλείο	e·na viv·li·o·po·*li*·o
camera shop	ένα κατάστημα φωτογραφικών ειδών	e·na ka·*ta*·sti·ma fo·to·ghra·fi·*kon* i·*dhon*
department store	ένα κατάστημα	e·na ka·*ta*·sti·ma
grocery store	ένα οπωροπωλείο	e·na o·po·ro·po·*li*·o
kiosk	ένα περίπτερο	e·na pe·*rip*·te·ro
market	μια αγορά	mia a·gho·*ra*
newsagency	το εφημεριδοπωλείο	to e·fi·me·ri·dho·po·*li*·o
supermarket	ένα σούπερμάρκετ	e·na *su*·per·*mar*·ket

Where can I buy (a padlock)?
Που μπορώ να αγοράσω (μια κλειδαριά);
pu bo·*ro* na a·gho·*ra*·so (mia kli·dha·*ria*)

I'd like to buy ...
Θα ήθελα να αγοράσω ...
tha *i*·the·la na a·gho·*ra*·so ...

Can I look at it?
Μπορώ να το κοιτάξω;
bo·*ro* na to ki·*tak*·so

Do you have any others?
Έχετε άλλα;
e·he·te *a*·la

Does it have a guarantee?
Έχει εγγύηση;
e·hi e·*gi*·i·si

Can I have it sent overseas?
Μπορείς να το στείλεις στο εξωτερικό;
bo·*ris* na to *sti*·lis sto ek·so·te·ri·*ko*

Can I have ... repaired?
Μπορώ να επισκευάσω εδώ ...;
bo·*ro* na e·pi·ske·*va*·so e·*dho* ...

Can I have a bag, please?
Μπορώ να έχω μια τσάντα, παρακαλώ;
bo·*ro* na *e*·kho mia *tsa*·da pa·ra·ka·*lo*

It's faulty.
Είναι ελαττωματικό.
i·ne e·la·to·ma·ti·*ko*

I'd like ..., please.	Θα ήθελα ..., παρακαλώ.	tha *i*·the·la ... pa·ra·ka·*lo*
a refund	επιστροφή χρημάτων	e·pi·stro·*fi* khri·*ma*·ton
to return this	να επιστρέφω αυτό	na e·pi·*strep*·so af·*to*

paying

How much is it?
Πόσο κάνει;

po·so ka·ni

Can you write down the price?
Μπορείς να γράψεις την τιμή;

bo·ris na ghrap·sis tin ti·mi

That's too expensive.
Είναι πάρα πολύ ακριβό.

i·ne pa·ra po·li a·kri·vo

Can you lower the price?
Μπορείς να κατεβάσεις την τιμή;

bo·ris na ka·te·va·sis tin ti·mi

I'll give you (five) euros.
Θα σου δώσω (πέντε) ευρώ.

tha su dho·so (pe·de) ev·ro

There's a mistake in the bill.
Υπάρχει κάποιο λάθος
στο λογαριασμό.

i·par·hi ka·pio la·thos
sto lo·gha·riaz·mo

Do you accept ...?   Δέχεστε ...;   dhe·he·ste ...
   credit cards   πιστωτικές κάρτες   pi·sto·ti·kes kar·tes
   debit cards   χρεωτικές κάρτες   khre·o·ti·kes kar·tes
   travellers cheques   ταξιδιωτικές   tak·si·dhio·ti·kes
      επιταγές   e·pi·ta·yes

I'd like my change, please.
Θα ήθελα τα ρέστα μου, παρακαλώ.

tha i·the·la ta re·sta mu pa·ra·ka·lo

Can I have a receipt, please?
Μπορώ να έχω μια
απόδειξη, παρακαλώ;

bo·ro na e·kho mia
a·po·dhik·si pa·ra·ka·lo

clothes & shoes

Can I try it on?   Μπορώ να το προβάρω;   bo·ro na to pro·va·ro
My size is (40).   Το νούμερό μου είναι   to nu·me·ro mu i·ne
   (σαράντα).   (sa·ra·da)
It doesn't fit.   Δε μου κάνει.   dhe mu ka·ni

small   μικρό   mi·kro
medium   μεσαίο   me·se·o
large   μεγάλο   me·gha·lo

books & music

I'd like a ...	Θα ήθελα ...	tha *i*·the·la ...
newspaper	μια εφημερίδα	mia e·fi·me·*ri*·dha
(in English)	(στα Αγγλικά)	(sta ang·gli·*ka*)
pen	ένα στυλό	e·na sti·*lo*

Is there an English-language bookshop?
Υπάρχει ένα βιβλιοπωλείο   i·*par*·hi e·na viv·li·o·po·*li*·o
Αγγλικής γλώσσας;   ang·gli·*kis* ghlo·sas

I'm looking for something by (Anna Vissi).
Ψάχνω για κάτι (της Αννας Βίσση).   *psakh*·no yia *ka*·ti (tis *a*·nas *vi*·si)

Can I listen to this?
Μπορώ να το ακούσω;   bo·*ro* na to a·*ku*·so

photography

Can you ...?	Μπορείς να ...;	bo·*ris* na ...
develop this	εμφανίσεις αυτό	em·fa·*ni*·sis af·*to*
film	το φιλμ	to film
load my film	βάλεις το φιλμ	*va*·lis to film
	στη μηχανή μου	sti mi·kha·*ni* mu
transfer photos	μεταφέρεις	me·ta·*fe*·ris
from my	φωτογραφίες από	fo·to·ghra·*fi*·es a·*po*
camera to CD	την φωτογραφική	ti fo·to·ghra·fi·*ki*
	μου μηχανή στο CD	mu mi·kha·*ni* sto si·*di*

I need a/an ... film	Χρειάζομαι φιλμ ...	khri·*a*·zo·me film ...
for this camera.	για αυτή τη μηχανή.	yia af·*ti* ti mi·kha·*ni*
APS	APS	*e*·i·pi·es
B&W	μαυρόασπρο	mav·*ro*·a·spro
colour	έγχρωμο	*eng*·khro·mo
slide	σλάιντ	*sla*·id
(200) speed	ταχύτητα (διακοσίων)	ta·*hi*·ti·ta (dhia·ko·*si*·on)

When will it be ready? Πότε θα είναι έτοιμο;   *po*·te tha *i*·ne *e*·ti·mo

meeting people

greetings, goodbyes & introductions

Hello/Hi.	Γεια σου.	yia su
Good night.	Καληνύχτα.	ka·li·*nikh*·ta
Goodbye/Bye.	Αντίο.	a·*di*·o
Mr	Κύριε	*ki*·ri·e
Mrs	Κυρία	ki·*ri*·a
Miss	Δις	dhes·pi·*nis*
How are you?	Τι κάνεις;	ti *ka*·nis
Fine. And you?	Καλά. Εσύ;	ka·*la* e·si
What's your name?	Πως σε λένε;	pos se *le*·ne
My name is ...	Με λένε ...	me *le*·ne ...
I'm pleased to meet you.	Χαίρω πολύ.	*he*·ro po·*li*

This is my ...	Από εδώ ... μου.	a·*po* e·*dho* ... mu
boyfriend	ο φίλος	o *fi*·los
brother	ο αδερφός	o a·dher·*fos*
daughter	η κόρη	i *ko*·ri
father	ο πατέρας	o pa·*te*·ras
friend	ο φίλος/η φίλη m/f	o *fi*·los/i *fi*·li
girlfriend	η φιλενάδα	i fi·le·*na*·dha
husband	ο σύζυγός	o si·zi·*ghos*
mother	η μητέρα	i mi·*te*·ra
partner (intimate)	ο/η σύντροφός m/f	o/i si·dro·*fos*
sister	η αδερφή	i a·dher·*fi*
son	ο γιος	o yios
wife	η σύζυγός	i *si*·zi·ghos

Here's my ...	Εδώ είναι ... μου.	e·*dho* *i*·ne ... mu
What's your ...?	Ποιο είναι ... σου;	pio *i*·ne ... su
email address	το ημέιλ	to i·*me*·il
fax number	το φαξ	to faks
phone number	το τηλέφωνό	to ti·*le*·fo·*no*

Here's my address.

Εδώ είναι η διεύθυνσή μου.   e·*dho* *i*·ne i dhi·*ef*·thin·*si* mu

What's your address?

Ποια είναι η δική σου διεύθυνση;   pia *i*·ne i dhi·*ki* su dhi·*ef*·thin·si

occupations

What's your occupation?	Τι δουλειά κάνεις;	ti dhu·*lia ka*·nis
I'm a/an ...	Είμαι/Δουλεύω ...	*i*·me/dhou·*lev*·o ...
businessperson	επιχειρηματίας m&f	e·pi·hi·ri·ma·*ti*·as
farmer	γεωργός m&f	ye·or·*ghos*
manual worker	εργάτης/εργάτρια m/f	er·*gha*·tis/er·*gha*·tri·a
office worker	σε γραφείο	se ghra·*fi*·o
scientist	επιστήμονας m&f	e·pi·*sti*·mo·nas
tradesperson	έμπορος m&f	*e*·bo·ros

background

Where are you from?	Από που είσαι;	a·*po* pu *i*·se
I'm from ...	Είμαι από ...	*i*·me a·*po* ...
Australia	την Αυστραλία	tin af·stra·*li*·a
Canada	τον Καναδά	ton ka·na·*dha*
England	την Αγγλία	tin ang·*gli*·a
New Zealand	την Νέα Ζηλανδία	tin *ne*·a zi·lan·*dhi*·a
the USA	την Αμερική	tin A·me·ri·*ki*
Are you married?	Είσαι παντρεμένος/παντρεμένη; m/f	*i*·se pa·dre·*me*·nos/pa·dre·*me*·ni
I'm married.	Είμαι παντρεμένος/παντρεμένη. m/f	*i*·me pa·dre·*me*·nos/pa·dre·*me*·ni
I'm single.	Είμαι ανύπαντρος/ανύπαντρη. m/f	*i*·me a·*ni*·pa·dros/a·*ni*·pa·dri

age

How old ...?	Πόσο χρονών ...;	*po*·so khro·*non* ...
are you	είσαι	*i*·se
is your daughter	είναι η κόρη σου	*i*·ne i *ko*·ri su
is your son	είναι ο γιος σου	*i*·ne o yios su
I'm ... years old.	Είμαι ... χρονών.	*i*·me ... khro·*non*
He/She is ... years old.	Αυτός/αυτή είναι ... χρονών.	af·*tos*/af·*ti i*·ne ... khro·*non*

feelings

I'm (not) ...	(Δεν) Είμαι ...	(dhen) *i*·me ...
Are you ...?	Είσαι ...;	*i*·se ...
happy	ευτυχισμένος m	ef·ti·hiz·*me*·nos
	ευτυχισμένη f	ef·ti·hiz·*me*·ni
hot	ζεστός/ζεστή m/f	ze·*stos*/ze·*sti*
hungry	πεινασμένος m	pi·naz·*me*·nos
	πεινασμένη f	pi·naz·*me*·ni
sad	στενοχωρημένος m	ste·no·kho·ri·*me*·nos
	στενοχωρημένη f	ste·no·kho·ri·*me*·ni
thirsty	διψασμένος m	dhip·saz·*me*·nos
	διψασμένη f	dhip·saz·*me*·ni

entertainment

going out

Where can I find ...?	Που μπορώ να βρω ...;	pu bo·*ro* na vro ...
clubs	κλαμπ	klab
gay venues	Χώρους συνάντησης	*kho*·rus si·*na*·di·sis
	για γκέη	yia *ge*·i
pubs	μπυραρίες	bi·ra·*ri*·es
I feel like going	Εχω όρεξι να	*e*·kho *o*·rek·si na
to a/the ...	πάω σε ...	*pa*·o se ...
concert	κονσέρτο	kon·*ser*·to
the movies	φιλμ	film
party	πάρτυ	*par*·ti
restaurant	εστιατόριο	e·sti·a·*to*·ri·o
theatre	θέατρο	*the*·a·tro

interests

Do you like ...?	Σου αρέσει ...;	su a·*re*·si ...
I (don't) like ...	(Δεν) μου αρέσει ...	(dhen) mu a·*re*·si ...
cooking	η μαγειρική	i ma·yi·ri·*ki*
reading	το διάβασμα	to *dhia*·vaz·ma

Do you like ...?	Σου αρέσουν ...;	su a-*re*-sun ...
I (don't) like ...	(Δεν) μου αρέσουν τα ...	(dhen) mu a-*re*-sun ta ...
art	καλλιτεχνικά	ka-li-*tekh*-ni-*ka*
movies	φιλμ	film
nightclubs	νάιτ κλαμπ	*na*-it klab
sport	σπορ	spor
Do you like to ...?	Σου αρέσει να ...;	sou a-*re*-si na ...
dance	χορεύεις	kho-*re*-vis
go to concerts	πηγαίνεις σε κονσέρτα	pi-*ye*-nis se kon-*ser*-ta
listen to music	ακούς μουσική	a-*kus* mu-si-*ki*

food & drink

finding a place to eat

Can you	Μπορείς να	bo-*ris* na
recommend a ...?	συστήσεις ...;	si-*sti*-sis ...
bar	ένα μπαρ	*e*-na bar
café	μία καφετέρια	*mi*-a ka-fe-*te*-ria
restaurant	ένα εστιατόριο	e-sti-a-*to*-ri-o
I'd like ..., please.	Θα ήθελα ..., παρακαλώ.	tha *i*-thela ... pa-ra-ka-*lo*
a table for (five)	ένα τραπέζι για (πέντε)	*e*-na tra-*pe*-zi yia (*pe*-de)
the (non)smoking	στους (μη)	stus (mi)
section	καπνίζοντες	kap-*ni*-zo-des

ordering food

breakfast	πρόγευμα n	*pro*-yev-ma
lunch	γεύμα n	*yev*-ma
dinner	δείπνο n	*dhip*-no
snack	μεζεδάκι n	me-ze-*dha*-ki

What would you recommend?
Τι θα συνιστούσες;   ti tha si-ni-*stu*-ses

I'd like (a/the) ..., please.	θα ήθελα ..., παρακαλώ.	tha *i*·the·la ... pa·ra·ka·*lo*
bill	το λογαριασμό	to lo·gha·riaz·*mo*
drink list	τον κατάλογο	ton ka·*ta*·lo·gho
	με τα ποτά	me ta po·*ta*
menu	το μενού	to me·*nu*
that dish	εκείνο το φαγητό	e·*ki*·no to fa·yi·*to*

drinks

(cup of) coffee ...	(ένα φλυτζάνι) καφέ ...	(e·na fli·*dza*·ni) ka·*fe* ...
(cup of) tea ...	(ένα φλυτζάνι) τσάι ...	(e·na fli·*dza*·ni) *tsa*·i ...
with milk	με γάλα	me *gha*·la
without sugar	χωρίς ζάχαρη	kho·*ris* za·kha·ri
(orange) juice	χυμός (πορτοκάλι) m	hi·*mos* (por·to·*ka*·li)
soft drink	αναψυκτικό n	a·nap·sik·ti·*ko*
... water	... νερό	... ne·*ro*
hot	ζεστό	ze·*sto*
(sparkling) mineral	(γαζόζα) μεταλλικό	(gha·*zo*·za) me·ta·li·*ko*

in the bar

I'll have ...	θα πάρω ...	tha *pa*·ro ...
I'll buy you a drink.	θα σε κεράσω εγώ.	tha se ke·*ra*·so e·*gho*
What would you like?	Τι θα ήθελες;	ti tha *i*·the·les
Cheers!	Εις υγείαν!	is i·*yi*·an
brandy	μπράντι n	*bran*·di
champagne	σαμπάνια f	sam·*pa*·nia
a glass/bottle of	ένα ποτήρι/μπουκάλι	e·na po·*ti*·ri/bu·*ka*·li
beer	μπύρα	*bi*·ra
ouzo	ούζο n	*u*·zo
a shot of (whisky)	ένα (ουίσκι)	e·na (u·*i*·ski)
a glass/bottle	ένα ποτήρι/μπουκάλι	e·na po·*ti*·ri/bu·*ka*·li
of ... wine	... κρασί	... kra·*si*
red	κόκκινο	*ko*·ki·no
sparkling	σαμπάνια	sam·*pa*·nia
white	άσπρο	*a*·spro

What's the local speciality?
Ποιες είναι οι τοπικές λιχουδιές;   pies *i*·ne i to·pi·*kes* li·khu·*dhies*

What's that?
Τι είναι εκείνο;   ti *i*·ne e·*ki*·no

How much is (a kilo of cheese)?
Πόσο κάνει (ένα κιλό τυρί);   *po*·so *ka*·ni (*e*·na ki·*lo* ti·*ri*)

I'd like ...	Θα ήθελα ...	tha *i*·the·la ...
(100) grams	(εκατό) γραμμάρια	(e·ka·*to*) ghra·*ma*·ria
(two) kilos	(δύο) κιλά	(*dhi*·o) ki·*la*
(three) pieces	(τρία) κομμάτια	(*tri*·a) ko·*ma*·tia
(six) slices	(έξι) φέτες	(*ek*·si) *fe*·tes
Less.	Πιο λίγο.	pio *li*·gho
Enough.	Αρκετά.	ar·ke·*ta*
More.	Πιο πολύ.	pio po·*li*

special diets & allergies

Is there a vegetarian restaurant near here?
Υπάρχει ένα εστιατόριο χορτοφάγων   i·*par*·hi *e*·na e·sti·a·*to*·ri·o hor·to·*fa*·ghon
εδώ κοντά;   e·*dho* ko·*da*

Do you have vegetarian food?
Έχετε φαγητό για χορτοφάγους;   *e*·he·te fa·yi·*to* yia khor·to·*fa*·ghus

I don't eat ...	Δεν τρώγω ...	dhen *tro*·gho ...
butter	βούτυρο	*vu*·ti·ro
eggs	αβγά	av·*gha*
meat stock	ζουμί από κρέας	zu·*mi* a·po *kre*·as

I'm allergic to ...	Είμαι αλλεργικός/	*i*·me a·ler·yi·*kos*
	αλλεργική ... m/f	a·ler·yi·*ki* ...
dairy produce	στα γαλακτικά	sta gha·lak·ti·*ka*
gluten	στη γλουτένη	sti ghlu·*te*·ni
MSG	στο MSG	sto em es dzi
nuts	στους ξηρούς καρπούς	stus ksi·*rus* kar·*pus*
seafood	στα θαλασσινά	sta tha·la·si·*na*

menu decoder

αρνί κοκκινιστό n	ar·*ni* ko·ki·ni·*sto*	lamb braised in white wine
αστακός m	a·sta·*kos*	lobster, boiled or chargrilled
γιαουρτογλού f	yia·ur·to·*ghlu*	grilled meat & yogurt pie
γιουβέτσι n	yiu·*vet*·si	casserole of meat & seafood with tomatoes & pasta
δάχτυλα n pl	*dhakh*·ti·la	deep-fried, nut-filled pastries
ελιές τσακιστές f pl	e·*lies* tsa·ki·*stes*	marinated green olives
ελιές τουρσί f pl	e·*lies* tur·si	pickled olives
ιμάμ-μπαϊλντί n	i·*mam*·ba·il·*di*	stuffed eggplant
καβούρι βραστό n	ka·*vu*·ri vra·*sto*	boiled crab with dressing
κακαβιά f	ka·ka·*via*	saltwater fish soup
καλαμάρι Λεβριανά n	ka·la·*ma*·ri lev·ria·*na*	squid stewed in wine
καλαμάρι τηγανητό n	ka·la·*ma*·ri ti·gha·ni·*to*	battered & fried squid rings
καρυδόπιτα f	ka·ri·*dho*·pi·ta	rich moist walnut cake
καταΐφι n	ka·ta·*i*·fi	syrupy nut-filled rolls
κεφτέδες m pl	kef·*te*·dhes	lamb, pork or veal rissoles
κοντοσούβλι n	kon·do·*suv*·li	spit-roast pieces of lamb or pork
κοφίσι n	ko·*fi*·si	fish pie
κρεατόπιτα f	kre·a·*to*·pi·ta	lamb or veal pie
λάχανα με λαρδί n pl	*la*·kha·na me lar·*dhi*	greens & bacon casserole
μηλοπιτάκια n pl	mi·lo·pi·*ta*·kia	apple & walnut pies
μπακλαβάς m pl	ba·kla·*vas*	nut-filled pastry in honey syrup
μπάμιες γιαχνί f pl	*ba*·mies yia·*khni*	braised okra
μπιζελόσουπα f	bi·ze·*lo*·su·pa	fragrant pea soup with dill
μπουρδέτο n	bur·*dhe*·to	salt cod stew

μπριάμι n	bri-*a*-mi	mixed vegetables casserole
μπριζόλες f pl	bri-*zo*-les	chops · steak
μύδια κρασάτα n pl	*mi*-dhia kra-*sa*-ta	poached mussels in wine sauce
ντολμάδες m pl	dol-*ma*-dhes	stuffed vine or cabbage leaves
ντοματόσουπα f	do-ma-*to*-su-pa	tomato soup with pasta
παλικάρια n pl	pa-li-*ka*-ri-a	boiled legumes & grains
ρέγγα f	*reng*-ga	smoked herrings, plain or grilled
ριζάδα f	ri-*za*-dha	thick soup with rice & shellfish
σαλιγκάρια n pl	sa-ling-*ga*-ri-a	snails cooked in the shell
σουβλάκι n	suv-*la*-ki	seasoned or marinated meat or fish, skewered & chargrilled
σπανακόπιτα f	spa-na-*ko*-pi-ta	spinach pie
συκόψωμο n	si-*kop*-so-mo	heavy aromatic fig cake
ταβάς m	ta-*vas*	seasoned beef or lamb casserole
τζατζίκι n	dza-*dzi*-ki	cucumber, yogurt & garlic salad
τυρόπιτα f	ti-*ro*-pi-ta	cheese pie
φακές σούπα f pl	fa-*kes* su-pa	lentil soup
φασολάδα f	fa-so-*la*-dha	thick fragrant bean soup
χαλβάς m	khal-*vas*	sweet of sesame seeds & honey, with pistachio or almonds
χαμψοπίλαφο n	kham-pso-*pi*-la-fo	onion & anchovy pilau
χόρτα τσιγάρι n pl	*khor*-ta tsi-*gha*-ri	lightly fried wild greens
χορτόπιτα f	khor-*to*-pi-ta	pie with seasonal greens
χορτοσαλάτα f	khor-to-sa-*la*-ta	warm salad of greens & dressing
χταπόδι βραστό n	khta-*po*-dhi vra-*sto*	boiled octopus
χωριάτικη σαλάτα f	kho-ri-*a*-ti-ki sa-*la*-ta	salad of tomatoes, cucumber, olives & feta

emergencies

basics

Help!	Βοήθεια!	vo·*i*·thia
Stop!	Σταμάτα!	sta·*ma*·ta
Go away!	Φύγε!	*fi*·ye
Thief!	Κλέφτης!	*klef*·tis
Fire!	Φωτιά!	fo·*tia*
Watch out!	Πρόσεχε!	*pro*·se·he

Call ...!	Κάλεσε ...!	*ka*·le·se ...
an ambulance	το ασθενοφόρο	to as·the·no·*fo*·ro
the doctor	ένα γιατρό	*e*·na yia·*tro*
the police	την αστυνομία	tin a·sti·no·*mi*·a

It's an emergency.
Είναι μια έκτακτη ανάγκη.   *i*·ne mia *ek*·tak·ti a·*na*·gi

Could you help me, please?
Μπορείς να βοηθήσεις, παρακαλώ;   bo·*ris* na vo·i·*thi*·sis pa·ra·ka·*lo*

Can I make a phone call?
Μπορώ να κάνω ένα τηλεφώνημα;   bo·*ro* na *ka*·no *e*·na ti·le·*fo*·ni·ma

I'm lost.
Έχω χαθεί.   *e*·kho kha·*thi*

Where are the toilets?
Που είναι η τουαλέτα;   pu *i*·ne i tu·a·*le*·ta

police

Where's the police station?
Που είναι ο αστυνομικός σταθμός;   pu *i*·ne o a·sti·no·mi·*kos* stath·*mos*

I want to report an offence.
Θέλω να αναφέρω μια παρανομία.   *the*·lo na a·na·*fe*·ro mia pa·ra·no·*mi*·a

I have insurance.
Έχω ασφάλεια.   *e*·kho as·*fa*·li·a

I've been ...	Με έχουν ...	me *e*·khun ...
assaulted	κακοποιήσει	ka·ko·pi·*i*·si
raped	βιάσει	vi·*a*·si
robbed	ληστέψει	li·*step*·si

I've lost my ...	Έχασα ... μου.	e·kha·sa ... mu
My ... was/were stolen.	Έκλεψαν ... μου.	e·klep·san ... mu
backpack	το σακίδιό	to sa·ki·dhio
bags	τις βαλίτσες	tis va·lits·es
credit card	την πιστωτική	tin pi·sto·ti·ki
	κάρτα	kar·ta
handbag	την τσάντα	tin tsa·da
jewellery	τα κοσμήματά	ta koz·mi·ma·ta
money	τα χρήματά	ta khri·ma·ta
passport	το διαβατήριο	to dhia·va·ti·rio
travellers	τις ταξιδιωτικές	tis tak·si·dhio·ti·kes
cheques	επιταγές	e·pi·ta·yes
wallet	το πορτοφόλι	to por·to·fo·li
I want to contact	Θέλω να έρθω σε	the·lo na er·tho se
my ...	επαφή με ... μου.	e·pa·fi me ... mu
consulate	τηνπρεσβεία	tin prez·vi·a
embassy	το προξενείο	to pro·ksee·ni·o

health

medical needs

Where's the	Που είναι ο πιο	pu i·ne o pio
nearest ...?	κοντινός ...;	ko·di·nos ...
dentist	οδοντίατρος	o·dho·di·a·tros
doctor	γιατρός	yia·tros

Where's the	Που είναι το πιο	pu i·ne to pio
nearest ...?	κοντινό...;	ko·di·no ...
hospital	νοσοκομείο	no·so·ko·mi·o
(night) pharmacy	(νυχτερινό) φαρμακείο	(nikh·te·ri·no) far·ma·ki·o

I need a doctor (who speaks English).
Χρειάζομαι ένα γιατρό   khri·a·zo·me e·na yia·tro
(που να μιλάει αγγλικά).   (pu na mi·la·i ang·gli·ka)

Could I see a female doctor?
Μπορώ να δω μια γυναίκα γιατρό;   bo·ro na dho mia yi·ne·ka yia·tro

I've run out of my medication.
Μου έχουν τελειώσει τα φάρμακά μου.   mu e·khun te·li·o·si ta far·ma·ka mu

symptoms, conditions & allergies

I'm sick.	Είμαι άρρωστος/άρρωστη m/f	i·me a·ro·stos/a·ro·sti
It hurts here.	Πονάει εδώ.	po·na·i e·dho
I have (a/an) ...	Έχω ...	e·kho ...

asthma	άσθμα n	as·thma
bronchitis	βροχίτιδα f	vro·hi·ti·dha
constipation	δυσκοιλιότητα f	dhis·ki·li·o·ti·ta
cough	βήχα m	vi·kha
diarrhoea	διάρροια f	dhi·a·ri·a
fever	πυρετό m	pi·re·to
headache	πονοκέφαλο m	po·no·ke·fa·lo
heart condition	καρδιακή κατάσταση f	kar·dhi·a·ki ka·ta·sta·si
nausea	ναυτία f	naf·ti·a
pain	πόνο m	po·no
sore throat	πονόλαιμο m	po·no·le·mo
toothache	πονόδοντο	po·no·dho·do

I'm allergic to ...	Είμαι αλλεργικός/ αλλεργική ... m/f	i·me a·ler·yi·kos/ a·ler·yi·ki ...
antibiotics	στα αντιβιωτικά	sta a·di·vi·o·ti·ka
anti-inflammatories	στα αντιφλεγμονώδη	sta a·di·flegh·mo·no·dhi
aspirin	στην ασπιρίνη	stin as·pi·ri·ni
bees	στις μέλισσες	stis me·li·ses
codeine	στην κωδεΐνη	stin ko·dhe·i·ni
penicillin	στην πενικιλλίνη	stin pe·ni·ki·li·ni

antiseptic	αντισηπτικό n	a·di·sip·ti·ko
bandage	επίδεσμος m	e·pi·dhez·mos
condoms	προφυλακτικά n	pro·fi·lak·ti·ka
contraceptives	αντισυλληπτικά n pl	a·di·si·lip·ti·ka
diarrhoea medicine	φάρμακο διάροιας	far·ma·ko dhiar·ghias
insect repellent	εντομοαπωθητικό n	e·do·mo·a·po·thi·ti·ko
laxatives	καθαρτικό n	ka·thar·ti·ko
painkillers	παυσίπονα	paf·si·po·na
rehydration salts	ενυδρωτικά άλατα n pl	en·i·dhro·ti·ka a·la·ta
sleeping tablets	υπνωτικά χάπια n pl	ip·no·ti·ka kha·pia

english–greek dictionary

Greek nouns in this dictionary have their gender indicated by ⑩ (masculine), ① (feminine) or ⑪ (neuter). If it's a plural noun you'll also see pl. Adjectives are given in the masculine form only. Words are also marked as n (noun), a (adjective), v (verb), sg (singular), pl (plural), inf (informal) and pol (polite) where necessary.

A

accident ατύχημα ⑪ a-*ti*-hi-ma
accommodation κατάλυμα ⑪ ka-*ta*-li-ma
adaptor μετασχηματιστής ⑩ me-ta-shi-ma-ti-*stis*
address διεύθυνση ① dhi-*ef*-thin-si
aeroplane αεροπλάνο ⑪ a-e-ro-*pla*-no
after μετά me-*ta*
air-conditioned με έρκοντίσιον me er-kon-*di*-si-on
airport αεροδρόμιο ⑪ a-e-ro-*dhro*-mi-o
alcohol αλκοόλ ⑪ al-ko-*ol*
all όλοι ⑩ *o*-li
allergy αλλεργία ① a-ler-*yi*-a
ambulance νοσοκομειακό ⑪ no-so-ko-mi-a-*ko*
and και ke
ankle αστράγαλος ⑩ a-*stra*-gha-los
arm χέρι ⑪ *he*-ri
ashtray σταχτοθήκη ① stakh-to-*thi*-ki
ATM αυτόματη μηχανή χρημάτων ①
af-*to*-ma-ti mi-kha-*ni* khri-*ma*-ton

B

baby μωρό ⑪ mo-*ro*
back (body) πλάτη ① *pla*-ti
backpack σακίδιο ⑪ sa-*ki*-dhi-o
bad κακός ka-*kos*
bag σάκος ⑩ *sa*-kos
baggage claim παραλαβή αποσκευών ①
pa-ra-la-*vi* a-po-ske-*von*
bank τράπεζα ① *tra*-pe-za
bar μπαρ ⑩ bar
bathroom μπάνιο ⑪ *ba*-nio
battery μπαταρία ① ba-ta-*ri*-a
beautiful όμορφος o-mor-fos
bed κρεβάτι ⑪ kre-*va*-ti
beer μπύρα ① *bi*-ra
before πριν prin
behind πίσω *pi*-so
bicycle ποδήλατο ⑪ po-*dhi*-la-to
big μεγάλος me-*gha*-los

bill λογαριασμός ⑩ lo-gha-riaz-*mos*
black a μαύρος *mav*-ros
blanket κουβέρτα ① ku-*ver*-ta
blood group ομάδα αίματος ① o-*ma*-dha *e*-ma-tos
blue a μπλε ble
boat βάρκα ① *var*-ka
book (make a reservation) v κλείσω θέση *kli*-so *the*-si
bottle μπουκάλι ⑪ bu-*ka*-li
bottle opener ανοιχτήρι ⑪ a-nikh-*ti*-ri
boy αγόρι ⑪ a-*gho*-ri
brakes (car) φρένα ⑪ pl *fre*-na
breakfast πρωινό ⑪ pro-i-no
broken (faulty) ελαττωματικός e-la-to-ma-ti-*kos*
bus λεωφορείο ⑪ le-o-fo-*ri*-o
business επιχείρηση ① e-pi-*hi*-ri-si
buy αγοράζω a-gho-*ra*-zo

C

café καφετέρια ① ka-fe-*te*-ria
camera φωτογραφική μηχανή ①
fo-to-ghra-fi-*ki* mi-kha-*ni*
camp site χώρος για κάμπινγκ ⑩ *kho*-ros yia *kam*-ping
cancel ακυρώνω a-ki-*ro*-no
can opener ανοιχτήρι ⑪ a-nikh-*ti*-ri
car αυτοκίνητο ⑪ af-to-*ki*-ni-to
cash μετρητά ⑪ pl me-tri-*ta*
cash (a cheque) v εξαργυρώνω ek-sar-yi-*ro*-no
cell phone κινητό ⑪ ki-ni-to
centre κέντρο ⑪ *ke*-dro
change (money) v αλλάζω a-*la*-zo
cheap φτηνός fti-nos
check (bill) λογαριασμός ⑩ lo-gha-riaz-*mos*
check-in ρεσεψιόν ① re-sep-*sion*
chest στήθος ⑪ *sti*-thos
child παιδί ⑪ pe-*dhi*
cigarette τσιγάρο ⑪ tsi-*gha*-ro
city πόλη ① *po*-li
clean a καθαρός ka-tha-ros
closed κλεισμένος kliz-*me*-nos
coffee καφές ⑩ ka-fes
coins κέρματα ⑪ pl *ker*-ma-ta
cold a κρυωμένος kri-o-*me*-nos

collect call κλήση με αντιστροφή της επιβάρυνσης ①
kli-si me a-dis-tro-*fi* tis e-pi-*va*-rin-sis
come έρχομαι er-kho-me
computer κομπιούτερ ⑩ kom-*piu*-ter
condom προφυλακτικό ⑩ pro-fi-lak-ti-*ko*
contact lenses φακοί επαφής ⑩ pl fa-*ki* e-pa-*fis*
cook v μαγειρεύω ma-yi-*re*-vo
cost τιμή ① ti-*mi*
credit card πιστωτική κάρτα ① pi-sto-ti-*ki kar*-ta
cup φλιτζάνι ⑩ fli-*dza*-ni
currency exchange τιμή συναλλάγματος ①
ti-*mi* si-na-*lagh*-ma-tos
customs (immigration) τελωνείο ⑩ te-lo-*ni*-o
Cypriot (nationality) Κύπριος/Κύπρια ⑩/①
ki-pri-os/*ki*-pri-a
Cypriot a κυπριακός/κυπριακή ⑩/①
ki-pri-a-*kos*/ki-pri-a-*ki*
Cyprus Κύπρος ① *ki*-pros

D

dangerous επικίνδυνος e-pi-*kin*-di-nos
date (time) ημερομηνία ① i-me-ro-mi-*ni*-a
day ημέρα ① i-*me*-ra
delay καθυστέρηση ① ka-thi-*ste*-ri-si
dentist οδοντίατρος ⑩&① o-dho-*di*-a-tros
depart αναχωρώ a-na-kho-*ro*
diaper πάνα ① *pa*-na
dictionary λεξικό ⑩ lek-si-*ko*
dinner δείπνο ① *dhip*-no
direct άμεσος *a*-me-sos
dirty βρώμικος *vro*-mi-kos
disabled ανάπηρος a-*na*-pi-ros
discount έκπτωση ① *ek*-pto-si
doctor γιατρός ⑩&① yia-*tros*
double bed διπλό κρεβάτι ⑩ dhi-*plo* kre-*va*-ti
double room διπλό δωμάτιο ⑩ dhi-*plo* dho-*ma*-ti-o
drink ποτό ⑩ po-*to*
drive v οδηγώ o-dhi-*gho*
drivers licence άδεια οδήγησης ① *a*-dhi-a o-*dhi*-yi-sis
drugs (illicit) ναρκωτικό ⑩ nar-ko-ti-*ko*
dummy (pacifier) πιπίλα ① pi-*pi*-la

E

ear αφτί ⑩ af-*ti*
east ανατολή ① a-na-to-*li*
eat τρώγω *tro*-gho
economy class τουριστική θέση ① tu-ri-sti-*ki the*-si
electricity ηλεκτρισμός ⑩ i-lek-triz-*mos*

elevator ασανσέρ ⑩ a-san-*ser*
email ημέιλ ① i-me-il
embassy πρεσβεία ① pre-*zvi*-a
emergency έκτακτη ανάγκη ① ek-tak-ti a-*na*-gi
English (language) Αγγλικά ⑩ ang-gli-*ka*
entrance είσοδος ① *i*-so-dhos
evening βράδι ⑩ *vra*-dhi
exchange rate τιμή συναλλάγματος ①
ti-*mi* si-na-*lagh*-ma-tos
exit έξοδος ① *ek*-so-dhos
expensive ακριβός a-kri-*vos*
express mail επείγον ταχυδρομείο ⑩
e-*pi*-ghon ta-hi-dhro-*mi*-o
eye μάτι ⑩ *ma*-ti

F

far μακριά ma-kri-*a*
fast γρήγορος *ghri*-gho-ros
father πατέρας ⑩ pa-*te*-ras
film (camera) φιλμ ⑩ film
finger δάκτυλο ⑩ *dhak*-ti-lo
first-aid kit κυτίο πρώτων βοηθειών ⑩
ki-*ti*-o pro-ton vo-i-*thi*-on
first class πρώτη τάξη ① *pro*-ti tak-si
fish ψάρι ⑩ *psa*-ri
food φαγητό ⑩ fa-yi-*to*
foot πόδι ⑩ *po*-dhi
fork πιρούνι ⑩ pi-*ru*-ni
free (of charge) δωρεάν dho-re-*an*
friend φίλος/φίλη ⑩/① *fi*-los/*fi*-li
fruit φρούτα ⑩ pl *fru*-ta
full γεμάτο ye-*ma*-to
funny αστείος a-*sti*-os

G

gift δώρο ⑩ *dho*-ro
girl κορίτσι ⑩ ko-*rit*-si
glass (drinking) ποτήρι ⑩ po-*ti*-ri
glasses γυαλιά ⑩ yia-*lia*
go πηγαίνω pi-*ye*-no
good καλός ka-*los*
Greece Ελλάδα ① e-*la*-dha
Greek (language) Ελληνικά ⑩ e-li-ni-*ka*
Greek (nationality) Έλληνες ⑩ pl *e*-li-nes
green πράσινος *pra*-si-nos
guide οδηγός ⑩&① o-dhi-*ghos*

H

half μισό ⓝ mi-*so*
hand χέρι ⓝ *he*-ri
handbag τσάντα ⓕ *tsa*-da
happy ευτυχισμένος ef-ti-hiz-*me*-nos
have έχω *e*-kho
he αυτός ⓜ af-*tos*
head κεφάλι ⓝ ke-*fa*-li
heart καρδιά ⓕ kar-*dhia*
heat ζέστη ⓕ ze-sti
heavy βαρύς va-*ris*
help v βοηθώ vo-i-*tho*
here εδώ e-*dho*
high ψηλός psi-*los*
highway δημόσιος δρόμος ⓜ dhi-*mo*-si-os *dhro*-mos
hike v πεζοπορώ pe-zo-po-*ro*
holiday διακοπές ⓕ pl dhia-ko-*pes*
homosexual ομοφυλόφιλος ⓜ o-mo-fi-*lo*-fi-los
hospital νοσοκομείο ⓝ no-so-ko-*mi*-o
hot ζεστός ze-*stos*
hotel ξενοδοχείο ⓝ kse-no-dho-*hi*-o
hungry πεινασμένος pi-naz-*me*-nos
husband σύζυγος ⓜ *si*-zi-ghos

I

I εγώ e-*gho*
identification (card) ταυτότητα ⓕ taf-*to*-ti-ta
ill άρρωστος *a*-ro-stos
important σπουδαίος spu-*dhe*-os
included συμπεριλαμβανομένου si-be-ri-lam-va-no-*me*-nu
injury πληγή ⓕ pli-*yi*
insurance ασφάλεια ⓕ as-*fa*-li-a
Internet διαδίκτυο ⓝ dhia-*dhik*-ti-o
interpreter διερμηνέας ⓜ & ⓕ dhi-er-mi-*ne*-as

J

jewellery κοσμήματα ⓝ pl koz-*mi*-ma-ta
job δουλειά ⓕ dhu-*lia*

K

key κλειδί ⓝ kli-*dhi*
kilogram χιλιόγραμμο ⓝ hi-*lio*-gra-mo
kitchen κουζίνα ⓕ ku-*zi*-na
knife μαχαίρι ⓝ ma-*he*-ri

L

laundry (place) πλυντήριο ⓝ pli-*di*-ri-o
lawyer δικηγόρος ⓜ & ⓕ dhi-ki-*gho*-ros
left (direction) αριστερός ⓜ a-ri-ste-*ros*
left-luggage office γραφείο φύλαξη αποσκευών ⓝ gra-*fi*-o fi-lak-si a-po-ske-*von*
leg πόδι ⓝ *po*-dhi
lesbian λεσβία ⓕ les-*vi*-a
less λιγότερο li-*gho*-te-ro
letter (mail) γράμμα ⓝ *ghra*-ma
lift (elevator) ασανσέρ ⓝ a-san-*ser*
light φως ⓝ fos
like v μου αρέσει mu a-*re*-si
lock κλειδαριά ⓕ kli-dha-*ria*
long μακρύς ma-*kris*
lost χαμένος kha-*me*-nos
lost-property office γραφείο απωλεσθέντων αντικειμένων ⓝ gra-*fi*-o a-po-les-*the*-don a-di-ki-*me*-non
love v αγαπώ a-gha-*po*
luggage αποσκευές ⓕ pl a-po-ske-*ves*
lunch μεσημεριανό φαγητό ⓝ me-si-me-ria-*no* fa-yi-*to*

M

mail (letters) αλληλογραφία ⓕ a-li-lo-ghra-*fi*-a
mail (postal system) ταχυδρομείο ⓝ ta-hi-dhro-*mi*-o
man άντρας ⓜ *a*-dras
map χάρτης ⓜ *khar*-tis
market αγορά ⓕ a-gho-*ra*
matches σπίρτα ⓝ pl *spir*-ta
meat κρέας ⓝ *kre*-as
medicine φάρμακο ⓝ *far*-ma-ko
menu μενού ⓝ me-*nu*
message μήνυμα ⓝ *mi*-ni-ma
milk γάλα ⓝ *gha*-la
minute λεπτό ⓝ lep-*to*
mobile phone κινητό ⓝ ki-ni-*to*
money χρήματα ⓝ *khri*-ma-ta
month μήνας ⓜ *mi*-nas
morning πρωί ⓝ pro-*i*
mother μητέρα ⓕ mi-*te*-ra
motorcycle μοτοσυκλέτα ⓕ mo-to-si-*kle*-ta
motorway αυτοκινητόδρομος ⓜ af-to-ki-ni-*to*-dhro-mos
mouth στόμα ⓝ *sto*-ma
music μουσική ⓕ mu-si-*ki*

N

name όνομα ⓝ *o*-no-ma
napkin πετσετάκι ⓝ pet-se-*ta*-ki
nappy πάνα ⓕ *pa*-na

near κοντά ko-*da*
neck λαιμός m le-*mos*
new νέος *ne*-os
news νέα f *ne*-a
newspaper εφημερίδα f e-fi-me-*ri*-dha
night νύχτα f *nikh*-ta
no όχι o-hi
noisy a θορυβώδης tho-ri-*vo*-dhis
nonsmoking μη καπνίζοντες mi kap-*ni*-zo-des
north βοράς m vo-*ras*
nose μύτη f *mi*-ti
now τώρα *to*-ra
number αριθμός m a-rith-*mos*

O

oil (engine) λάδι αυτοκινήτου n *la*-dhi af-to-ki-*ni*-tu
old παλιός pa-*lios*
one-way ticket απλό εισιτήριο n a-*plo* i-si-*ti*-ri-o
open a ανοιχτός a-nikh-*tos*
outside έξω *ek*-so

P

package πακέτο n pa-*ke*-to
paper χαρτί n khar-*ti*
park (car) v παρκάρω par-*ka*-ro
passport διαβατήριο n dhia-va-*ti*-ri-o
pay v πληρώνω pli-*ro*-no
pen στυλό n sti-*lo*
petrol πετρέλαιο n pe-*tre*-le-o
pharmacy φαρμακείο n far-ma-*ki*-o
phonecard τηλεκάρτα f ti-le-*kar*-ta
photo φωτογραφία f fo-to-gra-*fi*-a
plate πιάτο n *pia*-to
police αστυνομία f a-sti-no-*mi*-a
postcard κάρτα f *kar*-ta
post office ταχυδρομείο n ta-hi-dhro-*mi*-o
pregnant έγκυος *e*-gi-os
price τιμή f ti-*mi*

Q

quiet ήσυχος *i*-si-khos

R

rain βροχή vro-*hi*
razor ξυριστική μηχανή f ksi-ri-sti-*ki* mi-kha-*ni*
receipt απόδειξη f a-*po*-dhik-si

red κόκκινο *ko*-ki-no
refund n επιστροφή χρημάτων f
   e-pi-stro-*fi* khri-*ma*-ton
registered mail συστημένο sis-ti-*me*-no
rent v ενοικιάζω e-ni-ki-*a*-zo
repair v επισκευάζω e-pi-ske-*va*-zo
reservation κράτηση f *kra*-ti-si
restaurant εστιατόριο f e-sti-a-*to*-ri-o
return v επιστρέφω e-pi-*stre*-fo
return ticket εισιτήριο μετ' επιστροφής n
   i-si-*ti*-ri-o me-te-pis-tro-*fis*
right (direction) δεξιός dhek-si-*os*
road δρόμος m *dhro*-mos
room δωμάτιο n dho-*ma*-ti-o

S

safe a ασφαλής as-fa-*lis*
sanitary napkin πετσετάκι υγείας n pet-se-*ta*-ki i-*yi*-as
seat θέση f *the*-si
send στέλνω *stel*-no
service station βενζινάδικο n ven-zi-*na*-dhi-ko
sex σεξ n seks
shampoo σαμπουάν n sam-*pu*-an
share (a dorm) μοιράζομαι mi-*ra*-zo-me
shaving cream κρέμα ξυρίσματος f
   kre-ma ksi-*riz*-ma-tos
she αυτή af-*ti*
sheet (bed) σεντόνι n se-*do*-ni
shirt πουκάμισο n pu-*ka*-mi-so
shoes παπούτσια n pl pa-*put*-si-a
shop μαγαζί n ma-gha-*zi*
short κοντός ko-*dos*
shower ντους f duz
single room μονό δωμάτιο n mo-*no* dho-*ma*-tio
skin δέρμα n *dher*-ma
skirt φούστα f *fu*-sta
sleep v κοιμάμαι ki-*ma*-me
slowly αργά ar-*gha*
small μικρός mi-*kros*
smoke (cigarettes) v καπνίζω kap-*ni*-zo
soap σαπούνι n sa-*pu*-ni
some μερικοί me-ri-*ki*
soon σύντομα *si*-do-ma
south νότος *no*-tos
souvenir shop κατάστημα για σουβενίρ n
   ka-*ta*-sti-ma yia su-ve-*nir*
speak μιλάω mi-*la*-o
spoon κουτάλι n ku-*ta*-li
stamp γραμματόσημο n ghra-ma-*to*-si-mo

stand-by ticket εισιτήριο σταντ μπάι ⓝ i-si-*ti*-ri-o stand *ba*-i
station (train) σταθμός ⓜ stath-*mos*
stomach στομάχι ⓝ sto-*ma*-hi
stop v σταματάω sta-ma-*ta*-o
stop (bus) στάση ⓕ *sta*-si
street οδός ⓕ o-*dhos*
student σπουδαστής/σπουδάστρια ⓜ/ⓕ spu-dhas-*stis*/spu-*dha*-stri-a
sun ήλιος ⓜ *i*-li-os
sunscreen αντιηλιακό ⓝ a-di-i-li-a-*ko*
swim v κολυμπώ ko-li-*bo*

T

tampon ταμπόν ⓝ ta-*bon*
taxi ταξί ⓝ tak-*si*
teaspoon κουτάλι τσαγιού ⓝ ku-*ta*-li tsa-*yiu*
teeth δόντια ⓝ *dho*-dia
telephone τηλέφωνο ⓝ ti-*le*-fo-no
television τηλεόραση ⓕ ti-le-*o*-ra-si
temperature (weather) θερμοκρασία ⓕ ther-mo-kra-*si*-a
tent τέντα ⓕ *te*-da
that (one) εκείνο e-*ki*-no
they αυτοί af-*ti*
thirsty διψασμένος dhip-saz-*me*-nos
this (one) αυτός ⓜ af-*tos*
throat λαιμός ⓜ le-*mos*
ticket εισιτήριο ⓝ i-si-*ti*-ri-o
time ώρα ⓕ *o*-ra
tired κουρασμένος ku-raz-*me*-nos
tissues χαρτομάντηλα ⓝ pl khar-to-*ma*-di-la
today σήμερα *si*-me-ra
toilet τουαλέτα ⓕ tu-a-*le*-ta
tomorrow αύριο *av*-ri-o
tonight απόψε a-*pop*-se
toothbrush οδοντόβουρτσα ⓕ o-dho-*do*-vur-tsa
toothpaste οδοντόπαστα ⓕ o-dho-*do*-pa-sta
torch (flashlight) φακός ⓜ fa-*kos*
tour περιήγηση ⓕ pe-ri-*i*-yi-si
tourist office τουριστικό γραφείο ⓝ tu-ri-sti-*ko* ghra-*fi*-o
towel πετσέτα ⓕ pet-*se*-ta
train τρένο ⓝ *tre*-no
translate v μεταφράζω me-ta-*fra*-zo
travel agency ταξιδιωτικό γραφείο ⓝ tak-si-dhi-o-ti-*ko* ghra-*fi*-o
travellers cheque ταξιδιωτική επιταγή ⓕ tak-si-dhi-o-ti-*ki* e-pi-ta-*yi*

trousers παντελόνι ⓝ pa-de-*lo*-ni
twin beds δίκλινο δωμάτιο ⓝ *dhi*-kli-no dho-*ma*-ti-o
tyre λάστιχο ⓝ *la*-sti-kho

U

underwear εσώρουχα ⓝ pl e-*so*-ru-kha
urgent επείγον e-*pi*-ghon

V

vacant ελεύθερος e-*lef*-the-ros
vacation διακοπές ⓕ dhia-ko-*pes*
vegetable λαχανικά ⓝ pl la-kha-ni-*ka*
vegetarian n χορτοφάγος ⓜ&ⓕ khor-to-*fa*-ghos
visa βίζα ⓕ *vi*-za

W

waiter γκαρσόν ⓝ gar-*son*
walk v περπατάω per-pa-*ta*-o
wallet πορτοφόλι ⓝ por-to-*fo*-li
warm a ζεστός ze-*stos*
wash (something) v πλένω *ple*-no
watch ρολόι ⓝ ro-*lo*-i
water νερό ⓝ ne-*ro*
we εμείς e-*mis*
weekend Σαββατοκύριακο ⓝ sa-va-to-*ki*-ria-ko
west δύση ⓕ *dhi*-si
wheelchair αναπηρική καρέκλα ⓕ a-na-pi-ri-*ki* ka-*re*-kla
when όταν *o*-tan
where πού pu
white άσπρος *as*-pros
who ποιος *pios*
why γιατί yia-*ti*
wife σύζυγος ⓕ *si*-zi-ghos
window παράθυρο ⓝ pa-*ra*-thi-ro
wine κρασί ⓝ kra-*si*
with με me
without χωρίς kho-*ris*
woman γυναίκα ⓕ yi-*ne*-ka
write v γράφω *ghra*-fo

Y

yellow a κίτρινος *ki*-tri-nos
yes ναι ne
yesterday χτες khtes
you sg inf εσύ e-*si*
you sg pol & pl εσείς e-*sis*

Italian

italian alphabet

A a a	B b bee	C c chee	D d dee	E e e
F f e·fe	G g jee	H h a·ka	I i ee	L l e·le
M m e·me	N n e·ne	O o o	P p pee	Q q koo
R r e·re	S s e·se	T t tee	U u oo	V v voo
Z z tse·ta				

italian

ITALIANO

introduction

All you need for *la dolce vita* is to be able to tell your *Moschino* from your *macchiato* and your *Fellini* from your *fettuccine*. Happily, you'll find Italian (*italiano* ee·ta·*lya*·no) an easy language to start speaking as well as a beautiful one to listen to. When even a simple sentence sounds like an aria it can be difficult to resist striking up a conversation – and thanks to widespread migration and the huge popularity of Italian culture and cuisine, you're probably familiar with words like *ciao*, *pasta* and *bella* already.

There are also many similarities between Italian and English which smooth the way for language learners. Italian is a Romance language – a descendent of Latin, the language of the Romans (as are French, Spanish, Portuguese and Romanian), and English has been heavily influenced by Latin, particularly via contact with French.

Up until the 19th century, Italy was a collection of autonomous states, rather than a nation-state. As a result, Italian has many regional dialects, including Sardinian and Sicilian. Some dialects are so different from standard Italian as to be considered distinct languages in their own right. It wasn't until the 19th century that the Tuscan dialect – the language of Dante, Boccaccio and Petrarch – became the standard language of the nation, and the official language of schools, media and administration. 'Standard Italian' is the variety that will take you from the top of the boot to the very toe – all the language in this phrasebook is in standard Italian.

The majority of the approximately 65 million people who speak Italian live, of course, in Italy. However, the language also has official status in San Marino, Vatican City, parts of Switzerland, Slovenia and the Istrian peninsula of Croatia. Italian was the official language of Malta during the period of the Knights of St John (1530–1798) and afterwards shared that status with English during the British rule. Only in 1934 was Italian withdrawn and substituted with the native Maltese language. Today, Maltese people are generally fluent in Italian. It might surprise you to learn that Italian is also spoken in the African nation of Eritrea, which was a colony of Italy from 1880 until 1941. Most Eritreans nowadays speak Italian only as a second language. Italian is widely used in Albania, Monaco and France, and spoken by large communities of immigrants worldwide. This chapter is designed to help you on your adventures in the Italian-speaking world – so, as the Italians would say, *In bocca al lupo!* een bo·ka·*loo*·po (lit: in the mouth of the wolf) – good luck!

pronunciation

vowel sounds

Italian vowel sounds are generally shorter than those in English. They also tend not to run together to form vowel sound combinations (diphthongs), though it can often sound as if they do to English speakers.

symbol	english equivalent	italian example	transliteration
a	father	*pane*	*pa*·ne
ai	aisle	*mai*	mai
ay	say	*vorrei*	vo·*ray*
e	bet	*letto*	*le*·to
ee	see	*vino*	*vee*·no
o	pot	*molo*	*mo*·lo
oo	zoo	*frutta*	*froo*·ta
oy	toy	*poi*	poy
ow	how	*ciao, autobus*	chow, *ow*·to·boos

word stress

In Italian, you generally emphasise the second-last syllable of a word. When a written word has an accent marked on a vowel, though, the stress is on that syllable. The stressed syllable is always italicised in our pronunciation guides. The characteristic sing-song quality of an Italian sentence is created by pronouncing the syllables evenly and rhythmically, then swinging down on the last word.

consonant sounds

In addition to the sounds described on the next page, Italian consonants can also have a stronger, more emphatic pronunciation. The actual sounds are basically the same, though meaning can be altered between a normal consonant sound and this double consonant sound. The phonetic guides in this book don't distinguish between the two forms. Refer to the written Italian beside each phonetic guide as the cue –

if the word is written with a double consonant, use the stronger form. Even if you never distinguish them, you'll always be understood in context. Here are some examples where this 'double consonant' effect can make a difference:

sonno	son·no	**sleep**	sono	so·no	**I am**
pappa	pap·pa	**baby food**	papa	pa·pa	**pope**

symbol	english equivalent	italian example	transliteration
b	**bed**	*bello*	*be*·lo
ch	**cheat**	*centro*	*chen*·tro
d	**dog**	*denaro*	*de*·na·ro
dz	**adds**	*mezzo, zaino*	*me*·dzo, *dzai*·no
f	**fat**	*fare*	*fa*·re
g	**go**	*gomma*	*go*·ma
j	**joke**	*cugino*	ku·*jee*·no
k	**kit**	*cambio, quanto*	*kam*·byo, *kwan*·to
l	**lot**	*linea*	*lee*·ne·a
ly	**million**	*figlia*	*fee*·lya
m	**man**	*madre*	*ma*·dre
n	**not**	*numero*	*noo*·me·ro
ny	**canyon**	*bagno*	*ba*·nyo
p	**pet**	*pronto*	*pron*·to
r	**red** (stronger and rolled)	*ristorante*	ree·sto·*ran*·te
s	**sun**	*sera*	*se*·ra
sh	**shot**	*sciare*	*shya*·re
t	**top**	*teatro*	te·*a*·tro
ts	**hits**	*grazie, sicurezza*	*gra*·tsye, see·koo·re·*tsa*
v	**very**	*viaggio*	*vya*·jo
w	**win**	*uomo*	*wo*·mo
y	**yes**	*italiano*	ee·ta·*lya*·no
z	**zero**	*casa*	*ka*·za

basics

language difficulties

Do you speak English?
Parla inglese?   par·la een·gle·ze

Do you understand?
Capisce?   ka·pee·she

I (don't) understand.
(Non) capisco.   (non) ka·pee·sko

What does (*giorno*) mean?
Che cosa vuol dire (giorno)?   ke ko·za vwol dee·re (jor·no)

How do you ...?	*Come si ...?*	ko·me see ...
pronounce this	*pronuncia questo*	pro·noon·cha kwe·sto
write (*arrivederci*)	*scrive (arrivederci)*	skree·ve (a·ree·ve·der·chee)

Could you please ...?	*Può ... per favore?*	pwo ... per fa·vo·re
repeat that	*ripeterlo*	ree·pe·ter·lo
speak more	*parlare più*	par·la·re pyoo
slowly	*lentamente*	len·ta·men·te
write it down	*scriverlo*	skree·ver·lo

essentials

Yes.	*Sì.*	see
No.	*No.*	no
Please.	*Per favore.*	per fa·vo·re
Thank you (very much).	*Grazie (mille).*	gra·tsye (mee·le)
You're welcome.	*Prego.*	pre·go
Excuse me.	*Mi scusi.* pol	mee skoo·zee
	Scusami. inf	skoo·za·mee
Sorry.	*Mi dispiace.*	mee dees·pya·che

numbers

0	zero	dze-ro	16	sedici	se-dee-chee
1	uno	oo-no	17	diciassette	dee-cha-se-te
2	due	doo-e	18	diciotto	dee-cho-to
3	tre	tre	19	diciannove	dee-cha-no-ve
4	quattro	kwa-tro	20	venti	ven-tee
5	cinque	cheen-kwe	21	ventuno	ven-too-no
6	sei	say	22	ventidue	ven-tee-doo-e
7	sette	se-te	30	trenta	tren-ta
8	otto	o-to	40	quaranta	kwa-ran-ta
9	nove	no-ve	50	cinquanta	cheen-kwan-ta
10	dieci	dye-chee	60	sessanta	se-san-ta
11	undici	oon-dee-chee	70	settanta	se-tan-ta
12	dodici	do-dee-chee	80	ottanta	o-tan-ta
13	tredici	tre-dee-chee	90	novanta	no-van-ta
14	quattordici	kwa-tor-dee-chee	100	cento	chen-to
15	quindici	kween-dee-chee	1000	mille	mee-le

time & dates

What time is it?	Che ora è?	ke o-ra e
It's one o'clock.	È l'una.	e loo-na
It's (two) o'clock.	Sono le (due).	so-no le (doo-e)
Quarter past (one).	(L'una) e un quarto.	(loo-na) e oon kwar-to
Half past (one).	(L'una) e mezza.	(loo-na) e me-dza
Quarter to (eight).	(Le otto) meno un quarto.	(le o-to) me-no oon kwar-to
At what time ...?	A che ora ...?	a ke o-ra ...
At ...	Alle ...	a-le ...
am	di mattina	dee ma-tee-na
pm	di pomeriggio	dee po-me-ree-jo
Monday	lunedì	loo-ne-dee
Tuesday	martedì	mar-te-dee
Wednesday	mercoledì	mer-ko-le-dee
Thursday	giovedì	jo-ve-dee
Friday	venerdì	ve-ner-dee
Saturday	sabato	sa-ba-to
Sunday	domenica	do-me-nee-ka

January	gennaio	je·*na*·yo
February	febbraio	fe·*bra*·yo
March	marzo	*mar*·tso
April	aprile	a·*pree*·le
May	maggio	*ma*·jo
June	giugno	*joo*·nyo
July	luglio	*loo*·lyo
August	agosto	a·*gos*·to
September	settembre	se·*tem*·bre
October	ottobre	o·*to*·bre
November	novembre	no·*vem*·bre
December	dicembre	dee·*chem*·bre

What date is it today?
Che giorno è oggi?   ke *jor*·no e *o*·jee

It's (15 December).
È (il quindici) dicembre.   e (eel *kween*·dee·chee) dee·*chem*·bre

since (May)	da (maggio)	da (*ma*·jo)
until (June)	fino a (giugno)	*fee*·no a (*joo*·nyo)
yesterday	ieri	*ye*·ree
today	oggi	*o*·jee
tonight	stasera	sta·*se*·ra
tomorrow	domani	do·*ma*·nee

last ...		
night	ieri notte	*ye*·ree *no*·te
week	la settimana scorsa	la se·tee·*ma*·na *skor*·sa
month	il mese scorso	eel *me*·ze *skor*·so
year	l'anno scorso	*la*·no *skor*·so

next ...		
week	la settimana prossima	la se·tee·*ma*·na *pro*·see·ma
month	il mese prossimo	eel *me*·ze *pro*·see·mo
year	l'anno prossimo	*la*·no *pro*·see·mo

yesterday/tomorrow ...	ieri/domani ...	*ye*·ree/do·*ma*·nee ...
morning	mattina	ma·*tee*·na
afternoon	pomeriggio	po·me·*ree*·jo
evening	sera	*se*·ra

weather

What's the weather like?	Che tempo fa?	ke *tem*·po fa
It's ...		
cloudy	È nuvoloso.	e noo·vo·*lo*·zo
cold	Fa freddo.	fa *fre*·do
hot	Fa caldo.	fa *kal*·do
raining	Piove.	*pyo*·ve
snowing	Nevica.	ne·*vee*·ka
sunny	È soleggiato.	e so·le·*ja*·to
warm	Fa bel tempo.	fa bel *tem*·po
windy	Tira vento.	*tee*·ra *ven*·to
spring	primavera f	pree·ma·*ve*·ra
summer	estate f	es·*ta*·te
autumn	autunno m	ow·*too*·no
winter	inverno m	een·*ver*·no

border crossing

I'm here ...	Sono qui ...	*so*·no kwee ...
in transit	in transito	een *tran*·see·to
on business	per affari	per a·*fa*·ree
on holiday	in vacanza	een va·*kan*·tsa
I'm here for ...	Sono qui per ...	*so*·no kwee per ...
(10) days	(dieci) giorni	(*dye*·chee) *jor*·nee
(three) weeks	(tre) settimane	(tre) se·tee·*ma*·ne
(two) months	(due) mesi	(*doo*·e) me·zee

I'm going to (Perugia).
Vado a (Perugia).   *va*·do a (pe·*roo*·ja)

I'm staying at the (Minerva Hotel).
Alloggio al (Minerva).   a·*lo*·jo al (mee·*ner*·va)

I have nothing to declare.
Non ho niente da dichiarare.   non o *nyen*·te da dee·kya·*ra*·re

I have something to declare.
Ho delle cose da dichiarare.   o *de*·le *ko*·ze da dee·kya·*ra*·re

That's (not) mine.
(Non) è mio/mia. m/f   (non) e *mee*·o/*mee*·a

transport

tickets & luggage

Where can I buy a ticket?
Dove posso comprare un biglietto?   do·ve *po*·so kom·*pra*·re oon bee·*lye*·to

Do I need to book a seat?
Bisogna prenotare un posto?   bee·*zo*·nya pre·no·*ta*·re oon *pos*·to

One ... ticket (to Rome), please.	*Un biglietto ... (per Roma), per favore.*	oon bee·*lye*·to ... (per *ro*·ma) per fa·*vo*·re
one-way	*di sola andata*	dee *so*·la an·*da*·ta
return	*di andata e ritorno*	dee an·*da*·ta e ree·*tor*·no

I'd like to ... my ticket, please.	*Vorrei ... il mio biglietto, per favore.*	vo·*ray* ... eel *mee*·o bee·*lye*·to per fa·*vo*·re
cancel	*cancellare*	kan·che·*la*·re
change	*cambiare*	kam·*bya*·re
collect	*ritirare*	ree·tee·*ra*·re
confirm	*confermare*	kon·fer·*ma*·re

I'd like a ... seat, please.	*Vorrei un posto ..., per favore.*	vo·*ray* oon *pos*·to ... per fa·*vo*·re
nonsmoking	*per non fumatori*	per non foo·ma·*to*·ree
smoking	*per fumatori*	per foo·ma·*to*·ree

How much is it?
Quant'è?   kwan·*te*

Is there air conditioning?
C'è l'aria condizionata?   che *la*·rya kon·dee·tsyo·*na*·ta

Is there a toilet?
C'è un gabinetto?   che oon ga·bee·*ne*·to

How long does the trip take?
Quanto ci vuole?   *kwan*·to chee *vwo*·le

Is it a direct route?
È un itinerario diretto?   e oo·nee·tee·ne·*ra*·ryo dee·*re*·to

I'd like a luggage locker.
Vorrei un armadietto per il bagaglio.   vo·*ray* oon ar·ma·*dye*·to per eel ba·*ga*·lyo

My luggage	Il mio bagaglio	eel *mee*·o ba·*ga*·lyo
has been ...	è stato ...	e *sta*·to ...
damaged	danneggiato	da·ne·*ja*·to
lost	perso	*per*·so
stolen	rubato	roo·*ba*·to

getting around

Where does flight (004) arrive?
Dove arriva il volo (004)? do·ve a·*ree*·va eel *vo*·lo (*dze*·ro *dze*·ro *kwa*·tro)

Where does flight (004) depart?
Da dove parte il volo (004)? da *do*·ve *par*·te eel *vo*·lo (*dze*·ro *dze*·ro *kwa*·tro)

Where's the ...?	Dove sono ...?	*do*·ve *so*·no ...
arrivalls hall	gli arrivi	lyee a·*ree*·vee
departures hall	le partenze	le par·*ten*·dze

Is this the ...	È questo/questa ...	e *kwes*·to/*kwes*·ta ...
to (Venice)?	per (Venezia)? m/f	per (ve·*ne*·tsya)
boat	la nave f	la *na*·ve
bus	l'autobus m	*low*·to·boos
plane	l'aereo m	la·*e*·re·o
train	il treno m	eel *tre*·no

What time's	A che ora passa	a ke *o*·ra *pa*·sa
the ... bus?	... autobus?	... *ow*·to·boos
first	il primo	eel *pree*·mo
last	l'ultimo	*lool*·tee·mo
next	il prossimo	eel *pro*·see·mo

At what time does it arrive/leave?
A che ora arriva/parte? a ke *o*·ra a·*ree*·va/*par*·te

How long will it be delayed?
Di quanto ritarderà? dee *kwan*·to ree·tar·de·*ra*

What station/stop is this?
Che stazione/fermata è questa? ke sta·*tsyo*·ne/fer·*ma*·ta e *kwe*·sta

What's the next station/stop?
Qual'è la prossima stazione/ kwa·*le* la *pro*·see·ma sta·*tsyo*·ne/
fermata? fer·*ma*·ta

Does it stop at (Milan)?
Si ferma a (Milano)? see *fer*·ma a (mee·*la*·no)

Please tell me when we get to (Taranto).
Mi dica per favore quando   mee *dee*-ka per fa-*vo*-re *kwan*-do
arriviamo a (Taranto).   a-ree-*vya*-mo a (ta-*ran*-to).

How long do we stop here?
Per quanto tempo ci fermiamo qui?   per *kwan*-to *tem*-po chee fer-*mya*-mo kwee

Is this seat available?
È libero questo posto?   e *lee*-be-ro *kwe*-sto *pos*-to

That's my seat.
Quel posto è mio.   kwel *pos*-to e *mee*-o

I'd like a taxi ...	*Vorrei un tassì ...*	vo-*ray* oon ta-*see* ...
at (9am)	*alle (nove*	*a*-le (*no*-ve
	di mattina)	dee ma-*tee*-na)
now	*adesso*	a-*de*-so
tomorrow	*domani*	do-*ma*-nee

Is this taxi available?
È libero questo tassì?   e *lee*-be-ro *kwe*-sto ta-*see*

How much is it to ...?
Quant'è per ...?   kwan-*te* per ...

Please put the meter on.
Usi il tassametro, per favore.   *oo*-zee eel ta-sa-*me*-tro per fa-*vo*-re

Please take me to (this address).
Mi porti a (questo indirizzo),   mee *por*-tee a (*kwe*-sto een-dee-*ree*-tso)
per piacere.   per pya-*che*-re

Please ...	*..., per favore.*	... per fa-*vo*-re
slow down	*Rallenti*	ra-*len*-tee
stop here	*Si fermi qui*	see *fer*-mee kwee
wait here	*Mi aspetti qui*	mee as-*pe*-tee kwee

car, motorbike & bicycle hire

I'd like to hire a/an ...	*Vorrei noleggiare ...*	vo-*ray* no-le-*ja*-re ...
bicycle	*una bicicletta*	*oo*-na bee-chee-*kle*-ta
car	*una macchina*	*oo*-na *ma*-kee-na
motorbike	*una moto*	*oo*-na *mo*-to

with ...	*con ...*	kon ...
a driver	*un'autista*	oo-now-*tee*-sta
air conditioning	*aria condizionata*	*a*-rya kon-dee-tsyo-*na*-ta

How much for ... hire?	Quanto costa ...?	kwan·to kos·ta ...
hourly	all'ora	a·lo·ra
daily	al giorno	al jor·no
weekly	alla settimana	a·la se·tee·ma·na

air	aria f	a·rya
oil	olio m	o·lyo
petrol	benzina f	ben·dzee·na
tyres	gomme f pl	go·me

I need a mechanic.
Ho bisogno di un meccanico.   o bee·zo·nyo dee oon me·ka·nee·ko

I've run out of petrol.
Ho esaurito la benzina.   o e·zow·ree·to la ben·dzee·na

I have a flat tyre.
Ho una gomma bucata.   o oo·na go·ma boo·ka·ta

directions

Where's the ...?	Dov'è ...?	do·ve ...
bank	la banca	la ban·ka
city centre	il centro città	eel chen·tro chee·ta
hotel	l'albergo	lal·ber·go
market	il mercato	eel mer·ka·to
police station	il posto di polizia	eel pos·to dee po·lee·tsee·a
post office	l'ufficio postale	loo·fee·cho pos·ta·le
public toilet	il gabinetto pubblico	eel ga·bee·ne·to poo·blee·ko
tourist office	l'ufficio del turismo	loo·fee·cho del too·reez·mo

Is this the road to (Milan)?
Questa strada porta a (Milano)?   kwe·sta stra·da por·ta a (mee·la·no)

Can you show me (on the map)?
Può mostrarmi (sulla pianta)?   pwo mos·trar·mee (soo·la pyan·ta)

What's the address?
Qual'è l'indirizzo?   kwa·le leen·dee·ree·tso

How far is it?
Quant'è distante?   kwan·te dees·tan·te

How do I get there?
Come ci si arriva?   ko·me chee see a·ree·va

Turn ...	Giri ...	jee-ree ...
at the corner	all'angolo	a-lan-go-lo
at the traffic lights	al semaforo	al se-ma-fo-ro
left/right	a sinistra/destra	a see-nee-stra/de-stra

It's ...	È ...	e ...
behind ...	dietro ...	dye-tro ...
far away	lontano	lon-ta-no
here	qui	kwee
in front of ...	davanti a ...	da-van-tee a ...
left	a sinistra	a see-nee-stra
near (to ...)	vicino (a ...)	vee-chee-no (a ...)
next to ...	accanto a ...	a-kan-to a ...
on the corner	all'angolo	a lan-go-lo
opposite ...	di fronte a ...	dee fron-te a ...
right	a destra	a de-stra
straight ahead	sempre diritto	sem-pre dee-ree-to
there	là	la

by bus	con l'autobus	kon low-to-boos
by taxi	con il tassì	ko-neel ta-see
by train	con il treno	ko-neel tre-no
on foot	a piedi	a pye-dee

north	nord m	nord
south	sud m	sood
east	est m	est
west	ovest m	o-vest

signs

Entrata/Uscita	en-tra-ta/oo-shee-ta	Entrance/Exit
Aperto/Chiuso	a-per-to/kyoo-zo	Open/Closed
Camere Libere	ka-me-re lee-be-re	Rooms Available
Completo	kom-ple-to	No Vacancies
Informazioni	een-for-ma-tsyo-nee	Information
Posto di Polizia	pos-to dee po-lee-tsee-a	Police Station
Proibito	pro-ee-bee-to	Prohibited
Gabinetti	ga-bee-ne-tee	Toilets
Uomini	wo-mee-nee	Men
Donne	do-ne	Women
Caldo/Freddo	kal-do/fre-do	Hot/Cold

accommodation

finding accommodation

Where's a/an ...?	Dov'è ...?	do·ve ...
camping ground	un campeggio	oon kam·pe·jo
guesthouse	una pensione	oo·na pen·syo·ne
inn	una locanda	oo·na lo·kan·da
hotel	un albergo	oo·nal·ber·go
youth hostel	un ostello della gioventù	oo·nos·te·lo de·la jo·ven·too

Can you recommend somewhere ...?	Può consigliare qualche posto ...?	pwo kon·see·lya·re kwal·ke pos·to ...
cheap	economico	e·ko·no·mee·ko
good	buono	bwo·no
nearby	vicino	vee·chee·no

I'd like to book a room, please.
Vorrei prenotare una camera, vo·ray pre·no·ta·re oo·na ka·me·ra
per favore. per fa·vo·re

I have a reservation.
Ho una prenotazione. o oo·na pre·no·ta·tsyo·ne

My name's ...
Mi chiamo ... mee kya·mo ...

Do you have a ... room?	Avete una camera ...?	a·ve·te oo·na ka·me·ra ...
single	singola	seen·go·la
double	doppia con letto matrimoniale	do·pya kon le·to ma·tree·mo·nya·le
twin	doppia a due letti	do·pya a doo·e le·tee

How much is it per ...?	Quanto costa per ...?	kwan·to kos·ta per ...
night	una notte	oo·na no·te
person	persona	per·so·na

Can I pay by ...?	Posso pagare con ...?	po·so pa·ga·re kon ...
credit card	la carta di credito	la kar·ta dee kre·dee·to
travellers cheque	un assegno di viaggio	oo·na·se·nyo dee vee·a·jo

I'd like to stay for (two) nights.
Vorrei rimanere (due) notti.   vo·*ray* ree·ma·*ne*·re (*doo*·e) *no*·tee

From (July 2) to (July 6).
Dal (due luglio) al (sei luglio).   dal (*doo*·e *loo*·lyo) al (say *loo*·lyo)

Can I see it?
Posso vederla?   *po*·so ve·*der*·la

Am I allowed to camp here?
Si può campeggiare qui?   see pwo kam·pe·*ja*·re kwee

Is there a camp site nearby?
C'è un campeggio qui vicino?   che oon kam·*pe*·jo kwee vee·*chee*·no

requests & queries

When's breakfast served?
A che ora è la prima colazione?   a ke *o*·ra e la *pree*·ma ko·la·*tsyo*·ne

Where's breakfast served?
Dove si prende la prima colazione?   *do*·ve see *pren*·de la *pree*·ma ko·la·*tsyo*·ne

Please wake me at (seven).
Mi svegli alle (sette), per favore.   mee *sve*·lyee *a*·le (*se*·te) per fa·*vo*·re

Could I have my key, please?
Posso avere la chiave, per favore?   *po*·so a·*ve*·re la *kya*·ve per fa·*vo*·re

Can I get another (blanket)?
Può darmi un altra (coperta)?   pwo *dar*·mee oo·*nal*·tra (ko·*per*·ta)

This (sheet) isn't clean.
Questo (lenzuolo) non è pulito.   *kwe*·sto (len·*tzwo*·lo) non e poo·*lee*·to

Is there a/an ...?	*C'è ...?*	che ...
elevator	*un ascensore*	oo·na·shen·*so*·re
safe	*una cassaforte*	oo·na ka·sa·*for*·te
The room is too ...	*La camera è troppo ...*	la *ka*·me·ra e *tro*·po ...
expensive	*cara*	*ka*·ra
noisy	*rumorosa*	roo·mo·*ro*·za
small	*piccola*	*pee*·ko·la
The ... doesn't work.	*... non funziona.*	... non foon·*tsyo*·na
air conditioning	*L'aria condizionata*	*la*·rya kon·dee·tsyo·*na*·ta
fan	*Il ventilatore*	eel ven·tee·la·*to*·re
toilet	*Il gabinetto*	eel ga·bee·*ne*·to

checking out

What time is checkout?
A che ora si deve lasciar   a ke o·ra see de·ve la·shar
libera la camera?   lee·be·ra la ka·me·ra

Can I leave my luggage here?
Posso lasciare ili mio bagaglio qui?   po·so la·sha·re eel mee·o ba·ga·lyo kwee

Could I have my ..., please?	Posso avere ..., per favore?	po·so a·ve·re ... per fa·vo·re
deposit	la caparra	la ka·pa·ra
passport	il mio passaporto	eel mee·o pa·sa·por·to
valuables	i miei oggetti	ee myay o·je·tee
	di valore	dee va·lo·re

communications & banking

the internet

Where's the local Internet café?
Dove si trova l'Internet point?   do·ve see tro·va leen·ter·net poynt

How much is it per hour?
Quanto costa all'ora?   kwan·to kos·ta a·lo·ra

I'd like to ...	Vorrei ...	vo·ray ...
check my email	controllare le mie email	kon·tro·la·re le mee·e e·mayl
get Internet access	usare Internet	oo·za·re een·ter·net
use a printer	usare una stampante	oo·za·re oo·na stam·pan·te
use a scanner	scandire	skan·dee·re

mobile/cell phone

I'd like a ...	Vorrei ...	vo·ray ...
mobile/cell phone for hire	un cellulare da noleggiare	oon che·loo·la·re da no·le·ja·re
SIM card for your network	un SIM card per la rete telefonica	oon seem kard per la re·te te·le·fo·nee·ka

What are the rates?
Quali sono le tariffe?   kwa·lee so·no le ta·ree·fe

telephone

What's your phone number?
Qual'è il Suo/tuo numero   kwa·*le* eel *soo*·o/*too*·o *noo*·me·ro
di telefono? pol/inf   dee te·*le*·fo·no

The number is ...
Il numero è ...   eel *noo*·me·ro e ...

Where's the nearest public phone?
Dov'è il telefono pubblico   do·*ve* eel te·*le*·fo·no poo·blee·ko
più vicino?   pyoo vee·*chee*·no

I'd like to buy a phonecard.
Vorrei comprare una   vo·*ray* kom·*pra*·re *oo*·na
scheda telefonica.   *ske*·da te·le·*fo*·nee·ka

I want to ...	*Vorrei ...*	vo·*ray* ...
call (Singapore)	*fare una chiamata*	*fa*·re *oo*·na kya·*ma*·ta
	a (Singapore)	a (seen·ga·*po*·re)
make a local call	*fare una chiamata*	*fa*·re *oo*·na kya·*ma*·ta
	locale	lo·*ka*·le
reverse the charges	*fare una chiamata a*	*fa*·re *oo*·na kya·*ma*·ta a
	carico del destinatario	ka·ree·ko del des·tee·na·*ta*·ryo

How much does ... cost?	*Quanto costa ...?*	kwan·to *kos*·ta ...
a (three)-minute	*una telefonata*	*oo*·na te·le·fo·*na*·ta
call	*di (tre) minuti*	dee (tre) mee·*noo*·tee
each extra minute	*ogni minuto in più*	*o*·nyee mee·*noo*·to een pyoo

It's (one euro) per (minute).
(Un euro) per (un minuto).   (oon e·*oo*·ro) per (oon mee·*noo*·to)

post office

I want to send a ...	*Vorrei mandare ...*	vo·*ray* man·*da*·re ...
fax	*un fax*	oon faks
letter	*una lettera*	*oo*·na *le*·te·ra
parcel	*un pacchetto*	oon pa·*ke*·to
postcard	*una cartolina*	*oo*·na kar·to·*lee*·na

I want to buy ...	*Vorrei comprare ...*	vo·*ray* kom·*pra*·re ...
an envelope	*una busta*	*oo*·na *boo*·sta
stamps	*dei francobolli*	day fran·ko·*bo*·lee

Please send it (to Australia) by ...	Lo mandi ... (in Australia), per favore.	lo man·dee ... (een ow·stra·lya) per fa·vo·re
airmail	via aerea	vee·a a·e·re·a
express mail	posta prioritaria	pos·ta pryo·ree·ta·rya
registered mail	posta raccomandata	pos·ta ra·ko·man·da·ta
surface mail	posta ordinaria	pos·ta or·dee·na·rya
Is there any mail for me?	C'è posta per me?	che pos·ta per me

bank

Where's a/an ...?	Dov'è ... più vicino?	do·ve ... pyoo vee·chee·no
ATM	il Bancomat	eel ban·ko·mat
foreign exchange office	il cambio	eel kam·byo

I'd like to ...	Vorrei ...	vo·ray ...
Where can I ...?	Dove posso ...?	do·ve po·so ...
arrange a transfer	trasferire soldi	tras·fe·ree·re sol·dee
cash a cheque	riscuotere un assegno	ree·skwo·te·re oo·na·se·nyo
change a travellers cheque	cambiare un assegno di viaggio	kam·bya·re oo·na·se·nyo dee vee·a·jo
change money	cambiare denaro	kam·bya·re de·na·ro
get a cash advance	prelevare con carta di credito	pre·le·va·re kon kar·ta dee kre·dee·to
withdraw money	fare un prelievo	fa·re oon pre·lye·vo

What's the ...?	Quant'è ...?	kwan·te ...
commission	la commissione	la ko·mee·syo·ne
exchange rate	il cambio	eel kam·byo

It's ...	È ...	e ...
(12) euros	(dodici) euro	(do·dee·chee) e·oo·ro
free	gratuito	gra·too·ee·to

What's the charge for that?
Quanto costa? kwan·to kos·ta

What time does the bank open?
A che ora apre la banca? a ke o·ra a·pre la ban·ka

Has my money arrived yet?
È arrivato il mio denaro? e a·ree·va·to eel mee·o de·na·ro

sightseeing

getting in

What time does it open/close?
A che ora apre/chiude?
a ke *o*·ra *a*·pre/*kyoo*·de

What's the admission charge?
Quant'è il prezzo d'ingresso?
kwan·*te* eel *pre*·tso deen·*gre*·so

Is there a discount for children/students?
C'è uno sconto per
bambini/studenti?
che *oo*·no *skon*·to per
bam·*bee*·nee/stoo·*den*·tee

I'd like a ...	*Vorrei ...*	vo·*ray* ...
catalogue	*un catalogo*	oon ka·*ta*·lo·go
guide	*una guida*	*oo*·na *gwee*·da
local map	*una cartina*	*oo*·na kar·*tee*·na
	della zona	de·la *dzo*·na

I'd like to see ...	*Vorrei vedere ...*	vo·*ray* ve·*de*·re ...
What's that?	*Cos'è?*	ko·*ze*
Can I take a photo?	*Posso fare una foto?*	*po*·so *fa*·re *oo*·na *fo*·to

tours

When's the	*A che ora parte la*	a ke *o*·ra *par*·te la
next ...?	*prossima ...?*	*pro*·see·ma ...
day trip	*escursione*	es·koor·*syo*·ne
	in giornata	een jor·*na*·ta
tour	*gita turistica*	*jee*·ta too·*ree*·stee·ka

Is ... included?	*È incluso ...?*	e een·*kloo*·zo ...
accommodation	*l'alloggio*	la·*lo*·jo
the admission charge	*il prezzo d'ingresso*	eel *pre*·tso deen·*gre*·so
food	*il vitto*	eel *vee*·to
transport	*il trasporto*	eel tras·*por*·to

How long is the tour?
Quanto dura la gita?
kwan·to *doo*·ra la *jee*·ta

What time should we be back?
A che ora dovremmo ritornare?
a ke *o*·ra dov·*re*·mo ree·tor·*na*·re

castle	castello m	kas-*te*-lo
cathedral	duomo m	*dwo*-mo
church	chiesa f	*kye*-za
main square	piazza principale f	*pya*-tsa preen-chee-*pa*-le
monastery	monastero m	mo-nas-*te*-ro
monument	monumento m	mo-noo-*men*-to
museum	museo m	moo-*ze*-o
old city	centro storico m	*chen*-tro sto-ree-ko
palace	palazzo m	pa-*la*-tso
ruins	rovine f pl	ro-*vee*-ne
stadium	stadio m	*sta*-dyo
statues	statue f pl	*sta*-too-e

shopping

enquiries

Where's a ... ?	Dov'è ... ?	do-*ve* ...
bank	la banca	la *ban*-ka
bookshop	la libreria	la lee-bre-*ree*-a
camera shop	il fotografo	eel fo-*to*-gra-fo
department store	il grande magazzino	eel *gran*-de ma-ga-*dzee*-no
grocery store	la drogheria	la dro-ge-*ree*-a
market	il mercato	eel mer-*ka*-to
newsagency	l'edicola	le-*dee*-ko-la
supermarket	il supermercato	eel soo-per-mer-*ka*-to

Where can I buy (a padlock)?
Dove posso comprare (un lucchetto)? do-ve po-so kom-*pra*-re (oon loo-*ke*-to)

I'm looking for ...
Sto cercando ... sto cher-*kan*-do ...

Can I look at it?
  Posso dare un'occhiata? · po·so da·re oo·no·kya·ta

Do you have any others?
  Ne avete altri? · ne a·ve·te al·tree

Does it have a guarantee?
  Ha la garanzia? · a la ga·ran·tsee·a

Can I have it sent overseas?
  Può spedirlo all'estero? · pwo spe·deer·lo a·les·te·ro

Can I have my ... repaired?
  Posso far aggiustare ... qui? · po·so far a·joo·sta·re ... kwee

It's faulty.
  È difettoso. · e dee·fe·to·zo

I'd like (a) ..., please.	*Vorrei ..., per favore.*	vo·ray ... per fa·vo·re
bag	*un sacchetto*	oon sa·ke·to
refund	*un rimborso*	oon reem·bor·so
to return this	*restituire questo*	res·tee·twee·re kwe·sto

paying

How much is it?
  Quant'è? · kwan·te

Can you write down the price?
  Può scrivere il prezzo? · pwo skree·ve·re eel pre·tso

That's too expensive.
  È troppo caro. · e tro·po ka·ro

Can you lower the price?
  Può farmi lo sconto? · pwo far·mee lo skon·to

I'll give you (five) euros.
  Le offro (cinque) euro. · le o·fro (cheen·kwe) e·oo·ro

There's a mistake in the bill.
  C'è un errore nel conto. · che oon e·ro·re nel kon·to

Do you accept ...?	*Accettate ...?*	a·che·ta·te ...
credit cards	*la carta di credito*	la kar·ta dee kre·dee·to
debit cards	*la carta di debito*	la kar·ta dee de·bee·to
travellers cheques	*gli assegni di viaggio*	lyee a·se·nyee dee vee·a·jo

I'd like ..., please.	Vorrei ..., per favore.	vo·ray ... per fa·vo·re
a receipt	una ricevuta	oo·na ree·che·voo·ta
my change	il mio resto	eel mee·o res·to

clothes & shoes

Can I try it on?	Potrei provarmelo?	po·tray pro·var·me·lo
My size is (40).	Sono una taglia (quaranta).	so·no oo·na ta·lya (kwa·ran·ta)
It doesn't fit.	Non va bene.	non va be·ne
small	piccola	pee·ko·la
medium	media	me·dya
large	forte	for·te

books & music

I'd like a ...	Vorrei ...	vo·ray ...
newspaper	un giornale	oon jor·na·le
(in English)	(in inglese)	(een een·gle·ze)
pen	una penna	oo·na pe·na

Is there an English-language bookshop?

C'è una libreria specializzata che oo·na lee·bre·ree·a spe·cha·lee·dza·ta
in lingua inglese? een leen·gwa een·gle·ze

I'm looking for something by (Alberto Moravia).

Sto cercando qualcosa di sto cher·kan·do kwal·ko·za dee
(Alberto Moravia). (al·ber·to mo·ra·vee·a)

Can I listen to this?

Potrei ascoltarlo? po·tray as·kol·tar·lo

photography

Can you ...?	Potrebbe ...?	po·tre·be ...
burn a CD from	masterizzare un	mas·te·ree·tsa·re oon
my memory card	CD dalla mia	chee dee da·la mee·a
	memory card	me·mo·ree kard
develop this	sviluppare	svee·loo·pa·re
film	questo rullino	kwe·sto roo·lee·no
load my film	inserire il	een·se·ree·re eel
	mio rullino	mee·o roo·lee·no

I need a/an … film for this camera.	Vorrei un rullino … per questa macchina fotografica.	vo-*ray* oon roo-*lee*-no … per *kwe*-sta ma-*kee*-na fo-to-*gra*-fee-ka
APS	da APS	da a-pee-*e*-se
B&W	in bianco e nero	een *byan*-ko e *ne*-ro
colour	a colori	a *ko*-lo-ree
slide	per diapositive	per dee-a-po-zee-*tee*-ve
(200) speed	da (duecento) ASA	da (*doo*-e *chen*-to) *a*-za
When will it be ready?	Quando sarà pronto?	*kwan*-do sa-*ra* *pron*-to

meeting people

greetings, goodbyes & introductions

Hello.	Buongiorno.	bwon-*jor*-no
Hi.	Ciao.	chow
Good night.	Buonanotte.	bwo-na-*no*-te
Goodbye.	Arrivederci.	a-ree-ve-*der*-chee
Bye.	Ciao.	chow
See you later.	A più tardi.	a pyoo *tar*-dee
Mr	Signore	see-*nyo*-re
Mrs	Signora	see-*nyo*-ra
Miss	Signorina	see-nyo-*ree*-na
How are you?	Come sta? pol	*ko*-me sta
	Come stai? inf	*ko*-me stai
Fine. And you?	Bene. E Lei? pol	*be*-ne e lay
	Bene. E tu? inf	*be*-ne e too
What's your name?	Come si chiama? pol	*ko*-me see *kya*-ma
	Come ti chiami? inf	*ko*-me tee *kya*-mee
My name is …	Mi chiamo …	mee *kya*-mo …
I'm pleased to meet you.	Piacere.	pya-*che*-re

This is my ...	Le/Ti presento ... pol/inf	le/tee pre·zen·to ...
boyfriend	mio ragazzo	mee·o ra·ga·tso
brother	mio fratello	mee·o fra·te·lo
daughter	mia figlia	mee·a fee·lya
father	mio padre	mee·o pa·dre
friend	il mio amico m	eel mee·o a·mee·ko
	la mia amica f	la mee·a a·mee·ka
girlfriend	mia ragazza	mee·a ra·ga·tsa
husband	mio marito	mee·o ma·ree·to
mother	mia madre	mee·a ma·dre
partner (intimate)	il mio compagno m	eel mee·o kom·pa·nyo
	la mia compagna f	la mee·a kom·pa·nya
sister	mia sorella	mee·a so·re·la
son	mio figlio	mee·o fee·lyo
wife	mia moglie	mee·a mo·lye

Here's my ...	Ecco il mio ...	e·ko eel mee·o ...
What's your ...?	Qual'è il	kwa·le eel
	Suo/tuo ...? pol/inf	soo·o/too·o ...
address	indirizzo	een·dee·ree·tso
email address	indirizzo di email	een·dee·ree·tso dee e·mayl
fax number	numero di fax	noo·me·ro dee faks
phone number	numero di telefono	noo·me·ro dee te·le·fo·no

occupations

What's your occupation?	Che lavoro fa/fai? pol/inf	ke la·vo·ro fa/fai
I'm a/an ...	Sono ...	so·no ...
artist	artista m&f	ar·tees·ta
business person	uomo/donna	wo·mo/do·na
	d'affari m/f	da·fa·ree
farmer	agricoltore m	a·gree·kol·to·re
	agricoltrice f	a·gree·kol·tree·che
manual worker	manovale m&f	ma·no·va·le
office worker	impiegato/a m/f	eem·pye·ga·to/a
scientist	scienziato/a m/f	shen·tsee·a·to/a
student	studente m	stoo·den·te
	studentessa f	stoo·den·te·sa
tradesperson	operaio/a m/f	o·pe·ra·yo/a

background

Where are you from?	*Da dove viene/vieni?* pol/inf	da *do*·ve vye·ne/*vye*·nee
I'm from ...	*Vengo ...*	*ven*·go ...
Australia	*dall'Australia*	dal·ow·*stra*·lya
Canada	*dal Canada*	dal *ka*·na·da
England	*dall'Inghilterra*	da·leen·geel·*te*·ra
New Zealand	*dalla Nuova Zelanda*	*da*·la *nwo*·va ze·*lan*·da
the USA	*dagli Stati Uniti*	*da*·lyee *sta*·tee oo·*nee*·tee
Are you married?	*È sposato/a?* m/f pol	e spo·*za*·to/a
	Sei sposato/a? m/f inf	say spo·*za*·to/a
I'm married.	*Sono sposato/a.* m/f	*so*·no spo·*za*·to/a
I'm single.	*Sono celibe/nubile.* m/f	*che*·lee·be/*noo*·bee·le

age

How old ...?	*Quanti anni ...?*	*kwan*·tee *a*·nee ...
are you	*ha/hai* pol/inf	a/ai
is your daughter	*ha Sua/tua*	a *soo*·a/*too*·a
	figlia pol/inf	*fee*·lya
is your son	*ha Suo/tuo*	a *soo*·o/*too*·o
	figlio pol/inf	*fee*·lyo
I'm ... years old.	*Ho ... anni.*	o ... *a*·nee
He/She is ... years old.	*Ha ... anni.*	a ... *a*·nee

feelings

I'm (not) ...	*(Non) Ho ...*	(non) o ...
Are you ...?	*Ha/Hai ...?* pol/inf	a/ai ...
cold	*freddo*	*fre*·do
hot	*caldo*	*kal*·do
hungry	*fame*	*fa*·me
thirsty	*sete*	*se*·te
I'm (not) ...	*(Non) Sono ...*	(non) *so*·no ...
Are you ...?	*È/Sei ...?* pol/inf	e/say ...
happy	*felice*	fe·*lee*·che
sad	*triste*	*tree*·ste

entertainment

going out

Where can I find ...?	*Dove sono ...?*	do·ve so·no ...
clubs	*dei clubs*	day kloob
gay venues	*dei locali gay*	day lo·ka·lee ge
pubs	*dei pub*	day pab
I feel like going to a/the ...	*Ho voglia d'andare ...*	o vo·lya dan·da·re ...
concert	*a un concerto*	a oon kon·cher·to
movies	*al cinema*	al chee·nee·ma
party	*a una festa*	a oo·na fes·ta
restaurant	*in un ristorante*	een oon rees·to·ran·te
theatre	*a teatro*	a te·a·tro

interests

Do you like ...?	*Ti piace/ piacciono ...?* sg/pl	tee pya·che/ pya·cho·no ...
I (don't) like ...	*(Non) Mi piace/ piacciono ...* sg/pl	(non) mee pya·che/ pya·cho·no ...
art	*l'arte* sg	lar·te
cooking	*cucinare* sg	koo·chee·na·re
movies	*i film* pl	ee feelm
nightclubs	*le discoteche* pl	le dees·ko·te·ke
reading	*leggere* sg	le·je·re
shopping	*lo shopping* sg	lo sho·ping
sport	*lo sport* sg	lo sport
travelling	*viaggiare* sg	vee·a·ja·re
Do you like to ...?	*Ti piace ...?*	tee pya·che ...
dance	*ballare*	ba·la·re
go to concerts	*andare ai concerti*	an·da·re ai kon·cher·tee
listen to music	*ascoltare la musica*	as·kol·ta·re la moo·zee·ka

food & drink

finding a place to eat

Can you recommend a ...?	*Potrebbe consigliare un ...?*	po·*tre*·be kon·see·*lya*·re oon ...
bar	*locale*	lo·*ka*·le
café	*bar*	bar
restaurant	*ristorante*	rees·to·*ran*·te
I'd like ..., please.	*Vorrei ..., per favore.*	vo·*ray* ... per fa·*vo*·re
a table for (four)	*un tavolo per (quattro)*	oon *ta*·vo·lo per (*kwa*·tro)
the (non)smoking section	*(non) fumatori*	(non) foo·ma·*to*·ree

ordering food

breakfast	*prima colazione* f	*pree*·ma ko·la·*tsyo*·ne
lunch	*pranzo* m	*pran*·dzo
dinner	*cena* f	*che*·na
snack	*spuntino* m	spoon·*tee*·no

What would you recommend?
Cosa mi consiglia? ko·za mee kon·*see*·lya

I'd like (the) ..., please.	*Vorrei ..., per favore.*	vo·*ray* ... per fa·*vo*·re
bill	*il conto*	eel *kon*·to
drink list	*la lista delle bevande*	la *lee*·sta *de*·le be·*van*·de
menu	*il menù*	eel me·*noo*
that dish	*questo piatto*	*kwe*·sto *pya*·to

drinks

(cup of) coffee ...	(un) caffè ...	(oon) ka-fe ...
(cup of) tea ...	(un) tè ...	(oon) te ...
with milk	con latte	kon la-te
without sugar	senza zucchero	sen-tsa tsoo-ke-ro
orange juice (bottled)	succo d'arancia m	soo-ko da-ran-cha
orange juice (fresh)	spremuta d'arancia f	spre-moo-ta da-ran-cha
soft drink	bibita f	bee-bee-ta
... water	acqua ...	a-kwa ...
boiled	bollita	bo-lee-ta
mineral	minerale	mee-ne-ra-le
sparkling mineral	frizzante	free-tsan-te
still mineral	naturale	na-too-ra-le

in the bar

I'll have ...	Prendo ...	pren-do ...
I'll buy you a drink.	Ti offro da bere. inf	tee of-ro da be-re
What would you like?	Cosa prendi?	ko-za pren-dee
Cheers!	Salute!	sa-loo-te
brandy	cognac m	ko-nyak
champagne	champagne m	sham-pa-nye
cocktail	cocktail m	kok-tayl
a shot of (whisky)	un sorso di (whisky)	oon sor-so dee (wee-skee)
a ... of beer	... di birra	... dee bee-ra
bottle	una bottiglia	oo-na bo-tee-lya
glass	un bicchiere	oon bee-kye-re
a bottle of ...	una bottiglia di	oo-na bo-tee-lya dee
wine	vino ...	vee-no ...
a glass of ...	un bicchiere di	oon bee-kye-re dee
wine	vino ...	vee-no ...
red	rosso	ro-so
sparkling	spumante	spoo-man-te
white	bianco	byan-ko

self-catering

What's the local speciality?
 Qual'è la specialità　　　　　kwa-*le* la spe-cha-lee-*ta*
 di questa regione?　　　　　dee *kwe*-sta re-*jo*-ne

What's that?
 Cos'è?　　　　　　　　　ko-*ze*

How much is (a kilo of cheese)?
 Quanto costa (un chilo　　　*kwan*-to *kos*-ta (oon *kee*-lo
 di formaggio)?　　　　　　dee for-*ma*-jo)

I'd like ...	*Vorrei ...*	vo-*ray* ...
100 grams	*un etto*	oo-*ne*-to
(two) kilos	*(due) chili*	(*doo*-e) *kee*-lee
(three) pieces	*(tre) pezzi*	(tre) *pe*-tsee
(six) slices	*(sei) fette*	(say) *fe*-te
Less.	*Meno.*	*me*-no
Enough.	*Basta.*	*bas*-ta
More.	*Più.*	pyoo

special diets & allergies

Is there a vegetarian restaurant near here?
 C'è un ristorante vegetariano　che oon rees-to-*ran*-te ve-je-ta-*rya*-no
 qui vicino?　　　　　　　kwee vee-*chee*-no

Do you have vegetarian food?
 Avete piatti vegetariani?　　a-*ve*-te *pya*-tee ve-je-ta-*rya*-nee

Could you prepare	*Potreste preparare*	po-*tres*-te pre-pa-*ra*-re
a meal without ...?	*un pasto senza ...?*	oon *pas*-to *sen*-tsa ...
butter	*burro*	*boo*-ro
eggs	*uova*	*wo*-va
meat stock	*brodo di carne*	*bro*-do dee *kar*-ne
I'm allergic to ...	*Sono allergico/a ...* **m/f**	*so*-no a-*ler*-jee-ko/a ...
dairy produce	*ai latticini*	ai la-tee-*chee*-nee
gluten	*al glutine*	al *gloo*-tee-ne
MSG	*al glutammato*	al glu-ta-*ma*-to
	monosodico	mo-no-*so*-dee-ko
nuts	*alle noci*	*a*-le *no*-chee
seafood	*ai frutti di mare*	ai *froo*-tee dee *ma*-re

menu decoder

acciughe f pl	a-*choo*-ge	anchovies
arancini m pl	a-ran-*chee*-nee	rice balls stuffed with a meat mixture
babà m	ba-*ba*	dessert containing sultanas
baccalà m	ba-ka-*la*	dried salted cod
bagna cauda f	*ban*-ya *cow*-da	anchovy, olive oil & garlic dip
brioche m	bree-*osh*	breakfast pastry
bruschetta f	broos-*ke*-ta	toasted bread with olive oil & toppings
budino m	boo-*dee*-no	milk-based pudding
cacciucco m	ka-*choo*-ko	seafood stew with wine, garlic & herbs
cannelloni m pl	ka-ne-*lo*-nee	pasta stuffed with spinach, minced roast veal, ham, eggs, parmesan & spices
caponata f	ka-po-*na*-ta	eggplant with a tomato sauce
ciabatta f	cha-*ba*-ta	crisp, flat & long bread
conchiglie f pl	kon-*kee*-lye	pasta shells
costine f pl	kos-*tee*-ne	ribs
cozze f pl	*ko*-tse	mussels
crostata f	kro-*sta*-ta	fruit tart
crostini m pl	kro-*stee*-nee	bread toasted with savoury toppings
farinata f	fa-ree-*na*-ta	thin, flat bread made from chickpea flour
fettuccine f pl	fe-too-*chee*-ne	long ribbon-shaped pasta
focaccia f	fo-*ka*-cha	flat bread filled or topped with cheese, ham, vegetables & other ingredients
frittata f	free-*ta*-ta	thick omelette slice, served hot or cold
funghi m pl	*foon*-gee	mushrooms
gamberoni m pl	gam-be-*ro*-nee	prawns
gelato m	je-*la*-to	ice cream

gnocchi m pl	*nyo*-kee	small (usually potato) dumplings
grappa f	*gra*-pa	distilled grape must
involtini m pl	een-vol-*tee*-nee	stuffed rolls of meat or fish
linguine f pl	leen-*gwee*-ne	long thin ribbons of pasta
lumache f pl	loo-*ma*-ke	snails
maccheroni m pl	ma-ke-*ro*-nee	refers to any tube pasta
mascarpone m	mas-kar-*po*-ne	very soft & creamy cheese
minestrone m	mee-ne-*stro*-ne	traditional vegetable soup
ostriche f pl	*os*-tree-ke	oysters
pancetta f	pan-*che*-ta	salt-cured bacon
panzanella f	pan-tsa-*ne*-la	tomato, onion, garlic, olive oil, bread & basil salad
penne f pl	*pe*-ne	short & tubular pasta
pesto m	*pes*-to	paste of garlic, basil, pine nuts & parmesan
polpette m	pol-*pe*-te	meatballs
prosciutto m	pro-*shoo*-to	any type of thinly sliced ham
quattro formaggi	*kwa*-tro for-*ma*-jee	pasta sauce with four different cheeses
quattro stagioni	*kwa*-tro sta-*jo*-nee	pizza with different toppings on each quarter
ragù m	ra-*goo*	meat sauce (sometimes vegetarian)
ravioli m pl	ra-vee-*o*-lee	pasta squares usually stuffed with meat, parmesan cheese & breadcrumbs
rigatoni m pl	ree-ga-*to*-nee	short, fat tubes of pasta
risotto m	ree-*zo*-to	rice dish cooked in broth
spaghetti m pl	spa-*ge*-tee	ubiquitous long thin strands of pasta
tagliatelle f	ta-lya-*te*-le	long, ribbon-shaped pasta
tiramisù m	tee-ra-mee-*soo*	layered sponge cake soaked in coffee
tortellini m pl	tor-te-*lee*-nee	pasta filled with meat, parmesan & egg
vongole f pl	*von*-go-le	clams

emergencies

basics

Help!	*Aiuto!*	ai-*yoo*-to
Stop!	*Fermi!*	*fer*-mee
Go away!	*Vai via!*	vai *vee*-a
Thief!	*Ladro!*	*la*-dro
Fire!	*Al fuoco!*	al *fwo*-ko
Watch out!	*Attenzione!*	a-ten-*tsyo*-ne
Call ...!	*Chiami ...!*	*kya*-mee ...
a doctor	*un medico*	oon *me*-dee-ko
an ambulance	*un'ambulanza*	o-nam-boo-*lan*-tsa
the police	*la polizia*	la po-lee-*tsee*-a

It's an emergency!
È un'emergenza!   e oo-ne-mer-*jen*-tsa

Could you help me, please?
Mi può aiutare, per favore?   mee pwo ai-yoo-*ta*-re per fa-*vo*-re

I have to use the telephone.
Devo fare una telefonata.   *de*-vo *fa*-re *oo*-na te-le-fo-*na*-ta

I'm lost.
Mi sono perso/a. m/f   mee *so*-no *per*-so/a

Where are the toilets?
Dove sono i gabinetti?   *do*-ve *so*-no ee ga-bee-*ne*-tee

police

Where's the police station?
Dov'è il posto di polizia?   do-*ve* eel *pos*-to dee po-lee-*tsee*-a

I want to report an offence.
Voglio fare una denuncia.   *vo*-lyo *fa*-re *oo*-na de-*noon*-cha

I have insurance.
Ho l'assicurazione.   o la-see-koo-ra-*tsyo*-ne

I've been ...	*Sono stato/a ...* m/f	*so*-no *sta*-to/a ...
assaulted	*aggredito/a* m/f	a-gre-*dee*-to/a
raped	*violentato/a* m/f	vyo-len-*ta*-to/a
robbed	*derubato/a* m/f	roo-*ba*-to/a

I've lost my ...	Ho perso ...	o *per*·so ...
My ... was/were stolen.	Mi hanno rubato ...	mee *a*·no roo·*ba*·to ...
backpack	il mio zaino	eel *mee*·o *dzai*·no
bags	i miei bagagli	ee mee·*ay* ba·*ga*·lyee
credit card	la mia carta di credito	la *mee*·a *kar*·ta dee *kre*·dee·to
handbag	la mia borsa	la *mee*·a *bor*·sa
jewellery	i miei gioielli	ee mee·*ay* jo·*ye*·lee
money	i miei soldi	ee mee·*ay* *sol*·dee
passport	il mio passaporte	eel *mee*·o pa·sa·*por*·te
travellers cheques	i miei assegni di viaggio	ee mee·*ay* a·*se*·nyee dee vee·*a*·jo
wallet	portafoglio	por·ta·*fo*·lyo
I want to contact my ...	Vorrei contattare ...	vo·*ray* kon·ta·*ta*·re ...
consulate	il mio consolato	eel *mee*·o kon·so·*la*·to
embassy	la mia ambasciata	la *mee*·a am·ba·*sha*·ta

health

medical needs

Where's the nearest ...?	Dov'è ... più vicino/a? m/f	do·*ve* ... pyoo vee·*chee*·no/a
dentist	il dentista m	eel den·*tee*·sta
doctor	il medico m	eel *me*·dee·ko
hospital	l'ospedale m	los·pe·*da*·le
(night) pharmacist	la farmacia (di turno) f	la far·ma·*chee*·a (dee *toor*·no)

I need a doctor (who speaks English).
Ho bisogno di un medico (che parli inglese).
o bee·*zo*·nyo dee oon *me*·dee·ko (ke *par*·lee een·*gle*·ze)

Could I see a female doctor?
Posso vedere una dottoressa?
po·so ve·*de*·re *oo*·na do·to·*re*·sa

I've run out of my medication.
Ho finito la mia medicina.
o fee·*nee*·to la *mee*·a me·dee·*chee*·na

symptoms, conditions & allergies

I'm sick.   *Mi sento male.*   mee *sen*·to *ma*·le
It hurts here.   *Mi fa male qui.*   mee fa *ma*·le kwee

I have (a) ...   *Ho ...*   o ...

asthma	*asma*	*as*·ma
bronchitis	*la bronchite*	la bron·*kee*·te
constipation	*la stitichezza*	la stee·tee·*ke*·tsa
cough	*la tosse*	la *to*·se
diarrhoea	*la diarrea*	la dee·a·*re*·a
fever	*la febbre*	la *fe*·bre
headache	*mal di testa*	mal dee *tes*·ta
heart condition	*un problema cardiaco*	oon pro·*ble*·ma kar·*dee*·a·ko
nausea	*la nausea*	la *now*·ze·a
pain	*un dolore*	oon do·*lo*·re
sore throat	*mal di gola*	mal dee *go*·la
toothache	*mal di denti*	mal dee *den*·tee

I'm allergic to ...   *Sono allergico/a ...* m/f   *so*·no a·*ler*·jee·ko/a ...

antibiotics	*agli*	*a*·lyee
	antibiotici	an·tee·bee·*o*·tee·chee
anti-inflammatories	*agli*	*a*·lyee
	antinfiammatori	an·teen·fya·ma·*to*·ree
aspirin	*all'aspirina*	a·las·pee·*ree*·na
bees	*alle api*	*a*·le *a*·pee
codeine	*alla codeina*	*a*·la ko·de·*ee*·na
penicillin	*alla penicillina*	*a*·la pe·nee·chee·*lee*·na

antiseptic	*antisettico* m	an·tee·*se*·tee·ko
bandage	*fascia* f	*fa*·sha
condoms	*preservativi* m pl	pre·zer·va·*tee*·vee
contraceptives	*contraccettivi* m pl	kon·tra·che·*tee*·vee
diarrhoea medicine	*antidissenterico* m	an·tee·dee·sen·*te*·ree·ko
insect repellent	*repellente per gli insetti* m	re·pe·*len*·te per lyee een·*se*·tee
laxatives	*lassativi* m pl	la·sa·*tee*·vee
painkillers	*analgesico* m	a·nal·*je*·zee·ko
rehydration salts	*sali minerali* m pl	*sa*·lee mee·ne·*ra*·lee
sleeping tablets	*sonniferi* m pl	so·*nee*·fe·ree

english–italian dictionary

Italian nouns in this dictionary, and adjectives affected by gender, have their gender indicated by ⓜ (masculine) or ⓕ (feminine). If it's a plural noun, you'll also see pl. Words are also marked as n (noun), a (adjective), v (verb), sg (singular), pl (plural), inf (informal) and pol (polite) where necessary.

A

accident *incidente* ⓜ een-chee-*den*-te
accommodation *alloggio* ⓜ a-*lo*-jo
adaptor *presa multipla* ⓕ *pre*-sa mool-*tee*-pla
address *indirizzo* ⓜ een-dee-*ree*-tso
after *dopo* *do*-po
air-conditioned *ad aria condizionata*
    ad *a*-rya kon-dee-tsyo-*na*-ta
airplane *aereo* ⓜ a-e-*re*-o
airport *aeroporto* ⓜ a-e-ro-*por*-to
alcohol *alcol* ⓜ *al*-kol
all a *tutto/a* *too*-to/a
allergy *allergia* ⓕ a-ler-*jee*-a
ambulance *ambulanza* ⓕ am-boo-*lan*-tsa
and *e* e
ankle *caviglia* ⓕ ka-*vee*-lya
arm *braccio* ⓜ *bra*-cho
ashtray *portacenere* ⓜ por-ta-*che*-ne-re
ATM *Bancomat* ⓜ *ban*-ko-mat

B

baby *bimbo/a* ⓜ/ⓕ *beem*-bo/a
back (body) *schiena* ⓕ *skye*-na
backpack *zaino* ⓜ *dzai*-no
bad *cattivo/a* ⓜ/ⓕ ka-*tee*-vo/a
bag *borsa* ⓕ *bor*-sa
baggage claim *ritiro bagagli* ⓜ ree-*tee*-ro ba-*ga*-lyee
bank *banca* ⓕ *ban*-ka
bar *locale* ⓜ lo-*ka*-le
bathroom *bagno* ⓜ *ba*-nyo
battery *pila* ⓕ *pee*-la
beautiful *bello/a* ⓜ/ⓕ *be*-lo/a
bed *letto* ⓜ *le*-to
beer *birra* ⓕ *bee*-ra
before *prima* *pree*-ma
behind *dietro* *dye*-tro
bicycle *bicicletta* ⓕ bee-chee-*kle*-ta
big *grande* *gran*-de
bill *conto* ⓜ *kon*-to

black *nero/a* ⓜ/ⓕ *ne*-ro/a
blanket *coperta* ⓕ ko-*per*-ta
blood group *gruppo sanguigno* ⓜ *groo*-po san-*gwee*-nyo
blue *azzurro/a* ⓜ/ⓕ a-*dzoo*-ro/a
boat *barca* ⓕ *bar*-ka
book (make a reservation) v *prenotare* pre-no-*ta*-re
bottle *bottiglia* ⓕ bo-*tee*-lya
bottle opener *apribottiglie* ⓜ a-pree-bo-*tee*-lye
boy *ragazzo* ⓜ ra-*ga*-tso
brakes (car) *freno* ⓜ *fre*-no
breakfast (prima) colazione ⓕ (*pree*-ma) ko-la-*tsyo*-ne
broken (faulty) *rotto/a* ⓜ/ⓕ *ro*-to/a
bus *autobus* ⓜ *ow*-to-boos
business *affari* ⓜ pl a-*fa*-ree
buy *comprare* kom-*pra*-re

C

café *bar* ⓜ bar
camera *macchina fotografica* ⓕ
    ma-kee-na fo-to-*gra*-fee-ka
camp site *campeggio* ⓜ kam-*pe*-jo
can opener *apriscatole* ⓜ a-pree-*ska*-to-le
cancel *cancellare* kan-che-*la*-re
car *macchina* ⓕ *ma*-kee-na
cash *soldi* ⓜ pl *sol*-dee
cash (a cheque) v *riscuotere un assegno*
    ree-*skwo*-te-re oon a-*se*-nyo
cell phone *telefono cellulare* ⓜ te-*le*-fo-no che-loo-*la*-re
centre *centro* ⓜ *chen*-tro
change (money) v *cambiare* kam-*bya*-re
cheap *economico/a* ⓜ/ⓕ e-ko-*no*-mee-ko/a
check (bill) *conto* ⓜ *kon*-to
check-in *registrazione* ⓕ re-jee-stra-*tsyo*-ne
chest *petto* ⓜ *pe*-to
child *bambino/a* ⓜ/ⓕ bam-*bee*-no/a
cigarette *sigaretta* ⓕ see-ga-*re*-ta
city *città* ⓕ chee-*ta*
clean a *pulito/a* poo-*lee*-to/a
closed *chiuso/a* ⓜ/ⓕ *kyoo*-zo/a
coffee *caffè* ⓜ ka-*fe*
coins *monete* ⓕ pl mo-*ne*-te

cold a *freddo/a* ⓜ/ⓕ *fre*-do/a
collect call *chiamata a carico del destinatario* ⓕ
   kya-*ma*-ta a ka-*ree*-ko del des-tee-na-*ta*-ryo
come *venire* ve-*nee*-re
computer *computer* ⓜ kom-*pyoo*-ter
condom *preservativo* ⓜ pre-zer-va-*tee*-vo
contact lenses *lenti a contatto* ⓕ pl *len*-tee a kon-*ta*-to
cook ∨ *cucinare* koo-chee-*na*-re
cost *prezzo* ⓜ *pre*-tso
credit card *carta di credito* ⓕ *kar*-ta dee *kre*-dee-to
cup *tazza* ⓕ *ta*-tsa
currency exchange *cambio valuta* ⓜ *kam*-byo va-*loo*-ta
customs (immigration) *dogana* ⓕ do-*ga*-na

D

dangerous *pericoloso/a* ⓜ/ⓕ pe-ree-ko-*lo*-zo/a
date (time) *data* ⓕ *da*-ta
day *giorno* ⓜ *jor*-no
delay *ritardo* ⓜ ree-*tar*-do
dentist *dentista* ⓕ den-*tee*-sta
depart *partire* par-*tee*-re
diaper *pannolino* ⓜ pa-no-*lee*-no
dictionary *vocabolario* ⓜ vo-ka-bo-*la*-ryo
dinner *cena* ⓕ *che*-na
direct *diretto/a* ⓜ/ⓕ dee-*re*-to/a
dirty *sporco/a* ⓜ/ⓕ *spor*-ko/a
disabled *disabile* dee-*za*-bee-le
discount *sconto* ⓜ *skon*-to
doctor *medico* ⓜ *me*-dee-ko
double bed *letto matrimoniale* ⓜ *le*-to-ma-tree-mo-*nya*-le
double room *camera doppia* ⓕ *ka*-mer-a *do*-pya
drink *bevanda* ⓕ be-*van*-da
drive ∨ *guidare* gwee-*da*-re
drivers licence *patente di guida* ⓕ pa-*ten*-te dee *gwee*-da
drugs (illicit) *droga* ⓕ *dro*-ga
dummy (pacifier) *ciucciotto* ⓜ choo-*cho*-to

E

ear *orecchio* ⓜ o-*re*-kyo
east *est* ⓜ est
eat *mangiare* man-*ja*-re
economy class *classe turistica* ⓕ *kla*-se too-*ree*-stee-ka
electricity *elettricità* ⓕ e-le-tree-chee-*ta*
elevator *ascensore* ⓜ a-shen-*so*-re
email *email* ⓜ e-mayl
embassy *ambasciata* ⓕ am-ba-*sha*-ta
emergency *emergenza* ⓕ e-mer-*jen*-tsa
English (language) *inglese* een-*gle*-ze

entrance *entrata* ⓕ en-*tra*-ta
evening *sera* ⓕ *se*-ra
exchange rate *tasso di cambio* ⓜ *ta*-so dee *kam*-byo
exit *uscita* ⓕ *ta*-so dee *kam*-byo
expensive *caro/a* ⓜ/ⓕ *ka*-ro/a
express mail *posta prioritaria* ⓕ *pos*-ta pree-o-ree-*ta*-rya
eye *occhio* ⓜ *o*-kyo

F

far *lontano/a* ⓜ/ⓕ lon-*ta*-no/a
fast *veloce* ve-*lo*-che
father *padre* ⓜ *pa*-dre
film (camera) *rullino* ⓜ roo-*lee*-no
finger *dito* ⓜ *dee*-to
first-aid kit *valigetta del pronto soccorso* ⓕ
   va-lee-*je*-ta del *pron*-to so-*kor*-so
first class *prima classe* ⓕ *pree*-ma *kla*-se
fish ∩ *pesce* ⓜ *pe*-she
food *cibo* ⓜ *chee*-bo
foot *piede* ⓜ *pye*-de
fork *forchetta* ⓕ for-*ke*-ta
free (of charge) *gratuito/a* ⓜ/ⓕ gra-*too*-ee-to/a
friend *amico/a* ⓜ/ⓕ a-*mee*-ko/a
fruit *frutta* ⓕ *froo*-ta
full *pieno/a* ⓜ/ⓕ *pye*-no/a
funny *divertente* dee-ver-*ten*-te

G

gift *regalo* ⓜ re-*ga*-lo
girl *ragazza* ⓕ ra-*ga*-tsa
glass (drinking) *bicchiere* ⓜ bee-*kye*-re
glasses *occhiali* ⓜ pl o-*kya*-lee
go *andare* an-*da*-re
good *buono/a* ⓜ/ⓕ *bwo*-no/a
green *verde* ver-de
guide ∩ *guida* ⓕ *gwee*-da

H

half *mezzo* ⓜ *me*-dzo
hand *mano* ⓕ *ma*-no
handbag *borsetta* ⓕ bor-*se*-ta
happy *felice* ⓜ/ⓕ fe-*lee*-che
have *avere* a-*ve*-re
he *lui* loo-ee
head *testa* ⓕ *tes*-ta
heart *cuore* ⓜ *kwo*-re
heat ∩ *caldo* ⓜ *kal*-do

heavy *pesante* pe-*zan*-te
help v *aiutare* a-yoo-*ta*-re
here *qui* kwee
high *alto/a* ⓜ/ⓕ *al*-to/a
highway *autostrada* ⓕ ow-to-*stra*-da
hike v *fare un'escursione a piedi*
  fa-re oon es-koor-*syo*-ne a *pye*-de
holiday *vacanze* ⓕ pl va-*kan*-tse
homosexual n *omosessuale* ⓜ&ⓕ o-mo-se-*swa*-le
hospital *ospedale* ⓜ os-pe-*da*-le
hot *caldo/a* ⓜ/ⓕ *kal*-do/a
hotel *albergo* ⓜ al-*ber*-go
hungry *affamato/a* ⓜ/ⓕ a-fa-*ma*-to
husband *marito* ⓜ ma-*ree*-to

I

I *io* ee-o
identification (card) *carta d'identità* ⓕ
  kar-ta dee-den-tee-*ta*
ill *malato/a* ⓜ/ⓕ ma-*la*-to/a
important *importante* eem-por-*tan*-te
included *compreso/a* ⓜ/ⓕ kom-*pre*-zo/a
injury *ferita* ⓕ fe-*ree*-ta
insurance *assicurazione* ⓕ a-see-koo-ra-*tsyo*-ne
Internet *Internet* ⓜ een-ter-net
interpreter *interprete* ⓜ/ⓕ een-*ter*-pre-te
Italy *Italia* ⓕ ee-*ta*-lya
Italian (language) *italiano* ⓜ ee-ta-*lya*-no

J

jewellery *gioielli* ⓜ pl jo-*ye*-lee
job *lavoro* ⓜ la-*vo*-ro

K

key *chiave* ⓕ *kya*-ve
kilogram *chilo* ⓜ *kee*-lo
kitchen *cucina* ⓕ koo-*chee*-na
knife *coltello* ⓜ kol-*te*-lo

L

laundry (place) *lavanderia* ⓕ la-van-de-*ree*-a
lawyer *avvocato/a* ⓜ/ⓕ a-vo-*ka*-to/a
left (direction) *sinistra* see-*nee*-stra
left-luggage office *deposito bagagli* ⓜ
  de-*po*-zee-to ba-*ga*-lyee
leg *gamba* ⓕ *gam*-ba

lesbian n *lesbica* ⓕ *lez*-bee-ka
less *(di) meno* (dee) *me*-no
letter (mail) *lettera* ⓕ *le*-te-ra
lift (elevator) *ascensore* ⓜ a-shen-*so*-re
light *luce* ⓕ *loo*-che
like v *piacere* pya-*che*-re
lock *serratura* ⓕ se-ra-*too*-ra
long *lungo/a* ⓜ/ⓕ *loon*-go/a
lost *perso/a* ⓜ/ⓕ *per*-so/a
lost-property office *ufficio oggetti smarriti* ⓜ
  oo-*fee*-cho o-*je*-tee sma-*ree*-tee
love v *amare* a-*ma*-re
luggage *bagaglio* ⓜ ba-*ga*-lyo
lunch *pranzo* ⓜ *pran*-dzo

M

mail *posta* ⓕ *pos*-ta
man *uomo* ⓜ *wo*-mo
map *pianta* ⓕ *pyan*-ta
market *mercato* ⓜ mer-*ka*-to
matches *fiammiferi* ⓜ pl fya-*mee*-fe-ree
meat *carne* ⓕ *kar*-ne
medicine *medicina* ⓕ me-dee-*chee*-na
menu *menu* ⓜ me-*noo*
message *messaggio* ⓜ me-*sa*-jo
milk *latte* ⓕ *la*-te
minute *minuto* ⓜ mee-*noo*-to
mobile phone *telefono cellulare* ⓜ te-*le*-fo-no che-loo-*la*-re
money *denaro* ⓜ de-*na*-ro
month *mese* ⓜ *me*-ze
morning *mattina* ⓕ ma-*tee*-na
mother *madre* ⓕ *ma*-dre
motorcycle *moto* ⓕ *mo*-to
motorway *autostrada* ⓕ ow-to-*stra*-da
mouth *bocca* ⓕ *bo*-ka
music *musica* ⓕ *moo*-zee-ka

N

name *nome* ⓜ *no*-me
napkin *tovagliolo* ⓜ to-va-*lyo*-lo
nappy *pannolino* ⓜ pa-no-*lee*-no
near *vicino (a)* vee-*chee*-no (a)
neck *collo* ⓜ *ko*-lo
new *nuovo/a* ⓜ/ⓕ *nwo*-vo/a
news *notizie* ⓕ pl no-*tee*-tsye
newspaper *giornale* ⓜ jor-*na*-le
night *notte* ⓕ *no*-te
no *no* no

noisy *rumoroso/a* ⑩/① roo-mo-ro-zo/a
nonsmoking *non fumatore* non foo-ma-to-re
north *nord* ⑩ nord
nose *naso* ⑩ na-zo
now *adesso* a-de-so
number *numero* ⑩ noo-me-ro

O

oil (engine) *olio* ⑩ o-lyo
old *vecchio/a* ⑩/① ve-kyo/a
one-way ticket *biglietto di solo andata*
    bee-*lye*-to dee so-lo an-*da*-ta
open a *aperto/a* ⑩/① a-*per*-to/a
outside *fuori* fwo-ree

P

package *pacchetto* ⑩ pa-*ke*-to
paper *carta* ① kar-ta
park (car) v *parcheggiare* par-ke-*ja*-re
passport *passaporto* ⑩ pa-sa-*por*-to
pay *pagare* pa-*ga*-re
pen *penna (a sfera)* ① pe-na (a *sfe*-ra)
petrol *benzina* ① ben-*dzee*-na
pharmacy *farmacia* ① far-ma-*chee*-a
phonecard *scheda telefonica* ① *ske*-da te-le-fo-nee-ka
photo *foto* ① fo-to
plate *piatto* ⑩ pya-to
police *polizia* ① po-lee-*tsee*-a
postcard *cartolina* ① kar-to-*lee*-na
post office *ufficio postale* ⑩ oo-fee-cho pos-*ta*-le
pregnant *incinta* een-*cheen*-ta
price *prezzo* ⑩ pre-tso

Q

quiet *tranquillo/a* ⑩/① tran-*kwee*-lo/a

R

rain n *pioggia* ① *pyo*-ja
razor *rasoio* ① ra-zo-yo
receipt *ricevuta* ① re-che-*voo*-ta
red *rosso/a* ⑩/① ro-so/a
refund *rimborso* ⑩ reem-*bor*-so
registered mail *posta raccomandata* ①
    pos-ta ra-ko-man-*da*-ta
rent v *prendere in affitto* pren-de-re een a-*fee*-to
repair v *riparare* ree-pa-*ra*-re

reservation *prenotazione* ① pre-no-ta-*tsyo*-ne
restaurant *ristorante* ⑩ rees-to-*ran*-te
return v *ritornare* ree-tor-*na*-re
return ticket *biglietto di andata e ritorno*
    bee-*lye*-to dee an-*da*-ta e ree-*tor*-no
right (direction) *destra* de-stra
road *strada* ① *stra*-da
room *camera* ① *ka*-me-ra

S

safe a *sicuro/a* ⑩/① see-koo-ro/a
sanitary napkins *assorbenti igienici* ⑩ pl
    as-or-*ben*-tee ee-je-nee-chee
seat *posto* ⑩ pos-to
send *mandare* man-*da*-re
service station *stazione di servizio* ①
    sta-*tsyo*-ne dee ser-*vee*-tsyo
sex *sesso* ⑩ se-so
shampoo *shampoo* ⑩ sham-poo
share (a dorm) *condividere* kon-dee-vee-de-re
shaving cream *crema da barba* ① *kre*-ma da *bar*-ba
she *lei* lay
sheet (bed) *lenzuolo* ⑩ len-*tswo*-lo
shirt *camicia* ① ka-*mee*-cha
shoes *scarpe* ① pl skar-pe
shop *negozio* ⑩ ne-go-tsyo
short *corto/a* ⑩/① kor-to/a
shower *doccia* ① do-cha
single room *camera singola* ① *ka*-me-ra seen-go-la
skin *pelle* ① pe-le
skirt *gonna* ① go-na
sleep v *dormire* dor-*mee*-re
slowly *lentamente* len-ta-*men*-te
small *piccolo/a* ⑩/① pee-ko-lo/a
smoke (cigarettes) v *fumare* foo-*ma*-re
soap *sapone* ⑩ sa-*po*-ne
some *alcuni/e* ⑩/① pl al-koo-nee/al-koo-ne
soon *fra poco* fra po-ko
south *sud* ⑩ sood
souvenir shop *negozio di souvenir* ⑩
    ne-*go*-tsyo dee soo-ve-neer
speak *parlare* par-*la*-re
spoon *cucchiaio* ⑩ koo-*kya*-yo
stamp *francobollo* ⑩ fran-ko-*bo*-lo
stand-by ticket *in lista d'attesa* een *lee*-sta da-*te*-za
station (train) *stazione* ① sta-*tsyo*-ne
stomach *stomaco* ⑩ sto-ma-ko
stop v *fermare* fer-*ma*-re
stop (bus) *fermata* ① fer-*ma*-ta

street *strada* ① *stra*-da
student *studente/studentessa* ⓜ/①
  stoo-*den*-te/stoo-den-*te*-sa
sun *sole* ⓜ *so*-le
sunscreen *crema solare* ① *kre*-ma so-*la*-re
swim v *nuotare* nwo-*ta*-re
Switzerland *Svizzera* ① svee-*tse*-ra

T

tampons *assorbenti interni* ⓜ pl
  a-sor-*ben*-tee een-*ter*-nee
taxi *tassì* ⓜ ta-*see*
teaspoon *cucchiaino* ⓜ koo-kya-*ee*-no
teeth *denti* ⓜ pl *den*-tee
telephone *telefono* ⓜ te-*le*-fo-no
television *televisione* ① te-le-vee-*zyo*-ne
temperature (weather) *temperatura* ①
  tem-pe-ra-*too*-ra
tent *tenda* ① *ten*-da
that (one) *quello/a* ⓜ/① *kwe*-lo/a
they *loro* *lo*-ro
thirsty *assetato/a* ⓜ/① a-se-*ta*-to
this (one) *questo/a* ⓜ/① *kwe*-sto/a
throat *gola* ① *go*-la
ticket *biglietto* ⓜ bee-*lye*-to
time *tempo* ⓜ *tem*-po
tired *stanco/a* ⓜ/① *stan*-ko/a
tissues *fazzolettini di carta* ⓜ pl
  fa-tso-le-*tee*-nee dee *kar*-ta
today *oggi* o-jee
toilet *gabinetto* ⓜ ga-bee-*ne*-to
tomorrow *domani* do-*ma*-nee
tonight *stasera* sta-*se*-ra
toothbrush *spazzolino da denti* ⓜ
  spa-tso-*lee*-no da *den*-tee
toothpaste *dentifricio* ⓜ den-tee-*free*-cho
torch (flashlight) *torcia elettrica* ① *tor*-cha e-*le*-tree-ka
tour *gita* ① *jee*-ta
tourist office *ufficio del turismo* ⓜ
  oo-*fee*-cho del too-*reez*-mo
towel *asciugamano* ⓜ a-shoo-ga-*ma*-no
train *treno* ⓜ *tre*-no
translate *tradurre* tra-*doo*-re
travel agency *agenzia di viaggio* ①
  a-jen-*tsee*-a dee vee-*a*-jo
travellers cheque *assegno di viaggio* ⓜ
  a-*se*-nyo dee vee-*a*-jo
trousers *pantaloni* ⓜ pl pan-ta-*lo*-nee

twin beds *due letti* doo-e le-tee
tyre *gomma* ① *go*-ma

U

underwear *biancheria intima* ⓜ byan-ke-*ree*-a een-*tee*-ma
urgent *urgente* ⓜ/① oor-*jen*-te

V

vacant *libero/a* ⓜ/① *lee*-be-ro/a
vacation *vacanza* ① va-*kan*-tsa
vegetable *verdura* ① ver-*doo*-ra
vegetarian a *vegetariano/a* ⓜ/① ve-je-ta-*rya*-no/a
visa *visto* ⓜ *vee*-sto

W

waiter *cameriere/a* ⓜ/① ka-mer-*ye*-re/a
walk v *camminare* ka-mee-*na*-re
wallet *portafoglio* ⓜ/① por-ta-*fo*-lyo
warm a *tiepido/a* ⓜ/① *tye*-pee-do/a
wash (something) *lavare* la-*va*-re
watch *orologio* ⓜ o-ro-*lo*-jo
water *acqua* ① *a*-kwa
we *noi* noy
weekend *fine settimana* ① *fee*-ne se-tee-*ma*-na
west *ovest* *o*-vest
wheelchair *sedia a rotelle* ① *se*-dya a ro-*te*-le
when *quando* kwan-do
where *dove* *do*-ve
white *bianco/a* ⓜ/① *byan*-ko/a
who *chi* kee
why *perché* per-*ke*
wife *moglie* ① *mo*-lye
window *finestra* ① fee-*nes*-tra
wine *vino* ⓜ *vee*-no
with *con* kon
without *senza* *sen*-tsa
woman *donna* ① *do*-na
write *scrivere* skree-ve-re

Y

yellow *giallo/a* ⓜ/① *ja*-lo/a
yes *sì* see
yesterday *ieri* ye-ree
you sg inf *tu* too
you sg pol *Lei* lay
you pl *voi* voy

Macedonian

macedonian alphabet

А а a	Б б buh	В в vuh	Г г guh	Д д duh	Ѓ ѓ gyuh
Е е e	Ж ж zhuh	З з zuh	Ѕ ѕ dzuh	И и i	Ј ј yuh
К к kuh	Л л luh	Љ љ lyuh	М м muh	Н н nuh	Њ њ nyuh
О о o	П п puh	Р р ruh	С с suh	Т т tuh	Ќ ќ kyuh
У у u	Ф ф fuh	Х х huh	Ц ц tsuh	Ч ч chuh	Џ џ juh
Ш ш shuh					

МАКЕДОНСКИ

macedonian

MACEDONIAN
македонски

introduction

Macedonian (македонски ma·ke·don·ski), the language spoken in the Balkan peninsula to the north of Greece, shares only the name with the ancient language usually thought of in relation to the empire of Alexander the Great. The present-day Macedonian is a South Slavic language (with Bulgarian and Serbian its closest relatives) and the official language of Macedonia, the former Yugoslav republic which became an independent state in 1992. For the speakers of Macedonian – about 2 million people living in Macedonia and the neighbouring countries, as well as the diaspora – it has extreme significance as a confirmation of their national identity.

From the arrival of the Slavs to the Balkans in the 6th century AD until the Turkish conquest in the 15th century, the present-day Macedonia was passed back and forth between Byzantium and the medieval Bulgarian and Serbian kingdoms, and the heavy interaction between the three Slavic languages explains many of their common features. Most notably, Macedonian and Bulgarian differ from the other Slavic languages in the absence of noun cases. During the five centuries of Turkish rule in the Ottoman Empire, Turkish linguistic influence on Macedonian (mostly in the vocabulary) was rivalled only by Greek, as the liturgic language of the Greek Orthodox Church. Stronger exposure to Serbian within the Yugoslav state for most of the 20th century is reflected in the vocabulary (particularly slang) of Macedonian today.

The history of the Macedonian literary language is centred around Old Church Slavonic and the Cyrillic alphabet. The Byzantine Orthodox missionaries, St Cyril and Methodius, themselves from Salonica in Aegean Macedonia and speakers of a Slavic dialect of the region, invented the Glagolitic alphabet in the 9th century. They translated Greek religious literature into Old Church Slavonic, the language of the earliest written records from which the modern South Slavic literary languages all evolved. The Cyrillic alphabet was later developed by the disciples of the two missionaries, using the Greek and Glagolitic characters. The Macedonian Cyrillic alphabet in its present form is phonetic and very similar to the Serbian alphabet, with only a few different letters.

The creation of a modern literary standard started in the latter half of the 19th century and ended with the official codification in 1945 of a standard based on the west-central dialects. This form is the most distinct from Bulgarian and Serbian, whose boundaries with Macedonian can often be blurry.

introduction – MACEDONIAN

pronunciation

vowel sounds

The Macedonian vowel system is very straightforward – it consists of the five basic vowels.

symbol	english equivalent	macedonian example	transliteration
a	father	здраво	*zdra*·vo
e	bet	вера	*ve*·ra
i	hit	син	sin
o	pot	добро	*dob*·ro
u	put	југ	yug

word stress

In the Macedonian literary standard the stress usually falls on the third syllable from the end in words with three syllables or more. If the word has only two syllables, the first is usually stressed. There are exceptions to this rule, such as with many new borrowings and other words of foreign origin – eg литература li·te·ra·*tu*·ra, not li·te·*ra*·tu·ra (literature). Just follow our coloured pronunciation guide, in which the stressed syllable is indicated in italics.

consonant sounds

The consonant sounds in Macedonian mostly have equivalents in English. You might need a little practice with the 'soft' ѓ gy and ќ ky sounds. Don't be intimidated by the consonant clusters as in црква *tsrk*·va (church) or брзо *br*·zo (fast) – try putting a slight 'uh' sound before the r, which serves as a semi-vowel.

symbol	english equivalent	macedonian example	transliteration
b	**b**ed	билет	*bi*·let
ch	**ch**eat	чист	chist
d	**d**og	мед	med
dz	a**dds**	ѕид	dzid
f	**f**at	кафе	*ka*·fe
g	**g**o	гуми	*gu*·mi
gy	le**g**ume	госпоѓа	*gos*·po·*gya*
h	**h**at	храм	hram
j	**j**oke	џамија	*ja*·mi·ya
k	**k**it	компир	*kom*·pir
ky	**c**ure	ноќ	noky
l	**l**ot	леб	leb
ly	mi**ll**ion	љубов	*lyu*·bov
m	**m**an	месо	*me*·so
n	**n**ot	бензин	*ben*·zin
ny	ca**ny**on	бања	*ba*·nya
p	**p**et	писмо	*pis*·mo
r	**r**un	стар	star
s	**s**un	сега	*se*·ga
sh	**sh**ot	туш	tush
t	**t**op	исток	*is*·tok
ts	ha**ts**	деца	*de*·tsa
v	**v**ery	север	*se*·ver
y	**y**es	јас	yas
z	**z**ero	пазар	*pa*·zar
zh	plea**s**ure	плажа	*pla*·zha

basics

language difficulties

Do you speak English?
Зборувате ли англиски?

zbo·*ru*·va·te li *an*·glis·ki

Do you understand?
Разбирате ли?

raz·*bi*·ra·te li

I (don't) understand.
Јас (не) разбирам.

yas (ne) *raz*·bi·ram

What does (добро) mean?
Што значи (добро)?

shto *zna*·chi (*dob*·ro)

How do you ...? | Како се ...? | *ka*·ko se ...
pronounce this | изговара ова | iz·*go*·va·ra *o*·va
write (утре) | пишува (утре) | *pi*·shu·va (*ut*·re)

Could you please ...? | ..., ве молам. | ... ve *mo*·lam
repeat that | Повторете го тоа | pov·to·*re*·te go *to*·a
speak more slowly | Зборувајте полека | zbo·*ru*·vay·te *po*·le·ka
write it down | Напишете го тоа | na·pi·*she*·te go *to*·a

essentials

Yes.	Да.	da
No.	Не.	ne
Please.	Молам.	*mo*·lam
Thank you (very much).	Благодарам. pol	bla·*go*·da·ram
Thanks a lot.	Фала многу. inf	*fa*·la *mno*·gu
You're welcome.	Нема зошто.	ne·ma *zosh*·to
Excuse me.	Извинете.	iz·*vi*·ne·te
Sorry.	Простете.	*pros*·te·te

numbers

0	нула	*nu*·la	15	петнаесет	pet·*na*·e·set
1	еден/една m/f	e·den/*ed*·na	16	шеснаесет	shes·*na*·e·set
	едно n	*ed*·no	17	седумнаесет	se·dum·*na*·e·set
2	два m	dva	18	осумнаесет	o·sum·*na*·e·set
	две f&n	dve	19	деветнаесет	de·vet·*na*·e·set
3	три	tri	20	дваесет	*dva*·e·set
4	четири	*che*·ti·ri	21	дваесет и еден	*dva*·e·set i e·den
5	пет	pet	22	дваесет и два	*dva*·e·set i dva
6	шест	shest	30	триесет	*tri*·e·set
7	седум	*se*·dum	40	четириесет	che·ti·*ri*·e·set
8	осум	*o*·sum	50	педесет	*pe*·de·set
9	девет	*de*·vet	60	шеесет	*she*·e·set
10	десет	*de*·set	70	седумдесет	se·*dum*·de·set
11	единаесет	e·di·*na*·e·set	80	осумдесет	o·*sum*·de·set
12	дванаесет	dva·*na*·e·set	90	деведесет	de·*ve*·de·set
13	тринаесет	tri·*na*·e·set	100	сто	sto
14	четиринаесет	che·ti·ri·*na*·e·set	1000	илјада	il·*ya*·da

time & dates

What time is it?	Колку е часот?	*kol*·ku e *cha*·sot
It's one o'clock.	Часот е еден.	*cha*·sot e e·den
It's (two) o'clock.	Часот е (два).	*cha*·sot e (dva)
Quarter past (one).	(Еден) и петнаесет.	(e·den) i pet·*na*·e·set
Half past (one).	(Еден) и пол.	(e·den) i pol
Quarter to (eight).	Петнаесет до (осум).	pet·*na*·e·set do (*o*·sum)
At what time ...?	Во колку часот ...?	vo *kol*·ku *cha*·sot ...
At ...	Во ...	vo ...
am	претпладне	*pret*·plad·ne
pm	попладне	*po*·plad·ne
Monday	понеделник	po·*ne*·del·nik
Tuesday	вторник	*vtor*·nik
Wednesday	среда	*sre*·da
Thursday	четврток	*chet*·vr·tok
Friday	петок	*pe*·tok
Saturday	сабота	*sa*·bo·ta
Sunday	недела	*ne*·de·la

January	јануари	ya·nu·*a*·ri
February	февруари	fev·ru·*a*·ri
March	март	mart
April	април	*ap*·ril
May	мај	may
June	јуни	*yu*·ni
July	јули	*yu*·li
August	август	*av*·gust
September	септември	sep·*tem*·vri
October	октомври	ok·*tom*·vri
November	ноември	no·*em*·vri
December	декември	de·*kem*·vri

What date is it today?
Кој датум е денес? koy *da*·tum e *de*·nes

It's (15 December).
Денес е (петнаесетти декември). *de*·nes e (pet·na·e·*set*·ti de·*kem*·vri)

| since (May) | од (мај) | od (may) |
| until (June) | до (јуни) | do (*yu*·ni) |

last ...

night	синоќа	*si*·no·kya
week	минатата недела	mi·*na*·ta·ta ne·de·la
month	минатиот месец	mi·*na*·ti·ot *me*·sets
year	минатата година	mi·*na*·ta·ta go·di·na

next ...

week	следната недела	*sled*·na·ta ne·de·la
month	следниот месец	*sled*·ni·ot *me*·sets
year	следната година	*sled*·na·ta go·di·na

yesterday/tomorrow ... вчера/утре ... *vche*·ra/*ut*·re ...

morning	наутро	*na*·ut·ro
afternoon	попладне	*pop*·lad·ne
evening	вечер	*ve*·cher

weather

What's the weather like?	Какво е времето?	*kak*·vo e *vre*·me·to
It' snowing.	Паѓа снег.	*pa*·gya sneg

It's...	Времето е ...	*vre*·me·to e ...
cloudy	облачно	*ob*·lach·no
cold	студено	*stu*·de·no
hot	жешко	*zhesh*·ko
raining	врнежливо	vr·*nezh*·li·vo
sunny	сончево	*son*·che·vo
warm	топло	*top*·lo
windy	ветровито	vet·*ro*·vi·to

spring	пролет f	*pro*·let
summer	лето n	*le*·to
autumn	есен m	*e*·sen
winter	зима f	*zi*·ma

border crossing

I'm here ...	Јас сум овде ...	yas sum *ov*·de ...
in transit	транзит	*tran*·zit
on business	службено	*sluzh*·be·no
on holiday	на одмор	na *od*·mor

I'm here for ...	Јас овде останувам ...	yas *ov*·de os·*ta*·nu·vam ...
(10) days	(десет) дена	(*de*·set) *de*·na
(two) months	(два) месеца	(dva) *me*·se·tsa
(three) weeks	(три) недели	(tri) *ne*·de·li

I'm going to (Ohrid).
Јас одам во (Охрид). yas *o*·dam vo (*oh*·rid)

I'm staying at the (Hotel Park).
Јас престојувам во (хотел 'Парк'). yas pres·*to*·yu·vam vo (*ho*·tel park)

I have nothing to declare.
Јас немам да пријавам ништо. yas *ne*·mam da *pri*·ya·vam *nish*·to

I have something to declare.
Јас имам нешто да пријавам. yas *i*·mam *nesh*·to da *pri*·ya·vam

That's (not) mine.
Тоа (не) е мое. *to*·a (ne) e *mo*·e

transport

tickets & luggage

Where can I buy a ticket?
Каде можам да купам билет?   ka·de mo·zham da ku·pam bi·let

Do I need to book a seat?
Ми треба ли резервација?   mi tre·ba li re·zer·va·tsi·ya

One ... ticket (to Ohrid), please.	Еден ... (за Охрид), ве молам.	e·den ... (za oh·rid) ve mo·lam
one-way	билет во еден правец	bi·let vo e·den pra·vets
return	повратен билет	pov·ra·ten bi·let

I'd like to ... my ticket, please.	Сакам да го ... мојот билет, ве молам.	sa·kam da go ... mo·yot bi·let ve mo·lam
cancel	откажам	ot·ka·zham
change	променам	pro·me·nam
collect	земам	ze·mam
confirm	потврдам	pot·vr·dam

I'd like a ... seat, please.	Сакам едно седиште за ..., ве молам.	sa·kam ed·no se·dish·te za ... ve mo·lam
nonsmoking	непушачи	ne·pu·sha·chi
smoking	пушачи	pu·sha·chi

How much is it?
Колку чини тоа?   kol·ku chi·ni to·a

Is there air conditioning?
Дали има клима уред?   da·li i·ma kli·ma u·red

Is there a toilet?
Дали има тоалет?   da·li i·ma to·a·let

How long does the trip take?
Колку време се патува?   kol·ku vre·me se pa·tu·va

Is it a direct route? (train/bus)
Дали е овој воз/автобус директен?   da·li e o·voy voz/av·to·bus di·rek·ten

I'd like a luggage locker.
Сакам шкаф за багаж.   sa·kam shkaf za ba·gazh

My luggage has been ...	Мојот багаж е ...	*mo*·yot *ba*·gazh e ...
damaged	оштетен	*osh*·te·ten
lost	загубен	*za*·gu·ben
stolen	украден	*uk*·ra·den

getting around

Where does flight (912) arrive/depart?
Каде слетува/полетува
авионот со лет (912)?
ka·de *sle*·tu·va/po·*le*·tu·va
a·vi·*o*·not so let (*de*·vet *e*·den dva)

Where's (the) ...?	Каде е ...?	*ka*·de e ...
arrivals hall	чекалната за	che·*kal*·na·ta za
	пристигнување	pris·*tig*·*nu*·va·nye
departures hall	чекалната за	che·*kal*·na·ta za
	заминување	za·mi·*nu*·va·nye
duty-free shop	дјутифри	*dyu*·ti·fri
	продавницата	pro·dav·*ni*·tsa·ta
gate (12)	излезот (дванаесет)	*iz*·le·zot (dva·*na*·e·set)

Is this the ... to (Bitola)?	Дали овој ... оди за (Битола)?	*da*·li *o*·voy ... *o*·di za (*bi*·to·la)
boat	брод	brod
bus	автобус	*av*·to·bus
plane	авион	a·vi·*on*
train	воз	voz

What time's the ... bus?	Кога поаѓа ... автобус?	*ko*·ga *po*·a·gya ... *av*·to·bus
first	првиот	*pr*·vi·ot
last	последниот	pos·*led*·ni·ot
next	следниот	*sled*·ni·ot

At what time does it arrive/leave?
Кога пристигнува/поаѓа?
ko·ga pris·*tig*·nu·va/*po*·a·gya

How long will it be delayed?
Колку време ќе доцни?
kol·ku *vre*·me kye *dots*·ni

What station/stop is this?
Која е оваа станица?
ko·ya e *o*·va·a *sta*·ni·tsa

What's the next station/stop?
Која е следната станица?
ko·ya e *sled*·na·ta *sta*·ni·tsa

Does it stop at (Prilep)?
Дали застанува во (Прилеп)? — *da*·li zas·*ta*·nu·va vo (*pri*·lep)

Please tell me when we get to (Skopje).
Ве молам кажете ми кога
ќе стигнеме во (Скопје). — ve *mo*·lam ka·*zhe*·te mi *ko*·ga
kye *stig*·ne·me vo (*skop*·ye)

How long do we stop here?
Колку долго ќе стоиме овде? — *kol*·ku *dol*·go kye *sto*·i·me *ov*·de

Is this seat available?
Дали е ова седиште слободно? — *da*·li e *o*·va se·*dish*·te *slo*·bod·no

That's my seat.
Тоа е мое седиште. — *to*·a e *mo*·e se·*dish*·te

I'd like a taxi …	Сакам такси …	*sa*·kam *tak*·si …
at (9am)	во (девет претпладне)	vo (*de*·vet *pret*·plad·ne)
now	сега	*se*·ga
tomorrow	утре	*ut*·re

Is this taxi available?
Дали е ова такси слободно? — *da*·li e *o*·va *tak*·si *slo*·bod·no

How much is it to …?
Колку ќе чини до …? — *kol*·ku kye *chi*·ni do …

Please put the meter on.
Ве молам вклучете го
таксиметарот. — ve *mo*·lam vklu·*che*·te go
tak·si·*me*·ta·rot

Please take me to (this address).
Ве молам одвезете ме до
(оваа адреса). — ve *mo*·lam od·ve·*ze*·te me do
(*o*·va·a *a*·dre·sa)

Please …	Ве молам …	ve *mo*·lam …
slow down	возете побавно	vo·*ze*·te *po*·bav·no
stop here	застанете овде	zas·*ta*·ne·te *ov*·de
wait here	причекајте овде	pri·*che*·kay·te *ov*·de

car, motorbike & bicycle hire

I'd like to hire a …	Сакам да изнајмам …	*sa*·kam da *iz*·nay·mam …
bicycle	точак	*to*·chak
car	кола	*ko*·la
motorbike	моторцикл	mo·tor·*tsikl*

with ...	со ...	so ...
a driver	возач	*vo*-zach
air conditioning	клима уред	*kli*-ma *u*-red
antifreeze	антифриз	*an*-ti-friz
snow chains	синџири за снег	*sin*-ji-ri za sneg

How much for ... hire?	Колку чини ...?	*kol*-ku *chi*-ni ...
hourly	на час	na chas
daily	дневно	*dnev*-no
weekly	неделно	*ne*-del-no

air	воздух m	*voz*-duh
oil	масло n	*mas*-lo
petrol	бензин m	*ben*-zin
tyres	гуми f pl	*gu*-mi

I need a mechanic.
Ми треба механичар.
mi *tre*-ba me-*ha*-ni-char

I've run out of petrol.
Останав без бензин.
os-*ta*-nav bez *ben*-zin

I have a flat tyre.
Имам издишена гума.
i-mam iz-*di*-she-na *gu*-ma

directions

Where's the ...?	Каде е ...?	*ka*-de e ...
bank	банката	*ban*-ka-ta
city centre	центарот на градот	*tsen*-ta-rot na *gra*-dot
hotel	хотелот	*ho*-te-lot
market	пазарот	*pa*-za-rot
police station	полициската	po-li-*tsis*-ka-ta
	станица	*sta*-ni-tsa
post office	поштата	*posh*-ta-ta
public toilet	јавниот тоалет	*yav*-ni-ot to-a-*let*
tourist office	туристичкото биро	tu-*ris*-tich-ko-to bi-*ro*

Is this the road to (Bitola)?
Дали овој пат води до (Битола)?
da-li o-*voy* pat *vo*-di do (*bi*-to-la)

Can you show me (on the map)?
Можете ли да ми покажете
(на картава)?
mo-zhe-te li da mi po-*ka*-zhe-te
(na *kar*-ta-va)

What's the address?
Која е адресата? — *ko·ya e ad·re·sa·ta*

How far is it?
Колку е тоа далеку? — *kol·ku e to·a da·le·ku*

How do I get there?
Како да стигнам до таму? — *ka·ko da stig·nam do ta·mu*

Turn ...	Свртете ...	*svr·te·te ...*
at the corner	на аголот	*na a·go·lot*
at the traffic lights	на семафорите	*na se·ma·fo·ri·te*
left/right	лево/десно	*le·vo/des·no*

It's ...	Тоа е ...	*to·a e ...*
behind ...	зад ...	*zad ...*
far away	далеку	*da·le·ku*
here	овде	*ov·de*
in front of ...	пред ...	*pred ...*
left	лево	*le·vo*
near (to ...)	блиску (до ...)	*blis·ku (do ...)*
next to ...	веднаш до ...	*ved·nash do ...*
on the corner	на аголот	*na a·go·lot*
opposite ...	спроти ...	*spro·ti ...*
right	десно	*des·no*
straight ahead	право напред	*pra·vo nap·red*
there	таму	*ta·mu*

by bus	со автобус	so *av·to·bus*
by taxi	со такси	so *tak·si*
by train	со воз	so voz
on foot	пешки	*pesh·ki*

north	север	*se·ver*
south	југ	yug
east	исток	*is·tok*
west	запад	*za·pad*

Влез/Излез	vlez/iz·lez	Entrance/Exit
Отворено/Затворено	ot·vo·re·no/zat·vo·re·no	Open/Closed
Соби за издавање	so·bi za iz·da·va·nye	Rooms Available
Нема место	ne·ma mes·to	No Vacancies
Информации	in·for·ma·tsi·i	Information
Полициска станица	po·li·tsis·ka sta·ni·tsa	Police Station
Забрането	za·bra·ne·to	Prohibited
Тоалети	to·a·le·ti	Toilets
Машки	mash·ki	Men
Женски	zhen·ski	Women
Топло/Ладно	top·lo/lad·no	Hot/Cold

accommodation

finding accommodation

Where's a ...?	Каде има ...?	ka·de i·ma ...
camping ground	камп	kamp
guesthouse	приватно сместување	pri·vat·no smes·tu·va·nye
hotel	хотел	ho·tel
youth hostel	младинско	mla·din·sko
	пренокиште	pre·no·kyish·te

Can you recommend somewhere ...?	Можете ли да ми препорачате нешто ...?	mo·zhe·te li da mi pre·po·ra·cha·te nesh·to ...
cheap	поевтино	po·ev·ti·no
good	добро	dob·ro
nearby	близу	bli·zu

I'd like to book a room, please.
Сакам да резервирам соба, ве молам.
sa·kam da re·zer·vi·ram so·ba ve mo·lam

I have a reservation.
Јас имам резервација.
yas i·mam re·zer·va·tsi·ya

My name's ...
Јас се викам ...
yas se vi·kam ...

Do you have a ... room?	Дали имате...?	da·li i·ma·te ...
single	еднокреветна соба	ed·no·kre·vet·na so·ba
double	соба со брачен	so·ba so bra·chen
	кревет	kre·vet
twin	двокреветна соба	dvo·kre·vet·na so·ba

How much is it per ...?	Која е цената за ...?	ko·ya e tse·na·ta za ...
night	ноќ	noky
person	еден	e·den

Can I pay ...?	Примате ли ...?	pri·ma·te li ...
by credit card	кредитни картички	kre·dit·ni kar·tich·ki
with a travellers cheque	патнички чекови	pat·nich·ki che·ko·vi

I'd like to stay for (two) nights.
Сакам да останам (две) ноќи.
sa·kam da os·ta·nam (dve) no·kyi

From (2 July) to (6 July).
Од (втори јули) до (шести јули).
od (vto·ri yu·li) do (shes·ti yu·li)

Can I see it?
Може ли да ја видам?
mo·zhe li da ya vi·dam

Am I allowed to camp here?
Може ли да кампувам овде?
mo·zhe li da kam·pu·vam ov·de

Is there a camp site nearby?
Дали во близината има камп?
da·li vo bli·zi·na·ta i·ma kamp

requests & queries

When's breakfast served?
Кога е појадокот?
ko·ga e po·ya·do·kot

Where's breakfast served?
Каде се појадува?
ka·de se po·ya·du·va

Please wake me at (seven).
Ве молам разбудете ме
во (седум).
ve mo·lam raz·bu·de·te me
vo (se·dum)

Could I have my key, please?
Може ли да го добијам
клучот, ве молам?
mo·zhe li da go do·bi·yam
klu·chot ve mo·lam

Is there a/an ...?	Дали има ...?	*da*·li *i*·ma ...
elevator	лифт	lift
safe	сеф	sef

The room is too ...	Собата е премногу ...	*so*·ba·ta e *prem*·no·gu ...
expensive	скапа	*ska*·pa
noisy	бучна	*buch*·na
small	мала	*ma*·la

The ... doesn't work.	Не работи ...	ne *ra*·bo·ti ...
air conditioning	клима уредот	*kli*·ma *u*·re·dot
fan	фенот	*fe*·not
toilet	тоалетот	to·a·*le*·tot

This ... isn't clean.	Овој ... не е чист.	*o*·voy ... ne e chist
sheet	чаршаф	*char*·shaf
towel	пешкир	*pesh*·kir

This pillow isn't clean.
Оваа перница не е чиста. · *o*·va·a *per*·ni·tsa ne e *chis*·ta

Can I get another (blanket)?
Може ли да добијам уште · *mo*·zhe li da *do*·bi·yam *ush*·te
едно (ќебе)? · *ed*·no (*kye*·be)

checking out

What time is checkout?
Во колку часот треба да се · vo *kol*·ku *cha*·sot *tre*·ba da se
одјавам? · *od*·ya·vam

Can I leave my luggage here?
Може ли да го оставам мојот · *mo*·zhe li da go *os*·ta·vam *mo*·yot
багаж овде? · *ba*·gazh *ov*·de

Could I have my valuables, please?
Може ли да ги добијам моите · *mo*·zhe li da gi *do*·bi·yam *mo*·i·te
вредни предмети, ве молам? · *vred*·ni *pred*·me·ti ve *mo*·lam

Could I have my ..., please?	Може ли да го добијам мојот..., ве молам?	*mo*·zhe li da go *do*·bi·yam *mo*·yot ... ve *mo*·lam
deposit	депозит	de·*po*·zit
passport	пасош	*pa*·sosh

communications & banking

the internet

Where's the local Internet café?
Каде има тука интернет кафе? — *ka*·de *i*·ma *tu*·ka *in*·ter·net ka·*fe*

How much is it per hour?
Колку чини на час? — *kol*·ku *chi*·ni na chas

I'd like to ...	Сакам да ...	*sa*·kam da ...
check my email	си ја проверам електронската пошта	si ya *pro*·ve·ram e·lek·*tron*·ska·ta *posh*·ta
get Internet access	добијам пристап на интернет	*do*·bi·yam *pris*·tap na *in*·ter·net
use a printer	користам печатар	ko·*ris*·tam pe·*cha*·tar
use a scanner	користам скенер	ko·*ris*·tam *ske*·ner

mobile/cell phone

I'd like to buy ...	Сакам да купам ...	*sa*·kam da *ku*·pam ...
a mobile/cell phone	мобилен телефон	*mo*·bi·len *te*·le·fon
SIM card for your network	СИМ картичка за вашата мрежа	sim *kar*·tich·ka za *va*·sha·ta *mre*·zha

What are the rates?
Кои се цените? — *ko*·i se *tse*·ni·te

telephone

What's your phone number?
Кој е вашиот телефонски број? — koy e *va*·shi·ot te·le·*fon*·ski broy

The number is ...
Бројот е ... — *bro*·yot e ...

Where's the nearest public phone?
Каде е најблиската јавна говорница? — *ka*·de e nay·*blis*·ka·ta *yav*·na go·*vor*·ni·tsa

I'd like to buy a phonecard.
Сакам да купам телефонска картичка. — *sa*·kam da *ku*·pam te·le·*fon*·ska *kar*·tich·ka

I want to ...	Сакам да ...	sa·kam da ...
call (Singapore)	се јавам во (Сингапур)	se ya·vam vo (sin·ga·pur)
make a local call	телефонирам локално	te·le·fo·ni·ram lo·kal·no
reverse the charges	телефонирам на нивна сметка	te·le·fo·ni·ram na niv·na smet·ka

How much does ... cost?	Колку чини ...?	kol·ku chi·ni ...
a (three)-minute call	разговор од (три) минути	raz·go·vor od (tri) mi·nu·ti
each extra minute	секоја наредна минута	se·ko·ya na·red·na mi·nu·ta

(Ten) denars per minute.
(Десет) денари за минута.   (de·set) de·na·ri za mi·nu·ta

post office

I want to send a ...	Сакам да испратам ...	sa·kam da is·pra·tam ...
letter	писмо	pis·mo
parcel	пакет	pa·ket
postcard	разгледница	raz·gled·ni·tsa

I want to buy ...	Сакам да купам ...	sa·kam da ku·pam ...
an envelope	плик	plik
stamps	поштенски марки	posh·ten·ski mar·ki

Please send it (to Australia) by ...	Ве молам испратете го (во Австралија) ...	ve mo·lam is·pra·te·te go (vo av·stra·li·ya) ...
airmail	авионски	a·vi·on·ski
express mail	експресно	eks·pres·no
registered mail	препорачано	pre·po·ra·cha·no
surface mail	обично	o·bich·no

Is there any mail for me?
Дали има пошта за мене?   da·li i·ma posh·ta za me·ne

bank

Where's a/an ...?	Каде има ...?	ka·de i·ma ...
ATM	банкомат	ban·ko·mat
foreign exchange office	менувачница	me·nu·vach·ni·tsa

I'd like to ...	Сакам да ...	*sa*-kam da ...
Where can I ...?	Каде можам да ...?	*ka*-de *mo*-zham da ...
arrange a transfer	направам трансфер	*na*-pra-vam *trans*-fer
cash a cheque	разменам чек	*raz*-me-nam chek
change a travellers cheque	разменам патнички чекови	*raz*-me-nam *pat*-nich-ki *che*-ko-vi
change money	разменам пари	*raz*-me-nam *pa*-ri
get a cash advance	добијам кредит	*do*-bi-yam *kre*-dit
withdraw money	извадам пари	*iz*-va-dam *pa*-ri

What's the ...?	Колку ...?	*kol*-ku ...
charge for that	се наплаќа за тоа	se *na*-pla-kya za *to*-a
commission	е провизијата	e pro-vi-*zi*-ya-ta
exchange rate	е курсот	e *kur*-sot

| It's (12) denars. | (Дванаесет) денари. | (dva-*na*-e-set) *de*-na-ri |
| It's free. | Бесплатно е. | *bes*-plat-no e |

What time does the bank open?
Кога се отвора банката? — *ko*-ga se ot-*vo*-ra *ban*-ka-ta

Has my money arrived yet?
Дали пристигнаа моите пари? — *da*-li pris-*tig*-na-a *mo*-i-te *pa*-ri

sightseeing

getting in

What time does it open/close?
Кога се отвора/затвора? — *ko*-ga se ot-*vo*-ra/zat-*vo*-ra

What's the admission charge?
Колку чини влезница? — *kol*-ku *chi*-ni *vlez*-ni-tsa

Is there a discount for students/children?
Има ли попуст за студенти/деца? — *i*-ma li *po*-pust za stu-*den*-ti/*de*-tsa

I'd like a ...	Сакам ...	*sa*-kam ...
catalogue	каталог	*ka*-ta-log
guide	водич	*vo*-dich
local map	локална карта	*lo*-kal-na *kar*-ta

I'd like to see …
Сакам да видам…   *sa*-kam da *vi*-dam …

What's that?
Што е ова?   shto e *o*-va

Can I take a photo?
Може ли да сликам?   *mo*-zhe li da *sli*-kam

tours

When's the next …?	Кога е следната …?	*ko*-ga e *sled*-na-ta …
day trip	целодневна тура	tse-*lo*-dnev-na *tu*-ra
tour	тура	*tu*-ra
Is … included?	Дали е …?	*da*-li e …
accommodation	вклучено	*vklu*-che-no
	сместувањето	smes-tu-*va*-nye-to
the admission	вклучена цената	*vklu*-che-na *tse*-na-ta
charge	на влезниците	na vlez-*ni*-tsi-te
food	вклучена храна	*vklu*-che-na *hra*-na
transport	вклучен превоз	*vklu*-chen *pre*-voz

How long is the tour?
Колку долго трае турата?   kol-ku *dol*-go *tra*-e *tu*-ra-ta

What time should we be back?
Во колку часот ќе се вратиме?   vo *kol*-ku *cha*-sot kye se *vra*-ti-me

sightseeing

castle	тврдина f	*tvr*-di-na
church	црква f	*tsrk*-va
main square	главен плоштад m	*gla*-ven *plosh*-tad
monastery	манастир m	*ma*-nas-tir
monument	споменик m	*spo*-me-nik
mosque	џамија f	*ja*-mi-ya
museum	музеј m	*mu*-zey
old city	стар град m	star grad
palace	палата f	pa-*la*-ta
ruins	урнатини f pl	ur-*na*-ti-ni
stadium	стадион m	sta-di-*on*
statue	статуа f	*sta*-tu-a

shopping

enquiries

Where's a ...?	Каде има ...?	ka·de i·ma ...
bank	банка	ban·ka
bookshop	книжарница	kni·zhar·ni·tsa
camera shop	продавница за фотоапарати	pro·dav·ni·tsa za fo·to·a·pa·ra·ti
department store	стоковна куќа	sto·kov·na ku·kya
grocery store	бакалница	ba·kal·ni·tsa
market	пазар	pa·zar
newsagency	киоск за весници	ki·osk za ves·ni·tsi
supermarket	супермаркет	su·per·mar·ket

Where can I buy (a padlock)?
Каде можам да купам (катинар)?
ka·de mo·zham da ku·pam (ka·ti·nar)

I'm looking for ...
Барам ...
ba·ram ...

Can I look at it?
Може ли да ја видам?
mo·zhe li da ya vi·dam

Do you have any others?
Имате ли други?
i·ma·te li dru·gi

Does it have a guarantee?
Дали има гаранција?
da·li i·ma ga·ran·tsi·ya

Can I have it sent abroad?
Може ли да ми го испратите во странство?
mo·zhe li da mi go is·pra·ti·te vo strans·tvo

Can I have my ... repaired?
Може ли да ми го поправите ...?
mo·ze li da mi go pop·ra·vi·te ...

It's faulty.
Расипан е.
ra·si·pan e

I'd like ..., please.	Јас би сакал ..., ве молам.	yas bi sa·kal ... ve mo·lam
a bag	торба	tor·ba
a refund	да ми ги вратите парите	da mi gi vra·ti·te pa·ri·te
to return this	да го вратам ова	da go vra·tam o·va

paying

How much is it?
Колку чини тоа?
kol·ku *chi*·ni *to*·a

Can you write down the price?
Можете ли да ми ја напишете
ценатa?
mo·zhe·te li da mi ya na·*pi*·she·te
tse·na·ta

That's too expensive.
Тоа е многу скапо.
to·a e *mno*·gu *ska*·po

What's your lowest price?
Која е вашата најниска цена?
ko·ya e *va*·sha·ta *nai*·nis·ka *tse*·na

I'll give you (five) denars.
Јас ќе ви дадам (пет) денари.
yas kye vi *da*·dam (pet) *de*·na·ri

There's a mistake in the bill.
Има грешка во сметката.
i·ma *gresh*·ka vo *smet*·ka·ta

Do you accept ...?	Примате ли ...?	*pri*·ma·te li ...
credit cards	кредитни картички	*kre*·dit·ni *kar*·tich·ki
debit cards	дебитни картички	*de*·bit·ni *kar*·tich·ki
travellers cheques	патнички чекови	*pat*·nich·ki *che*·ko·vi
I'd like ..., please.	Сакам ..., ве молам.	*sa*·kam ... ve *mo*·lam
a receipt	признаница	*priz*·na·ni·tsa
my change	кусур	*ku*·sur

clothes & shoes

Can I try it on?
Може ли да го пробам тоа?
mo·zhe li da go *pro*·bam *to*·a

My size is (42).
Јас носам (четириесет и два).
yas *no*·sam (che·ti·*ri*·e·set i dva)

It doesn't fit.
Не ми е точно.
ne mi e *toch*·no

small	мал	*mal*
medium	среден	*sre·den*
large	голем	*go·lem*

books & music

I'd like a ...	Сакам ...	*sa·kam ...*
newspaper	весник	*ves·nik*
(in English)	(на англиски)	(na *an*·glis·ki)
pen	пенкало	*pen·ka·lo*

Is there an English-language bookshop?
Дали има англиска книжарница?   *da·li i·ma an·glis·ka kni·zhar·ni·tsa*

I'm looking for something by (Simon Trpcheski/Blazhe Koneski).
Барам нешто од (Симон   *ba·ram nesh·to od (si·mon*
Трпчески/Блаже Конески).   *trp·ches·ki/bla·zhe ko·nes·ki)*

Can I listen to this?
Може ли да го слушнам ова?   *mo·zhe li da go slush·nam o·va*

photography

Can you ...?	Можете ли ...?	*mo·zhe·te li ...*
burn a CD from	да преснимите од ЦД	da pres·*ni*·mi·te od *tse*·de
my memory card	од мојата картичка	od *mo*·ya·ta *kar*·tich·ka
	со меморија	so me·*mo*·ri·ya
develop this	да го развиете овој	da go raz·*vi*·e·te *o*·voy
film	филм	film
load my film	да го ставите филмот	da go *sta*·vi·te *fil*·mot
	во апаратот	vo a·pa·*ra*·tot

I need a/an ... film	Сакам ... за овој	*sa*·kam ... za *o*·voy
for this camera.	фотоапарат.	*fo*·to·a·pa·*rat*
APS	АПС филм	*a*·pe·es film
B&W	црно-бел филм	*tsr*·no·bel film
colour	филм во боја	film vo *bo*·ya
slide	слајд филм	slayd film
(200) speed	филм со брзина	film so *br*·zi·na
	(двеста)	(*dves*·ta)

When will it be ready? Кога ќе биде готов?   *ko*·ga kye *bi*·de *go*·tov

meeting people

greetings, goodbyes & introductions

Hello/Hi.	Здраво/Чао.	zdra·vo/cha·o
Good night.	Добра ноќ.	dob·ra noky
Goodbye/Bye.	До гледање/Чао.	do gle·da·nye/cha·o
See you later.	Се гледаме.	se gle·da·me
Mr	Господин	gos·po·din
Mrs	Госпоѓа	gos·po·gya
Miss	Госпоѓица	gos·po·gyi·tsa
How are you?	Како сте/си? pol/inf	ka·ko ste/si
Fine. And you?	Добро. А вие/ти? pol/inf	dob·ro a vi·e/ti
What's your name?	Како се викате/	ka·ko se vi·ka·te/
	викаш? pol/inf	vi·kash
My name is ...	Јас се викам ...	yas se vi·kam ...
I'm pleased to	Драго ми е што	dra·go mi e shto
meet you.	се запознавме.	se za·poz·nav·me

This is my ...	Ова е ...	o·va e ...
boyfriend	моето момче	mo·e·to mom·che
brother	мојот брат	mo·yot brat
daughter	мојата ќерка	mo·ya·ta kyer·ka
father	мојот татко	mo·yot tat·ko
friend	мојот пријател m	mo·yot pri·ya·tel
	мојата пријателка f	mo·ya·ta pri·ya·tel·ka
girlfriend	мојата девојка	mo·ya·ta de·voy·ka
husband	мојот сопруг	mo·yot sop·rug
mother	мојата мајка	mo·ya·ta may·ka
partner (intimate)	мојот партнер m&f	mo·yot part·ner
sister	мојата сестра	mo·ya·ta ses·tra
son	мојот син	mo·yot sin
wife	мојата сопруга	mo·ya·ta so·pru·ga

Here's my ...	Ова е мојата ...	o·va e mo·ya·ta ...
What's your ...?	Која е вашата ...?	ko·ya e va·sha·ta ...
address	адреса	ad·re·sa
email address	имеил адреса	i·me·il ad·re·sa

Here's my ...	Ова е мојот ...	*o*·va e *mo*·yot ...
What's your ...?	Кој е вашиот ...?	koy e *va*·shi·ot ...
fax number	број на факс	broy na faks
phone number	телефонски број	te·le·*fon*·ski broy

occupations

What's your occupation?	Што работите?	shto ra·*bo*·ti·te
I'm a/an ...	Јас сум ...	yas sum ...
artist	уметник **m&f**	*u*·met·nik
farmer	фармер **m&f**	*far*·mer
office worker	службеник **m**	*sluzh*·be·nik
	службеничка **f**	sluzh·be·*nich*·ka
scientist	научник **m&f**	*na*·uch·nik
tradesperson	трговец **m&f**	*tr*·go·vets

background

Where are you from?	Од каде сте?	od *ka*·de ste
I'm from ...	Јас сум од ...	yas sum od ...
Australia	Австралија	av·*stra*·li·ya
Canada	Канада	*ka*·na·da
England	Англија	*an*·gli·ya
New Zealand	Нов Зеланд	nov *ze*·land
the USA	Америка	a·*me*·ri·ka
Are you married?	Дали сте женет/	*da*·li ste *zhe*·net/
	мажена? **m/f**	*ma*·zhe·na
I'm married.	Јас сум женет/	yas sum *zhe*·net/
	мажена. **m/f**	*ma*·zhe·na
I'm single.	Јас сум неженет/	yas sum ne·*zhe*·net/
	немажена. **m/f**	ne·*ma*·zhe·na

age

How old ...?	Колку години ...?	*kol*·ku *go*·di·ni ...
are you	имате/имаш **pol/inf**	*i*·ma·te/*i*·mash
is your daughter	има вашата ќерка	*i*·ma *va*·sha·ta *kyer*·ka
is your son	има вашиот син	*i*·ma *va*·shi·ot sin

I'm ... years old.	Јас имам ... години.	yas *i*·mam ... *go*·di·ni
He/She is ... years old.	Тој/Таа има ... години.	toy/*ta*·a *i*·ma ... *go*·di·ni

feelings

I'm (not) ...	Јас (не) сум ...	yas (ne) sum ...
Are you ...?	Дали си ...?	*da*·li si ...
happy	среќен/среќна m/f	*sre*·kyen/*sreky*·na
hungry	гладен/гладна m/f	*gla*·den/*glad*·na
sad	тажен/тажна m/f	*ta*·zhen/*tazh*·na
thirsty	жеден/жедна m/f	*zhe*·den/*zhed*·na

I'm ...	Мене ми е ...	*me*·ne mi e ...
I'm not ...	Не ми е ...	ne mi e ...
Are you ...?	Дали ти е ...?	*da*·li ti e ...
cold	студено	*stu*·de·no
hot	топло	*top*·lo

entertainment

going out

Where can I find ...?	Каде можам да најдам ...?	*ka*·de *mo*·zham da *nay*·dam ...
clubs	клубови	*klu*·bo·vi
gay venues	собиралишта на хомосексуалци	so·bi·*ra*·lish·ta na ho·mo·sek·su·*al*·tsi
pubs	пабови	*pa*·bo·vi

I feel like going to a/the ...	Ми се оди ...	mi se o·di ...
concert	на концерт	na *kon*·tsert
movies	на кино	na *ki*·no
party	на забава	na *za*·ba·va
restaurant	во ресторан	vo res·to·*ran*
theatre	на театар	na te·*a*·tar

interests

Do you like …?	Дали сакате …?	*da*·li *sa*·ka·te …
I (don't) like …	Jac (не) сакам …	yas (ne) *sa*·kam …
art	уметност	*u*·met·nost
cooking	готвење	*got*·ve·nye
movies	филмови	*fil*·mo·vi
reading	читање	*chi*·ta·nye
shopping	купување	*ku*·pu·va·nye
sport	спорт	sport
travelling	патување	*pa*·tu·va·nye

Do you like to …?	Дали сакате да …?	*da*·li *sa*·ka·te da …
dance	танцувате	tan·*tsu*·va·te
go to concerts	одите на концерти	*o*·di·te na *kon*·tsert
listen to music	слушате музика	*slu*·sha·te *mu*·zi·ka

food & drink

finding a place to eat

Can you recommend a …?	Можете ли да ми препорачате …?	*mo*·zhe·te li da mi pre·po·*ra*·cha·te …
bar	некој бар	*ne*·koy bar
café	некое кафе	*ne*·ko·e ka·*fe*
restaurant	некој ресторан	*ne*·koy res·to·*ran*

I'd like …, please.	Сакам …, ве молам.	*sa*·kam … ve *mo*·lam
a table for (four)	маса за (четворица)	*ma*·sa za (chet·*vo*·ri·tsa)
the (non)smoking section	на место за (не)пушачи	na *mes*·to za (ne·)*pu*·sha·chi

ordering food

breakfast	појадок m	*po*·ya·dok
lunch	ручек m	*ru*·chek
dinner	вечера f	*ve*·che·ra
snack	закуска f	*za*·kus·ka
today's special	специјалитет на денот m	spe·tsi·ya·li·*tet* na *de*·not

What would you recommend?
Што препорачувате вие? shto pre·po·ra·*chu*·va·te *vi*·e

I'd like (the) …, please.	Ве молам …	ve *mo*·lam …
bill	сметката	*smet*·ka·ta
drink list	листа со пијалаци	*lis*·ta so pi·*ya*·la·tsi
menu	мени	me·*ni*
that dish	ова јадење	*o*·va *ya*·de·nye

drinks

(cup of) coffee …	(шоља) кафе …	(*sho*·lya) *ka*·fe …
(cup of) tea …	(шоља) чај …	(*sho*·lya) chay …
with milk	со млеко	so *mle*·ko
without sugar	без шеќер	bez *she*·kyer
(orange) juice	сок (од поморанџа) m	sok (od po·mo·*ran*·ja)
soft drink	безалкохолен пијалак m	bez·al·*ko*·ho·len *pi*·ya·lak
… water	… вода	… *vo*·da
boiled	превриена	pre·*vri*·e·na
mineral	минерална	mi·ne·*ral*·na

in the bar

I'll have …	Јас ќе земам …	yas kye *ze*·mam …
I'll buy you a drink.	Јас ќе ви/ти купам	yas kye vi/ti *ku*·pam
	пијалак. **pol/inf**	*pi*·ya·lak
What would you like?	Што сакате вие/ти? **pol/inf**	shto *sa*·ka·te *vi*·e/ti
Cheers!	На здравје!	na *zdrav*·ye
brandy	ракија f	*ra*·ki·ya
cocktail	коктел m	kok·*tel*
cognac	коњак m	*ko*·nyak
a bottle/glass of beer	шише/чаша пиво	*shi*·she/*cha*·sha *pi*·vo
a shot of (whisky)	чашка (виски)	*chash*·ka (*vis*·ki)
a bottle/glass	шише/чаша	*shi*·she/*cha*·sha
of … wine	… вино	… *vi*·no
red	црвено	*tsr*·ve·no
sparkling	пенливо	*pen*·li·vo
white	бело	*be*·lo

self-catering

What's the local speciality?
Што е локален специјалитет?   shto e *lo*·ka·len spe·tsi·ya·li·*tet*

What's that?
Што е тоа?   shto e *to*·a

How much is (a kilo of cheese)?
Колку чини (кило сирење)?   *kol*·ku *chi*·ni (*ki*·lo *si*·re·nye)

I'd like ...	Сакам ...	*sa*·kam ...
(100) grams	(сто) грама	(sto) *gra*·ma
(two) kilos	(две) кила	(dve) *ki*·la
(three) pieces	(три) парчиња	(tri) *par*·chi·nya
(six) slices	(шест) парчиња	(shest) *par*·chi·nya

Less.	Помалку.	*po*·mal·ku
Enough.	Доволно.	*do*·vol·no
More.	Повеќе.	*po*·ve·kye

special diets & allergies

Is there a vegetarian restaurant near here?
Дали овде близу има   *da*·li *ov*·de *bli*·zu *i*·ma
вегетаријански ресторан?   ve·ge·ta·ri·*yan*·ski res·to·*ran*

Do you have vegetarian food?
Дали имате вегетаријанска храна?   *da*·li *i*·ma·te ve·ge·ta·ri·*yan*·ska *hra*·na

Could you prepare a meal without ...?	Може ли да подготвите јадење без ...?	*mo*·zhe li da pod·*got*·vi·te *ya*·de·nye bez ...
butter	путер	*pu*·ter
eggs	јајца	*yay*·tsa
meat stock	производи од месо	pro·*iz*·vo·di od *me*·so

I'm allergic to ...	Јас сум алергичен/ алергична на ... m/f	yas sum a·*ler*·gi·chen/ a·*ler*·gich·na na ...
dairy produce	млечни производи	*mlech*·ni pro·*iz*·vo·di
gluten	глутен	glu·*ten*
MSG	МСГ	muh suh guh
nuts	ореви, бадеми, лешници	o·*re*·vi *ba*·de·mi *lesh*·ni·tsi
seafood	морска храна	*mor*·ska *hra*·na

menu decoder

ајвар m	*ay·var*	*spicy mixture of grilled, ground & fried red peppers (sometimes with eggplant and/or carrots added)*
алва f	*al·va*	*sesame seeds crushed in honey*
баклава f	*bak·la·va*	*flaky pastry with nuts, soaked in syrup*
бурек m	*bu·rek*	*flaky pastry with layers of cheese, spinach, potato or minced meat & onion*
ѓувеч m	*gyu·vech*	*stew made of meat (usually chicken), rice, peppers, carrots & onion, baked in the oven*
зелник m	*zel·nik*	*thin, flaky pastry filled with leek, spinach, cabbage or potatoes, with cheese & eggs added*
качамак m	*ka·cha·mak*	*a paste-like entrée, made of ground maize cooked in salt water & served with feta cheese & fried bacon*
мусака f	*mu·sa·ka*	*alternate layers of minced meat & potato or eggplant*
пастрмајлија f	*pas·tr·may·li·ya*	*similar to a pizza, with meat (usually pork) & eggs*
пилав m	*pi·lav*	*meat cut into small pieces & mixed with seasoned rice before being cooked in the oven*
пилешка супа f	*pi·lesh·ka su·pa*	*chicken soup*
пинџур m	*pin·jur*	*a mixture of baked, ground or crushed & stir-fried green peppers, tomatoes, eggplant & garlic*
пита/баница f	*pi·ta/ba·ni·tsa*	*flaky pastry filled with spinach & cheese, eggs, or pumpkin*

плескавица f	ples-*ka*-vi-tsa	burger of minced pork, beef or lamb
подварок m	*pod*-va-rok	finely shredded sour cabbage cooked in the oven with slices of meat
полнети пиперки f pl	*pol*-ne-ti *pi*-per-ki	peppers stuffed with minced beef or pork & rice
рибја чорба f	*rib*-ya *chor*-ba	fish soup
сарма f	*sar*-ma	minced meat rolled in sour cabbage leaves
селско месо n	*sel*-sko *me*-so	fried meat, meatballs, smoked meat, mushrooms, tomatoes & onions, cooked in a clay pot in the oven
сирење n	*si*-re-nye	white cheese
скара f	*ska*-ra	barbecue (chicken, lamb or pork)
слатко n	*slat*-ko	fruit (either cherries, grapes, plums etc) cooked in sugar to get a thick mixture, kept in small jars & served with water
сутлијаш m	*sut*-li-yash	rice pudding garnished with almonds & cinnamon
тавче гравче n	*tav*-che *grav*-che	boiled beans cooked in a clay pot in the oven
таратор m	*ta*-ra-tor	cold appetiser made of yogurt, cucumbers & garlic
телешка чорба f	te-*lesh*-ka *chor*-ba	veal soup
турли тава f	*tur*-li *ta*-va	stew of meat (pork, veal & mutton) & vegetables, cooked in the oven
ќофтиња n pl	*kyof*-ti-nya	meatballs
шампити f pl	*sham*-pi-ti	whisked egg whites with sugar placed in a thick layer on baked pastry
шопска салата f	*shop*-ska sa-*la*-ta	salad of peppers, cucumbers, tomatoes, onions & feta cheese

emergencies

basics

Help!	Помош!	*po*·mosh
Stop!	Застани!	*za*·sta·ni
Go away!	Одете си!	o·*de*·te si
Thief!	Крадец!	*kra*·dets
Fire!	Пожар!	*po*·zhar
Watch out!	Внимавајте!	vni·*ma*·vay·te
It's an emergency!	Итно е!	*it*·no e
I'm lost.	Се загубив.	se *za*·gu·biv
Where are the toilets?	Каде се тоалетите?	*ka*·de se to·a·*le*·ti·te
Call ...!	Викнете ...!	*vik*·ne·te ...
a doctor	лекар	*le*·kar
an ambulance	брза помош	*br*·za *po*·mosh
the police	полиција	po·*li*·tsi·ya

Could you help me, please?
Може ли да ми помогнете,
ве молам?
mo·zhe li da mi po·*mog*·ne·te ve *mo*·lam

I have to use the telephone.
Треба да телефонирам.
tre·ba da te·le·fo·*ni*·ram

police

Where's the police station?
Каде е полициската станица?
ka·de e po·li·*tsis*·ka·ta *sta*·ni·tsa

I want to report an offence.
Сакам да пријавам престап.
sa·kam da *pri*·ya·vam *pres*·tap

I have insurance.
Имам осигурување.
i·mam o·si·gu·*ru*·va·nye

I've been ...	Бев ...	bev ...
assaulted	нападнат m	*na*·pad·nat
	нападната f	na·*pad*·na·ta
raped	силуван/силувана m/f	si·*lu*·van/si·*lu*·va·na
robbed	опљачкан m	*op*·lyach·kan
	опљачкана f	op·*lyach*·ka·na

I've lost my ...	Го загубив мојот ...	go za·gu·biv mo·yot ...
My ...was stolen.	Мојот ... беше украден.	mo·yot ... be·she uk·ra·den
jewellery	накит	na·kit
passport	пасош	pa·sosh
wallet	паричник	pa·rich·nik

I've lost my ...	Ја загубив мојата ...	ya za·gu·biv mo·ya·ta ...
My ...was stolen.	Мојата ... беше украдена.	mo·ya·ta ... be·she uk·ra·de·na
credit card	кредитна картичка	kre·dit·na kar·tich·ka
handbag	чанта	chan·ta

I've lost my ...	Ги загубив моите ...	gi za·gu·biv mo·i·te ...
My ...were stolen.	Моите ... беа украдени.	mo·i·te ... be·a uk·ra·de·ni
bags	торби	tor·bi
travellers cheques	патнички чекови	pat·nich·ki che·ko·vi

I want to contact my ...	Сакам да се јавам во ...	sa·kam da se ya·vam vo ...
consulate	мојот конзулат	mo·yot kon·zu·lat
embassy	мојата амбасада	mo·ya·ta am·ba·sa·da

health

medical needs

Where's the nearest ...?	Каде има најблиску ...?	ka·de i·ma nay·blis·ku ...
dentist	заболекар	za·bo·le·kar
doctor	лекар	le·kar
hospital	болница	bol·ni·tsa
(night) pharmacist	(дежурна) аптека	(de·zhur·na) ap·te·ka

I need a doctor (who speaks English).

Ми треба доктор (што зборува англиски). — mi tre·ba dok·tor (shto zbo·ru·va an·glis·ki)

Could I see a female doctor?

Може ли да одам кај докторка? — mo·zhe li da o·dam kay dok·tor·ka

I've run out of my medication.

Останав без лекови. — os·ta·nav bez le·ko·vi

symptoms, conditions & allergies

| I'm sick. | Јас сум болен/болна. m/f | yas sum bo·len/bol·na |
| It hurts here. | Овде ме боли. | ov·de me bo·li |

I have (a) ...	Имам ...	i·mam ...
asthma	астма	ast·ma
bronchitis	бронхитис	bron·hi·tis
constipation	конститупација	kon·sti·pa·tsi·ya
cough	кашлица	kash·li·tsa
diarrhoea	пролив	pro·liv
fever	треска	tres·ka
headache	главоболка	gla·vo·bol·ka
heart condition	тешкотии со срцето	tesh·ko·ti·i so sr·tse·to
nausea	лошење	lo·she·nye
pain	болка	bol·ka
sore throat	воспаление на грлото	vos·pa·le·ni·e na gr·lo·to
toothache	забоболка	za·bo·bol·ka

I'm allergic to ...	Јас сум алергичен/	yas sum a·ler·gi·chen/
	алергична на ... m/f	a·ler·gich·na na ...
antibiotics	антибиотици	an·ti·bi·o·ti·tsi
anti-inflammatories	анти-инфламатори	an·ti·in·fla·ma·to·ri
aspirin	аспирин	as·pi·rin
bees	пчели	pche·li
codeine	кодеин	ko·de·in
penicillin	пеницилин	pe·ni·tsi·lin

antiseptic	антисептик m	an·ti·sep·tik
bandage	завој m	za·voy
condoms	кондоми m pl	kon·do·mi
contraceptives	средства за	sreds·tva za
	контрацепција n pl	kon·tra·tsep·tsi·ya
diarrhoea medicine	лекови против	le·ko·vi pro·tiv
	пролив m pl	pro·liv
insect repellent	средство против	sreds·tvo pro·tiv
	инсекти n	in·sek·ti
laxatives	лаксативи m pl	lak·sa·ti·vi
painkillers	средства против болки n pl	sreds·tva pro·tiv bol·ki
rehydration salts	соли за рехидрирање f pl	so·li za re·hid·ri·ra·nye
sleeping tablets	таблети за спиење f pl	tab·le·ti za spi·e·nye

english–macedonian dictionary

Macedonian nouns in this dictionary have their gender indicated by ⓜ (masculine), ⓕ (feminine) or ⓝ (neuter). If it's a plural noun, you'll also see pl. Adjectives are given in the masculine form only. Words are also marked as a (adjective), v (verb), sg (singular), pl (plural), inf (informal) or pol (polite) where necessary.

A

accident несреќа ⓝ *nes-re-kya*
accommodation сместување ⓝ *smes-tu-va-nye*
adaptor адаптер ⓜ *a-dap-ter*
address адреса ⓕ *a-dre-sa*
after потоа *po-to-a*
air-conditioned климатизиран kli-ma-ti-*zi*-ran
airplane авион ⓜ *a-vi-on*
airport аеродром ⓜ *a-e-ro-drom*
alcohol алкохол ⓜ *al-ko-hol*
all сите *si-te*
allergy алергија ⓕ *a-ler-gi-ya*
ambulance брза помош ⓕ *br-za po-mosh*
and и *i*
ankle зглоб ⓜ zglob
arm рака ⓕ *ra-ka*
ashtray пепелник ⓜ *pe-pel-nik*
ATM банкомат ⓜ ban-ko-*mat*

B

baby бебе ⓝ *be-be*
back (body) грб ⓜ grb
backpack ранец ⓜ *ra-nets*
bad лош losh
bag торба ⓕ *tor-ba*
baggage claim подигање на багаж ⓝ *po-di-ga*-nye na *ba-gazh*
bank банка ⓕ *ban-ka*
bar бар ⓜ bar
bathroom бања ⓕ *ba-nya*
battery батерија ⓕ ba-*te-ri*-ya
beautiful убав *u-bav*
bed кревет ⓜ *kre-vet*
beer пиво ⓝ *pi-vo*
before пред pred
behind зад zad
bicycle точак ⓜ *to-chak*
big голем *go-lem*
bill сметка ⓕ *smet-ka*
black црн tsrn
blanket ќебе ⓝ *kye-be*

blood group крвна група ⓕ *krv-na gru-pa*
blue син sin
boat брод ⓜ brod
book (make a reservation) v резервира re-zer-*vi*-ra
bottle шише ⓝ *shi-she*
bottle opener отворач за шишиња ⓜ *o-tvo-rach za shi-shi-nya*
boy момче ⓝ *mom-che*
brakes (car) кочници ⓜ pl *koch-ni-tsi*
breakfast појадок ⓜ *po-ya-dok*
broken (faulty) расипан *ra-si-pan*
bus автобус ⓜ *av-to-bus*
business бизнис ⓜ *biz-nis*
buy купува *ku-pu-va*

C

café кафуле ⓝ *ka-fu-le*
camera фото апарат ⓜ *fo-to a-pa-rat*
camp site камп ⓜ kamp
cancel откажува ot-*ka-zhu*-va
can opener отворач за конзерви ⓜ *o-tvo-rach za kon-zer-vi*
car автомобил ⓜ *av-to-mo-bil*
(pay) cash (плаќа) во готово (*pla-kya*) vo *go-to-vo*
cash (a cheque) v менува (чек) *me-nu-va* (chek)
cell phone мобилен телефон ⓜ *mo-bi-len te-le-fon*
centre центар ⓜ *tsen-tar*
change (money) v разменува (пари) raz-*me-nu-va* (*pa-ri*)
cheap евтин *ev-tin*
check (bill) сметка ⓕ *smet-ka*
check-in пријавување ⓝ pri-*ya-vu*-va-nye
chest гради ⓕ *gra-di*
child дете ⓝ *de-te*
cigarette цигара ⓕ *tsi-ga-ra*
city град ⓜ grad
clean a чист chist
closed затворен zat-*vo-ren*
coffee кафе ⓝ *ka-fe*
coins метални пари ⓜ pl *me-tal-ni pa-ri*
cold a студен *stu-den*
collect call разговор платен од примачот ⓜ *raz-go-vor pla-ten od pri-ma-chot*

come доаѓа *do*-a-gya
computer компјутер ⓜ komp-*yu*-ter
condom кондом ⓜ *kon*-dom
contact lenses контактни леќи ⓕ pl
   kon-takt-ni *le*-kyi
cook v готви *got*-vi
cost цена ⓕ *tse*-na
credit card кредитна картичка ⓕ
   kre-dit-na *kar*-tich-ka
cup шолја ⓕ *sho*-lya
currency exchange курс на валути *kurs na va-lu*-ti
customs (immigration) царинарница ⓕ
   tsa-ri-*nar*-ni-tsa

D

dangerous опасен *o*-pa-sen
date (time) датум ⓜ *da*-tum
day ден den
delay n доцнење ⓕ *dots*-nye
dentist забар ⓜ *za*-bar
depart заминува za-*mi*-nu-va
diaper пелена ⓕ *pe*-le-na
dictionary речник ⓜ *rech*-nik
dinner вечера ⓕ *ve*-che-ra
direct директен di-*rek*-ten
dirty нечист *ne*-chist
disabled (person) инвалид ⓜ in-va-*lid*
discount попуст *po*-pust
doctor доктор ⓜ *dok*-tor
double bed брачен кревет ⓜ *bra*-chen *kre*-vet
double room двокреветна соба ⓕ
   dvo-*kre*-vet-na *so*-ba
drink пијалак ⓜ *pi*-ya-lak
drive v вози *vo*-zi
drivers licence возачка дозвола ⓕ
   vo-zach-ka *doz*-vo-la
drug (illicit) дрога ⓕ *dro*-ga
dummy (pacifier) цуцла ⓕ *tsuts*-la

E

ear уво ⓝ *u*-vo
east исток ⓜ *is*-tok
eat јаде *ya*-de
economy class економска класа ⓕ
   e-*ko*-nom-ska *kla*-sa
electricity електрична струја ⓕ
   e-*lek*-trich-na *stru*-ya
elevator лифт ⓜ lift
email имеил ⓜ *i*-me-il
embassy амбасада ⓕ am-ba-*sa*-da
emergency итна ситуација ⓕ *it*-na si-tu-*a*-tsi-ya

English (language) англиски ⓜ *an*-glis-ki
entrance влез ⓜ vlez
evening вечер ⓕ *ve*-cher
exchange rate курс ⓜ kurs
exit излез ⓜ *iz*-lez
expensive скап skap
express mail брза пошта ⓕ *br*-za *posh*-ta
eye око ⓝ *o*-ko

F

far далеку *da*-le-ku
fast брз brz
father татко ⓜ *tat*-ko
film (camera) филм ⓜ film
finger прст ⓜ prst
first-aid kit кутија за прва помош ⓕ
   ku-ti-ya za *pr*-va *po*-mosh
first class прва класа ⓕ *pr*-va *kla*-sa
fish риба ⓕ *ri*-ba
food храна ⓕ *hra*-na
foot нога ⓕ *no*-ga
fork вилушка ⓕ vi-*lyush*-ka
free (of charge) бесплатен bes-*pla*-ten
friend пријател/пријателка ⓜ/ⓕ
   pri-*ya*-tel/pri-*ya*-tel-ka
fruit овошје ⓝ *o*-vosh-ye
full полн poln
funny смешен *sme*-shen

G

gift подарок ⓜ *po*-da-rok
girl девојка ⓕ *de*-voy-ka
glass (drinking) чаша ⓕ *cha*-sha
glasses очила ⓝ pl *o*-chi-la
go оди *o*-di
good добар *do*-bar
green зелен *ze*-len
guide водич ⓜ *vo*-dich

H

half половина ⓕ *po*-lo-vi-na
hand рака ⓕ *ra*-ka
handbag женска чанта ⓕ *zhen*-ska *chan*-ta
happy среќен *sre*-kyen
have има *i*-ma
he тој toy
head глава ⓕ *gla*-va
heart срце ⓝ *sr*-tse
heat топлина ⓕ *to*-pli-na

heavy тежок *te*-zhok
help v помага po-*ma*-ga
here овде *ov*-de
high висок *ví*-sok
highway автопат ⓜ *av*-to-pat
hike v планинари pla-*ni*-na-ri
holiday годишен одмор ⓜ go-di-shen *od*-mor
homosexual хомосексуалец ⓜ ho-mo-sek-su-*a*-lets
hospital болница ⓕ *bol*-ni-tsa
hot жежок *zhe*-zhok
hotel хотел ⓜ *ho*-tel
hungry гладен *gla*-den
husband сопруг ⓜ *sop*-rug

I

I jac yas
identification (card) лична карта ⓕ *lich*-na *kar*-ta
ill болен *bo*-len
important важен *va*-zhen
included вклучен *vklu*-chen
injury повреда ⓕ po-*vre*-da
insurance осигурување ⓝ o-si-gu-*ru*-va-nye
Internet интернет ⓜ *in*-ter-net
interpreter толкувач ⓜ *tol*-ku-vach

J

jewellery накит ⓜ *na*-kit
job работа ⓕ *ra*-bo-ta

K

key клуч ⓜ kluch
kilogram килограм ⓜ *ki*-lo-gram
kitchen кујна ⓕ *kuy*-na
knife нож ⓜ nozh

L

laundry (place) перална ⓕ pe-*ral*-na
lawyer адвокат ⓜ ad-vo-*kat*
left (direction) лево *le*-vo
left-luggage office место за чување багаж ⓝ mes-to za chu-*va*-nye *ba*-gazh
leg нога ⓕ *no*-ga
lesbian лезбејка ⓕ *lez*-bey-ka
less помалку po-*mal*-ku
letter (mail) писмо ⓝ *pis*-mo
lift (elevator) лифт ⓜ lift
light светлина ⓕ *svet*-li-na

like v сака *sa*-ka
lock катанец ⓜ *ka*-ta-nets
long долг dolg
lost загубен za-*gu*-ben
lost-property office биро за загубени работи ⓝ bi-ro za za-gu-*be*-ni *ra*-bo-ti
love v љуби *lyu*-bi
luggage багаж ⓜ *ba*-gazh
lunch ручек ⓜ *ru*-chek

M

Macedonia Македонија ⓕ ma-ke-*do*-ni-ya
Macedonian (language) македонски ⓜ ma-ke-*don*-ski
Macedonian a македонски ma-ke-*don*-ski
mail пошта ⓕ *posh*-ta
man маж ⓜ mazh
map мапа ⓕ *ma*-pa
market пазар ⓜ *pa*-zar
matches кибрит ⓜ *kib*-rit
meat месо ⓝ *me*-so
medicine лек ⓜ lek
menu мени ⓝ *me*-ni
message порака ⓕ *po*-ra-ka
milk млеко ⓝ *mle*-ko
minute минута ⓕ *mi*-nu-ta
mobile phone мобилен телефон ⓜ mo-bi-len te-le-*fon*
money пари ⓕ pl *pa*-ri
month месец ⓜ *me*-sets
morning утро ⓝ *ut*-ro
mother мајка ⓕ *may*-ka
motorcycle мотор ⓜ *mo*-tor
motorway автопат ⓜ *av*-to-pat
mouth уста ⓕ *us*-ta
music музика ⓕ *mu*-zi-ka

N

name име ⓝ *i*-me
napkin салфета ⓕ sal-*fe*-ta
nappy пелена ⓕ *pe*-le-na
near блиску *blis*-ku
neck врат ⓜ vrat
new нов nov
news вести ⓕ pl *ves*-ti
newspaper весник ⓜ *yes*-nik
night ноќ ⓕ noky
no не ne
noisy бучен *bu*-chen
nonsmoking за непушачи za ne-*pu*-sha-chi

north север ⓜ *se*-ver
nose нос ⓜ nos
now сега *se*-ga
number број ⓜ broy

O

oil (engine) масло ⓝ *mas*-lo
old стар ⓜ star
one-way ticket билет во еден правец ⓜ
  bi-let vo e-den *pra*-vets
open a отворен *ot*-vo-ren
outside надвор *nad*-vor

P

package пакет ⓜ *pa*-ket
paper хартија ⓕ *har*-ti-ya
park (car) v паркира par-*ki*-ra
passport пасош ⓜ *pa*-sosh
pay плаќа *pla*-kya
pen пенкало ⓝ *pen*-ka-lo
petrol бензин ⓜ *ben*-zin
pharmacy аптека ⓕ *ap*-te-ka
phonecard телефонска картичка ⓕ
  te-le-*fon*-ska *kar*-tich-ka
photo фотографија ⓕ fo-to-*gra*-fi-ya
plate чинија ⓕ *chi*-ni-ya
police полиција ⓕ po-*li*-tsi-ya
postcard поштенска картичка ⓕ
  posh-ten-ska *kar*-tich-ka
post office пошта ⓕ *posh*-ta
pregnant бремена ⓕ *bre*-me-na
price цена ⓕ *tse*-na

Q

quiet тивок *ti*-vok

R

rain дожд ⓜ dozhd
razor жилет ⓜ *zhi*-let
receipt белешка ⓕ *be*-lesh-ka
red црвен *tsr*-ven
refund враќање на пари ⓝ vra-*kya*-nye na *pa*-ri
registered mail препорачано писмо ⓝ
  pre-po-*ra*-cha-no *pis*-mo
rent v изнајмува iz-*nay*-mu-va
repair v поправа *pop*-ra-va
reservation резервација ⓕ re-zer-*va*-tsi-ya

restaurant ресторан ⓜ res-to-*ran*
return v враќа *vra*-kya
return ticket повратен билет ⓜ po-*vra*-ten *bi*-let
right (direction) десно *des*-no
road пат ⓜ pat
room соба ⓕ *so*-ba

S

safe a безбеден *bez*-be-den
sanitary napkin хигиенска влошка ⓕ
  hi-gi-*en*-ska *vlosh*-ka
seat седиште ⓝ *se*-dish-te
send испраќа is-*pra*-kya
service station бензинска пумпа ⓕ
  ben-zin-ska *pum*-pa
sex секс ⓜ seks
shampoo шампон ⓜ sham-*pon*
share (a dorm) дели *de*-li
shaving cream крем за бричење ⓝ
  krem za *bri*-che-nye
she таа *ta*-a
sheet (bed) чаршаф ⓜ *char*-shaf
shirt кошула ⓕ *ko*-shu-la
shoes чевли ⓜ pl *chev*-li
shop продавница ⓕ *pro*-dav-ni-tsa
short кус kus
shower туш ⓜ tush
single room еднокреветна соба ⓕ
  ed-no-*kre*-vet-na *so*-ba
skin кожа ⓕ *ko*-zha
skirt здолниште ⓝ *zdol*-nish-te
sleep v спие *spi*-e
slowly полека po-*le*-ka
small мал mal
smoke (cigarettes) v пуши *pu*-shi
soap сапун ⓜ *sa*-pun
some неколку *ne*-kol-ku
soon наскоро *nas*-ko-ro
south југ ⓜ yug
souvenir shop продавница за сувенири ⓕ
  pro-dav-ni-tsa za su-ve-*ni*-ri
speak зборува *zbo*-ru-va
spoon лажица ⓕ *la*-zhi-tsa
stamp марка ⓕ *mar*-ka
stand-by ticket стендбај билет ⓜ *stend*-bay *bi*-let
station (train) (железничка) станица ⓕ
  (zhe-*lez*-nich-ka) *sta*-ni-tsa
stomach стомак ⓜ *sto*-mak
stop v запира *za*-pi-ra
(bus) stop (автобуска) станица ⓕ
  (av-to-*bus*-ka) *sta*-ni-tsa
street улица ⓕ *u*-li-tsa

student студент/студентка ⓜ/ⓕ
stu-dent/stu-*dent*-ka
sun сонце ⓝ *son*-tse
sunscreen лосион за сончање ⓜ
lo-si-*on* za son-*cha*-nye
swim v плива *pli*-va

T

tampons тампони ⓜ pl tam-*po*-ni
taxi такси ⓝ *tak*-si
teaspoon лажиче ⓝ *la*-zhi-che
teeth заби ⓝ pl *za*-bi
telephone телефон ⓜ te-le-*fon*
television телевизија ⓕ te-le-*vi*-zi-ya
temperature (weather) температура ⓕ
tem-pe-ra-*tu*-ra
tent шатор ⓜ *sha*-tor
that (one) она *o*-na
they тие *ti*-e
thirsty жеден *zhe*-den
this (one) ова *o*-va
throat грло ⓝ *gr*-lo
ticket билет ⓜ *bi*-let
time време ⓝ *vre*-me
tired уморен u-*mo*-ren
tissues книжни марамчиња ⓝ pl
knizh-ni ma-*ram*-chi-nya
today денес *de*-nes
toilet тоалет ⓜ to-a-*let*
tomorrow утре *ut*-re
tonight вечерва *ve*-cher-va
toothbrush четка за заби ⓕ *chet*-ka za *za*-bi
toothpaste паста за заби ⓕ *pas*-ta za *za*-bi
torch (flashlight) џепна ламба ⓕ *jep*-na *lam*-ba
tour патување ⓝ pa-*tu*-va-nye
tourist office туристичко биро ⓝ tu-*ris*-tich-ko bi-*ro*
towel пешкир ⓜ *pesh*-kir
train воз ⓜ voz
translate преведува pre-*ve*-du-va
travel agency туристичка агенција ⓕ
tu-*ris*-tich-ka a-*gen*-tsi-ya
travellers cheque патнички чек ⓜ *pat*-nich-ki chek
trousers панталони ⓝ pl pan-ta-*lo*-ni
twin beds двоен кревет ⓜ *dvo*-en *kre*-vet
tyre гума ⓕ *gu*-ma

U

underwear долна облека ⓕ *dol*-na *ob*-le-ka
urgent итен *i*-ten

V

vacant слободен *slo*-bo-den
vacation годишен одмор ⓜ *go*-di-shen *od*-mor
vegetable зеленчук ⓜ ze-len-*chuk*
vegetarian a вегетаријански ve-ge-ta-ri-*yan*-ski
visa виза ⓕ *vi*-za

W

waiter келнер ⓜ *kel*-ner
walk v пешачи pe-*sha*-chi
wallet паричник ⓜ pa-*rich*-nik
warm a топол *to*-pol
wash (something) мие *mi*-e
watch часовник ⓜ *cha*-sov-nik
water вода ⓕ *vo*-da
we ние *ni*-e
weekend викенд ⓜ *vi*-kend
west запад ⓜ *za*-pad
wheelchair инвалидска количка ⓕ
in-va-*lid*-ska ko-*lich*-ka
when кога *ko*-ga
where каде *ka*-de
white бел bel
who кој koy
why зошто *zosh*-to
wife сопруга ⓕ *so*-pru-ga
window прозорец ⓜ *pro*-zo-rets
wine вино ⓝ *vi*-no
with со so
without без bez
woman жена ⓕ *zhe*-na
write пишува *pi*-shu-va

Y

yellow жолт zholt
yes да da
yesterday вчера *vche*-ra
you sg inf ти ti
you sg pol & pl вие *vi*-e

Portuguese

portuguese alphabet

A a aa	B b be	C c se	D d de	E e e
F f e·fe	G g je	H h a·gaah	I i ee	J j jo·ta
K k ka·pa	L l e·le	M m e·me	N n e·ne	O o o
P p pe	Q q ke	R r e·rre	S s e·se	T t te
U u oo	V v ve	W w da·blyoo	X x sheesh	Y y eeps·lon
Z z ze				

portuguese

introduction

Portuguese (*português* poor·too·*gesh*), the language which produced words such as *albino*, *brocade* and *molasses*, comes from the Romance language family and is closely related to Spanish, French and Italian. Descended from the colloquial Latin spoken by Roman soldiers, it's now used by over 200 million people worldwide.

Linguists believe that before the Roman invasion of the Iberian Peninsula in 218 BC, the locals of modern-day Portugal spoke a Celtic language. That local language was supplanted by the vernacular form of Latin (sometimes called 'Romance') spoken by the occupying forces under the Romans' 500-year rule of the province of Lusitania (present-day Portugal and Spanish Galicia). During this period, Portuguese also absorbed elements of the languages of invading Germanic tribes. The greatest influence on today's Portuguese, however, was a result of the Moorish invasion of the peninsula in AD 711. Arabic was imposed as the official language of the region until the expulsion of the Moors in 1249, and although Romance was still spoken by the masses, the Moorish language left its mark on the vocabulary. From the 16th century on, there were only minor changes to the language, mostly influences from France and Spain. The earliest written documents were composed in the 12th century, and the Portuguese used in 1572 by Luís de Camões (author of the first great Portuguese classic, *Os Lusíadas*) was already identifiable as the language of José Saramago's Nobel Prize-winning works in the 20th century.

The global distribution of the Portuguese language began during the period know as *Os Descobrimentos* (the Discoveries), the golden era of Portugal's colonial expansion into Africa, Asia and South America. In the 15th and 16th centuries, the peninsular nation was a world power and had enormous economic, cultural and political influence. The empire's reach can be seen today in the number of countries besides Portugal where Portuguese still has the status of an official language – Brazil, Madeira and the Azores in the Atlantic Ocean off Europe, Cape Verde, São Tomé and Príncipe, Guinea-Bissau, Angola and Mozambique (all in Africa), and Macau and East Timor in Asia.

While there are differences between European Portuguese and that spoken elsewhere, you shouldn't have many problems being understood throughout the Portuguese-speaking world. As the Portuguese say, *Quem não arrisca, não petisca* keng nowng a·*rreesh*·ka, nowng pe·*teesh*·ka (If you don't take a risk, you won't eat delicacies).

pronunciation

vowel sounds

The vowel sounds in Portuguese are quite similar to those found in English. Most vowel sounds in Portuguese also have a nasal version with an effect similar to the silent '-ng' ending in English, as in *amanhã* aa·ma·*nyang* (tomorrow), for example. The letter 'n' or 'm' at the end of a syllable or a tilde (~) in written Portuguese indicate that the vowel is nasal.

symbol	english equivalent	portuguese example	transliteration
a	run	*maçã*	ma·*sang*
aa	father	*tomate*	too·*maa*·te
ai	aisle	*pai*	pai
ay	say	*lei*	lay
e	bet	*cedo*	*se*·doo
ee	see	*fino*	*fee*·noo
o	pot	*sobre*	*so*·bre
oh	oh	*couve*	*koh*·ve
oo	book	*gato*	*ga*·too
ow	how	*Austrália*	ow·*shtraa*·lya
oy	toy	*noite*	*noy*·te

word stress

In Portuguese, stress generally falls on the second-to-last syllable of a word, though there are exceptions. If a written vowel has a circumflex (ˆ) or an acute (ˊ) or grave (ˋ) accent marked on it, this cancels the general rule and the stress falls on that syllable. When a word ends in a written *i*, *im*, *l*, *r*, *u*, *um* or *z*, or is pronounced with a nasalised vowel, the stress falls on the last syllable. Don't worry too much about it when using phrases from this book though – the stressed syllable is always italicised in our coloured pronunciation guides.

consonant sounds

Most of the consonant sounds in Portuguese are also found in English, and even *r* (rr) will be familiar to many people (it's similar to the French 'r'). Note that the letter ç ('c' with a cedilla) is pronounced as s rather than k.

symbol	english equivalent	portuguese example	transliteration
b	bed	*beber*	be·*ber*
d	dog	*dedo*	de·*doo*
f	fat	*faca*	faa·ka
g	go	*gasolina*	ga·zoo·lee·na
k	kit	*cama*	ka·ma
l	lot	*lixo*	lee·shoo
ly	million	*muralhas*	moo·raa·lyash
m	man	*macaco*	ma·kaa·koo
n	not	*nada*	naa·da
ng	ring (indicates the nasalisation of the preceding vowel)	*ambos,* *uns,* *amanhã*	ang·boosh, oongsh, aa·ma·*nyang*
ny	canyon	*linha*	lee·nya
p	pet	*padre*	paa·dre
r	like 'tt' in 'butter' said fast	*hora*	o·ra
rr	run (throaty)	*relva*	rrel·va
s	sun	*criança*	kree·ang·sa
sh	shot	*chave*	shaa·ve
t	top	*tacho*	taa·shoo
v	very	*vago*	vaa·goo
w	win	*água*	aa·gwa
y	yes	*edifício*	ee·dee·*fee*·syoo
z	zero	*camisa*	ka·mee·za
zh	pleasure	*cerveja*	serr·ve·zha

basics

language difficulties

Do you speak English?
Fala inglês?   faa·la eeng·*glesh*

Do you understand?
Entende?   eng·*teng*·de

I (don't) understand.
(Não) Entendo.   (nowng) eng·*teng*·doo

What does (*bem-vindo*) mean?
O que quer dizer (bem-vindo)?   oo ke ker dee·*zer* (beng·*veeng*·doo)

How do you ...?   *Como é que se ...?*   *ko*·moo e ke se ...
  pronounce this   *pronuncia isto*   proo·noong·*see*·a *esh*·too
  write (*ajuda*)   *escreve (ajuda)*   *shkre*·ve (a·*zhoo*·da)

Could you please ...? *Podia ..., por favor?*   poo·*dee*·a ... poor fa·*vor*
  repeat that   *repetir isto*   rre·pe·*teer eesh*·too
  speak more slowly *falar mais devagar*   fa·*laar* maish de·va·*gaar*
  write it down   *escrever isso*   shkre·*ver ee*·soo

essentials

Yes.	*Sim.*	seeng
No.	*Não.*	nowng
Please.	*Por favor.*	poor fa·*vor*
Thank you	*(Muito)*	(*mweeng*·too)
(very much).	*Obrigado/a.* m/f	o·bree·*gaa*·doo/a
You're welcome.	*De nada.*	de *naa*·da
Excuse me.	*Faz favor!*	faash fa·*vor*
Sorry.	*Desculpe.*	desh·*kool*·pe

numbers

0	zero	ze-roo	16	dezasseis	de-za-saysh
1	um	oong	17	dezassete	de-za-se-te
2	dois	doysh	18	dezoito	de-zoy-too
3	três	tresh	19	dezanove	de-za-no-ve
4	quatro	kwaa-troo	20	vinte	veeng-te
5	cinco	seeng-koo	21	vinte e um	veeng-te e oong
6	seis	saysh	22	vinte e dois	veeng-te e doysh
7	sete	se-te	30	trinta	treeng-ta
8	oito	oy-too	40	quarenta	kwa-reng-ta
9	nove	no-ve	50	cinquenta	seeng-kweng-ta
10	dez	desh	60	sessenta	se-seng-ta
11	onze	ong-ze	70	setenta	se-teng-ta
12	doze	do-ze	80	oitenta	oy-teng-ta
13	treze	tre-ze	90	noventa	no-veng-ta
14	catorze	ka-tor-ze	100	cem	seng
15	quinze	keeng-ze	1000	mil	meel

time & dates

What time is it?	Que horas são?	kee o-rash sowng
It's one o'clock.	É uma hora.	e oo-ma o-ra
It's (10) o'clock.	São (dez) horas.	sowng (desh) o-rash
Quarter past (10).	(Dez) e quinze.	(desh) e keeng-ze
Half past (10).	(Dez) e meia.	(desh) e may-a
Quarter to (10).	Quinze para as (dez).	keeng-ze pa-ra ash (desh)
At what time ...?	A que horas ...?	a ke o-rash ...
At ...	Às ...	ash ...
in the morning	da manhã	da ma-nyang
in the afternoon	da tarde	da taar-de
in the evening	da noite	da noy-te
Monday	segunda-feira	se-goong-da-fay-ra
Tuesday	terça-feira	ter-sa-fay-ra
Wednesday	quarta-feira	kwaar-ta-fay-ra
Thursday	quinta-feira	keeng-ta-fay-ra
Friday	sexta-feira	saysh-ta-fay-ra
Saturday	sábado	saa-ba-doo
Sunday	domingo	doo-meeng-goo

basics – PORTUGUESE

January	Janeiro	zha-*nay*-roo
February	Fevereiro	fe-*vray*-roo
March	Março	maar-soo
April	Abril	a-*breel*
May	Maio	maa-yoo
June	Junho	zhoo-nyoo
July	Julho	zhoo-lyoo
August	Agosto	a-*gosh*-too
September	Setembro	se-*teng*-broo
October	Outubro	oh-*too*-broo
November	Novembro	no-*veng*-broo
December	Dezembro	de-*zeng*-broo

What date is it today?
   Qual é a data de hoje?   kwaal e a *daa*-ta de o-zhe

It's (18 October).
   Hoje é dia (dezoito de Outubro).   o-zhe e *dee*-a (de-*zoy*-too de oh-*too*-broo)

| since (May) | desde (Maio) | desh-de (maa-yoo) |
| until (June) | até (Junho) | a-te (zhoo-nyoo) |

last ...
night	a noite passada	a noy-te pa-saa-da
week	a semana passada	a se-ma-na pa-saa-da
month	o mês passado	oo mesh pa-saa-doo
year	o ano passado	oo a-noo pa-saa-doo

next ...
week	na próxima semana	na pro-see-ma se-ma-na
month	no próximo mês	noo pro-see-moo mesh
year	no próximo ano	noo pro-see-moo a-noo

yesterday/tomorrow ... *ontem/amanhã ...* ong-teng/aa-ma-*nyang* ...
morning	de manhã	de ma-nyang
afternoon	à tarde	aa taar-de
evening	à noite	aa noy-te

weather

What's the weather like?	Como está o tempo?	ko·moo shtaa oo teng·poo
It's ...	Está ...	shtaa ...
cloudy	enublado	e·noo·blaa·doo
cold	frio	free·oo
hot	muito quente	mweeng·too keng·te
raining	a chover	a shoo·ver
snowing	a nevar	a ne·vaar
sunny	sol	sol
warm	quente	keng·te
windy	ventoso	veng·to·zoo
spring	primavera f	pree·ma·ve·ra
summer	verão m	ve·rowng
autumn	outono m	oh·to·noo
winter	inverno m	eeng·ver·noo

border crossing

I'm here ...	Estou ...	shtoh ...
in transit	em trânsito	eng trang·zee·too
on business	em negócios	eng ne·go·syoosh
on holiday	de férias	de fe·ree·ash
I'm here for ...	Vou ficar por ...	voh fee·kaar poor ...
(10) days	(dez) dias	(desh) dee·ash
(three) weeks	(três) semanas	(tresh) se·ma·nash
(two) months	(dois) meses	(doysh) me·zesh

I'm going to (Elvas).
Vou para (Elvas).
voh pa·ra (el·vash)

I'm staying at the (Hotel Lisbon).
Estou no (Hotel Lisboa).
shtoh noo (o·tel leezh·bo·a)

I have nothing to declare.
Não tenho nada a declarar.
nowng ta·nyoo naa·da a de·kla·raar

I have something to declare.
Tenho algo a declarar.
ta·nyoo al·goo a de·kla·raar

That's (not) mine.
Isto (não) é meu.
eesh·too (nowng) e me·oo

transport

tickets & luggage

Where can I buy a ticket?
Onde é que eu compro o bilhete?   ong·de e ke e·oo kong·proo oo bee·lye·te

Do I need to book a seat?
Preciso de fazer reserva?   pre·see·zoo de fa·zer rre·zer·va

One ... ticket (to Braga), please.	Um bilhete de ... (para Braga), por favor.	oong bee·lye·te de ... (pra braa·ga) poor fa·vor
one-way	ida	ee·da
return	ida e volta	ee·da ee vol·ta

I'd like to ... my ticket, please.	Queria ... o bilhete, por favor.	ke·ree·a ... oo bee·lye·te poor fa·vor
cancel	cancelar	kang·se·laar
change	trocar	troo·kaar
collect	cobrar	koo·braar
confirm	confirmar	kong·feer·maar

I'd like a ... seat, please.	Queria um lugar ... por favor.	ke·ree·a oong loo·gaar ... poor fa·vor
nonsmoking	de não fumadores	de nowng foo·ma·do·resh
smoking	para fumadores	pra foo·ma·do·resh

How much is it?
Quanto é?   kwang·too e

Is there air conditioning?
Tem ar condicionado?   teng aar kong·dee·syoo·naa·doo

Is there a toilet?
Tem casa de banho?   teng kaa·za de ba·nyoo

How long does the trip take?
Quanto tempo é que leva a viagem?   kwang·too teng·poo e ke le·va a vee·aa·zheng

Is it a direct route?
É uma rota directa?   e oo·ma rro·ta dee·re·ta

I'd like a luggage locker.
Queria o depósito de bagagens.   ke·ree·a oo de·po·zee·too de ba·gaa·zhengsh

My luggage has been ...	A minha bagagem ...	a *mee*-nya ba-*gaa*-zheng ...
damaged	foi danificada	foy da-nee-fee-*kaa*-da
lost	perdeu-se	per-*de*-oo-se
stolen	foi roubada	foy rroh-*baa*-da

getting around

Where does flight (TP 615) arrive/depart?

De onde pára/parte o voo (TP 615)?

de *ong*-de *paa*-ra/*paar*-te oo *vo*-oo (te pe saysh-*seng*-toosh e *keeng*-ze)

Where's (the) ...?	Onde é ...?	*ong*-de e ...
arrivals hall	a porta de chegada	a *por*-ta de she-*gaa*-da
departures hall	a porta de partida	a *por*-ta de par-*tee*-da
duty-free shop	a loja duty-free	a *lo*-zha doo-tee-free
gate (12)	a porta (doze)	a *por*-ta (*do*-ze)

Is this the ... to (Lisbon)?	Este é o ... para (Lisboa)?	*esh*-te e oo ... pra (leezh-*bo*-a)
boat	barco	*baar*-koo
bus	autocarro	ow-to-*kaa*-rroo
plane	avião	a-vee-*owng*
train	comboio	kong-*boy*-oo

What time's the ... bus?	Quando é que sai o ... autocarro?	*kwang*-doo e ke sai oo ... ow-to-*kaa*-rroo
first	primeiro	pree-*may*-roo
last	último	*ool*-tee-moo
next	próximo	*pro*-see-moo

At what time does it arrive/leave?

A que horas chega/sai?

a ke *o*-rash *she*-ga/sai

How long will it be delayed?

Quanto tempo é que vai chegar atrasado?

kwang-too *teng*-poo e ke vai she-*gaar* a-tra-*zaa*-doo

What station/stop is this?

Qual estação/paragem é este?

kwaal shta-*sowng*/pa-*raa*-zheng e *esh*-te

What's the next station/stop?

Qual é a próxima estação/ paragem?

kwaal e a *pro*-see-ma shta-*sowng*/ pa-*raa*-zheng

Does it stop at (Amarante)?
Pára em (Amarante)?
paa·ra eng (a·ma·*rang*·te)

Please tell me when we get to (Évora).
Por favor avise-me quando chegarmos a (Évora).
poor fa·*vor* a·*vee*·ze·me *kwang*·doo she·*gaar*·moosh a (*e*·voo·ra)

How long do we stop here?
Quanto tempo vamos ficar parados aqui?
kwang·too *teng*·poo va·moosh fee·*kaar* pa·*raa*·doosh a·*kee*

Is this seat available?
Este lugar está vago?
esh·te loo·*gaar* shtaa va·goo

That's my seat.
Este é o meu lugar.
esh·te e oo *me*·oo loo·*gaar*

I'd like a taxi ...
Queria chamar um táxi ...
ke·*ree*·a sha·*maar* oong *taak*·see ...

   at (9am)
   para as (nove da manhã)
   pra ash (*no*·ve da ma·*nyang*)

   now
   agora
   a·*go*·ra

   tomorrow
   amanhã
   aa·ma·*nyang*

Is this taxi available?
Este táxi está livre?
esh·te *taak*·see shtaa *lee*·vre

How much is it to ...?
Quanto custa até ao ...?
kwang·too *koosh*·ta a·*te* ow ...

Please put the meter on.
Por favor, ligue o taxímetro.
poor fa·*vor* *lee*·ge oo taak·*see*·me·troo

Please take me to (this address).
Leve-me para (este endereço), por favor.
le·ve·me *pa*·ra (*esh*·te eng·de·*re*·soo) poor fa·*vor*

Please ...
Por favor ...
poor fa·*vor* ...

   slow down
   vá mais devagar
   vaa maish de·va·*gaar*

   stop here
   pare aqui
   paa·re a·*kee*

   wait here
   espere aqui
   shpe·re a·*kee*

car, motorbike & bicycle hire

I'd like to hire a …	Queria alugar …	ke·ree·a a·loo·gaar …
bicycle	uma bicicleta	oo·ma bee·see·kle·ta
car	um carro	oong kaa·rroo
motorbike	uma mota	oo·ma mo·ta

with …	com …	kong …
a driver	motorista	moo·too·reesh·ta
air conditioning	ar condicionado	aar kong·dee·syoo·naa·doo

How much for … hire?	Quanto custa para alugar por …?	kwang·too koosh·ta pa·ra a·loo·gaar poor …
hourly	hora	o·ra
daily	dia	dee·a
weekly	semana	se·ma·na

air	ar m	aar
oil	óleo m	o·le·oo
petrol	gasolina f	ga·zoo·lee·na
tyres	pneus m pl	pe·ne·oosh

I need a mechanic.
Preciso de um mecânico.
pre·see·zoo de oong me·kaa·nee·koo

I've run out of petrol.
Estou sem gasolina.
shtoh seng ga·zoo·lee·na

I have a flat tyre.
Tenho um furo no pneu.
ta·nyoo oong foo·roo noo pe·ne·oo

directions

Where's the …?	Onde é …?	ong·de e …
bank	o banco	oo bang·koo
city centre	o centro da cidade	oo seng·troo da see·daa·de
hotel	o hotel	oo o·tel
market	o mercado	oo mer·kaa·doo
police station	a esquadra da polícia	a shkwaa·dra da poo·lee·sya
post office	o correio	oo koo·rray·oo
public toilet	a casa de banho pública	a kaa·za de ba·nyoo poo·blee·ka
tourist office	o escritório de turismo	oo shkree·to·ryoo de too·reezh·moo

Is this the road to (Sintra)?
Esta é a estrada para (Sintra)?   esh·ta e a shtraa·da pa·ra (seeng·tra)

Can you show me (on the map)?
Pode-me mostrar (no mapa)?   po·de·me moosh·traar (noo maa·pa)

How far is it?
A que distância fica?   a ke deesh·tang·sya fee·ka

How do I get there?
Como é que eu chego lá?   ko·moo e ke e·oo she·goo laa

Turn ...	*Vire ...*	vee·re ...
at the corner	*na esquina*	na shkee·na
at the traffic lights	*nos semáforos*	noosh se·maa·foo·roosh
left	*à esquerda*	aa shker·da
right	*à direita*	aa dee·ray·ta
It's ...	*É ...*	e ...
behind ...	*atrás de ...*	a·traash de ...
far away	*longe*	long·zhe
here	*aqui*	a·kee
in front of ...	*em frente de ...*	eng freng·te de ...
left	*à esquerda*	aa shker·da
near (to ...)	*perto (de ...)*	per·too (de ...)
next to ...	*ao lado de ...*	ow laa·doo de ...
on the corner	*na esquina*	na shkee·na
opposite ...	*do lado*	doo laa·doo
	oposto ...	oo·posh·too ...
right	*à direita*	aa dee·ray·ta
straight ahead	*em frente*	eng freng·te
there	*lá*	laa
by bus	*de autocarro*	de ow·to·kaa·rroo
by taxi	*de táxi*	de taak·see
by train	*de comboio*	de kong·boy·oo
on foot	*a pé*	a pe
north	*norte*	nor·te
south	*sul*	sool
east	*leste*	lesh·te
west	*oeste*	o·esh·te

Entrada/Saída	eng-*traa*-da/sa-*ee*-da	**Entrance/Exit**
Aberto/Fechado	a-*ber*-too/fe-*shaa*-doo	**Open/Closed**
Há Vaga	aa *vaa*-ga	**Rooms Available**
Não Há Vaga	nowng aa *vaa*-ga	**No Vacancies**
Informação	eeng-for-ma-*sowng*	**Information**
Esquadra da Polícia	shkwaa-dra da poo-*lee*-sya	**Police Station**
Proibido	pro-ee-*bee*-doo	**Prohibited**
Casa de Banho	*kaa*-za de ba-*nyoo*	**Toilets**
Homens	o-mengsh	**Men**
Mulheres	moo-*lye*-resh	**Women**
Quente/Frio	keng-te/*free*-oo	**Hot/Cold**

accommodation

finding accommodation

Where's a ...?	Onde é que há ...?	*ong*-de e ke aa ...
camping ground	um parque de	oong *paar*-ke de
	campismo	kang-*peezh*-moo
guesthouse	uma casa de hóspedes	oo-ma *kaa*-za de *osh*-pe-desh
hotel	um hotel	oong o-*tel*
youth hostel	uma pousada	oo-ma poh-*zaa*-da
	de juventude	de zhoo-veng-*too*-de

Can you recommend	Pode recomendar	po-de rre-koo-meng-*daar*
somewhere ...?	algum lugar ...?	aal-*goong* loo-*gaar* ...
cheap	barato	ba-*raa*-too
good	bom	bong
nearby	perto daqui	*per*-too da-*kee*

I'd like to book a room, please.
  Eu queria fazer uma   e-oo ke-*ree*-a fa-*zer* oo-ma
  reserva, por favor.   rre-*zer*-va poor fa-*vor*

I have a reservation.
  Eu tenho uma reserva.   e-oo ta-nyoo oo-ma rre-*zer*-va

My name's ...
  O meu nome é ...   oo me-oo no-me e ...

Do you have a ... room?	*Tem um quarto ...?*	teng oong *kwaar*·too ...
single	*de solteiro*	de sol·*tay*·roo
double	*de casal*	de ka·*zaal*
twin	*duplo*	*doo*·ploo

How much is it per ...?	*Quanto custa por ...?*	kwang·too koosh·ta poor ...
night	*noite*	*noy*·te
person	*pessoa*	pe·*so*·a

Can I pay by ...?	*Posso pagar com ...?*	po·soo pa·gaar kong ...
credit card	*cartão de crédito*	kar·*towng* de *kre*·dee·too
travellers cheque	*traveller cheque*	*tra*·ve·ler shek

I'd like to stay for (three) nights.
Para (três) noites. — pa·ra (tresh) *noy*·tesh

From (2 July) to (6 July).
De (dois de julho) até (seis de julho). — de (doysh de *zhoo*·lyoo) a·*te* (saysh de *zhoo*·lyoo)

Can I see it?
Posso ver? — po·soo ver

Am I allowed to camp here?
Posso acampar aqui? — po·soo a·kang·*paar* a·*kee*

Where can I find a camping ground?
Onde é o parque de campismo? — ong·de e oo *par*·ke de kang·*peesh*·moo

requests & queries

When/Where is breakfast served?
Quando/Onde é que servem o pequeno almoço? — kwang·doo/ong·de e ke *ser*·veng oo pe·*ke*·noo aal·*mo*·soo

Please wake me at (seven).
Por favor acorde-me às (sete). — poor fa·*vor* aa·*kor*·de·me aash (se·te)

Could I have my key, please?
Pode-me dar a minha chave, por favor? — po·de·me daar a *mee*·nya *shaa*·ve poor fa·*vor*

Can I get another (blanket)?
Pode-me dar mais um (cobertor)? — po·de·me daar maish oong (koo·ber·*tor*)

Is there a/an ...?	Tem ...?	teng ...
elevator	elevador	e·le·va·*dor*
safe	cofre	*ko*·fre

The room is too ...	É demasiado ...	e de·ma·zee·*aa*·doo ...
expensive	caro	*kaa*·roo
noisy	barulhento	ba·roo·*lyeng*·too
small	pequeno	pe·*ke*·noo

The ... doesn't work.	... não funciona.	... nowng foong·see·*o*·na
air conditioner	O ar condicionado	oo aar kong·dee·syoo·*naa*·doo
fan	A ventoínha	a veng·too·*ee*·na
toilet	A sanita	a sa·*nee*·ta

This ... isn't clean.	Esta ... está suja.	esh·ta ... shtaa *soo*·zha
pillow	almofada	aal·moo·*faa*·da
towel	toalha	*twaa*·lya

This sheet isn't clean.	Este lençol está sujo.	esh·te leng·*sol* shtaa *soo*·zho

checking out

What time is checkout?
A que horas é a partida? a ke *o*·rash e a par·*tee*·da

Can I leave my luggage here?
Posso deixar as minhas po·soo day·*shaar* ash *mee*·nyash
malas aqui? *maa*·lash a·*kee*

Could I have	Pode-me devolver	po·de·me de·vol·*ver*
my ..., please?	..., por favor?	... poor fa·*vor*
deposit	o depósito	oo de·*po*·zee·too
passport	o passaporte	oo paa·sa·*por*·te
valuables	os objectos	oosh o·be·*zhe*·toosh
	de valor	de va·*lor*

communications & banking

the internet

Where's the local Internet café?
Onde fica um café da internet nas redondezas?
ong·de *fee*·ka oong ka·*fe* da eeng·ter·*net* nash rre·dong·*de*·zash

How much is it per hour?
Quanto custa por hora?
kwang·too *koosh*·ta pooro·*ra*

I'd like to ...	*Queria ...*	ke·*ree*·a ...
check my email	*ler o meu email*	ler oo *me*·oo ee·*mayl*
get Internet access	*ter acesso à internet*	ter a·*se*·soo aa eeng·ter·*net*
use a printer	*usar uma impressora*	oo·*zaar* oo·ma eeng·pre·*so*·ra
use a scanner	*usar um digitalizador*	oo·*zaar* oong dee·zhee·ta·lee·za·*dor*

mobile/cell phone

I'd like a ...	*Queria ...*	ke·*ree*·a ...
mobile/cell phone for hire	*alugar um telemóvel*	a·loo·*gaar* oong te·le·*mo*·vel
SIM card for your network	*cartão SIM para a sua rede*	kar·*towng* seeng pa·ra a *soo*·a rre·de

What are the rates?
Qual é o valor cobrado?
kwaal e oo va·*lor* koo·*braa*·doo

telephone

What's your phone number?
Qual é o seu número de telefone?
kwaal e oo *se*·oo *noo*·me·roo de te·le·*fo*·ne

The number is ...
O número é ...
oo *noo*·me·roo e ...

Where's the nearest public phone?
Onde fica o telefone público mais perto?
ong·de *fee*·ka o te·le·*fo*·ne poo·*blee*·koo maish *per*·too

I'd like to buy a phonecard.
Quero comprar um cartão telefónico.
ke·roo kong·*praar* oong kar·*towng* te·le·*fo*·nee·koo

I want to ...	Quero ...	ke·roo ...
call (Singapore)	telefonar (para Singapura)	te·le·foo·naar (pa·ra seeng·ga·poo·ra)
make a local call	fazer uma chamada local	fa·zer oo·ma sha·maa·da loo·kaal
reverse the charges	fazer uma chamada a cobrar	fa·zer oo·ma sha·maa·da a koo·braar

How much does ... cost?	Quanto custa ...?	kwang·too koosh·ta ...
a (three)-minute call	uma ligação de (três) minutos	oo·ma lee·ga·sowng de (tresh) mee·noo·toosh
each extra minute	cada minuto extra	kaa·da mee·noo·too aysh·tra

It's (30c) per (30) seconds.
(Trinta cêntimos) por (trinta) segundos.
(treeng·ta seng·tee·moosh) poor (treeng·ta) se·goong·doosh

post office

I want to send a ...	Quero enviar ...	ke·roo eng·vee·aar ...
fax	um fax	oong faks
letter	uma carta	oo·ma kaar·ta
parcel	uma encomenda	oo·ma eng·koo·meng·da
postcard	um postal	oong poosh·taal

I want to buy a/an ...	Quero comprar um ...	ke·roo kong·praar oong ...
envelope	envelope	eng·ve·lo·pe
stamp	selo	se·loo

Please send it (to Australia) by ...	Por favor envie isto (para Australia) por ...	poor fa·vor eng·vee·e eesh·too (pa·ra owsh·traa·lya) poor ...
airmail	via aérea	vee·a a·e·ree·a
express mail	correio azul	koo·rray·oo a·zool
registered mail	registado/a m/f	rre·zheesh·taa·doo/a
surface mail	via terrestre	vee·a te·rresh·tre

Is there any mail for me?
Há alguma correspondência para mim?
aa aal·goo·ma koo·rresh·pong·deng·sya pa·ra meeng

Where's a/an ...?	Onde é que há ...?	ong-de e ke aa ...
ATM	um caixa	oong kai-sha
	automático	ow-too-maa-tee-koo
foreign exchange office	um câmbio	oong kang-byoo
I'd like to ...	Queria ...	ke-ree-a ...
Where can I ...?	Onde é que posso ...?	ong-de e ke po-soo ...
arrange a transfer	fazer uma	faa-zer oo-ma
	transferencia	trans-fe-reng-sya
cash a cheque	trocar um cheque	troo-kaar oong she-ke
change a travellers cheque	trocar traveller cheque	troo-kaar tra-ve-ler shek
change money	trocar dinheiro	troo-kaar dee-nyay-roo
get a cash advance	fazer um levantamento adiantado	fa-zer oong le-vang-ta-meng-too a-dee-ang-taa-doo
withdraw money	levantar dinheiro	le-vang-taar dee-nyay-roo
What's the ...?	Qual é ...?	kwaal e ...
commission	a comissão	a koo-mee-sowng
charge for that	o imposto	oo eeng-posh-too
exchange rate	o câmbio do dia	oo kang-byoo doo dee-a
It's ...	É ...	e ...
(12) euros	(doze) euros	(do-ze) e-oo-roosh
free	gratuito	gra-twee-too

What time does the bank open?
A que horas é que abre o banco? a ke o-rash e ke aa-bre oo bang-koo

Has my money arrived yet?
O meu dinheiro já chegou? oo me-oo dee-nyay-roo zhaa she-goh

sightseeing

getting in

What time does it open/close?
A que horas abre/fecha? — a ke o-rash aa-bre/fe-sha

What's the admission charge?
Qual é o preço de entrada? — kwaal e oo pre-soo de eng-traa-da

Is there a discount for children/students?
Tem desconto para crianças/ estudantes? — teng desh-kong-too pa-ra kree-ang-sash/ shtoo-dang-tesh

I'd like a ...	Queria um ...	ke-ree-a oong ...
catalogue	catálogo	ka-taa-loo-goo
guide	guia	gee-a
local map	mapa local	maa-pa loo-kaal

I'd like to see ...	Eu gostava de ver ...	e-oo goosh-taa-va de ver ...
What's that?	O que é aquilo?	oo ke e a-kee-loo
Can I take a photo?	Posso tirar uma fotografia?	po-soo tee-raar oo-ma foo-too-gra-fee-a

tours

When's the next ...?	Quando é ...?	kwang-doo e ...
day trip	o próximo passeio	oo pro-see-moo pa-say-oo
tour	a próxima excursão	a pro-see-ma shkoor-sowng

Is ... included?	Inclui ...?	eeng-kloo-ee ...
accommodation	hospedagem	osh-pe-daa-zheng
the admission charge	preço de entrada	pre-soo de eng-traa-da
food	comida	koo-mee-da
transport	transporte	trangsh-por-te

How long is the tour?
Quanto tempo dura a excursão? — kwang-too teng-poo doo-ra a shkoor-sowng

What time should we be back?
A que hora é que devemos estar de volta? — a ke o-ra e ke de-ve-moosh shtaar de vol-ta

sightseeing

castle	*castelo* m	kash·*te*·loo
cathedral	*catedral* f	ka·te·*draal*
church	*igreja* f	ee·*gre*·zha
main square	*praça principal* f	*praa*·sa preeng·see·*paal*
monastery	*mosteiro* m	moosh·*tay*·roo
monument	*monumento* m	moo·noo·*meng*·too
museum	*museu* m	moo·ze·oo
old city	*cidade antiga* f	see·*daa*·de ang·*tee*·ga
palace	*palácio* m	pa·*laa*·syoo
ruins	*ruínas* f pl	rroo·*ee*·nash
stadium	*estádio* m	*shtaa*·dyoo
statues	*estátuas* f pl	shtaa·too·ash

shopping

enquiries

Where's a ...?	*Onde é ...?*	ong·de e ...
bank	*o banco*	oo *bang*·koo
bookshop	*a livraria*	a lee·vra·*ree*·a
department store	*loja de departamentos*	*lo*·zha de de·par·ta·*meng*·toosh
grocery store	*a mercearia*	a mer·see·a·*ree*·a
market	*o mercado*	oo mer·*kaa*·doo
newsagency	*o quiosque*	oo kee·*osh*·ke
supermarket	*o supermercado*	oo soo·per·mer·*kaa*·doo

Where can I buy (a padlock)?
Onde é que posso comprar (um cadeado)?
ong·de e ke *po*·soo kong·*praar* (oong ka·de·*aa*·doo)

I'm looking for ...
Estou à procura de ...
shtoh aa proo·*koo*·ra de ...

Can I look at it?
Posso ver?
po·soo ver

Do you have any others?
Tem outros?
teng *oh*·troosh

Does it have a guarantee?
Tem garantia? — teng ga·rang·*tee*·a

Can I have it sent overseas?
Podem enviar para o estrangeiro? — po·deng eng·vee·*aar* pa·ra oo shtrang·*zhay*·roo

Can I have my ... repaired?
Vocês consertam ...? — vo·*sesh* kong·*ser*·tang ...

It's faulty.
Tem defeito. — teng de·*fay*·too

I'd like ..., please.	*Queria ..., por favor.*	ke·*ree*·a ... poor fa·*vor*
a bag	*um saco*	oong *saa*·koo
a refund	*ser reembolsado/a* m/f	ser rre·eng·bol·*saa*·doo/a
to return this	*devolver isto*	de·vol·*ver* eesh·too

paying

How much is it?
Quanto custa? — kwang·too *koosh*·ta

Can you write down the price?
Pode escrever o preço? — po·de shkre·*ver* oo *pre*·soo

That's too expensive.
Está muito caro. — shtaa *mweeng*·too *kaa*·roo

What's your lowest price?
Qual é o seu último preço? — kwaal e oo *se*·oo *ool*·tee·moo *pre*·soo

I'll give you (five) euros.
Dou-lhe (cinco) euros. — *doh*·lye (*seeng*·koo) e·oo·roosh

There's a mistake in the bill.
Há um erro na conta. — aa oong *e*·rroo na *kong*·ta

Do you accept ...?	*Aceitam ...?*	a·*say*·tang ...
credit cards	*cartão de crédito*	kar·*towng* de *kre*·dee·too
debit cards	*multibanco*	mool·tee·*bang*·koo
travellers cheques	*travellers cheques*	tra·ve·ler *she*·kesh

I'd like ..., please.	*Queria ..., por favor.*	ke·*ree*·a ... poor fa·*vor*
a receipt	*um recibo*	oong rre·*see*·boo
my change	*o troco*	oo *tro*·koo

clothes & shoes

Can I try it on?	*Posso experimentar?*	po·soo shpree·meng·*taar*
My size is (40).	*O meu número é (quarenta).*	oo *me*·oo *noo*·me·roo e (kwa·*reng*·ta)
It doesn't fit.	*Não serve.*	nowng *ser*·ve
small	*pequeno/pequena* m/f	pe·*ke*·noo/pe·*ke*·na
medium	*meio/meia* m/f	*may*·oo/*may*·a
large	*grande* m&f	*grang*·de

books & music

I'd like a ...	*Queria comprar ...*	ke·*ree*·a kong·*praar* ...
newspaper	*um jornal*	oong zhor·*naal*
(in English)	*(em inglês)*	(eng eeng·*glesh*)
pen	*uma caneta*	*oo*·ma ka·*ne*·ta

Is there an English-language bookshop?

Há uma livraria de língua inglesa?

aa *oo*·ma lee·vra·*ree*·a de *leeng*·gwa eeng·*gle*·za

I'm looking for something by (Fernando Pessoa).

Estou à procura de qualquer coisa do (Fernando Pessoa).

shtoh aa proo·*koo*·ra de kwaal·*ker koy*·za doo (fer·*nang*·doo pe·*so*·a)

Can I listen to this?

Posso ouvir?

po·soo oh·*veer*

photography

I need a/an ... film for this camera.	*Preciso de filme ... para esta máquina.*	pre·*see*·zoo de *feel*·me ... *pa*·ra esh·ta *maa*·kee·na
APS	*sistema APS*	seesh·*te*·ma aa pe *e*·se
B&W	*a preto e branco*	a *pre*·too e *brang*·koo
colour	*a cores*	a *ko*·resh
slide	*de diapositivos*	de dee·a·po·zee·*tee*·voosh
(200) ASA	*de (duzentos) ASA*	de (doo·*zeng*·toosh) *aa*·za
When will it be ready?	*Quando fica pronto?*	*kwang*·doo *fee*·ka *prong*·too

Can you ...?	Pode ...?	po·de ...
develop this film	revelar este filme	rre·ve·laar esh·te feel·me
load my film	carregar o filme	kaa·rre·gaar oo feel·me
transfer photos from my camera to CD	transferir as fotografias da minha máquina para um CD	trangsh·fe·reer ash foo·too·gra·fee·ash da mee·nya maa·kee·na pa·ra oong se·de

meeting people

greetings, goodbyes & introductions

Hello/Hi.	Olá.	o·laa
Good night.	Boa noite.	bo·a noy·te
Goodbye/Bye.	Adeus.	a·de·oosh
See you later.	Até logo.	a·te lo·goo
Mr	Senhor	se·nyor
Mrs	Senhora	se·nyo·ra
Ms	Senhorita	se·nyo·ree·ta
How are you?	Como está?	ko·moo shtaa
Fine. And you?	Bem. E você?	beng e vo·se
What's your name?	Qual é o seu nome?	kwaal e oo se·oo no·me
My name is ...	O meu nome é ...	oo me·oo no·me e ...
I'm pleased to meet you.	Prazer em conhecê-lo/ conhecê-la. m/f	pra·zer eng koo·nye·se·lo/ koo·nye·se·la
This is my ...	Este é o meu ... m Esta é a minha ... f	esh·te e oo me·oo ... esh·ta e a mee·nya ...
brother	irmão	eer·mowng
daughter	filha	fee·lya
father	pai	pai
friend	amigo/a m/f	a·mee·goo/a
husband	marido	ma·ree·doo
mother	mãe	maing
partner (intimate)	companheiro/a m/f	kong·pa·nyay·roo/a
sister	irmã	eer·mang
son	filho	fee·lyoo
wife	esposa	shpo·za

Here's my ...	Aqui está o meu ...	a·*kee* shtaa oo *me*·oo ...
What's your ...?	Qual é o seu ...?	kwaal e oo *se*·oo ...
address	endereço	eng·de·*re*·soo
email address	email	ee·*mayl*
fax number	número de fax	*noo*·me·roo de faaks
phone number	número de telefone	*noo*·me·roo de te·le·*fo*·ne

occupations

| What's your occupation? | | |
| Qual é a sua profissão? | | kwaal e a *soo*·a proo·fee·*sowng* |

I'm a/an ...	Sou ...	soh ...
artist	artista m&f	ar·*teesh*·ta
business person	homem/mulher de	o·meng/moo·*lyer* de
	negócios m/f	ne·*go*·syoosh
farmer	agricultor m&f	a·gree·kool·*tor*
manual worker	trabalhador m	tra·ba·lya·*dor*
	trabalhadora f	tra·ba·lya·*do*·ra
office worker	empregado/a	eng·pre·*gaa*·doo/a
	de escritório m/f	de shkree·*to*·ryoo
scientist	cientista m&f	see·eng·*teesh*·ta
student	estudante m&f	shtoo·*dang*·te
tradesperson	comerciante m&f	koo·mer·see·*aang*·te

background

| Where are you from? | De onde é? | dong·de e |

I'm from ...	Eu sou ...	e·oo soh ...
Australia	da Austrália	da owsh·*traa*·lya
Canada	do Canadá	doo ka·na·*daa*
England	da Inglaterra	da eeng·gla·*te*·rra
New Zealand	da Nova Zelândia	da *no*·va ze·*lang*·dya
the USA	dos Estados	doosh *shtaa*·doosh
	Unidos	oo·*nee*·doosh

| Are you married? | É casado/a? m/f | e ka·*zaa*·doo/a |

I'm ...	Eu sou ...	e·oo soh ...
married	casado/a m/f	ka·*zaa*·doo/a
single	solteiro/a m/f	sol·*tay*·roo/a

age

How old ...?	Quantos anos ...?	kwang-toosh a-noosh ...
are you	tem	teng
is your daughter	tem a sua filha	teng a soo-a fee-lya
is your son	tem o seu filho	teng oo se-oo fee-lyoo
I'm ... years old.	Tenho ... anos.	ta-nyoo ... a-noosh
He/She is ... years old.	Ele/Ela tem ... anos.	e-le/e-la teng ... a-noosh

feelings

I'm (not) ...	(Não) Estou ...	(nowng) shtoh ...
Are you ...?	Está ...	shtaa ...
cold	com frio	kong free-oo
happy	feliz	fe-leesh
hot	com calor	kong ka-lor
hungry	com fome	kong fo-me
OK	bem	beng
sad	triste	treesh-te
thirsty	com sede	kong se-de
tired	cansado/a m/f	kang-saa-doo/a

entertainment

going out

Where can I find ...?	Onde é que há ...?	ong-de e ke aa ...
clubs	discotecas	deesh-koo-te-kash
gay/lesbian	lugares de	loo-gaa-resh de
venues	gays/lésbicas	gaysh/lezh-bee-kash
pubs	bares	ba-resh
I feel like	Está-me a	shtaa-me a
going to a ...	apetecer ir a ...	a-pe-te-ser eer a ...
concert	um concerto	oong kong-ser-too
movies	um filme	oong feel-me
party	uma festa	oo-ma fesh-ta
restaurant	um restaurante	oong rresh-tow-rang-te
theatre	uma peça de teatro	oo-ma pe-sa de tee-aa-troo

interests

Do you like ...?	Gosta de ...?	gosh-ta de ...
I (don't) like ...	Eu (não) gosto de ...	e-oo (nowng) gosh-too de ...
art	arte	aar-te
cooking	cozinhar	koo-zee-nyaar
movies	ver filmes	ver feel-mesh
reading	ler	ler
sport	fazer desporto	fa-zer desh-por-too
travelling	viajar	vee-a-zhaar
Do you like to ...?	Costuma ...?	koosh-too-ma ...
dance	ir dançar	eer dang-saar
go to concerts	ir a concertos	eer a kong-ser-toosh
listen to music	ouvir música	oh-veer moo-zee-ka

food & drink

finding a place to eat

Can you	Pode-me	po-de-me
recommend a ...?	recomendar um ...?	rre-koo-meng-daar oong ...
bar	bar	bar
café	café	ka-fe
restaurant	restaurante	rresh-tow-rang-te
I'd like ..., please.	Queria uma ..., por favor.	ke-ree-a oo-ma ... poor fa-vor
a table for (five)	mesa para (cinco)	me-za pa-ra (seeng-koo)
the (non)smoking	mesa de (não)	me-za de (nowng)
section	fumador	foo-ma-dor

ordering food

breakfast	pequeno almoço m	pe-ke-noo aal-mo-soo
lunch	almoço m	aal-mo-soo
dinner	jantar m	zhang-taar
snack	lanche m	lang-she

What would you recommend?
O que é que recomenda?   oo ke e ke rre-koo-meng-da

I'd like (the) ..., please.	Queria ..., por favor.	ke-*ree*-a ...poor fa-*vor*
bill	a conta	a *kong*-ta
drink list	a lista das bebidas	a *leesh*-ta dash be-*bee*-dash
menu	um menu	oong me-*noo*
that dish	aquele prato	a-*ke*-le *praa*-too

drinks

(cup of) coffee ...	(chávena de) café ...	(*shaa*-ve-na de) ka-*fe* ...
(cup of) tea ...	(chávena de) chá ...	(*shaa*-ve-na de) shaa ...
with milk	com leite	kong *lay*-te
without sugar	sem açúcar	seng a-*soo*-kar

| (orange) juice | sumo (de laranja) m | *soo*-moo (de la-*rang*-zha) |
| soft drink | refrigerante m | rre-*free*-zhe-*rang*-te |

... water	água ...	*aa*-gwa ...
hot	quente	*keng*-te
(sparkling) mineral	mineral (com gás)	mee-ne-*raal* (kong gaash)

in the bar

I'll have ...	Eu queria ...	e-oo ke-*ree*-a ...
I'll buy you a drink.	Eu pago-lhe uma bebida.	e-oo *paa*-goo-lye *oo*-ma be-*bee*-da
What would you like?	O que é que quer?	oo ke e ke ker
Cheers!	À nossa!	aa *no*-sa

brandy	brandy f	*brang*-dee
cocktail	cocktail m	kok-*tayl*
a shot of (whisky)	um copinho de (uísque)	oong koo-*pee*-nyoo de (oo-*eesh*-kee)

a ... of beer	... de cerveja	... de ser-*ve*-zha
bottle	uma garrafa	*oo*-ma ga-*rraa*-fa
glass	um copo	oong *ko*-poo

a bottle of ... wine	uma garrafa de vinho ...	*oo*-ma ga-*rraa*-fa de *vee*-nyoo ...
a glass of ... wine	um copo de vinho ...	oong *ko*-poo de *vee*-nyoo ...
red	tinto	*teeng*-too
sparkling	espumante	shpoo-*mang*-te
white	branco	*brang*-koo

self-catering

What's the local speciality?
Qual é a especialidade local?
kwaal e a shpe·see·a·lee·*daa*·de loo·*kaal*

What's that?
O que é aquilo?
oo ke e a·*kee*·loo

How much is (a kilo of cheese)?
Quanto é (um quilo de queijo)?
kwang·too e (oong *kee*·loo de *kay*·zhoo)

I'd like ...	*Eu queria ...*	e·oo ke·*ree*·a ...
(200) grams	*(duzentos) gramas*	(doo·*zeng*·toosh) *graa*·mash
(two) kilos	*(dois) quilos*	(doysh) *kee*·loosh
(three) pieces	*(três) peças*	(tresh) pe·sash
(six) slices	*(seis) fatias*	(saysh) fa·*tee*·ash

Less.	*Menos.*	me·noosh
Enough.	*Chega.*	she·ga
More.	*Mais.*	maish

special diets & allergies

Is there a vegetarian restaurant near here?
Há algum restaurante
vegetariano perto daqui?
aa aal·*goong* rresh·tow·*rang*·te
ve·zhe·ta·ree·*aa*·noo per·too da·*kee*

Do you have vegetarian food?
Tem comida vegetariana?
teng koo·*mee*·da ve·zhe·ta·ree·*aa*·na

Could you prepare	*Pode preparar*	*po*·de pre·pa·*raar*
a meal without ...?	*sem ...?*	seng ...
butter	*manteiga*	mang·*tay*·ga
eggs	*ovos*	o·voosh
meat stock	*caldo de carne*	*kaal*·doo de *kaar*·ne

I'm allergic to ...	*Eu sou alérgico/a*	e·oo soh a·*ler*·zhee·koo/a
	a ... m/f	a ...
dairy produce	*produtos lácteos*	pro·*doo*·toosh *laak*·tee·oosh
gluten	*glúten*	*gloo*·teng
MSG	*MSG*	e·me·e·se·*zhe*
nuts	*oleaginosas*	o·lee·a·zhee·*no*·zash
seafood	*marisco*	ma·*reesh*·koo

menu decoder

açorda f	a-*sor*-da	bread-based thick soup, flavoured with garlic, coriander & olive oil
alheiras f pl	a-*lyay*-rash	bread, garlic, chilli & meat sausage
arroz árabe m	a-*rrosh aa*-ra-be	rice with raisins, nuts & dried fruit
arroz de bacalhau m	a-*rrosh* de ba-ka-*lyow*	rice with shredded salt cod
assado de peixe m	a-*saa*-doo de *pay*-she	mix of roasted or baked fish
bacalhau no borralho m	ba-ka-*lyow* noo boo-*rraa*-lyoo	salt cod steak wrapped in cabbage leaves & bacon
bacalhau roupa-velha m	ba-ka-*lyow* rroh-pa-*ve*-lya	mixture of cabbage, salt cod & potatoes, sautéed in olive oil & garlic
bifana no pão f	bee-*fa*-na noo powng	thin pork steak sandwich
bitoque m	bee-*to*-ke	steak or fillet with a fried egg on top
bolo de mel m	*bo*-loo de mel	rich molasses & spice cake with candied fruit & almonds
borrachões m pl	boo-rra-*shoyngsh*	fried ring-shaped biscuits flavoured with brandy or white wine & cinnamon
caldeirada f	kaal-day-*raa*-da	soup-like stew, usually with fish
chanfana f	shang-*fa*-na	hearty stew with goat or mutton in heavy red wine sauce
chouriço m	shoh-*ree*-soo	garlicky pork sausage flavoured with red pepper paste
coelho à caçador m	koo-e-lyoo aa ka-sa-*dor*	rabbit stewed with wine & tomato
cozido à Portuguesa m	koo-zee-doo aa poor-too-*ge*-za	hearty meal with chunks of meats & sausages, vegetables, beans & rice
dobrada f	doo-*braa*-da	tripe with white beans & rice
duchesse f	doo-*shes*	puff pastry filled with whipped cream & topped with fruit

escabeche m	shka-be-she	raw meat or fish pickled in olive oil, vinegar, garlic & bay leaf
favada à Portuguesa f	fa-vaa-da aa poor-too-ge-za	stew of fava beans, sausage & sometimes poached eggs
feijoada f	fay-zhwaa-da	bean stew with sausages or other meat
francesinha f	frang-se-zee-nya	ham, sausage & cheese in a tomato-cream sauce, on slices of bread
gaspacho m	gash-paa-shoo	chilled tomato & garlic bread soup with olive oil, vinegar & oregano
jesuítas m pl	zhe-zoo-ee-tash	puff pastry with baked meringue icing
manjar branco m	mang-zhaar brang-koo	coconut-milk & prunes pudding with syrup poured over the top
migas f pl	mee-gash	a side dish, usually bread flavoured with olive oil, garlic & spices & fried
morgados m pl	mor-gaa-doosh	sweetmeats made with almonds & figs
pastéis de feijão m pl	pash-taysh de fay-zhowng	rich lima bean & almond mixture in flaky pastry shells
pataniscas de bacalhau f pl	pa-ta-neesh-kash de ba-ka-lyow	seasoned salt cod fritters
prato de grão m	praa-too de growng	chickpea stew flavoured with tomato, garlic, bay leaf & cumin
salada de atum f	sa-laa-da de a-toong	salad of tuna, potato, peas, carrots & eggs in an olive oil & vinegar dressing
salame de chocolate m	sa-la-me de shoo-koo-laa-te	dense chocolate fudge roll studded with bits of biscuits, served sliced
sopa de pedra f	so-pa de pe-dra	vegetable soup with red beans, onions, potatoes, pig's ear, bacon & sausages
tecolameco m	te-koo-la-me-koo	rich orange & almond cake
tripas à moda do Porto f pl	tree-pash aa mo-da doo por-too	slow-cooked dried beans, trotters, tripe, chicken, vegetables & sausages

emergencies

basics

Help!	Socorro!	soo·ko·rroo
Stop!	Stop!	stop
Go away!	Vá-se embora!	vaa·se eng·bo·ra
Thief!	Ladrão!	la·drowng
Fire!	Fogo!	fo·goo
Watch out!	Cuidado!	kwee·daa·doo

Call ...!	Chame ...!	shaa·me ...
a doctor	um médico	oong me·dee·koo
an ambulance	uma ambulância	oo·ma ang·boo·lang·sya
the police	a polícia	a poo·lee·sya

It's an emergency.
É uma emergência. — e oo·ma ee·mer·zheng·sya

Could you help me, please?
Pode ajudar, por favor? — po·de a·zhoo·daar poor fa·vor

Can I use the telephone?
Posso usar o seu telefone? — po·soo oo·zaar oo se·oo te·le·fo·ne

I'm lost.
Estou perdido/a. m/f — shtoh per·dee·doo/a

Where are the toilets?
Onde é a casa de banho? — ong·de e a kaa·za de ba·nyoo

police

Where's the police station?
Onde é a esquadra da polícia? — ong·de e a shkwaa·dra da poo·lee·sya

I want to report an offence.
Eu quero denunciar um crime. — e·oo ke·roo de·noong·see·aar oong kree·me

I have insurance.
Eu estou coberto/a pelo seguro. m/f — e·oo shtoh koo·ber·too/a pe·loo se·goo·roo

I've been assaulted.	Eu fui agredido/a. m/f	e·oo fwee a·gre·dee·doo/a
I've been raped.	Eu fui violado/a. m/f	e·oo fwee vee·oo·laa·doo/a
I've been robbed.	Eu fui roubado/a. m/f	e·oo fwee rroh·baa·doo/a

I've lost my ...	Eu perdi ...	e·oo per·dee
My ... was/were stolen.	Roubaram ...	rroh·baa·rang ...
backpack	a minha mochila	a meeng·nya moo·shee·la
bags	os meus sacos	oosh me·oosh saa·koosh
credit card	o meu cartão de crédito	oo me·oo kar·towng de kre·dee·too
handbag	a minha bolsa	a mee·nya bol·sa
jewellery	as minhas jóias	ash mee·nyash zhoy·ash
money	o meu dinheiro	oo me·oo dee·nyay·roo
passport	o meu passaporte	oo me·oo paa·sa·por·te
travellers cheques	os meus travellers cheques	oosh me·oosh tra·ve·ler she·kesh
wallet	a minha carteira	a mee·nya kar·tay·ra
I want to contact my ...	Eu quero contactar com ...	e·oo ke·roo kong·tak·taar kong ...
consulate	o meu consulado	oo me·oo kong·soo·laa·doo
embassy	a minha embaixada	a mee·nya eng·bai·shaa·da

health

medical needs

Where's the nearest ...?	Qual é ... mais perto?	kwaal e ... maish per·too
dentist	o dentista	oo deng·teesh·ta
doctor	o médico m	oo me·dee·koo
	a médica f	a me·dee·ka
hospital	o hospital	oo osh·pee·taal
(night) pharmacist	a farmácia (de serviço)	a far·maa·sya (de ser·vee·soo)

I need a doctor (who speaks English).
Eu preciso de um médico
(que fale inglês).

e·oo pre·see·zoo de oong me·dee·koo
(que faa·le eeng·glesh)

Could I see a female doctor?
Posso ser vista por uma médica?

po·soo ser veesh·ta poor oo·ma me·dee·ka

I've run out of my medication.
Os meus medicamentos
acabaram.

oosh me·oosh me·dee·ka·meng·toosh
a·ka·baa·rowng

symptoms, conditions & allergies

| I'm sick. | Estou doente. | shtoh doo·eng·te |
| It hurts here. | Dói-me aqui. | doy·me a·kee |

I have (a) ...	Eu tenho ...	e·oo ta·nyoo ...
asthma	asma	ash·ma
bronchitis	bronquite	brong·kee·te
constipation	prisão de ventre	pree·zowng de veng·tre
cough	tosse	to·se
diarrhoea	diarreia	dee·a·rray·a
fever	febre	fe·bre
headache	dor de cabeça	dor de ka·be·sa
heart condition	problemas cardíacos	proo·ble·mash kar·dee·a·koosh
nausea	náusea	now·zee·a
pain	dor	dor
sore throat	dores de garganta	do·resh de gar·gang·ta
toothache	uma dor de dentes	oo·ma dor de deng·tesh

I'm allergic to ...	Eu sou alérgico/a a ... m/f	e·oo soh a·ler·zhee·koo/a a ...
antibiotics	antibióticos	ang·tee·bee·o·tee·koosh
anti-inflammatories	anti-inflamatórios	ang·tee·eeng·fla·ma·to·ryoosh
aspirin	aspirina	ash·pee·ree·na
bees	abelhas	a·be·lyash
codeine	codeína	ko·de·ee·na
penicillin	penicilina	pe·nee·see·lee·na

antiseptic	antiséptico m	ang·tee·se·tee·koo
bandage	ligadura f	lee·ga·doo·ra
condoms	preservativos m pl	pre·zer·va·tee·voosh
contraceptives	contraceptivos m pl	kong·tra·se·tee·voosh
diarrhoea medicine	remédio para diarreia m	re·me·dyo pa·ra dee·a·rray·a
insect repellent	repelente m	rre·pe·leng·te
laxatives	laxantes m pl	la·shang·tesh
painkillers	comprimidos para as dores m pl	kong·pree·mee·doosh pa·ra ash do·resh
rehydration salts	sais rehidratantes m pl	saish rre·ee·dra·tang·tesh
sleeping tablets	pílulas para dormir f pl	pee·loo·laash pa·ra door·meer

english–portuguese dictionary

Portuguese nouns and adjectives in this dictionary have their gender indicated with ⓜ (masculine) and ⓕ (feminine). If it's a plural noun, you'll also see pl. Words are also marked as v (verb), n (noun), a (adjective), pl (plural), sg (singular), inf (informal) and pol (polite) where necessary.

A

accident *acidente* ⓜ a-see-*deng*-te
accommodation *hospedagem* ⓕ osh-pe-*daa*-zheng
adaptor *adaptador* ⓜ a-da-pe-ta-*dor*
address *endereço* ⓜ eng-de-re-*soo*
after *depois* de-*poysh*
air conditioned *com ar condicionado* kong aar kong-dee-syoo-*naa*-doo
airplane *avião* ⓜ a-vee-*owng*
airport *aeroporto* ⓜ a-e-ro-*por*-too
alcohol *álcool* ⓜ al-ko-ol
all *a todo/a* ⓜ/ⓕ to-doo/a
allergy *alergia* ⓕ a-ler-*zhee*-a
ambulance *ambulância* ⓕ ang-boo-*lang*-sya
and *e* e
ankle *tornozelo* ⓜ toor-noo-*ze*-loo
arm *braço* ⓜ *braa*-soo
ashtray *cinzeiro* ⓜ seeng-*zay*-roo
ATM *caixa automático* ⓜ *kai*-sha ow-too-*maa*-tee-koo

B

baby *bebé* ⓜ & ⓕ be-*be*
back (body) *costas* ⓕ pl *kosh*-tash
backpack *mochila* ⓕ moo-*shee*-la
bad *mau/má* ⓜ/ⓕ *ma*-oo/*maa*
bag *saco* ⓜ *saa*-koo
baggage claim *balcão de bagagens* ⓜ bal-*kowng* de ba-*gaa*-zhengsh
bank *banco* ⓜ *bang*-koo
bar *bar* ⓜ baar
bathroom *casa de banho* ⓕ *kaa*-za de *ba*-nyoo
battery *pilha* ⓕ *pee*-lya
beautiful *bonito/a* ⓜ/ⓕ boo-*nee*-too/a
bed *cama* ⓕ *ka*-ma
beer *cerveja* ⓕ ser-*ve*-zha
before *antes* *ang*-tesh
behind *atrás* a-*traash*
bicycle *bicicleta* ⓕ bee-see-*kle*-ta
big *grande* ⓜ & ⓕ *grang*-de

bill *conta* ⓕ *kong*-ta
black *preto/a* ⓜ/ⓕ *pre*-too/a
blanket *cobertor* ⓜ koo-ber-*tor*
blood group *grupo sanguíneo* ⓜ *groo*-poo sang-*gwee*-nee-oo
blue *azul* a-*zool*
boat *barco* ⓜ *baar*-koo
book (make a reservation) v *reservar* rre-zer-*vaar*
bottle *garrafa* ⓕ ga-*rraa*-fa
bottle opener *saca-rolhas* ⓕ *saa*-ka-rro-lyash
boy *menino* ⓜ me-*nee*-noo
brake (car) *travão* ⓜ tra-*vowng*
breakfast *pequeno almoço* ⓜ pe-*ke*-noo aal-*mo*-soo
broken (faulty) *defeituoso/a* ⓜ/ⓕ de-fay-too-o-*zoo*/a
bus *autocarro* ⓜ ow-to-*kaa*-roo
business *negócios* ⓜ pl ne-*go*-syoosh
buy *comprar* kong-*praar*

C

café *café* ⓜ ka-*fe*
camera *máquina fotográfica* ⓕ *maa*-kee-na foo-too-*graa*-fee-ka
camp site *parque de campismo* ⓜ *paar*-ke de kang-*peezh*-moo
cancel *cancelar* kang-se-*laar*
can opener *abre latas* ⓕ *aa*-bre *laa*-tash
car *carro* ⓜ *kaa*-rroo
cash *dinheiro* ⓜ dee-*nyay*-roo
cash (a cheque) v *levantar (um cheque)* le-vang-*taar* (oong she-ke)
cell phone *telemóvel* ⓜ te-le-*mo*-vel
centre *centro* ⓜ *seng*-troo
change (money) v *trocar* troo-*kaar*
cheap *barato/a* ba-*raa*-too/a
check (bill) *conta* ⓕ *kong*-ta
check-in *check-in* ⓜ shek-*eeng*
chest *peito* ⓜ *pay*-too
child *criança* ⓜ & ⓕ kree-*ang*-sa
cigarette *cigarro* ⓜ see-*gaa*-rroo
city *cidade* ⓕ see-*daa*-de
clean a *limpo/a* ⓜ/ⓕ *leeng*-poo/a

closed *fechado/a* ⓜ/ⓕ fe-*shaa*-doo/a
coffee *café* ⓜ ka-*fe*
coins *moedas* ⓕ pl moo-e-dash
cold a *frio/a* ⓜ/ⓕ *free*-oo/a
collect call *ligação a cobrar* ⓕ lee-ga-*sowng* a koo-*braar*
come *vir* veer
computer *computador* ⓜ kong-poo-ta-*dor*
condom *preservativo* ⓜ pre-zer-va-*tee*-voo
contact lenses *lentes de contacto* ⓜ pl
   leng-tesh de kong-*taak*-too
cook v *cozinhar* koo-zee-*nyaar*
cost *preço* ⓜ *pre*-soo
credit card *cartão de crédito* ⓜ kar-*towng* de *kre*-dee-too
cup *chávena* ⓕ *shaa*-ve-na
currency exchange *câmbio* ⓜ *kang*-byoo
customs (immigration) *alfândega* ⓕ aal-*fang*-de-ga

D

dangerous *perigoso/a* ⓜ/ⓕ pe-ree-*go*-zoo/a
date (time) *data* ⓕ *daa*-ta
day *dia* ⓜ *dee*-a
delay n *atraso* a-*traa*-zoo
dentist *dentista* ⓜ&ⓕ deng-*teesh*-ta
depart *partir* par-*teer*
diaper *fralda* ⓕ *fraal*-da
dictionary *dicionário* ⓜ dee-syoo-*naa*-ryoo
dinner *jantar* ⓜ zhang-*taar*
direct *directo/a* ⓜ/ⓕ dee-*re*-too/a
dirty *sujo/a* ⓜ/ⓕ *soo*-zhoo/a
disabled *deficiente* de-fee-see-*eng*-te
discount *desconto* ⓜ desh-*kong*-too
doctor *médico/a* ⓜ/ⓕ *me*-dee-koo/a
double bed *cama de casal* ⓕ *ka*-ma de ka-*zaal*
double room *quarto de casal* ⓜ *kwaar*-too de ka-*zaal*
drink *bebida* ⓕ be-*bee*-da
drive v *conduzir* kong-doo-*zeer*
drivers licence *carta de condução* ⓕ
   kaar-ta de kong-doo-*sowng*
drugs (illicit) *droga* ⓕ *dro*-ga
dummy (pacifier) *chupeta* ⓕ shoo-*pe*-ta

E

ear *orelha* ⓕ o-*re*-lya
east *leste* *lesh*-te
eat *comer* koo-*mer*
economy class *classe económica* ⓕ
   klaa-se ee-koo-*no*-mee-ka
electricity *electricidade* ⓕ ee-le-tree-see-*daa*-de

elevator *elevador* ⓜ ee-le-va-*dor*
email *email* ⓜ ee-*mayl*
embassy *embaixada* ⓕ eng-bai-*shaa*-da
emergency *emergência* ⓕ ee-mer-*zheng*-sya
English (language) *inglês* ⓜ eeng-*glesh*
entrance *entrada* ⓕ eng-*traa*-da
evening *noite* ⓕ *noy*-te
exchange rate *taxa de câmbio* ⓕ *taa*-sha de *kang*-byoo
exit *saída* ⓕ saa-*ee*-da
expensive *caro/a* ⓜ/ⓕ *kaa*-roo/a
express mail *correio azul* ⓜ koo-*rray*-oo a-*zool*
eye *olho* ⓜ *o*-lyoo

F

far *longe* *long*-zhe
fast *rápido/a* ⓜ/ⓕ *rraa*-pee-doo/a
father *pai* ⓜ pai
film (camera) *filme* ⓜ *feel*-me
finger *dedo* ⓜ *de*-doo
first-aid kit *estojo de primeiros socorros* ⓜ
   shto-zhoo de pree-*may*-roosh so-ko-*rroosh*
first class *primeira classe* ⓕ pree-*may*-ra *klaa*-se
fish *peixe* ⓜ *pay*-she
food *comida* ⓕ koo-*mee*-da
foot *pé* ⓜ pe
fork *garfo* ⓜ *gaar*-foo
free (of charge) ⓐ *grátis* *graa*-teesh
friend *amigo/a* ⓜ/ⓕ a-*mee*-goo/a
fruit *fruta* ⓕ *froo*-ta
full *cheio/a* ⓜ/ⓕ *shay*-oo/a
funny *engraçado/a* ⓜ/ⓕ eng-gra-*saa*-doo/a

G

gift *presente* ⓜ pre-*zeng*-te
girl *menina* ⓕ me-*nee*-na
glass (drinking) *copo* ⓜ *ko*-poo
glasses *óculos* ⓜ pl o-koo-*loosh*
go *ir* eer
good *bom/boa* ⓜ/ⓕ *bong*/*bo*-a
green *verde* *ver*-de
guide n *guia* ⓜ *gee*-a

H

half *metade* ⓕ me-*taa*-de
hand *mão* ⓕ mowng
handbag *mala de mão* ⓕ *maa*-la de mowng
happy *feliz* ⓜ&ⓕ fe-*leesh*

D

english–portuguese

285

have *ter* ter
he *ele* e-le
head *cabeça* ① ka-*be*-sa
heart *coração* ⓜ koo-ra-*sowng*
heat *calor* ⓜ ka-*lor*
heavy *pesado/a* ⓜ/① pe-*zaa*-doo/a
help v *ajudar* a-zhoo-*daar*
here *aqui* a-*kee*
high *alto/a* ⓜ/① *aal*-too/a
highway *autoestrada* ① ow-to-*shtraa*-da
hike v *caminhar* ka-mee-*nyaar*
holiday *feriado* ⓜ fe-ree-*aa*-doo
homosexual n&a *homosexual* ⓜ&①
    o-mo-sek-soo-*aal*
hospital *hospital* ⓜ osh-pee-*taal*
hot *quente* *keng*-te
hotel *hotel* ⓜ o-*tel*
hungry *faminto/a* ⓜ/① fa-*meeng*-too/a
husband *marido* ⓜ ma-*ree*-doo

I

I *eu* e-*oo*
identification (card) *bilhete de identidade* ⓜ
    bee-*lye*-te de ee-deng-tee-*daa*-de
ill *doente* ⓜ&① doo-*eng*-te
important *importante* ⓜ&① eeng-por-*tang*-te
included/a *incluído/a* ⓜ/① eeng-kloo-ee-doo/a
injury *ferimento* ⓜ fe-ree-*meng*-too
insurance *seguro* ⓜ se-*goo*-roo
Internet *internet* ① eeng-ter-*net*
interpreter *intérprete* ⓜ&① eeng-*ter*-pre-te

J

jewellery *ourivesaria* ① oh-ree-ve-za-*ree*-a
job *emprego* ⓜ eng-*pre*-goo

K

key *chave* ① *shaa*-ve
kilogram *quilograma* ⓜ kee-loo-*graa*-ma
kitchen *cozinha* ① koo-*zee*-nya
knife *faca* ① *faa*-ka

L

laundry (place) *lavandaria* ① la-vang-da-*ree*-a
lawyer *advogado/a* ⓜ/① a-de-voo-*gaa*-doo/a
left (direction) *esquerda* ① *shker*-da

left-luggage office *perdidos e achados* ⓜ pl
    per-*dee*-doosh ee aa-*shaa*-doosh
leg *perna* ① *per*-na
lesbian n&a *lésbica* ① *lezh*-bee-ka
less *menos* me-*noosh*
letter (mail) *carta* ① *kaar*-ta
lift (elevator) *elevador* ① ee-le-va-*dor*
light *luz* ① loosh
like v *gostar* goosh-*taar*
lock *tranca* ① *trang*-ka
long *longo/a* ⓜ/① *long*-goo/a
lost *perdido/a* ⓜ/① per-*dee*-doo/a
lost-property office *gabinete de perdidos e achados* ⓜ
    gaa-bee-*ne*-te de per-*dee*-doosh ee a-*shaa*-doosh
love v *amar* a-*maar*
luggage *bagagem* ① ba-*gaa*-zheng
lunch *almoço* ⓜ aal-*mo*-soo

M

mail *correio* ⓜ koo-*rray*-oo
man *homem* ⓜ *o*-meng
map *mapa* ⓜ *maa*-pa
market *mercado* ⓜ mer-*kaa*-doo
matches *fósforos* ⓜ pl fosh-foo-roosh
meat *carne* ① *kaar*-ne
medicine *medicamentos* ⓜ pl me-dee-ka-*meng*-toosh
menu *ementa* ① ee-*meng*-ta
message *mensagem* ① meng-*saa*-zheng
milk *leite* ① *lay*-te
minute *minuto* ⓜ mee-*noo*-too
mobile phone *telemóvel* ⓜ te-le-*mo*-vel
money *dinheiro* ⓜ dee-*nyay*-roo
month *mês* mesh
morning *manhã* ① ma-*nyang*
mother *mãe* ① maing
motorcycle *mota* ① *mo*-ta
motorway *autoestrada* ① ow-to-*shtraa*-da
mouth *boca* ① *bo*-ka
music *música* ① *moo*-zee-ka

N

name *nome* ⓜ *no*-me
napkin *guardanapo* ⓜ gwar-da-*naa*-poo
nappy *fralda* ① *fraal*-da
near *perto* per-too
neck *pescoço* ⓜ pesh-*ko*-soo
new *novo/a* ⓜ/① *no*-voo/a
news *notícias* ① pl noo-tee-syash

ewspaper *jornal* ⓜ zhor-*naal*
night *noite* ⓕ *noy*-te
no *não* nowng
noisy *barulhento/a* ⓜ/ⓕ ba-roo-*lyeng*-too/a
nonsmoking *não-fumador* nowng-foo-ma-*dor*
north *norte* *nor*-te
nose *nariz* ⓜ na-*reesh*
now *agora* a-*go*-ra
number *número* ⓜ *noo*-me-roo

O

oil (engine) *petróleo* ⓜ pe-*tro*-lyoo
old *velho/a* ⓜ/ⓕ *ve*-lyoo/a
one-way ticket *bilhete de ida* ⓜ bee-*lye*-te de *ee*-da
open a *aberto/a* ⓜ/ⓕ a-*ber*-too/a
outside *fora* *fo*-ra

P

package *embrulho* ⓜ eng-*broo*-lyoo
paper *papel* ⓜ pa-*pel*
park (car) v *estacionar* shta-syoo-*naar*
passport *passaporte* ⓜ paa-sa-*por*-te
pay *pagar* pa-*gaar*
pen *caneta* ⓕ ka-*ne*-ta
petrol *gasolina* ⓕ ga-zoo-*lee*-na
pharmacy *farmácia* ⓕ far-*maa*-sya
phonecard *cartão telefónico* ⓜ
  kar-*towng* te-le-*fo*-nee-koo
photo *fotografia* ⓕ foo-too-gra-*fee*-a
plate *prato* ⓜ *praa*-too
police *polícia* ⓕ poo-*lee*-sya
Portugal *Portugal* ⓜ poor-too-*gaal*
Portuguese (language) *português* ⓜ poor-too-*gesh*
postcard *postal* ⓜ poosh-*taal*
post office *correio* ⓜ koo-*rray*-oo
pregnant *grávida* ⓕ *graa*-vee-da
price *preço* ⓜ *pre*-soo

Q

quiet *calado/a* ⓜ/ⓕ ka-*laa*-doo/a

R

rain *chuva* ⓕ *shoo*-va
razor *gilete* ⓕ zhee-*le*-te
receipt *recibo* ⓜ rre-*see*-boo
red *vermelho/a* ⓜ/ⓕ ver-*me*-lyoo/a

refund *reembolso* ⓜ rre-eng-*bol*-soo
registered mail *correio registado* ⓜ
  koo-*rray*-oo re-zhee-*shtaa*-doo
rent v *alugar* a-loo-*gaar*
repair v *consertar* kong-ser-*taar*
reservation *reserva* ⓕ rre-*zer*-va
restaurant *restaurante* ⓜ rresh-tow-*rang*-te
return v *voltar* vol-*taar*
return ticket *bilhete de ida e volta* ⓜ
  bee-*lye*-te de *ee*-da ee *vol*-ta
right (direction) *direita* ⓕ dee-*ray*-ta
road *estrada* ⓕ *shtraa*-da
room *quarto* ⓜ *kwaar*-too

S

safe a *seguro/a* ⓜ/ⓕ se-*goo*-roo/a
sanitary napkin *penso higiénico* ⓜ
  peng-soo ee-zhee-e-nee-koo
seat *assento* ⓜ a-*seng*-too
send *enviar* eng-vee-*aar*
service station *posto de gasolina* ⓜ
  posh-too de ga-zoo-*lee*-na
sex *sexo* ⓜ *sek*-soo
shampoo *champô* ⓜ shang-*poo*
share (a dorm) *partilhar* par-tee-*lyaar*
shaving cream *creme de barbear* ⓜ
  kre-me de bar-bee-*aar*
she *ela* *e*-la
sheet (bed) *lençol* ⓜ leng-*sol*
shirt *camisa* ⓕ ka-*mee*-za
shoes *sapatos* ⓜ pl sa-*paa*-toosh
shop n *loja* ⓕ *lo*-zha
short *curto/a* ⓜ/ⓕ *koor*-too/a
shower n *chuveiro* ⓜ shoo-*vay*-roo
single room *quarto de solteiro* ⓜ
  kwaar-too de sol-*tay*-roo
skin *pele* ⓕ *pe*-le
skirt *saia* ⓕ *sai*-a
sleep v *dormir* door-*meer*
slowly *vagarosamente* va-ga-ro-za-*meng*-te
small *pequeno/a* ⓜ/ⓕ pe-*ke*-noo/a
smoke (cigarettes) v *fumar* foo-*maar*
soap *sabonete* ⓜ sa-boo-*ne*-te
some *uns/umas* ⓜ/ⓕ pl oongsh/*oo*-mash
soon *em breve* eng *bre*-ve
south *sul* sool
souvenir shop *loja de lembranças* ⓕ
  lo-zha de leng-*brang*-sash
speak *falar* fa-*laar*

spoon *colher* ① koo-*lyer*
stamp *selo* ⑩ *se*-loo
stand-by ticket *bilhete sem garantia* ⑩
bee-*lye*-te seng ga-rang-*tee*-a
station (train) *estação* ① shta-*sowng*
stomach *estômago* ⑩ shto-ma-goo
stop v *parar* pa-*raar*
stop (bus) *paragem* ① pa-*raa*-zheng
street *rua* ① *rroo*-a
student *estudante* ⑩&① shtoo-*dang*-te
sun *sol* ⑩ sol
sunscreen *protecção anti-solar* ①
proo-te-*sowng* ang-tee-soo-*laar*
swim v *nadar* na-*daar*

T

tampons *tampões* ⑩ pl tang-*powngsh*
taxi *táxi* ⑩ *taak*-see
teaspoon *colher de chá* ① koo-*lyer* de shaa
teeth *dentes* ⑩ pl *deng*-tesh
telephone *telefone* ⑩ te-le-*fo*-ne
television *televisão* ① te-le-vee-*zowng*
temperature (weather) *temperatura* ①
teng-pe-ra-*too*-ra
tent *tenda* ① *teng*-da
that (one) *aquele/a* ⑩/① a-*ke*-le/a
they *eles/elas* ⑩/① *e*-lesh/e-lash
thirsty *sedento/a* ⑩/① se-*deng*-too/a
this (one) *este/a* ⑩/① *esh*-te/a
throat *garganta* ① gar-*gang*-ta
ticket *bilhete* ⑩ bee-*lye*-te
time *tempo* ⑩ *teng*-poo
tired *cansado/a* ⑩/① kang-*saa*-doo/a
tissues *lenços de papel* ⑩ pl *leng*-soosh de pa-*pel*
today *hoje* o-*zhe*
toilet *casa de banho* ① *kaa*-za de ba-nyoo
tomorrow *amanhã* aa-ma-*nyang*
tonight *hoje à noite* o-zhe aa *noy*-te
toothbrush *escova de dentes* ① shko-va de *deng*-tesh
toothpaste *pasta de dentes* ① *paash*-ta de *deng*-tesh
torch (flashlight) *lanterna eléctrica* ①
lang-*ter*-na ee-*le*-tree-ka
tour n *excursão* ① shkoor-*sowng*
tourist office *escritório de turismo* ⑩
shkree-*to*-ryoo de too-*reezh*-moo
towel *toalha* ① *twaa*-lya
train *comboio* ⑩ kong-*boy*-oo
translate *traduzir* tra-doo-*zeer*

travel agency *agência de viagens* ①
a-*zheng*-sya de vee-*aa*-zhengsh
travellers cheque *travellers cheque* ⑩ *tra*-ve-ler shek
trousers *calças* ① pl *kaal*-sash
twin beds *camas gémeas* ① pl *ka*-mash zhe-me-ash
tyre *pneu* ⑩ pe-*ne*-oo

U

underwear *roupa interior* ① rroh-pa eeng-te-ree-*or*
urgent *urgente* ⑩&① oor-*zheng*-te

V

vacant *vago/a* ⑩/① *vaa*-goo/a
vacation *férias* ① pl *fe*-ree-ash
vegetable *legume* ⑩ le-*goo*-me
vegetarian a *vegetariano/a* ⑩/① ve-zhe-ta-ree-*a*-noo/a
visa *visto* ⑩ *veesh*-too

W

waiter *criado/a de mesa* ⑩/① kree-*aa*-doo/a de *me*-za
walk v *caminhar* ka-mee-*nyaar*
wallet *carteira* ① kar-*tay*-ra
warm a *morno/a* ⑩/① *mor*-noo/a
wash (something) *lavar* la-*vaar*
watch *relógio* ⑩ rre-*lo*-zhyoo
water *água* ① *aa*-gwa
we *nós* nosh
weekend *fim-de-semana* ⑩ feeng-de-se-*ma*-na
west *oeste* o-*esh*-te
wheelchair *cadeira de rodas* ① ka-*day*-ra de *rro*-dash
when *quando* *kwang*-doo
where *onde* ong-de
white *branca/a* ⑩/① *brang*-koo/a
who *quem* keng
why *porquê* poor-*ke*
wife *esposa* ① *shpo*-za
window *janela* ① zha-*ne*-la
wine *vinho* ⑩ *vee*-nyoo
with *com* kong
without *sem* seng
woman *mulher* ① moo-*lyer*
write *escrever* shkre-*ver*

Y

yellow *amarelo/a* ⑩/① a-ma-re-*loo*/a
yes *sim* seeng
yesterday *ontem* ong-teng
you inf sg/pl *tu/vocês* too/vo-*sesh*
you pol sg/pl *você/vás* vo-se/vosh

Slovene

slovene alphabet

A a a	B b buh	C c tsuh	Č č chuh	D d duh
E e e	F f fuh	G g guh	H h huh	I i ee
J j yuh	K k kuh	L l luh	M m muh	N n nuh
O o o	P p puh	R r ruh	S s suh	Š š shuh
T t tuh	U u oo	V v vuh	Z z zuh	Ž ž zhuh

slovene

introduction

The language spoken by about 2 million people 'on the sunny side of the Alps', Slovene (*slovenščina* slo-*vensh*-chee-na) is sandwiched between German, Italian and Hungarian, against the backdrop of its wider South Slavic family. Its distinctive geographical position parallels its unique evolution, beginning with Slav settlement in this corner of Europe back in the 6th century, then becoming the official language of Slovenia – first as a part of Yugoslavia and since 1991 an independent republic.

Although Croatian and Serbian are its closest relatives within the South Slavic group, Slovene is nevertheless much closer to Croatia's northwestern and coastal dialects. It also shares some features with the more distant West Slavic languages (through contact with a dialect of Slovak, from which it was later separated by the arrival of the Hungarians to Central Europe in the 9th century). Unlike any other modern Slavic language, it has preserved the archaic Indo-European dual grammatical form, which means, for example, that instead of *pivo pee*-vo (a beer) or *piva pee*-va (beers), you and a friend could simply order *pivi pee*-vee (two beers).

German, Italian and Hungarian words entered Slovene during the centuries of foreign rule (in the Austro-Hungarian Empire or under the control of Venice), as these were the languages of the elite, while the common people spoke one of the Slovene dialects. Croatian and Serbian influence on Slovene was particularly significant during the 20th century when all three countries coexisted within the Yugoslav state.

For a language with a relatively small number of speakers, Slovene abounds in regional variations – eight major dialect groups have been identified, which are further divided into fifty or so regional dialects. Some of these cover the neighbouring areas of Austria, Italy and Hungary. The modern literary language is based largely on the central dialects and was shaped through a gradual process that lasted from the 16th to the 19th century.

Slovenia has been called 'a nation of poets', and what better way to get immersed in that spirit than to plunge into this beautiful language first? While you're soaking up the atmosphere of the capital, Ljubljana (whose central square is graced with a monument in honour of the nation's greatest poet, France Prešeren), remember that its name almost equals 'beloved' (*ljubljena lyoob*-lye-na) in Slovene!

pronunciation

vowel sounds

The vowels in Slovene can be pronounced differently, depending on whether they're stressed or unstressed, long or short. Don't worry about these distinctions though, as you shouldn't have too much trouble being understood if you follow our coloured pronunciation guides. Note that we've used the symbols oh and ow to help you pronounce vowels followed by the letters *l* and *v* in written Slovene – when they appear at the end of a syllable, these combinations sometimes produce a sound similar to the 'w' in English.

symbol	english equivalent	slovene example	transliteration
a	father	*dan*	dan
ai	aisle	*srajca*	srai·tsa
e	bet	*center*	tsen·ter
ee	see	*riba*	ree·ba
o	pot	*oče*	o·che
oh	oh	*pol, nov*	poh, noh
oo	zoo	*jug*	yoog
ow	how	*ostal, prav*	os·tow, prow
uh	ago	*pes*	puhs

word stress

Slovene has free stress, which means there's no general rule regarding which syllable the stress falls on – it simply has to be learned. You'll be fine if you just follow our coloured pronunciation guides, in which the stressed syllable is always in italics.

consonant sounds

Most Slovene consonant sounds are pronounced more or less as they are in English. Don't be intimidated by the vowel-less words such as *trg* tuhrg (square) or *vrt* vuhrt (garden) – we've put a slight 'uh' sound before the *r*, which serves as a semi-vowel between the two other consonants.

symbol	english equivalent	slovene example	transliteration
b	bed	*brat*	brat
ch	cheat	*hči*	hchee
d	dog	*datum*	da·toom
f	fat	*telefon*	te·le·fon
g	go	*grad*	grad
h	hat	*hvala*	hva·la
k	kit	*karta*	kar·ta
l	lot	*ulica*	oo·lee·tsa
m	man	*mož*	mozh
n	not	*naslov*	nas·loh
p	pet	*pošta*	po·shta
r	run (rolled)	*brez*	brez
s	sun	*sin*	seen
sh	shot	*tuš*	toosh
t	top	*sto*	sto
ts	hats	*cesta*	tse·sta
v	very	*vlak*	vlak
y	yes	*jesen*	ye·sen
z	zero	*zima*	zee·ma
zh	pleasure	*žena*	zhe·na
'	a slight y sound	*kašelj, manj*	ka·shel', man'

basics

language difficulties

Do you speak English?
Ali govorite angleško?
a·lee go·vo·*ree*·te ang·*lesh*·ko

Do you understand?
Ali razumete?
a·lee ra·*zoo*·me·te

I (don't) understand.
(Ne) Razumem.
(ne) ra·*zoo*·mem

What does (*danes*) mean?
Kaj pomeni (danes)?
kai po·*me*·nee (*da*·nes)

Could you repeat that?
Lahko ponovite?
lah·ko po·no·*vee*·te

How do you ...?
Kako se ...?
ka·*ko* se ...

  pronounce this word
izgovori to besedo
eez·go·vo·*ree* to be·*se*·do

  write (*hvala*)
napiše (hvala)
na·*pee*·she (*hva*·la)

Could you please ...?
Prosim ...
pro·seem ...

  speak more slowly
govorite počasneje
go·vo·*ree*·te po·cha·*sne*·ye

  write it down
napišite
na·*pee*·shee·te

essentials

Yes.	*Da.*	da
No.	*Ne.*	ne
Please.	*Prosim.*	*pro*·seem
Thank you (very much).	*Hvala (lepa).*	*hva*·la (*le*·pa)
You're welcome.	*Ni za kaj.*	nee za kai
Excuse me.	*Dovolite.*	do·vo·*lee*·te
Sorry.	*Oprostite.*	op·ros·*tee*·te

numbers

0	nula	*noo*-la	16	šestnajst	*shest*-naist
1	en/ena m/f	en/*e*-na	17	sedemnajst	se-*dem*-naist
2	dva/dve m/f	dva/dve	18	osemnajst	*o*-sem-naist
3	trije/tri m/f	*tree*-ye/tree	19	devetnajst	de-*vet*-naist
4	štirje m	*shtee*-rye	20	dvajset	*dvai*-set
	štiri f	*shtee*-ree	21	enaindvajset	*e*-na-een-*dvai*-set
5	pet	pet	22	dvaindvajset	*dva*-een-*dvai*-set
6	šest	shest	30	trideset	*tree*-de-set
7	sedem	se-*dem*	40	štirideset	*shtee*-ree-de-set
8	osem	*o*-sem		deset	de-set
9	devet	de-*vet*	50	petdeset	*pet*-de-set
10	deset	de-set	60	šestdeset	*shest*-de-set
11	enajst	e-*naist*	70	sedemdeset	se-*dem*-de-set
12	dvanajst	*dva*-naist	80	osemdeset	*o*-sem-de-set
13	trinajst	*tree*-naist	90	devetdeset	de-*vet*-de-set
14	štirinajst	*shtee*-ree-naist	100	sto	sto
15	petnajst	*pet*-naist	1000	tisoč	*tee*-soch

time & dates

What time is it?	Koliko je ura?	ko-*lee*-ko ye *oo*-ra
It's one o'clock.	Ura je ena.	*oo*-ra ye *e*-na
It's (10) o'clock.	Ura je (deset).	*oo*-ra ye (de-*set*)
Quarter past (one).	Četrt čez (ena).	che-*tuhrt* chez (*e*-na)
Half past (one).	Pol (dveh). (lit: half two)	pol (dveh)
Quarter to (one).	Petnajst do (enih).	*pet*-naist do (*e*-neeh)
At what time ...?	Ob kateri uri ...?	ob ka-*te*-ree *oo*-ree ...
At ...	Ob ...	ob ...
am	dopoldne	do-*poh*-dne
pm	popoldne	po-*poh*-dne
Monday	ponedeljek	po-ne-*del*-yek
Tuesday	torek	*to*-rek
Wednesday	sreda	*sre*-da
Thursday	četrtek	che-*tuhr*-tek
Friday	petek	*pe*-tek
Saturday	sobota	so-*bo*-ta
Sunday	nedelja	ne-*del*-ya

January	*januar*	*ya*·noo·ar
February	*februar*	*feb*·roo·ar
March	*marec*	*ma*·rets
April	*april*	ap·*reel*
May	*maj*	mai
June	*junij*	*yoo*·neey
July	*julij*	*yoo*·leey
August	*avgust*	av·*goost*
September	*september*	sep·*tem*·ber
October	*oktober*	ok·*to*·ber
November	*november*	no·*vem*·ber
December	*december*	de·*tsem*·ber

What date is it today?
   Katerega smo danes?   ka·*te*·re·ga smo *da*·nes

It's (18 October).
   Smo (osemnajstega oktobra).   smo (o·sem·*nai*·ste·ga) ok·*tob*·ra

| since (May) | *od (maja)* | od (*ma*·ya) |
| until (June) | *do (junija)* | do (*yoo*·nee·ya) |

last ...
night	*prejšnji večer*	*preysh*·nyee ve·*cher*
week	*prejšnji teden*	*preysh*·nyee *te*·den
month	*prejšnji mesec*	*preysh*·nyee *me*·sets
year	*prejšnje leto*	*preysh*·nye *le*·to

next ...
week	*naslednji teden*	nas·*led*·nyee *te*·den
month	*naslednji mesec*	nas·*led*·nyee *me*·sets
year	*naslednje leto*	nas·*led*·nye *le*·to

yesterday/tomorrow ...
včeraj/jutri ...	vche·rai/yoot·ree ...
morning	*zjutraj*	*zyoot*·rai
afternoon	*popoldne*	po·*poh*·dne
evening	*zvečer*	zve·*cher*

weather

What's the weather like?	*Kakšno je vreme?*	kak·shno ye vre·me
It's raining/snowing.	*Dežuje/Sneži.*	de·zhoo·ye/sne·zhee

It's	*... je.*	... ye
cloudy	*Oblačno*	ob·lach·no
cold	*Mrzlo*	muhr·zlo
hot	*Vroče*	vro·che
sunny	*Sončno*	sonch·no
warm	*Toplo*	top·lo
windy	*Vetrovno*	vet·roh·no

spring	*pomlad* f	pom·lad
summer	*poletje* n	po·let·ye
autumn	*jesen* f	ye·sen
winter	*zima* f	zee·ma

border crossing

I'm here ...	*Tu sem ...*	too sem ...
on business	*poslovno*	pos·lov·no
on holiday	*na počitnicah*	na po·cheet·nee·tsah

I'm here for ...	*Ostanem ...*	os·ta·nem ...
(10) days	*(deset) dni*	(de·set) dnee
(two) months	*(dva) meseca*	(dva) me·se·tsa
(three) weeks	*(tri) tedne*	(tree) ted·ne

I'm going to ...
Namenjen/Namenjena sem v ... m/f na·men·yen/na·men·ye·na sem v ...

I'm staying at the (Slon).
Stanujem v (Slonu). sta·noo·yem v (slo·noo)

I have nothing to declare.
Ničesar nimam za prijaviti. nee·che·sar nee·mam za pree·ya·vee·tee

I have something to declare.
Nekaj imam za prijaviti. ne·kai ee·mam za pree·ya·vee·tee

That's mine.
To je moje. to ye mo·ye

That's not mine.
To ni moje. to nee mo·ye

transport

tickets & luggage

Where can I buy a ticket?
Kje lahko kupim vozovnico?   kye lah·*ko* koo·peem vo·*zov*·nee·tso

Do I need to book a seat?
Ali moram rezervirati sedež?   a·lee *mo*·ram re·zer·*vee*·ra·tee se·dezh

One ... ticket to (Koper), please.	*... vozovnico do (Kopra), prosim.*	... vo·*zov*·nee·tso do (*ko*·pra) *pro*·seem
one-way	*Enosmerno*	e·no·*smer*·no
return	*Povratno*	pov·*rat*·no

I'd like to ... my ticket, please.	*Želim ... vozovnico, prosim.*	zhe·*leem* ... vo·*zov*·nee·tso *pro*·seem
cancel	*preklicati*	prek·*lee*·tsa·tee
change	*zamenjati*	za·*men*·ya·tee
collect	*dvigniti*	*dveeg*·nee·tee
confirm	*potrditi*	po·tuhr·*dee*·tee

I'd like a ... seat, please.	*Želim ... sedež, prosim.*	zhe·*leem* ... se·dezh *pro*·seem
nonsmoking	*nekadilski*	ne·ka·*deel*·skee
smoking	*kadilski*	ka·*deel*·skee

How much is it?
Koliko stane?   ko·lee·ko *sta*·ne

Is there air conditioning?
Ali ima klimo?   a·lee ee·*ma* klee·mo

Is there a toilet?
Ali ima stranišče?   a·lee ee·*ma* stra·*neesh*·che

How long does the trip take?
Kako dolgo traja potovanje?   ka·ko *dol*·go *tra*·ya po·to·*van*·ye

Is it a direct route?
Je to direktna proga?   ye to dee·*rekt*·na *pro*·ga

I'd like a luggage locker.
Želim garderobno omarico.   zhe·*leem* gar·de·*rob*·no o·*ma*·ree·tso

My luggage has been ...	Moja prtljaga je ...	mo·ya puhrt·lya·ga ye ...
damaged	poškodovana	posh·ko·do·va·na
lost	izgubljena	eez·goob·lye·na
stolen	ukradena	oo·kra·de·na

getting around

Where does flight (AF 46) arrive/depart?
Kje pristane/odleti let — kye pree·sta·ne/od·le·tee let
številka (AF 46)? — shte·veel·ka (a fuh shtee·ree shest)

Where's (the) ...?	Kje je/so ...? sg/pl	kye ye/so ...
arrivals hall	prihodi pl	pree·ho·dee
departures hall	odhodi pl	od·ho·dee
duty-free shop	brezcarinska	brez·tsa·reen·ska
	trgovina sg	tuhr·go·vee·na
gate (12)	izhod (dvanajst) sg	eez·hod (dva·naist)

Is this the ... to (Venice)?	Je to ... za (Benetke)?	ye to ... za (be·net·ke)
boat	ladja	lad·ya
bus	avtobus	av·to·boos
plane	letalo	le·ta·lo
train	vlak	vlak

What time's the ... bus?	Kdaj odpelje ... avtobus?	kdai od·pel·ye ... av·to·boos
first	prvi	puhr·vee
last	zadnji	zad·nyee
next	naslednji	nas·led·nyee

At what time does it arrive/leave?
Kdaj prispe/odpelje? — kdai prees·pe/od·pel·ye

How long will it be delayed?
Koliko je zamujen? — ko·lee·ko ye za·moo·yen

What station is this?
Katera postaja je to? — ka·te·ra pos·ta·ya ye to

What stop is this?
Katero postajališče je to? — ka·te·ro pos·ta·ya·leesh·che ye to

What's the next station?
Katera je naslednja postaja? — ka·te·ra ye nas·led·nya pos·ta·ya

What's the next stop?
Katero je naslednje postajališče? — ka·te·ro ye nas·led·nye pos·ta·ya·leesh·che

Does it stop at (Postojna)?
Ali ustavi v (Postojni)? a·lee oos·*ta*·vee v (pos·*toy*·nee)

Please tell me when we get to (Kranj).
Prosim povejte mi, pro·seem po·*vey*·te mee
ko prispemo v (Kranj). ko prees·*pe*·mo v (kran)

How long do we stop here?
Kako dolgo stojimo tu? ka·ko dol·go sto·*yee*·mo too

Is this seat available?
Je ta sedež prost? ye ta se·dezh prost

That's my seat.
To je moj sedež. to ye moy se·dezh

I'd like a taxi ... | *Želim taksi ...* | zhe·*leem* tak·see ...
at (9am) | *ob (devetih* | ob (de·*ve*·teeh
 | *dopoldne)* | do·*poh*·dne)
now | *zdaj* | zdai
tomorrow | *jutri* | *yoot*·ree

Is this taxi available?
Je ta taksi prost? ye ta *tak*·see prost

How much is it to ...?
Koliko stane do ...? ko·lee·ko *sta*·ne do ...

Please put the meter on.
Prosim, vključite taksimeter. pro·seem vklyoo·chee·te tak·see·*me*·ter

Please take me to (this address).
Prosim, peljite me na (ta naslov). pro·seem pel·*yee*·te me na (ta nas·*loh*)

Please ... | *Prosim ...* | pro·seem ...
slow down | *vozite počasneje* | vo·*zee*·te po·chas·*ne*·ye
stop here | *ustavite tukaj* | oos·*ta*·vee·te *too*·kai
wait here | *počakajte tukaj* | po·*cha*·kai·te *too*·kai

car, motorbike & bicycle hire

I'd like to hire a ... | *Želim najeti ...* | zhe·*leem* na·ye·tee ...
bicycle | *kolo* | ko·*lo*
car | *avto* | *av*·to
motorbike | *motor* | mo·*tor*

with ...	s ...	s ...
a driver	šoferjem	sho·fer·yem
air conditioning	klimo	klee·mo
antifreeze	sredstvom proti	sreds·tvom pro·tee
	zmrzovanju	zmuhr·zo·van·yoo
snow chains	snežnimi	snezh·nee·mee
	verigami	ve·ree·ga·mee

How much for	Koliko stane najem	ko·lee·ko sta·ne na·yem
... hire?	na ...?	na ...
hourly	uro	oo·ro
daily	dan	dan
weekly	teden	te·den

air	zrak m	zrak
oil	olje n	ol·ye
petrol	bencin m	ben·tseen
tyres	gume f	goo·me

I need a mechanic.
Potrebujem mehanika.   pot·re·boo·yem me·ha·nee·ka

I've run out of petrol.
Zmanjkalo mi je bencina.   zman'·ka·lo mee ye ben·tsee·na

I have a flat tyre.
Počila mi je guma.   po·chee·la mee ye goo·ma

directions

Where's the ...?	Kje je ...?	kye ye ...
bank	banka	ban·ka
city centre	center mesta	tsen·ter mes·ta
hotel	hotel	ho·tel
market	tržnica	tuhrzh·nee·tsa
police station	policijska	po·lee·tseey·ska
	postaja	pos·ta·ya
post office	pošta	posh·ta
public toilet	javno stranišče	yav·no stra·neesh·che
tourist office	turistični	too·rees·teech·nee
	urad	oo·rad

Is this the road to (Ptuj)?
Pelje ta cesta do (Ptuja)?   *pel·ye ta tses·ta do (ptoo·ya)*

Can you show me (on the map)?
Mi lahko pokažete   mee *lah·ko* po·*ka·*zhe·te
(na zemljevidu)?   (na zem·lye·*vee·*doo)

What's the address?
Na katerem naslovu je?   na ka·*te·*rem nas·*lo·*voo ye

How far is it?
Kako daleč je?   ka·*ko da·*lech ye

How do I get there?
Kako pridem tja?   ka·*ko pree·*dem tya

Turn ...	*Zavijte ...*	za·*veey·*te ...
at the corner	*na vogalu*	na vo·*ga·*loo
at the traffic lights	*pri semaforju*	pree se·ma·*for·*yoo
left/right	*levo/desno*	*le·*vo/*des·*no

It's ...		
behind ...	*Za ...*	za ...
far away	*Daleč.*	*da·*lech
here	*Tukaj.*	*too·*kai
in front of ...	*Pred ...*	pred ...
left	*Levo.*	*le·*vo
near (to ...)	*Blizu ...*	*blee·*zoo ...
next to ...	*Poleg ...*	*po·*leg ...
on the corner	*Na vogalu.*	na vo·*ga·*loo
opposite ...	*Nasproti ...*	nas·*pro·*tee ...
right	*Desno.*	*des·*no
straight ahead	*Naravnost naprej.*	na·*rav·*nost na·*prey*
there	*Tam.*	tam

by bus	*z avtobusom*	z av·to·*boo·*som
by taxi	*s taksijem*	s tak·*see·*yem
by train	*z vlakom*	z vla·*kom*
on foot	*peš*	pesh

north	*sever*	*se·*ver
south	*jug*	yoog
east	*vzhod*	vzhod
west	*zahod*	za·*hod*

Vhod/Izhod	vhod/eez·hod	**Entrance/Exit**
Odprto/Zaprto	od·puhr·to/za·puhr·to	**Open/Closed**
Proste sobe	pros·te so·be	**Rooms Available**
Ni prostih mest	nee pros·teeh mest	**No Vacancies**
Informacije	een·for·ma·tsee·ye	**Information**
Policijska postaja	po·lee·tseey·ska pos·ta·ya	**Police Station**
Prepovedano	pre·po·ve·da·no	**Prohibited**
Stranišče	stra·neesh·che	**Toilets**
Moški	mosh·kee	**Men**
Ženske	zhen·ske	**Women**
Vroče/Mrzlo	vro·che/muhr·zlo	**Hot/Cold**

accommodation

finding accommodation

Where's a ...?	*Kje je ... ?*	kye ye ...
camping ground	*kamp*	kamp
guesthouse	*gostišče*	gos·teesh·che
hotel	*hotel*	ho·tel
youth hostel	*mladinski hotel*	mla·deen·skee ho·tel
Can you recommend a ... hotel?	*Mi lahko priporočite ... hotel?*	mee lah·ko pree·po·ro·chee·te ... ho·tel
cheap	*poceni*	po·tse·nee
good	*dober*	do·ber

Can you recommend a hotel nearby?
Mi lahko priporočite hotel v bližini?
mee lah·ko pree·po·ro·chee·te ho·tel oo blee·zhee·nee

I'd like to book a room, please.
Želim rezervirati sobo, prosim.
zhe·leem re·zer·vee·ra·tee so·bo pro·seem

I have a reservation.
Imam rezervacijo.
ee·mam re·zer·va·tsee·yo

My name's ...
Ime mi je ...
ee·me mee ye ...

Do you have a twin room?
Imate sobo z ločenima posteljama?   ee·*ma*·te *so*·bo z *lo*·che·nee·ma *pos*·tel·ya·ma

Do you have a ... room?   *Ali imate ... sobo?*   *a*·lee ee·*ma*·te ... *so*·bo
   single   *enoposteljno*   e·no·*pos*·tel'·no
   double   *dvoposteljno*   dvo·*pos*·tel'·no

How much is it per ...?   *Koliko stane na ...?*   ko·lee·ko *sta*·ne na ...
   night   *noč*   noch
   person   *osebo*   o·*se*·bo

Can I pay by ...?   *Lahko plačam s ...?*   lah·*ko* pla·cham s ...
   credit card   *kreditno kartico*   kre·*deet*·no *kar*·tee·tso
   travellers cheque   *potovalnim čekom*   po·to·*val*·neem che·kom

I'd like to stay for (three) nights.
Rad bi ostal (tri) noči. m   rada bee os·*tow* (tree) no·*chee*
Rada bi ostala (tri) noči. f   *ra*·da bee os·*ta*·la (tree) no·*chee*

From (2 July) to (6 July).
Od (drugega julija)   od (*droo*·ge·ga *yoo*·lee·ya)
do (šestega julija).   do (*shes*·te·ga *yoo*·lee·ya)

Can I see the room?
Lahko vidim sobo?   lah·*ko* vee·deem *so*·bo

Am I allowed to camp here?
Smem tu kampirati?   smem too kam·*pee*·ra·tee

Is there a camp site nearby?
Je v bližini kakšen kamp?   ye v blee·*zhee*·nee *kak*·shen kamp

requests & queries

When/Where is breakfast served?
Kdaj/Kje strežete zajtrk?   kdai/kye *stre*·zhe·te *zai*·tuhrk

Please wake me at (seven).
Prosim, zbudite me ob (sedmih).   *pro*·seem zboo·*dee*·te me ob (*sed*·meeh)

Could I have my key, please?
Lahko prosim dobim ključ?   lah·*ko pro*·sim do·*beem* klyooch

Can I get another (blanket)?
Lahko dobim drugo (odejo)?   lah·*ko* do·*beem droo*·go (o·*de*·yo)

Is there an elevator/a safe?
Imate dvigalo/sef?   ee·*ma*·te dvee·*ga*·lo/sef

The room is too...	Soba je ...	so·ba ye ...
expensive	predraga	pre·dra·ga
noisy	prehrupna	pre·hroop·na
small	premajhna	pre·mai·hna

This ... isn't clean.	Ta ... ni čista.	ta ... nee chees·ta
pillow	blazina	bla·zee·na
sheet	rjuha	ryoo·ha
towel	brisača	bree·sa·cha

The fan doesn't work.
Ventilator je pokvarjen.   ven·tee·*la*·tor ye pok·*var*·yen
The air conditioning doesn't work.
Klima je pokvarjena.   klee·ma ye pok·*var*·ye·na
The toilet doesn't work.
Stranišče je pokvarjeno.   stra·*neesh*·che ye pok·*var*·ye·no

checking out

What time is checkout?
Kdaj se moram odjaviti?   kdai se *mo*·ram od·*ya*·vee·tee
Can I leave my luggage here?
Lahko pustim prtljago tu?   lah·*ko* poos·*teem* puhrt·*lya*·go too

Could I have my ..., please?	Lahko prosim dobim ...?	lah·ko pro·seem do·beem ...
deposit	moj polog	moy po·log
passport	moj potni list	moy pot·nee leest
valuables	moje dragocenosti	mo·ye dra·go·tse·nos·tee

communications & banking

the internet

Where's the local Internet café?
Kje je najbližja internetna kavarna?   kye ye nai·*bleezh*·ya een·ter·*net*·na ka·*var*·na
How much is it per hour?
Koliko stane ena ura?   ko·lee·ko *sta*·ne *e*·na *oo*·ra

I'd like to ...	Želim ...	zhe-leem ...
check my email	preveriti elektronsko pošto	pre-ve-ree-tee e-lek-tron-sko posh-to
get Internet access	dostop do interneta	dos-top do een-ter-ne-ta
use a printer	uporabiti tiskalnik	oo-po-ra-bee-tee tees-kal-neek
use a scanner	uporabiti optični čitalnik	oo-po-ra-bee-tee op-teech-nee chee-tal-neek

mobile/cell phone

I'd like a ...	Želim ...	zhe-leem ...
mobile/cell phone for hire	najeti mobilni telefon	na-ye-tee mo-beel-nee te-le-fon
SIM card for your network	SIM kartico za vaše omrežje	seem kar-tee-tso za va-she om-rezh-ye

What are the rates? *Kakšne so cene?* kak-shne so tse-ne

telephone

What's your phone number?
Lahko izvem vašo telefonsko številko? lah-ko eez-vem va-sho te-le-fon-sko shte-veel-ko

The number is ...
Številka je ... shte-veel-ka ye ...

Where's the nearest public phone?
Kje je najbližja govorilnica? kye ye nai-bleezh-ya go-vo-reel-nee-tsa

I'd like to buy a phonecard.
Želim kupiti telefonsko kartico. zhe-leem koo-pee-tee te-le-fon-sko kar-tee-tso

I want to ...	Želim ...	zhe-leem ...
call (Singapore)	poklicati (Singapur)	pok-lee-tsa-tee (seen-ga-poor)
make a local call	klicati lokalno	klee-tsa-tee lo-kal-no
reverse the charges	klicati na stroške klicanega	klee-tsa-tee na strosh-ke klee-tsa-ne-ga

How much does ... cost?	Koliko stane ...?	ko-lee-ko sta-ne ...
a (three)-minute call	(tri)minutni klic	(tree-)mee-noot-nee kleets
each extra minute	vsaka dodatna minuta	vsa-ka do-dat-na mee-noo-ta

SLOVENŠČINA – communications & banking

post office

I want to send a ...	Želim poslati ...	zhe-*leem* pos-*la*-tee ...
letter	pismo	*pees*-mo
parcel	paket	pa-*ket*
postcard	razglednico	raz-*gled*-nee-tso

I want to buy a/an ...	Želim kupiti ...	zhe-*leem* koo-*pee*-tee ...
envelope	kuverto	koo-*ver*-to
stamp	znamko	*znam*-ko

Please send it by ...	Prosim, pošljite ...	pro-*seem* posh-*lyee*-te ...
airmail	z letalsko pošto	z le-*tal*-sko *posh*-to
express mail	s hitro pošto	s *heet*-ro *posh*-to
registered mail	s priporočeno pošto	s pree-po-ro-*che*-no *posh*-to
surface mail	z navadno pošto	z na-*vad*-no *posh*-to

bank

Where's a/an ...?	Kje je ...?	kye ye ...?
ATM	bankomat	ban-ko-*mat*
foreign exchange office	menjalnica	men-*yal*-nee-tsa

I'd like to ...	Želim ...	zhe-*leem* ...
Where can I ...?	Kje je mogoče ...?	kye ye mo-*go*-che ...
cash a cheque	unovčiti ček	oo-*nov*-chee-tee chek
change a travellers cheque	zamenjati potovalni ček	za-*men*-ya-tee po-to-*val*-nee chek
change money	zamenjati denar	za-*men*-ya-tee de-*nar*
withdraw money	dvigniti denar	*dveeg*-nee-tee de-*nar*

What's the ...?	Kakšen/Kakšna je ...? m/f	kak-*shen*/kak-*shna* ye ...?
commission	provizija f	pro-*vee*-zee-ya
exchange rate	menjalni tečaj m	men-*yal*-nee te-*chai*

Can I arrange a transfer of money?
Lahko uredim prenos denarja?   lah-*ko* oo-re-*deem* pre-*nos* de-*nar*-ya

What time does the bank open?
Kdaj se banka odpre?   kdai se *ban*-ka od-*pre*

Has my money arrived yet?
Je moj denar že prispel?   ye moy de-*nar* zhe *prees*-pe-oo

sightseeing

getting in

What time does it open/close?
Kdaj se odpre/zapre? — kdai se od·*pre*/za·*pre*

What's the admission charge?
Koliko stane vstopnica? — *ko*·lee·ko *sta*·ne *vstop*·nee·tsa

Is there a discount for students/children?
Imate popust za — ee·*ma*·te po·*poost* za
študente/otroke? — shtoo·*den*·te/ot·*ro*·ke

I'd like a ...	*Želim ...*	zhe·*leem* ...
catalogue	*katalog*	ka·ta·*log*
guide	*vodnik*	vod·*neek*
local map	*zemljevid kraja*	zem·lye·*veed* kra·ya

I'd like to see ... — *Želim videti ...* — zhe·*leem* vee·de·tee ...
What's that? — *Kaj je to?* — kai ye to
Can I take a photo? — *Ali lahko fotografiram?* — a·lee lah·*ko* fo·to·gra·*fee*·ram

tours

When's the next ...?	*Kdaj je naslednji ...?*	kdai ye nas·*led*·nyee ...
boat trip	*izlet s čolnom*	eez·*let* s *choh*·nom
day trip	*dnevni izlet*	*dnev*·nee eez·*let*
tour	*izlet*	eez·*let*

Is ... included?	*Je ... vključena?*	ye ... *vklyoo*·che·na
accommodation	*nastanitev*	nas·ta·*nee*·tev
the admission charge	*vstopnina*	vstop·*nee*·na
food	*hrana*	*hra*·na

Is transport included?
Je prevoz vključen? — ye pre·*voz* vklyoo·chen

How long is the tour?
Koliko časa traja izlet? — *ko*·lee·ko *cha*·sa *tra*·ya eez·*let*

What time should we be back?
Kdaj naj se vrnemo? — kdai nai se *vuhr*·ne·mo

sightseeing

castle	*grad* m	grad
cathedral	*stolnica* f	*stol*·nee·tsa
church	*cerkev* f	*tser*·kev
main square	*glavni trg* m	*glav*·nee tuhrg
monastery	*samostan* m	sa·mos·*tan*
monument	*spomenik* m	spo·me·*neek*
museum	*muzej* m	moo·zey
old city	*staro mesto* n	*sta*·ro *mes*·to
palace	*palača* f	pa·*la*·cha
ruins	*ruševine* f	roo·she·*vee*·ne
stadium	*stadion* m	*sta*·dee·on
statue	*kip* m	keep

shopping

enquiries

Where's a ...?	*Kje je ...?*	kye ye ...
bank	*banka*	*ban*·ka
bookshop	*knjigarna*	knyee·*gar*·na
camera shop	*trgovina s*	tuhr·go·*vee*·na s
	fotografsko opremo	fo·to·*graf*·sko op·*re*·mo
department store	*blagovnica*	bla·*gov*·nee·tsa
grocery store	*trgovina s*	tuhr·go·*vee*·na s
	špecerijo	shpe·tse·*ree*·yo
market	*tržnica*	*tuhrzh*·nee·tsa
newsagency	*kiosk*	*kee*·osk
supermarket	*trgovina*	tuhr·go·*vee*·na

Where can I buy (a padlock)?

Kje lahko kupim (ključavnico)?   kye lah·ko koo·peem (klyoo·*chav*·nee·tso)

I'm looking for ...

Iščem ...   *eesh*·chem ...

Can I look at it?

Lahko pogledam?   lah·ko pog·*le*·dam

Do you have any others?
Imate še kakšnega/kakšno? m/f — ee·*ma*·te she *kak*·shne·ga/*kak*·shno

Does it have a guarantee?
Ali ima garancijo? — *a*·lee ee·*ma* ga·ran·*tsee*·yo

Can I have it sent abroad?
Mi lahko pošljete v tujino? — mee lah·*ko* posh·lye·te v too·*yee*·no

Can I have my ... repaired?
Mi lahko popravite ....? — mee lah·*ko* po·*pra*·vee·te ...

It's faulty.
Ne deluje. — ne de·*loo*·ye

I'd like ..., please.	*Želim ..., prosim.*	zhe·*leem* ... *pro*·seem
a bag	*vrečko*	*vrech*·ko
a refund	*vračilo denarja*	vra·*chee*·lo de·*nar*·ya
to return this	*vrniti tole*	vr·*nee*·tee *to*·le

paying

How much is this?
Koliko stane? — ko·lee·ko *sta*·ne

Can you write down the price?
Lahko napišete ceno? — lah·*ko* na·*pee*·she·te *tse*·no

That's too expensive.
To je predrago. — to ye pre·dra·*go*

What's your lowest price?
Povejte vašo najnižjo ceno. — po·*vey*·te *va*·sho nai·*neezh*·yo *tse*·no

I'll give you (five) euros.
Dam vam (pet) evrov. — dam vam (pet) *ev*·roh

There's a mistake in the bill.
Na računu je napaka. — na ra·*choo*·noo ye na·*pa*·ka

Do you accept ...?	*Ali sprejemate ...?*	*a*·lee spre·*ye*·ma·te ...
credit cards	*kreditne kartice*	kre·*deet*·ne *kar*·tee·tse
debit cards	*debetne kartice*	de·*bet*·ne *kar*·tee·tse
travellers cheques	*potovalne čeke*	po·to·*val*·ne *che*·ke

I'd like ..., please.	*Želim ..., prosim.*	zhe·*leem* ... *pro*·seem
a receipt	*račun*	ra·*choon*
my change	*drobiž*	dro·*beezh*

clothes & shoes

Can I try it on?	Lahko pomerim?	lah·ko po·me·reem
My size is (42).	Nosim številko	no·seem shte·veel·ko
	(dvainštirideset).	(dva·een·shtee·ree·de·set)
It doesn't fit.	Ni mi prav.	nee mee prow
... size	... številka	... shte·veel·ka
small	majhna	mai·hna
medium	srednja	sred·nya
large	velika	ve·lee·ka

books & music

I'd like a ...	Želim ...	zhe·leem ...
newspaper	časopis	cha·so·pees
(in English)	(v angleščini)	(v ang·lesh·chee·nee)
pen	pisalo	pee·sa·lo

I'm looking for an English-language bookshop.
Iščem angleško knjigarno.   eesh·chem ang·lesh·ko knyee·gar·no

I'm looking for a book/music by (Miha Mazzini/Zoran Predin).
Iščem knjigo/glasbo   eesh·chem knyee·go/glaz·bo
(Mihe Mazzinija/Zorana Predina).   (mee·he ma·tsee·nee·ya/zo·ra·na pre·dee·na)

Can I listen to this?
Lahko tole poslušam?   lah·ko to·le pos·loo·sham

photography

Can you ...?	Lahko ...?	lah·ko ...
burn a CD from	zapečete CD z moje	za·pe·che·te tse·de z mo·ye
my memory card	spominske kartice	spo·meen·ske kar·tee·tse
develop this film	razvijete ta film	raz·vee·ye·te ta feelm
load this film	vstavite ta film	vsta·vee·te ta feelm

I need a/an ... film	Potrebujem ... film	pot·re·boo·yem ... feelm
for this camera.	za ta fotoaparat.	za ta fo·to·a·pa·rat
APS	APS	a pe es
B&W	črno-bel	chuhr·no·be·oo
colour	barvni	barv·nee
(200) speed	(dvesto) ASA	(dve·sto) a·sa

I need a slide film for this camera.
Potrebujem film za diapozitive — pot·re·*boo*·yem feelm za dee·a·po·zee·*tee*·ve
za ta fotoaparat. — za ta fo·to·a·pa·*rat*

When will it be ready?
Kdaj bo gotovo? — kdai bo go·*to*·vo

meeting people

greetings, goodbyes & introductions

Hello/Hi.	*Zdravo.*	*zdra*·vo
Good night.	*Lahko noč.*	*lah*·ko noch
Goodbye/Bye.	*Na svidenje/Adijo.*	na *svee*·den·ye/a·*dee*·yo
See you later.	*Se vidiva.*	se *vee*·dee·va
Mr/Mrs	*gospod/gospa*	gos·*pod*/gos·*pa*
Miss	*gospodična*	gos·po·*deech*·na
How are you?	*Kako ste/si?* pol/inf	ka·*ko* ste/see
Fine, thanks.	*Dobro, hvala.*	*dob*·ro *hva*·la
And you?	*Pa vi/ti?* pol/inf	pa vee/tee
What's your name?	*Kako vam/ti je ime?* pol/inf	ka·*ko* vam/tee ye ee·*me*
My name is …	*Ime mi je …*	ee·*me* mee ye …
I'm pleased to meet you.	*Veseli me, da sem vas spoznal/spoznala.* m/f	ve·se·*lee* me da sem vas spoz·*now*/spoz·*na*·la
This is my …	*To je moj/moja …* m/f	to ye moy/*mo*·ya …
boyfriend	*fant*	fant
brother	*brat*	brat
daughter	*hči*	hchee
father	*oče*	*o*·che
friend	*prijatelj* m	pree·*ya*·tel'
	prijateljica f	pree·*ya*·tel·yee·tsa
girlfriend	*punca*	*poon*·tsa
husband	*mož*	mozh
mother	*mama*	*ma*·ma
partner (intimate)	*partner/partnerka* m/f	*part*·ner/*part*·ner·ka
sister	*sestra*	*ses*·tra
son	*sin*	seen
wife	*žena*	*zhe*·na

Here's my phone number.
Tu je moja telefonska številka.   too ye *mo*-ya te-le-*fon*-ska shte-*veel*-ka

What's your phone number?
Mi poveste vašo telefonsko številko?   mee po-*ves*-te *va*-sho te-le-*fon*-sko shte-*veel*-ko

Here's my ...	*Tu je moj/moja ...* m/f	too ye moy/*mo*-ya ...
What's your ...?	*Kakšen je vaš ...?* m	*kak*-shen ye vash ...
	Kakšna je vaša ...? f	*kak*-shna ye *va*-sha ...
(email) address	*(elektronski) naslov* m	(e-lek-*tron*-skee) nas-*loh*
fax number	*številka faksa* f	shte-*veel*-ka *fak*-sa

occupations

What's your occupation?	*Kaj ste po poklicu?*	kai ste po pok-*lee*-tsoo
I'm a/an ...	*... sem.*	... sem
artist	*Umetnik* m	oo-*met*-neek
	Umetnica f	oo-*met*-nee-tsa
farmer	*Kmet/Kmetica* m/f	kmet/kme-*tee*-tsa
office worker	*Uradnik* m	oo-*rad*-neek
	Uradnica f	oo-*rad*-nee-tsa
scientist	*Znanstvenik* m	znans-tve-neek
	Znanstvenica f	znans-tve-nee-tsa
student	*Študent/Študentka* m/f	shtoo-*dent*/ shtoo-*dent*-ka
tradesperson	*Trgovec/Trgovka* m/f	tuhr-*go*-vets/ tuhr-*gov*-ka

background

Where are you from?	*Od kod ste?*	od kod ste
I'm from ...	*Iz ... sem.*	eez ... sem
Australia	*Avstralije*	av-*stra*-lee-ye
Canada	*Kanade*	*ka*-na-de
England	*Anglije*	*an*-glee-ye
New Zealand	*Nove Zelandije*	*no*-ve ze-*lan*-dee-ye
the USA	*Združenih držav*	zdroo-zhe-neeh dr-*zhav*
Are you married?	*Ste poročeni?*	ste po-ro-*che*-nee
I'm married.	*Poročen/Poročena*	po-ro-*chen*/po-ro-*che*-na
	sem. m/f	sem
I'm single.	*Samski/Samska sem.* m/f	*sam*-skee/*sam*-ska sem

age

How old ...?	Koliko ...?	ko·lee·ko ...
are you	si star/stara m/f inf	see star/sta·ra
are you	ste stari m&f pol	ste sta·ree
is your daughter	je stara vaša hči	ye sta·ra va·sha hchee
is your son	je star vaš sin	ye star vash seen

| I'm ... years old. | Imam ... let. | ee·mam ... let |
| He/She is ... years old. | ... let ima. | ... let ee·ma |

feelings

I'm ...	... sem.	... sem
hungry	Lačen/Lačna m/f	la·chen/lach·na
thirsty	Žejen/Žejna m/f	zhe·yen/zhey·na
tired	Utrujen m	oot·roo·yen
	Utrujena f	oot·roo·ye·na

I'm not ...	Nisem ...	nee·sem ...
hungry	lačen/lačna m/f	la·chen/lach·na
thirsty	žejen/žejna m/f	zhe·yen/zhey·na
tired	utrujen/utrujena m/f	oot·roo·yen/oot·roo·ye·na

Are you ... ?	Ste ...?	ste ...
hungry	lačni	lach·nee
thirsty	žejni	zhey·nee
tired	utrujeni	oot·roo·ye·nee

I'm ...	... mi je.	... mee ye
hot	Vroče	vro·che
well	Dobro	dob·ro

I'm not ...	Ni mi ...	nee mee ...
Are you ...?	Vam je ...?	vam ye ...
hot	vroče	vro·che
well	dobro	dob·ro

| I'm (not) cold. | (Ne) Zebe me. | ne ze·be me |
| Are you cold? | Vas zebe? | vas ze·be |

entertainment

going out

Where can I find ...?	Kje je kakšen ...?	kye ye kak·shen ...
clubs	klub	kloob
gay venues	homoseksualski bar	ho·mo·sek·soo·al·skee bar
pubs	bar	bar
I feel like going to a/the ...	Želim iti	zhe·leem ee·tee ...
concert	na koncert	na kon·tsert
movies	v kino	oo kee·no
party	na zabavo	na za·ba·vo
restaurant	v restavracijo	oo res·tav·ra·tsee·yo
theatre	v gledališče	oo gle·da·leesh·che

interests

Do you like ...?	Vam je všeč ...?	vam ye vshech ...
I like ...	Všeč mi je ...	vshech mee ye ...
I don't like ...	Ni mi všeč ...	nee mee vshech ...
art	umetnost	oo·met·nost
cooking	kuhanje	koo·han·ye
reading	branje	bran·ye
shopping	nakupovanje	na·koo·po·van·ye
sport	šport	shport
Do you like ...?	So vam všeč ...?	so vam vshech ...
I like ...	Všeč so mi ...	vshech so mee ...
I don't like ...	Niso mi všeč ...	nee·so mee vshech ...
movies	filmi	feel·mee
nightclubs	nočni bari	noch·nee ba·ree
travelling	potovanja	po·to·van·ya
Do you like to ...?	Ali radi ...?	a·lee ra·dee ...
dance	plešete	ple·she·te
go to concerts	hodite na koncerte	ho·dee·te na kon·tser·te
listen to music	poslušate glasbo	pos·loo·sha·te glas·bo

food & drink

finding a place to eat

Can you recommend a ...?	Mi lahko priporočite ...?	mee lah-ko pree-po-ro-chee-te ...
bar	bar	bar
café	kavarno	ka-var-no
restaurant	restavracijo	res-tav-ra-tsee-yo
I'd like ..., please.	Želim ..., prosim.	zhe-leem ... pro-seem
a table for (five)	mizo za (pet)	mee-zo za (pet)
the (non)smoking section	prostor za (ne)kadilce	pros-tor za (ne-)ka-deel-tse

ordering food

breakfast	zajtrk m	zai-tuhrk
lunch	kosilo n	ko-see-lo
dinner	večerja f	ve-cher-ya
snack	malica f	ma-lee-tsa
today's special	danes nudimo	da-nes noo-dee-mo
What would you recommend?	Kaj priporočate?	kai pree-po-ro-cha-te
I'd like (the) ..., please.	Želim ..., prosim.	zhe-leem ... pro-seem
bill	račun	ra-choon
drink list	meni pijač	me-nee pee-yach
menu	jedilni list	ye-deel-nee leest
that dish	to jed	to yed

drinks

cup of coffee ...	skodelica kave ...	sko-de-lee-tsa ka-ve ...
cup of tea ...	skodelica čaja ...	sko-de-lee-tsa cha-ya ...
with milk	z mlekom	z mle-kom
without sugar	brez sladkorja	brez slad-kor-ya

(orange) juice	(pomarančni) sok m	(po·ma·*ranch*·nee) sok
soft drink	brezalkoholna	brez·al·ko·*hol*·na
	pijača f	pee·*ya*·cha
... water	... voda	... *vo*·da
boiled	prekuhana	pre·*koo*·ha·na
(sparkling)	mineralna	mee·ne·*ral*·na
mineral	(gazirana)	(ga·*zee*·ra·na)

in the bar

I'll have ...
Jaz bom ... yaz bom ...

I'll buy you a drink.
Povabim te na pijačo. inf po·*va*·beem te na pee·*ya*·cho

What would you like?
Kaj boš? inf kai bosh

Cheers!
Na zdravje! na *zdrav*·ye

brandy	vinjak m	*veen*·yak
champagne	šampanjec m	sham·*pan*·yets
cocktail	koktajl m	kok·*tail*
cognac	konjak m	*kon*·yak
a shot of (whisky)	kozarček (viskija)	ko·*zar*·chek (*vees*·kee·ya)
a ... of beer	... piva	... *pee*·va
glass	kozarec	ko·*za*·rets
jug	vrč	vuhrch
pint	vrček	*vuhr*·chek
a bottle/glass	steklenica/kozarec	stek·le·*nee*·tsa/ko·*za*·rets
of ... wine	... vina	... *vee*·na
red	rdečega	rde·*che*·ga
sparkling	penečega	pe·*ne*·che·ga
white	belega	*be*·le·ga

food & drink – SLOVENE

self-catering

What's the local speciality?
Kaj je lokalna specialiteta? — kai ye lo-*kal*-na spe-tsee-a-lee-*te*-ta

What's that?
Kaj je to? — kai ye to

How much is (a kilo of cheese)?
Koliko stane (kila sira)? — ko-lee-ko *sta*-ne (*kee*-la *see*-ra)

I'd like ...	Želim ...	zhe-*leem* ...
(200) grams	(dvesto) gramov	(*dve*-sto) *gra*-mov
(two) kilos	(dva) kilograma	(dva) kee-lo-*gra*-ma
(three) pieces	(tri) kose	(tree) *ko*-se
(six) slices	(šest) rezin	(shest) re-*zeen*

Less.	Manj.	man'
Enough.	Dovolj.	do-*vol*
More.	Več.	vech

special diets & allergies

Is there a vegetarian restaurant near here?
Je tu blizu vegetarijanska — ye too *blee*-zoo ve-ge-ta-ree-*yan*-ska
restavracija? — res-tav-*ra*-tsee-ya

Do you have vegetarian food?
Ali imate vegetarijansko hrano? — a-lee ee-*ma*-te ve-ge-ta-ree-*yan*-sko *hra*-no

Could you prepare	Lahko pripravite	lah-ko pree-*pra*-vee-te
a meal without ...?	obed brez ...?	o-*bed* brez ...
butter	masla	*mas*-la
eggs	jajc	yaits
meat stock	mesne osnove	*mes*-ne os-*no*-ve

I'm allergic to ...	Alergičen/Alergična	a-*ler*-gee-chen/a-*ler*-geech-na
	sem na ... m/f	sem na ...
dairy produce	mlečne izdelke	*mlech*-ne eez-*del*-ke
gluten	gluten	gloo-*ten*
MSG	MSG	em es ge
nuts	oreške	o-*resh*-ke
seafood	morsko hrano	*mor*-sko *hra*-no

318

menu decoder

bograč m	*bog*·rach	*beef goulash*
brancin na maslu m	bran·*tseen* na *mas*·loo	*sea bass in butter*
čebulna bržola f	che·*bool*·na br·*zho*·la	*braised beef with onions*
čevapčiči m	che·*vap*·chee·chee	*spicy beef or pork meatballs*
drobnjakovi štruklji m	drob·*nya*·ko·vee shtrook·lyee	*dumplings of cottage cheese & chives*
dunajski zrezek m	doo·nai·skee zre·zek	*breaded veal or pork cutlet*
francoska solata f	fran·*tsos*·ka so·*la*·ta	*diced potatoes & vegetables with mayonnaise*
gobova kremna juha f	*go*·bo·va *krem*·na *yoo*·ha	*creamed mushroom soup*
goveja juha z rezanci f	go·*ve*·ya *yoo*·ha z re·*zan*·tsee	*beef broth with little egg noodles*
jota f	*yo*·ta	*beans, sauerkraut & potatoes or barley cooked with pork*
kisle kumarice f	*kees*·le *koo*·ma·ree·tse	*pickled cucumbers*
kmečka pojedina f	*kmech*·ka po·*ye*·dee·na	*smoked meats with sauerkraut*
kranjska klobasa z gorčico f	*kran'*·ska klo·*ba*·sa z gor·*chee*·tso	*sausage with mustard*
kraški pršut z olivami m	*krash*·kee puhr·*shoot* z o·*lee*·va·mee	*air-dried ham with black olives*
krofi m	*kro*·fee	*jam-filled doughnuts*
kuhana govedina s hrenom f	*koo*·ha·na go·*ve*·dee·na s *hre*·nom	*boiled beef with horseradish*
kuhana postrv f	*koo*·ha·na pos·*tuhrv*	*boiled trout*
kumarična solata f	*koo*·ma·reech·na so·*la*·ta	*cucumber salad*
ljubljanski zrezek m	lyoob·*lyan*·skee zre·zek	*breaded cutlet with cheese*

mešano meso na žaru n	me·sha·no me·so na zha·roo	mixed grill
ocvrt oslič m	ots·vuhrt os·leech	fried cod
ocvrt piščanec m	ots·vuhrt peesh·cha·nets	fried chicken
orada na žaru f	o·ra·da na zha·roo	grilled sea bream
palačinke f	pa·la·cheen·ke	thin pancakes with marma-lade, nuts or chocolate
pečena postrv f	pe·che·na pos·tuhrv	grilled trout
pečene sardele f	pe·che·ne sar·de·le	grilled sardines
pleskavica f	ples·ka·vee·tsa	spicy meat patties
pariški zrezek m	pa·reesh·kee zre·zek	cutlet fried in egg batter
puranov zrezek s šampinjoni m	poo·ra·nov zre·zek s sham·peen·yo·nee	turkey steak with white mushrooms
ražnjiči m	razh·nyee·chee	shish kebab
riba v marinadi f	ree·ba v ma·ree·na·dee	marinated fish
ričet m	ree·chet	barley stew with smoked pork ribs
rižota z gobami f	ree·zho·ta z go·ba·mee	risotto with mushrooms
sadna kupa f	sad·na koo·pa	fruit salad with whipped cream
srbska solata f	suhrb·ska so·la·ta	salad of tomatoes & green peppers with onions & cheese
svinjska pečenka f	sveen'·ska pe·chen·ka	roast pork
škampi na žaru m	shkam·pee na zha·roo	grilled prawns
školjke f	shkol'·ke	clams
zelena solata f	ze·le·na so·la·ta	lettuce salad
zelenjavna juha f	ze·len·yav·na yoo·ha	vegetable soup

emergencies

basics

Help!	*Na pomoč!*	na po·*moch*
Stop!	*Ustavite (se)!*	oos·*ta*·vee·te (se)
Go away!	*Pojdite stran!*	poy·*dee*·te stran
Thief!	*Tat!*	tat
Fire!	*Požar!*	po·*zhar*
Watch out!	*Pazite!*	pa·*zee*·te
Call ...!	*Pokličite ...!*	pok·*lee*·chee·te ...
a doctor	*zdravnika*	zdrav·*nee*·ka
an ambulance	*rešilca*	re·*sheel*·tsa
the police	*policijo*	po·lee·*tsee*·yo

It's an emergency.
Nujno je. — *nooy*·no ye

Could you help me, please?
Pomagajte mi, prosim. — po·*ma*·gai·te mee *pro*·seem

I have to use the telephone.
Poklicati moram. — pok·*lee*·tsa·tee *mo*·ram

I'm lost.
Izgubil/Izgubila sem se. m/f — eez·*goo*·beew/eez·goo·*bee*·la sem se

Where are the toilets?
Kje je stranišče? — kye ye stra·*neesh*·che

police

Where's the police station?
Kje je policijska postaja? — kye ye po·lee·*tseey*·ska pos·*ta*·ya

I want to report an offence.
Želim prijaviti prestopek. — zhe·*leem* pree·*ya*·vee·tee pres·*to*·pek

I have insurance.
Zavarovan/Zavarovana sem. m/f — za·va·ro·*van*/za·va·ro·*va*·na sem

I've been ...	... so me.	... so me
assaulted	*Napadli*	na·*pad*·lee
raped	*Posilili*	po·*see*·lee·lee
robbed	*Oropali*	o·*ro*·pa·lee

I've lost my ...	Izgubil/Izgubila sem ... m/f	eez-goo-beew/eez-goo-bee-la sem ...
My ... was/were stolen.	Ukradli so mi ...	ook-rad-lee so mee ...
backpack	nahrbtnik	na-huhrbt-neek
bags	torbe	tor-be
credit card	kreditno kartico	kre-deet-no kar-tee-tso
handbag	ročno torbico	roch-no tor-bee-tso
jewellery	nakit	na-keet
money	denar	de-nar
passport	potni list	pot-nee leest
travellers cheques	potovalne čeke	po-to-val-ne che-ke
wallet	denarnico	de-nar-nee-tso
I want to contact my ...	Želim poklicati ... svoj/svojo ... m/f	zhe-leem pok-lee-tsa-tee ... svoy/svo-yo ...
consulate	konzulat m	kon-zoo-lat
embassy	ambasado f	am-ba-sa-do

health

medical needs

Where's the nearest ...?	Kje je najbližji/ najbližja ... ? m/f	kye ye nai-bleezh-yee/ nai-bleezh-ya ...
dentist	zobozdravnik m	zo-bo-zdrav-neek
doctor	zdravnik m	zdrav-neek
hospital	bolnišnica f	bol-neesh-nee-tsa
(night) pharmacist	(nočna) lekarna f	(noch-na) le-kar-na

I need a doctor (who speaks English).
Potrebujem zdravnika (ki govori angleško).
pot-re-boo-yem zdrav-nee-ka (kee go-vo-ree ang-lesh-ko)

Could I see a female doctor?
Bi me lahko pregledala zdravnica?
bee me lah-ko preg-le-da-la zdrav-nee-tsa

I've run out of my medication.

symptoms, conditions & allergies

I'm sick.	Bolan/Bolna sem. m/f	bo-*lan*/boh-na sem
It hurts here.	Tu me boli.	too me bo-*lee*

I have (a) ...	Imam ...	ee-*mam* ...
asthma	astmo	*ast*-mo
bronchitis	bronhitis	bron-*hee*-tees
constipation	zapeko	za-*pe*-ko
diarrhoea	drisko	*drees*-ko
fever	vročino	vro-*chee*-no
headache	glavobol	gla-vo-*bol*
heart condition	srčno bolezen	*suhr*-chno bo-*le*-zen
toothache	zobobol	zo-bo-*bol*
pain	bolečine	bo-le-*chee*-ne

I'm nauseous.	Slabo mi je.	sla-*bo* mee ye
I'm coughing.	Kašljam.	*kash*-lyam
I have a sore throat.	Boli me grlo.	bo-*lee* me *guhr*-lo

I'm allergic to ...	Alergičen/Alergična sem na ... m/f	a-*ler*-gee-chen/a-*ler*-geech-na sem na ...
antibiotics	antibiotike	an-tee-bee-*o*-tee-ke
anti-inflammatories	protivnetna zdravila	pro-teev-*net*-na zdra-*vee*-la
aspirin	aspirin	as-*pee*-reen
bees	čebelji pik	che-*bel*-yee peek
codeine	kodein	ko-de-*een*
penicillin	penicilin	pe-nee-tsee-*leen*

antiseptic	razkužilo n	raz-koo-*zhee*-lo
bandage	obveza f	ob-*ve*-za
condoms	kondomi m pl	kon-*do*-mee
contraceptives	kontracepcija f	kon-tra-*tsep*-tsee-ya
diarrhoea medicine	zdravilo za drisko n	zdra-*vee*-lo za *drees*-ko
insect repellent	sredstvo proti mrčesu n	*sreds*-tvo pro-tee muhr-*che*-soo
laxatives	odvajala n pl	od-va-*ya*-la
painkillers	analgetiki m pl	a-nal-*ge*-tee-kee
rehydration salts	sol za rehidracijo f	sol za re-heed-*ra*-tsee-yo
sleeping tablets	uspavalne tablete f pl	oos-pa-*val*-ne tab-*le*-te

english–slovene dictionary

Slovene nouns in this dictionary have their gender indicated by ⓜ (masculine), ⓕ (feminine) or ⓝ (neuter).
If it's a plural noun, you'll also see pl. Adjectives are given in the masculine form only. Words are also marked
as a (adjective), v (verb), sg (singular), pl (plural), inf (informal) or pol (polite) where necessary.

A

accident *nesreča* ⓕ nes-*re*-cha
accommodation *nastanitev* ⓕ na-sta-*nee*-tev
adaptor *adapter* ⓜ a-*dap*-ter
address *naslov* ⓜ nas-*loh*
after *po* po
air-conditioned *klimatiziran* klee-ma-tee-*zee*-ran
airplane *letalo* ⓝ le-*ta*-lo
airport *letališče* ⓝ le-ta-*leesh*-che
alcohol *alkohol* ⓜ al-ko-*hol*
all *vse* vse
allergy *alergija* ⓕ a-ler-*gee*-ya
ambulance *rešilni avto* re-*sheel*-nee *av*-to
and *in* een
ankle *gleženj* ⓜ *gle*-zhen'
arm *roka* ⓕ *ro*-ka
ashtray *pepelnik* ⓜ pe-*pel*-neek
ATM *bankomat* ⓜ ban-ko-*mat*

B

baby *dojenček* ⓜ do-*yen*-chek
back (body) *hrbet* ⓜ *huhr*-bet
backpack *nahrbtnik* ⓜ na-*huhrbt*-neek
bad *slab* slab
bag *torba* ⓕ *tor*-ba
baggage *prtljaga* ⓕ puhrt-*lya*-ga
baggage claim *prevzem prtljage* ⓕ
    prev-zem puhrt-*lya*-ge
bank *banka* ⓕ *ban*-ka
bar *bar* ⓜ bar
bathroom *kopalnica* ⓕ ko-*pal*-nee-tsa
battery *baterija* ⓕ ba-te-*ree*-ya
beautiful *lep* lep
bed *postelja* ⓕ *pos*-tel-ya
beer *pivo* ⓝ *pee*-vo
before *prej* prey
behind *zadaj* za-dai
bicycle *bicikel* ⓜ bee-*tsee*-kel
big *velik* ve-leek
bill *račun* ⓜ ra-*choon*
black *črn* chuhrn

blanket *odeja* ⓕ o-*de*-ya
blood group *krvna skupina* ⓕ *kuhrv*-na skoo-*pee*-na
blue *moder* mo-der
boat (ship) *ladja* ⓕ *lad*-ya
boat (small) *čoln* ⓜ chohn
book (make a reservation) v *rezervirati*
    re-zer-*vee*-ra-tee
bottle *steklenica* ⓕ stek-le-*nee*-tsa
bottle opener *odpirač* ⓜ od-*pee*-rach
boy *fant* ⓜ fant
brakes (car) *zavore* ⓕ pl za-*vo*-re
breakfast *zajtrk* ⓜ *zai*-tuhrk
broken (faulty) *pokvarjen* pok-*var*-yen
bus *avtobus* ⓜ av-to-*boos*
business *posel* ⓜ *po*-se-oo
buy *kupiti* koo-*pee*-tee

C

café *kavarna* ⓕ ka-*var*-na
camera *fotoaparat* ⓜ fo-to-a-pa-*rat*
camera shop *trgovina s fotografsko opremo* ⓕ
    tr-go-*vee*-na s fo-to-*graf*-sko o-*pre*-mo
campsite *kamp* ⓜ kamp
cancel *preklicati* prek-*lee*-tsa-tee
can opener *odpirač za pločevinke* ⓜ
    od-*pee*-rach za plo-che-*veen*-ke
car *avtomobil* ⓜ av-to-mo-*beel*
cash *gotovina* ⓕ go-to-*vee*-na
cash (a cheque) v *unovčiti (ček)* oo-*nov*-chee-tee (chek)
cell phone *mobilni telefon* ⓜ mo-*beel*-nee te-le-*fon*
centre *center* ⓜ *tsen*-ter
change (money) v *menjati (denar)* men-ya-tee (de-*nar*)
cheap *poceni* po-*tse*-nee
check (bill) *račun* ⓜ ra-*choon*
check-in *prijava za let* ⓕ pree-*ya*-va za let
chest *prsni koš* ⓜ *puhr*-snee kosh
child *otrok* ⓜ ot-rok
cigarette *cigareta* ⓕ tsee-ga-*re*-ta
city *mesto* ⓝ *mes*-to
clean a *čist* cheest
closed *zaprt* za-*puhrt*
coffee *kava* ⓕ *ka*-va
coins *kovanci* ⓜ pl ko-*van*-tsee

cold a *hladen* hla-den
collect call *klic na stroške klicanega* ⓜ
  kleets na strosh-ke klee-tsa-ne-ga
come *priti* pree-tee
computer *računalnik* ⓜ ra-choo-*nal*-neek
condom *kondom* ⓜ kon-*dom*
contact lenses *kontaktne leče* ① pl kon-*takt*-ne *le*-che
cook v *kuhati* koo-ha-tee
cost *strošek* ⓜ *stro*-shek
credit card *kreditna kartica* ① kre-*deet*-na *kar*-tee-tsa
cup *skodelica* ① sko-de-lee-tsa
currency exchange *menjava* ① men-*ya*-va
customs (immigration) *carina* ① tsa-*ree*-na

D

dangerous *nevaren* ne-*va*-ren
date (time) *datum* ⓜ *da*-toom
day *dan* ⓜ dan
delay *zamuda* ① za-*moo*-da
dentist *zobozdravnik* ⓜ zo-boz-*drav*-neek
depart *oditi* o-*dee*-tee
diaper *plenica* ① ple-*nee*-tsa
dictionary *slovar* ⓜ slo-*var*
dinner *večerja* ① ve-*cher*-ya
direct *direkten* dee-*rek*-ten
dirty *umazan* oo-ma-zan
disabled (person) *invaliden* een-va-*lee*-den
discount *popust* ⓜ po-*poost*
doctor *zdravnik* ⓜ *zdrav*-neek
double bed *dvojna postelja* ① *dvoy*-na *pos*-tel-ya
double room *dvoposteljna soba* ①
  dvo-*pos*-tel'-na *so*-ba
drink *pijača* ① pee-*ya*-cha
drive v *voziti* vo-*zee*-tee
drivers licence *vozniško dovoljenje* ⓜ
  voz-*neesh*-ko do-vol-*yen*-ye
drug (illicit) *mamilo* ⓜ ma-*mee*-lo
dummy (pacifier) *duda* ① *doo*-da

E

ear *uho* ⓝ *oo*-ho
east *vzhod* ⓜ vzhod
eat *jesti* yes-tee
economy class *turistični razred* ⓜ
  too-rees-*teech*-nee raz-red
electricity *elektrika* ① e-lek-*tree*-ka
elevator *dvigalo* ⓝ dvee-*ga*-lo
email *elektronska pošta* ① e-lek-*tron*-ska *posh*-ta
embassy *ambasada* ① am-ba-*sa*-da
emergency *nujen primer* ⓜ *noo*-yen pree-mer
english (language) *angleščina* ① ang-*lesh*-chee-na

entrance *vhod* ⓜ vhod
evening *večer* ⓜ ve-cher
exchange rate *menjalni tečaj* ⓜ men-*yal*-nee te-*chai*
exit *izhod* ⓜ eez-hod
expensive *drag* drag
express mail *hitra pošta* ① *heet*-ra *posh*-ta
eye *oko* ⓝ o-ko

F

far *daleč* da-lech
fast *hitro* heet-ro
father *oče* ⓜ o-che
film (camera) *film* ⓜ feelm
finger *prst* ⓜ puhrst
first-aid kit *komplet za prvo pomoč* ⓜ
  kom-*plet* za *puhr*-vo po-*moch*
first class *prvi razred* ⓜ *puhr*-vee *raz*-red
fish *riba* ① *ree*-ba
food *hrana* ① *hra*-na
foot *stopalo* ⓝ sto-*pa*-lo
fork *vilice* ① pl *vee*-lee-tse
free (of charge) *brezplačen* brez-*pla*-chen
friend *prijatelj/prijateljica* ⓜ/①
  pree-ya-*tel*/pree-ya-*tel*-yee-tsa
fruit *sadje* ⓝ pl *sad*-ye
full *poln* poln
funny *smešen* sme-shen

G

gift *darilo* ⓝ da-*ree*-lo
girl *dekle* ⓝ dek-le
glass (drinking) *kozarec* ⓜ ko-za-rets
glasses *očala* ⓝ pl o-*cha*-la
go *iti* ee-tee
good *dober* do-ber
green *zelen* ze-len
guide *vodnik* ⓜ vod-neek

H

half *pol* poh
hand *roka* ① *ro*-ka
handbag *ročna torbica* ① *roch*-na *tor*-bee-tsa
happy *srečen* sre-chen
have *imeti* ee-me-tee
he *on* ⓜ on
head *glava* ① *gla*-va
heart *srce* ⓝ suhr-tse
heat *vročina* ① vro-chee-na
heavy *težek* te-zhek

help v *pomagati* po-*ma*-ga-tee
here *tukaj* too-kai
high *visok* vee-sok
highway *hitra cesta* ⓕ *heet*-ra *tses*-ta
(go on a) holidays v *iti na pohod* ee-*tee* na po-*hod*
holidays *počitnice* ⓕ pl po-*cheet*-nee-tse
homosexual *homoseksualec* ⓜ ho-mo-sek-soo-*a*-lets
hospital *bolnišnica* ⓕ bol-*neesh*-nee-tsa
hot *vroč* vroch
hotel *hotel* ⓜ ho-*tel*
hungry *lačen* la-chen
husband *mož* ⓜ mozh

I

I *jaz* yaz
identification (card) *osebna izkaznica* ⓕ
   o-*seb*-na eez-*kaz*-nee-tsa
ill *bolan* bo-*lan*
important *pomemben* po-*mem*-ben
included *vključen* vklyoo-chen
injury *poškodba* ⓕ posh-*kod*-ba
insurance *zavarovanje* ⓝ za-va-ro-*van*-ye
Internet *internet* ⓜ een-ter-net
interpreter *tolmač* ⓜ tol-*mach*

J

jewellery *nakit* ⓜ na-*keet*
job *služba* ⓕ *sloozh*-ba

K

key *ključ* ⓜ klyooch
kilogram *kilogram* ⓜ kee-lo-*gram*
kitchen *kuhinja* ⓕ koo-heen-ya
knife *nož* ⓜ nozh

L

laundry (place) *pralnica* ⓕ *pral*-nee-tsa
lawyer *odvetnik* ⓜ od-*vet*-neek
left (direction) *levo* le-vo
left-luggage office *garderoba* ⓕ gar-de-ro-ba
leg *noga* ⓕ *no*-ga
lesbian *lezbijka* ⓕ lez-beey-ka
less *manj* man'
letter (mail) *pismo* ⓝ *pees*-mo
lift (elevator) *dvigalo* ⓝ dvee-ga-lo
light *svetloba* ⓕ svet-*lo*-ba
like v *všeč biti* vshech *bee*-tee

lock *ključavnica* ⓕ klyoo-*chav*-nee-tsa
long *dolg* dohg
lost *izgubljen* eez-goob-*lyen*
lost-property office *urad za izgubljene predmete* ⓜ
   oo-*rad* za eez-goob-*lye*-ne pred-*me*-te
love v *ljubiti* lyoo-bee-tee
luggage *prtljaga* ⓕ puhrt-*lya*-ga
lunch *kosilo* ⓝ ko-see-lo

M

mail *pošta* ⓕ *posh*-ta
man *moški* ⓜ *mosh*-kee
map *zemljevid* ⓜ zem-lye-*veed*
market *tržnica* ⓕ *tuhrzh*-nee-tsa
matches *vžigalice* ⓕ pl vzhee-*ga*-lee-tse
meat *meso* ⓝ me-*so*
medicine *zdravilo* ⓝ zdra-vee-lo
menu *jedilni list* ⓜ ye-*deel*-nee leest
message *sporočilo* ⓝ spo-ro-*chee*-lo
milk *mleko* ⓝ mle-ko
minute *minuta* ⓕ mee-noo-ta
mobile phone *mobilni telefon* ⓜ mo-*beel*-nee te-le-*fon*
money *denar* ⓜ de-*nar*
month *mesec* ⓜ me-sets
morning *dopoldne* ⓝ do-*pol*-dne
mother *mama* ⓕ *ma*-ma
motorcycle *motorno kolo* ⓝ mo-tor-no ko-lo
motorway *motorna cesta* ⓕ mo-tor-na tses-ta
mouth *usta* ⓕ *oos*-ta
music *glasba* ⓕ *glaz*-ba

N

name *ime* ⓝ ee-*me*
napkin *prtiček* ⓜ puhr-*tee*-chek
nappy *plenica* ⓕ ple-*nee*-tsa
near *blizu* blee-zoo
neck *vrat* ⓜ vrat
new *nov* noh
news *novice* ⓕ pl no-*vee*-tse
newspaper *časopis* ⓜ cha-so-*pees*
night *noč* ⓕ noch
no *ne* ne
noisy *hrupen* hroo-pen
nonsmoking *nekadilski* ne-ka-*deel*-skee
north *sever* ⓜ se-ver
nose *nos* ⓜ nos
now *zdaj* zdai
number *število* ⓝ shte-vee-lo

O

oil (engine) *olje* ⓝ *ol-ye*
old *star* star
one-way ticket *enosmerna vozovnica* ⓕ
e-no-*smer*-na vo-*zov*-nee-tsa
open a *odprt* od-*puhrt*
outside *zunaj* zoo-nai

P

package *paket* ⓜ pa-*ket*
paper *papir* ⓜ pa-*peer*
park (car) v *parkirati* par-*kee*-ra-tee
passport *potni list* ⓜ *pot*-nee leest
pay *plačati* pla-*cha*-tee
pen *pisalo* ⓝ pee-*sa*-lo
petrol *bencin* ⓜ ben-*tseen*
pharmacy *lekarna* ⓕ le-*kar*-na
phonecard *telefonska kartica* ⓕ
te-le-*fon*-ska *kar*-tee-tsa
photo *fotografija* ⓕ fo-to-*gra*-*fee*-ya
picnic *piknik* ⓜ *peek*-neek
plate *krožnik* ⓜ *krozh*-neek
police *policija* ⓕ po-lee-*tsee*-ya
postcard *razglednica* ⓕ raz-*gled*-nee-tsa
post office *pošta* ⓕ *posh*-ta
pregnant *noseča* no-se-cha
price *cena* ⓕ *tse*-na

Q

quiet *tih* teeh

R

rain *dež* ⓜ dezh
razor *brivnik* ⓜ *breev*-neek
receipt *račun* ⓜ ra-*choon*
red *rdeč* rdech
refund *vračilo denarja* ⓝ vra-*chee*-lo de-*nar*-ya
registered mail *priporočena pošta* ⓕ
pree-po-ro-che-na *posh*-ta
rent v *najeti* na-ye-tee
repair v *popraviti* pop-*ra*-vee-tee
reservation *rezervacija* ⓕ re-zer-*va*-tsee-ya
restaurant *restavracija* ⓕ res-tav-*ra*-tsee-ya
return v *vrniti* vr-nee-tee

return ticket *povratna vozovnica* ⓕ
pov-*rat*-na vo-*zov*-nee-tsa
right (direction) *desno* des-no
road *cesta* ⓕ *tses*-ta
room *soba* ⓕ *so*-ba

S

safe a *varen* va-ren
sanitary napkins *damski vložki* ⓜ pl
dam-skee *vlozh*-kee
seat *sedež* ⓜ se-dezh
send *poslati* pos-*la*-tee
service station *servis* ⓜ *ser*-vees
sex *seks* ⓜ seks
shampoo *šampon* ⓜ sham-*pon*
share (a dorm) *deliti (sobo)* de-lee-tee (*so*-bo)
shaving cream *krema za britje* ⓕ *kre*-ma za breet-ye
she *ona* ⓕ *o*-na
sheet (bed) *rjuha* ⓕ *ryoo*-ha
shirt *srajca* ⓕ *srai*-tsa
shoes *čevlji* ⓜ pl *chev*-lyee
shop *trgovina* ⓕ tuhr-*go*-vee-na
short *kratek* kra-tek
shower *prha* ⓕ *puhr*-ha
single room *enoposteljna soba* ⓕ
e-no-*pos*-tel'-na *so*-ba
skin *koža* ⓕ *ko*-zha
skirt *krilo* ⓝ *kree*-lo
sleep v *spati* *spa*-tee
Slovenia *Slovenija* ⓕ slo-ve-nee-ya
Slovene (language) *slovenščina* ⓕ slo-*vensh*-chee-na
Slovene a *slovenski* slo-ven-skee
slowly *počasi* po-cha-see
small *majhen* mai-hen
smoke (cigarettes) v *kaditi* ka-dee-tee
soap *milo* ⓝ *mee*-lo
some *nekaj* ne-kai
soon *kmalu* kma-loo
south *jug* ⓜ yoog
souvenir shop *trgovina s spominki* ⓕ
tuhr-go-vee-na s spo-meen-kee
speak *govoriti* go-vo-ree-tee
spoon *žlica* ⓕ zhlee-tsa
stamp *znamka* ⓕ znam-ka
stand-by ticket *stand-by vozovnica* ⓕ
stend-bai vo-zov-nee-tsa
station (train) *postaja* ⓕ pos-ta-ya
stomach *želodec* ⓜ zhe-lo-dets

stop v *ustaviti* oos-ta-vee-tee
stop (bus) *postajališče* ⓝ pos-ta-ya-leesh-che
street *ulica* ⓕ oo-lee-tsa
student *študent/študentka* ⓜ/ⓕ
  shtoo-dent/shtoo-dent-ka
sun *sonce* ⓝ son-tse
sunscreen *krema za sončenje* ⓕ kre-ma za son-chen-ye
swim v *plavati* pla-va-tee

T

tampons *tamponi* ⓜ pl tam-po-nee
taxi *taksi* ⓜ tak-see
teaspoon *čajna žlička* ⓕ chai-na zhleech-ka
teeth *zobje* zob-ye
telephone *telefon* ⓜ te-le-fon
television *televizija* ⓕ te-le-vee-zee-ya
temperature (weather) *temperatura* ⓕ
  tem-pe-ra-too-ra
tent *šotor* ⓜ sho-tor
that (one) *tisti* tees-tee
they *oni/one* ⓜ/ⓕ o-nee/o-ne
thirsty *žejen* zhe-yen
this (one) *ta* ta
throat *grlo* ⓝ guhr-lo
ticket (entrance) *vstopnica* ⓕ vstop-nee-tsa
ticket (travel) *vozovnica* ⓕ vo-zov-nee-tsa
time *čas* ⓜ chas
tired *utrujen* oo-troo-yen
tissues *robčki* ⓜ pl rob-chkee
today *danes* da-nes
toilet *stranišče* ⓝ stra-neesh-che
tomorrow *jutri* yoot-ree
tonight *nocoj* no-tsoy
toothbrush *zobna ščetka* ⓕ zob-na shchet-ka
toothpaste *zobna pasta* ⓕ zob-na pas-ta
torch (flashlight) *baterija* ⓕ ba-te-ree-ya
tour *izlet* ⓜ eez-let
tourist office *turistični urad* ⓜ too-rees-teech-nee oo-rad
towel *brisača* ⓕ bree-sa-cha
train *vlak* ⓜ vlak
translate *prevesti* pre-ves-tee
travel agency *potovalna agencija* ⓕ
  po-to-val-na a-gen-tsee-ya
travellers cheque *potovalni ček* ⓜ po-to-val-nee chek
trousers *hlače* ⓕ hla-che
twin beds *ločeni postelji* ⓕ pl lo-che-nee pos-tel-yee
tyre *guma* ⓕ goo-ma

U

underwear *spodnje perilo* ⓝ spod-nye pe-ree-lo
urgent *nujen* noo-yen

V

vacant *prost* prost
vacation *počitnice* ⓕ pl po-cheet-nee-tse
vegetable *zelenjava* ⓕ ze-len-ya-va
vegetarian a *vegetarijanski* ve-ge-ta-ree-yan-skee
visa *viza* ⓕ vee-za

W

waiter *natakar* ⓜ na-ta-kar
walk v *hoditi* ho-dee-tee
wallet *denarnica* ⓕ de-nar-nee-tsa
warm a *topel* to-pe-oo
wash (something) *prati* pra-tee
watch *zapestna ura* ⓕ za-pest-na oo-ra
water *voda* ⓕ vo-da
we *mi* mee
weekend *vikend* ⓜ vee-kend
west *zahod* ⓜ za-hod
wheelchair *invalidski voziček* ⓜ
  een-va-leed-skee vo-zee-chek
when *kdaj* kdai
where *kje* kye
white *bel* be-oo
who *kdo* kdo
why *zakaj* za-kai
wife *žena* ⓕ zhe-na
window *okno* ⓝ ok-no
wine *vino* ⓝ vee-no
with *z/s* z/s
without *brez* brez
woman *ženska* ⓕ zhen-ska
write *pisati* pee-sa-tee

Y

yellow *rumen* roo-men
yes *da* da
yesterday *včeraj* vche-rai
you sg inf/pol *ti/vi* tee/vee
you pl *vi* vee

Spanish

spanish alphabet

A a a	B b be	C c the	Ch ch che	D d de
E e e	F f e·fe	G g khe	H h a·che	I i ee
J j kho·ta	K k ka	L l e·le	LL ll e·lye	M m e·me
N n e·ne	Ñ ñ e·nye	O o o	P p pe	Q q koo
R r e·re	S s e·se	T t te	U u oo	V v oo·ve
W w oo·ve do·vle	X x e·kees	Y y ee·grye·ga	Z z the·ta	

■ spanish

introduction

The lively and picturesque language of Cervantes' *Don Quijote* and Almodóvar's movies, Spanish (*español* es·pa·*nyol*), or Castilian (*castellano* kas·te·*lya*·no), as it's also called in Spain, has over 390 million speakers worldwide. Outside Spain, it's the language of most of Latin America and the West Indies and is also spoken in the Philippines and Guam, in some areas of the African coast and in the US.

Spanish belongs to the Romance group of languages – the descendents of Latin – together with French, Italian, Portuguese and Romanian. It's derived from Vulgar Latin, which Roman soldiers and merchants brought to the Iberian Peninsula during the period of Roman conquest (3rd to 1st century BC). By 19 BC Spain had become totally Romanised and Latin became the language of the peninsula in the four centuries that followed. Thanks to the Arabic invasion in AD 711 and the Arabs' continuing presence in Spain during the next eight centuries, Spanish has also been strongly influenced by Arabic, although mostly in the vocabulary. Today's Castilian is spoken in the north, centre and south of Spain. Completing the colourful linguistic profile of the country, Basque (*euskera* e·*oos*·ke·ra), Catalan (*catalán* ka·ta·*lan*) and Galician (*gallego* ga·*lye*·go) are also official languages in Spain, though Castilian covers by far the largest territory.

Besides the shared vocabulary of Latin origin that English and Spanish have in common, there's also a large corpus of words from the indigenous American languages that have entered English via Spanish. After Columbus' discovery of the New World in 1492, America's indigenous languages had a considerable impact on Spanish, especially in words to do with flora, fauna and topography (such as *tobacco*, *chocolate*, *coyote*, *canyon*, to name a few).

Even if you're not familiar with the sound of Spanish through, say, the voices of José Carreras or Julio Iglesias, you'll be easily seduced by this melodic language and have fun trying to roll your *rr*'s like the locals. You may have heard the popular legend about one of the Spanish kings having a slight speech impediment which prompted all of Spain to mimic his lisp. Unfortunately, this charming explanation of the lisping 's' is only a myth – it's actually due to the way Spanish evolved from Latin and has nothing to do with lisping monarchs at all. So, when you hear someone say *gracias* gra·thyas, they're no more lisping than when you say 'thank you' in English.

pronunciation

vowel sounds

Vowels are pronounced short and fairly closed. The sound remains level, and each vowel is pronounced as an individual unit. There are, however, a number of cases where two vowel sounds become very closely combined (so-called diphthongs).

symbol	english equivalent	spanish example	transliteration
a	run	*agua*	a·gwa
ai	aisle	*bailar*	bai·*lar*
ay	say	*seis*	says
e	bet	*número*	noo·me·ro
ee	see	*día*	dee·a
o	pot	*ojo*	o·kho
oo	zoo	*gusto*	goo·sto
ow	how	*autobús*	ow·to·*boos*
oy	toy	*hoy*	oy

word stress

Spanish words have stress, which means you emphasise one syllable of a word over another. Here's a rule of thumb: when a written word ends in *n*, *s* or a vowel, the stress falls on the second-last syllable. Otherwise, the final syllable is stressed. If you see an accent mark over a syllable, it cancels out this rule and you just stress that syllable instead. You needn't worry about this though, as the stressed syllables are always italicised in our pronunciation guides .

consonant sounds

Remember that in Spanish the letter *h* is never pronounced. The Spanish *v* sounds more like a *b*, said with the lips pressed together. When ending a word, *d* is pronounced soft, like a *th*, or it's so slight it doesn't get pronounced at all. Finally, try to roll your *r*'s, especially at the start of a word and in words with *rr*.

symbol	english equivalent	spanish example	transliteration
b	**b**ed	*barco*	*bar*·ko
ch	**ch**eat	*chica*	*chee*·ka
d	**d**og	*dinero*	dee·*ne*·ro
f	**f**at	*fiesta*	*fye*·sta
g	**g**o	*gato*	*ga*·to
k	**k**it	*cabeza, queso*	ka·*be*·tha, *ke*·so
kh	lo**ch** (harsh and guttural)	*jardín, gente*	khar·*deen*, *khen*·te
l	**l**ot	*lago*	*la*·go
ly	mi**lli**on	*llamada*	lya·*ma*·da
m	**m**an	*mañana*	ma·*nya*·na
n	**n**ot	*nuevo*	*nwe*·vo
ny	ca**ny**on	*señora*	se·*nyo*·ra
p	**p**et	*padre*	*pa*·dre
r	like '**tt**' in 'bu**tt**er' said fast	*hora*	*o*·ra
rr	**r**un (but stronger and rolled)	*ritmo, burro*	*rreet*·mo, *boo*·rro
s	**s**un	*semana*	se·*ma*·na
t	**t**op	*tienda*	*tyen*·da
th	**th**in	*Barcelona, manzana*	bar·the·*lo*·na, man·*tha*·na
v	soft '**b**', between '**v**' and '**b**'	*abrir*	a·*vreer*
w	**w**in	*guardia*	*gwar*·dya
y	**y**es	*viaje*	*vya*·khe

basics

language difficulties

Do you speak English?
¿Habla inglés? *ab·*la een·*gles*

Do you understand?
¿Me entiende? me en·*tyen·*de

I (don't) understand.
(No) Entiendo. (no) een·*tyen·*do

What does (*cuenta*) mean?
¿Qué significa (cuenta)? ke seeg·nee·*fee·*ka (*kwen·*ta)

How do you ...? *¿Cómo se ...?* *ko·*mo se ...
  pronounce this *pronuncia esta* pro·*noon·*thya *es·*ta
  word *palabra* pa·*lab·*ra
  write (*ciudad*) *escribe (ciudad)* es·*kree·*be (thee·oo·*da*)

Could you *¿Puede ...,* *pwe·*de ...
please ...? *por favor?* por fa·*vor*
  repeat that *repetir* rre·pe·*teer*
  speak more slowly *hablar más despacio* ab·*lar* mas des·*pa·*thyo
  write it down *escribirlo* es·kree·*beer·*lo

---

essentials

Yes.	*Sí.*	see
No.	*No.*	no
Please.	*Por favor.*	por fa·*vor*
Thank you (very much).	*(Muchas) Gracias.*	(*moo·*chas) *gra·*thyas
You're welcome.	*De nada.*	de *na·*da
Excuse me.	*Perdón/Discúlpeme.*	per·*don*/dees·*kool·*pe·me
Sorry.	*Lo siento.*	lo *syen·*to

numbers

0	cero	*the*·ro	16	dieciséis	dye·thee·*seys*
1	uno	*oo*·no	17	diecisiete	dye·thee·*sye*·te
2	dos	dos	18	dieciocho	dye·thee·*o*·cho
3	tres	tres	19	diecinueve	dye·thee·*nwe*·ve
4	cuatro	*kwa*·tro	20	veinte	*veyn*·te
5	cinco	*theen*·ko	21	veintiuno	veyn·tee·*oo*·no
6	seis	seys	22	veintidós	veyn·tee·*dos*
7	siete	*sye*·te	30	treinta	*treyn*·ta
8	ocho	*o*·cho	40	cuarenta	kwa·*ren*·ta
9	nueve	*nwe*·ve	50	cincuenta	theen·*kwen*·ta
10	diez	dyeth	60	sesenta	se·*sen*·ta
11	once	*on*·the	70	setenta	se·*ten*·ta
12	doce	*do*·the	80	ochenta	o·*chen*·ta
13	trece	*tre*·the	90	noventa	no·*ven*·ta
14	catorce	ka·*tor*·the	100	cien	thyen
15	quince	*keen*·the	1000	mil	mil

time & dates

What time is it?	*¿Qué hora es?*	ke *o*·ra es
It's one o'clock.	*Es la una.*	es la *oo*·na
It's (10) o'clock.	*Son (las diez).*	son (las dyeth)
Quarter past (one).	*Es (la una) y cuarto.*	es (la *oo*·na) ee *kwar*·to
Half past (one).	*Es (la una) y media.*	es (la *oo*·na) ee *me*·dya
Quarter to (one).	*Es (la una) menos cuarto.*	es (la *oo*·na) *me*·nos *kwar*·to
At what time ...?	*¿A qué hora ...?*	a ke *o*·ra ...
At ...	*A las ...*	a las ...
am	*de la mañana*	de la ma·*nya*·na
pm	*de la tarde*	de la *tar*·de
Monday	*lunes*	*loo*·nes
Tuesday	*martes*	*mar*·tes
Wednesday	*miércoles*	*myer*·ko·les
Thursday	*jueves*	*khwe*·ves
Friday	*viernes*	*vyer*·nes
Saturday	*sábado*	*sa*·ba·do
Sunday	*domingo*	do·*meen*·go

January	*enero*	e·*ne*·ro
February	*febrero*	fe·*bre*·ro
March	*marzo*	*mar*·tho
April	*abril*	a·*breel*
May	*mayo*	*ma*·yo
June	*junio*	*khoo*·nyo
July	*julio*	*khoo*·lyo
August	*agosto*	a·*gos*·to
September	*septiembre*	sep·*tyem*·bre
October	*octubre*	ok·*too*·bre
November	*noviembre*	no·*vyem*·bre
December	*diciembre*	dee·*thyem*·bre

What date is it today?
  ¿Qué día es hoy?   ke *dee*·a es oy

It's (18 October).
  Es (el dieciocho de octubre).   es (el dye·thee·*o*·cho de ok·*too*·bre)

since (May)	*desde (mayo)*	*des*·de (*ma*·yo)
until (June)	*hasta (junio)*	*as*·ta (*khoo*·nyo)

last ...		
night	*anoche*	a·*no*·che
week	*la semana pasada*	la se·*ma*·na pa·*sa*·da
month	*el mes pasado*	el mes pa·*sa*·do
year	*el año pasado*	el *a*·nyo pa·*sa*·do

next ...	*... que viene*	... ke *vye*·ne
week	*la semana*	la se·*ma*·na
month	*el mes*	el mes
year	*el año*	el *a*·nyo

yesterday/tomorrow ...	*ayer/mañana por la ...*	a·*yer*/ma·*nya*·na por la ...
morning	*mañana*	ma·*nya*·na
afternoon	*tarde*	*tar*·de
evening	*noche*	*no*·che

weather

What's the weather like?	*¿Qué tiempo hace?*	ke *tyem*·po *a*·the

It's ...

cloudy	*Está nublado.*	es·*ta* noo·*bla*·do
cold	*Hace frío.*	*a*·the *free*·o
hot	*Hace calor.*	*a*·the ka·*lor*
raining	*Está lloviendo.*	es·*ta* lyo·*vyen*·do
snowing	*Está nevando.*	es·*ta* ne·*van*·do
sunny	*Hace sol.*	*a*·the sol
warm	*Hace calor.*	*a*·the ka·*lor*
windy	*Hace viento.*	*a*·the *vyen*·to

spring	*primavera* f	pree·ma·*ve*·ra
summer	*verano* m	ve·*ra*·no
autumn	*otoño* m	o·*to*·nyo
winter	*invierno* m	een·*vyer*·no

border crossing

I'm here ...	*Estoy aquí ...*	es·*toy* a·*kee* ...
in transit	*en tránsito*	en *tran*·see·to
on business	*de negocios*	de ne·*go*·thyos
on holiday	*de vacaciones*	de va·ka·*thyo*·nes

I'm here for ...	*Estoy aquí por ...*	es·*toy* a·*kee* por ...
(10) days	*(diez) días*	(dyeth) *dee*·as
(three) weeks	*(tres) semanas*	(tres) se·*ma*·nas
(two) months	*(dos) meses*	(dos) *me*·ses

I'm going to (Salamanca).
Voy a (Salamanca).   voy a (sa·la·*man*·ka)

I'm staying at the (Flores Hotel).
Me estoy alojando en (hotel Flores).   me es·*toy* a·lo·*khan*·do en (o·*tel flo*·res)

I have nothing to declare.
No tengo nada que declarar.   no *ten*·go *na*·da ke dek·la·*rar*

I have something to declare.
Quisiera declarar algo.   kee·*sye*·ra dek·la·*rar al*·go

That's (not) mine.
Eso (no) es mío.   eso (no) es *mee*·o

transport

tickets & luggage

Where can I buy a ticket?
¿Dónde puedo comprar un billete?   don·de pwe·do kom·prar oon bee·lye·te

Do I need to book a seat?
¿Tengo que reservar?   ten·go ke rre·ser·var

One ... ticket to (Barcelona), please.	*Un billete ... a (Barcelona), por favor.*	oon bee·lye·te ... a (bar·the·lo·na) por fa·vor
one-way	*sencillo*	sen·thee·lyo a
return	*de ida y vuelta*	de ee·da ee vwel·ta

I'd like to ... my ticket.	*Me gustaría ... mi billete.*	me goos·ta·ree·a ... mee bee·lye·te
cancel	*cancelar*	kan·the·lar
change	*cambiar*	kam·byar
confirm	*confirmar*	kon·feer·mar

How much is it?
¿Cuánto cuesta?   kwan·to kwes·ta

Is there air conditioning?
¿Hay aire acondicionado?   ai ai·re a·kon·dee·thyo·na·do

Is there a toilet?
¿Hay servicios?   ai ser·vee·thyos

How long does the trip take?
¿Cuánto se tarda?   kwan·to se tar·da

Is it a direct route?
¿Es un viaje directo?   es oon vya·khe dee·rek·to

I'd like a luggage locker.
Quisiera un casillero de consigna.   kee·sye·ra oon ka·see·lye·ro de kon·seeg·na

My luggage	Mis maletas	mees ma·*le*·tas
has been ...	han sido ...	an *see*·do ...
damaged	dañadas	da·*nya*·das
lost	perdidas	per·*dee*·das
stolen	robadas	rro·*ba*·das

getting around

Where does flight (G10) arrive/depart?
¿Dónde llega/sale el vuelo (G10)? don·de lye·ga/*sa*·le el *vwe*·lo (khe dyeth)

Where's the ...?	¿Dónde está...?	don·de es·*ta* ...
arrivals hall	el hall de partidas	el hol de par·*tee*·das
departures hall	el hall de llegadas	el hol de lye·*ga*·das
duty-free shop	la tienda libre de impuestos	la *tyen*·da *lee*·bre de eem·*pwe*·stos
gate (12)	la puerta (doce)	la *pwer*·ta (*do*·the)

Is this the ...	¿Es el ... para	es el ... *pa*·ra
to (Valencia)?	(Valencia)?	(va·*len*·thya)
boat	barco	*bar*·ko
bus	autobús	ow·to·*boos*
plane	avión	a·*vyon*
train	tren	tren

What time's	¿A qué hora es el	a ke *o*·ra es el
the ... bus?	... autobús?	... ow·to·*boos*
first	primer	pree·*mer*
last	último	*ool*·tee·mo
next	próximo	*prok*·see·mo

At what time does it arrive/leave?
¿A qué hora llega/sale? a ke *o*·ra lye·ga/*sa*·le

How long will it be delayed?
¿Cuánto tiempo se retrasará? *kwan*·to *tyem*·po se rre·tra·sa·*ra*

What station/stop is this?
¿Cuál es esta estación/parada? kwal es *es*·ta es·ta·*thyon*/pa·*ra*·da

What's the next station/stop?
¿Cuál es la próxima estación/parada? kwal es la *prok*·see·ma es·ta·*thyon*/pa·*ra*·da

Does it stop at (Aranjuez)?
¿Para en (Aranjuez)? *pa·ra en (a·ran·khweth)*

Please tell me when we get to (Seville).
¿Puede avisarme *pwe·de a·vee·sar·me*
cuando lleguemos a (Sevilla)? *kwan·do lye·ge·mos a (se·vee·lya)*

How long do we stop here?
¿Cuánto tiempo vamos a parar aquí? *kwan·to tyem·po va·mos a pa·rar a·kee*

Is this seat available?
¿Está libre este asiento? *es·ta lee·bre es·te a·syen·to*

That's my seat.
Ése es mi asiento. *e·se es mee a·syen·to*

I'd like a taxi ...	Quisiera un taxi ...	*kee·sye·ra oon tak·see ...*
at (9am)	a (las nueve	a (las nwe·ve
	de la mañana)	de la ma·nya·na)
now	ahora	a·o·ra
tomorrow	mañana	ma·nya·na

Is this taxi available?
¿Está libre este taxi? *es·ta lee·bre es·te tak·see*

How much is it to ...?
¿Cuánto cuesta ir a ...? *kwan·to kwes·ta eer a ...*

Please put the meter on.
Por favor, ponga el taxímetro. *por fa·vor pon·ga el tak·see·me·tro*

Please take me to (this address).
Por favor, lléveme a (esta dirección). *por fa·vor lye·ve·me a (es·ta dee·rek·thyon)*

Please ...	Por favor ...	*por fa·vor ...*
slow down	vaya más despacio	va·ya mas des·pa·thyo
stop here	pare aquí	pa·re a·kee
wait here	espere aquí	es·pe·re a·kee

car, motorbike & bicycle hire

I'd like to hire a ...	Quisiera alquilar ...	*kee·sye·ra al·kee·lar ...*
bicycle	una bicicleta	*oo·na bee·thee·kle·ta*
car	un coche	*oon ko·che*
motorbike	una moto	*oo·na mo·to*

with ...	con ...	kon ...
a driver	chófer	cho·fer
air conditioning	aire acondicionado	ai·re a·kon·dee·thyo·na·do
antifreeze	anticongelante	an·tee·kon·khe·lan·te
snow chains	cadenas de nieve	ka·de·nas de nye·ve

How much for ... hire?	¿Cuánto cuesta el alquiler por ...?	kwan·to kwes·ta el al·kee·ler por ...
hourly	hora	o·ra
daily	día	dee·a
weekly	semana	se·ma·na

air	aire m	ai·re
oil	aceite m	a·they·te
petrol	gasolina f	ga·so·lee·na
tyres	neumáticos f pl	ne·oo·ma·tee·kos

I need a mechanic.
Necesito un mecánico.
ne·the·see·to oon me·ka·nee·ko

I've run out of petrol.
Me he quedado sin gasolina.
me e ke·da·do sen ga·so·lee·na

I have a flat tyre.
Tengo un pinchazo.
ten·go oon peen·cha·tho

directions

Where's the ...?	¿Dónde está/ están ...? sg/pl	don·de es·ta/ es·tan ...
bank	el banco sg	el ban·ko
city centre	el centro de la ciudad sg	el then·tro de la theew·da
hotel	el hotel sg	el o·tel
market	el mercado sg	el mer·ka·do
police station	la comisaría sg	la ko·mee·sa·ree·a
post office	el correos sg	el ko·rre·os
public toilet	los servicios pl	los ser·vee·thyos
tourist office	la oficina de turismo sg	la o·fee·thee·na de too·rees·mo

Is this the road to (Valladolid)?
¿Se va a (Valladolid) por esta carretera?
se va a (va·lya·do·*lee*) por *es*·ta ka·rre·*te*·ra

Can you show me (on the map)?
¿Me lo puede indicar (en el mapa)?
me lo *pwe*·de een·dee·*kar* (en el *ma*·pa)

What's the address?
¿Cuál es la dirección?
kwal es la dee·rek·*thyon*

How far is it?
¿A cuánta distancia está?
a *kwan*·ta dees·*tan*·thya es·*ta*

How do I get there?
¿Cómo se llega ahí?
ko·mo se *lye*·ga a·*ee*

Turn ...	Doble ...	do·ble ...
at the corner	en la esquina	en la es·*kee*·na
at the traffic lights	en el semáforo	en el se·*ma*·fo·ro
left	a la izquierda	a la eeth·*kyer*·da
right	a la iderecha	a la de·*re*·cha

It's ...	Está ...	es·ta ...
behind ...	detrás de ...	de·*tras* de ...
far away	lejos	*le*·khos
here	aquí	a·*kee*
in front of ...	enfrente de ...	en·*fren*·te de ...
left	por la izquierda	por la eeth·*kyer*·da
near (to ...)	cerca (de ...)	*ther*·ka (de ...)
next to ...	al lado de ...	al *la*·do de ...
opposite ...	frente a ...	*fren*·te a ...
right	por la derecha	por la de·*re*·cha
straight ahead	todo recto	*to*·do *rrek*·to
there	ahí	a·*ee*

by bus	por autobús	por *ow*·to·boos
by taxi	por taxi	por *tak*·see
by train	por tren	por tren
on foot	a pie	a pye

north	norte m	*nor*·te
south	sur m	soor
east	este m	*es*·te
west	oeste m	o·*es*·te

Acceso/Salida	ak·*the*·so/sa·*lee*·da	Entrance/Exit
Abierto/Cerrado	a·*byer*·to/the·*rra*·do	Open/Closed
Hay Lugar	ai loo·*gar*	Rooms Available
No Hay Lugar	no ai loo·*gar*	No Vacancies
Información	een·for·ma·*thyon*	Information
Comisaría	ko·mee·sa·*ree*·a	Police Station
de Policía	de po·lee·*thee*·a	
Prohibido	pro·ee·*bee*·do	Prohibited
Servicios	ser·*vee*·thyos	Toilets
Caballeros	ka·ba·*lye*·ros	Men
Señoras	se·*nyo*·ras	Women
Caliente/Frío	ka·*lyen*·te/*free*·o	Hot/Cold

accommodation

finding accommodation

Where's a ...?	¿Dónde hay ...?	*don*·de ai ...
camping ground	un terreno de cámping	oon te·*rre*·no de *kam*·peeng
guesthouse	una pensión	*oo*·na pen·*syon*
hotel	un hotel	oon o·*tel*
youth hostel	un albergue juvenil	oon al·*ber*·ge khoo·ve·*neel*

Can you recommend somewhere ...?	¿Puede recomendar algún sitio ...?	*pwe*·de rre·ko·men·*dar* al·*goon* see·tio ...
cheap	barato	ba·*ra*·to
good	bueno	*bwe*·no
nearby	cercano	ther·*ka*·no

I'd like to book a room, please.
Quisiera reservar una habitación.　　kee·*sye*·ra rre·ser·*var* oo·na a·bee·ta·*thyon*

I have a reservation.
He hecho una reserva.　　e *e*·cho *oo*·na rre·*ser*·va

My name's ...
Me llamo ...　　me *lya*·mo ...

Do you have a ... room?	¿Tiene una habitación ...?	tye·ne oo·na a·bee·ta·thyon ...
single	individual	een·dee·vee·dwal
double	doble	do·ble
twin	con dos camas	kon dos ka·mas

How much is it per ...?	¿Cuánto cuesta por ...?	kwan·to kwes·ta por ...
night	noche	no·che
person	persona	per·so·na

Can I pay by ...?	¿Puedo pagar con ...?	pwe·do pa·gar con ...
credit card	tarjeta de crédito	tar·khe·ta de kre·dee·to
travellers cheque	cheque de viajero	che·ke de vya·khe·ro

I'd like to stay for (three) nights/weeks.
 Quisiera quedarme por (tres)   kee·sye·ra ke·dar·me por (tres)
 noches/semanas.   no·ches/se·ma·nas

From (July 2) to (July 6).
 Desde (el dos de julio)   des·de (el dos de khoo·lyo)
 hasta (el seis de julio).   as·ta (el seys de khoo·lyo)

Can I see it?
 ¿Puedo verla?   pwe·do ver·la

Am I allowed to camp here?
 ¿Se puede acampar aquí?   se pwe·de a·kam·par a·kee

Is there a camp site nearby?
 ¿Hay un terreno de cámping   ai oon te·rre·no de kam·peeng
 cercano?   ther·ka·no

requests & queries

When/Where's breakfast served?
 ¿Cuándo/Dónde se sirve el desayuno?   kwan·do/don·de se seer·ve el de·sa·yoo·no

Please wake me at (seven).
 Por favor, despiérteme a (las siete). por fa·vor des·pyer·te·me a (las sye·te)

Could I have my key, please?
 ¿Me puede dar la llave, por favor?   me pwe·de dar la lya·ve por fa·vor

Can I get another (blanket)?
 ¿Puede darme otra (manta)?   pwe·de dar·me ot·ra (man·ta)

Is there a/an ...?	¿Hay ...?	ai ...
elevator	ascensor	as·then·sor
safe	una caja fuerte	oo·na ka·kha fwer·te

The room is too ...	Es demasiado ...	es de·ma·sya·do ...
expensive	cara	ka·ra
noisy	ruidosa	rrwee·do·sa
small	pequeña	pe·ke·nya

The ... doesn't work.	No funciona ...	no foon·thyo·na ...
air conditioning	el aire	el ai·re
	acondicionado	a·kon·dee·thyo·na·do
fan	el ventilador	el ven·tee·la·dor
toilet	el retrete	el rre·tre·te

This ... isn't clean.	Esta ... no está limpia.	es·ta ... no es·ta leem·pya
pillow	almohada	al·mwa·da
sheet	sábana	sa·ba·na
towel	toalla	to·a·lya

checking out

What time is checkout?
¿A qué hora hay que dejar
libre la habitación?
a ke o·ra ai ke de·khar
lee·bre la a·bee·ta·thyon

Can I leave my luggage here?
¿Puedo dejar las maletas aquí?
pwe·do de·khar las ma·le·tas a·kee

Could I have ...,	¿Me puede dar ...,	me pwe·de dar ...
please?	por favor?	por fa·vor
my deposit	mi depósito	mee de·po·see·to
my passport	mi pasaporte	mee pa·sa·por·te
my valuables	mis objetos de valor	mees ob·khe·tos de va·lor

communications & banking

the internet

Where's the local Internet café?
¿Dónde hay un cibercafé cercano?
don·de ai oon thee·ber·ka·fe ther·ka·no

How much is it per hour?
¿Cuánto cuesta por hora?
kwan·to kwes·ta por o·ra

I'd like to ...	*Quisiera ...*	*kee·sye·ra ...*
check my email	*revisar mi correo electrónico*	*rre·vee·sar mee ko·re·o e·lek·tro·nee·ko*
get Internet access	*usar el Internet*	*oo·sar el een·ter·net*
use a printer	*usar una impresora*	*oo·sar oo·na eem·pre·so·ra*
use a scanner	*usar un escáner*	*oo·sar oon es·ka·ner*

mobile/cell phone

I'd like a ...	*Quisiera ...*	*kee·sye·ra ...*
mobile/cell phone for hire	*un móvil para alquilar*	*oon mo·veel pa·ra al·kee·lar*
SIM card for your network	*una tarjeta SIM para su red*	*oo·na tar·khe·ta seem pa·ra soo rred*

What are the rates?
¿Cuál es la tarifa?
kwal es la ta·ree·fa

telephone

What's your phone number?
¿Cuál es su/tu número de teléfono? pol/inf
kwal es soo/too noo·me·ro de te·le·fo·no

The number is ...
El número es ...
el noo·me·ro es ...

Where's the nearest public phone?
¿Dónde hay una cabina telefónica?
don·de ai oo·na ka·bee·na te·le·fo·nee·ka

I'd like to buy a phonecard.
Quiero comprar una tarjeta telefónica.
kye·ro kom·prar oo·na tar·khe·ta te·le·fo·nee·ka

I want to ...	Quiero ...	kye·ro ...
call (Singapore)	hacer una llamada (a Singapur)	a·ther oo·na lya·ma·da (a seen·ga·poor)
make a local call	hacer una llamada local	a·ther oo·na lya·ma·da lo·kal
reverse the charges	hacer una llamada a cobro revertido	a·ther oo·na lya·ma·da a ko·bro rre·ver·tee·do

How much does ... cost?	¿Cuánto cuesta ...?	kwan·to kwes·ta ...
a (three)-minute call	una llamada de (tres) minutos	oo·na lya·ma·da de (tres) mee·noo·tos
each extra minute	cada minuto extra	ka·da mee·noo·to ek·stra

It's (one euro) per (minute).
(Un euro) por (un minuto).

(oon e·oo·ro) por (oon mee·noo·to)

post office

I want to send a ...	Quisiera enviar ...	kee·sye·ra en·vee·ar ...
fax	un fax	oon faks
letter	una carta	oo·na kar·ta
parcel	un paquete	oon pa·ke·te
postcard	una postal	oo·na pos·tal

I want to buy ...	Quisiera comprar ...	kee·sye·ra kom·prar ...
an envelope	un sobre	oon so·bre
stamps	sellos	se·lyos

Please send it (to Australia) by ...	Por favor, mándelo (a Australia) por ...	por fa·vor man·de·lo (a ows·tra·lya) por ...
airmail	vía aérea	vee·a a·e·re·a
express mail	correo urgente	ko·rre·o oor·khen·te
registered mail	correo certificado	ko·rre·o ther·tee·fee·ka·do
surface mail	vía terrestre	vee·a te·rres·tre

Is there any mail for me?
¿Hay alguna carta para mí?

ai al·goo·na kar·ta pa·ra mee

bank

Where's a/an ...?	¿Dónde hay ...?	don·de ai ...
ATM	un cajero automático	oon ka·khe·ro ow·to·ma·tee·ko o
foreign exchange office	una oficina de cambio	oo·na o·fee·thee·na de kam·byo

I'd like to ...	Me gustaría ...	me goos·ta·ree·a ...
cash a cheque	cambiar un cheque	kam·byar oon che·ke
change a travellers cheque	cobrar un cheque de viajero	ko·brar oon che·ke de vee·a·khe·ro
change money	cambiar dinero	kam·byar dee·ne·ro
get a cash advance	obtener un adelanto	ob·te·ner oon a·de·lan·to
withdraw money	sacar dinero	sa·kar dee·ne·ro

What's the ...?	¿Cuál es ...?	kwal es ...
commission	la comisión	la ko·mee·syon
exchange rate	el tipo de cambio	el tee·po de kam·byo

| It's (12) euros. | Es (doce) euros. | es (do·the) e·oo·ros |
| It's free. | Es gratis. | es gra·tees |

What's the charge for that?
    ¿Cuánto hay que pagar por eso?   kwan·to ai ke pa·gar por e·so

What time does the bank open?
    ¿A qué hora abre el banco?   a ke o·ra a·bre el ban·ko

Has my money arrived yet?
    ¿Ya ha llegado mi dinero?   ya a lye·ga·do mee dee·ne·ro

sightseeing

getting in

What time does it open/close?
    ¿A qué hora abren/cierran?   a ke o·ra ab·ren/thye·rran

What's the admission charge?
    ¿Cuánto cuesta la entrada?   kwan·to kwes·ta la en·tra·da

Is there a discount for children/students?
    ¿Hay descuentos para niños/estudiantes?   ai des·kwen·tos pa·ra nee·nyos/es·too·dyan·tes

I'd like a ...	Quisiera ...	kee-sye-ra ...
catalogue	un catálogo	oon ka-ta-lo-go
guide	una guía	oo-na gee-a
(local) map	un mapa (de la zona)	oon ma-pa (de la tho-na)

I'd like to see ...	Me gustaría ver ...	me goos-ta-ree-a ver ...
What's that?	¿Qué es eso?	ke es e-so
Can I take a photo?	¿Puedo tomar un foto?	pwe-do to-mar un fo-to

tours

When's the next day trip?

*¿Cuándo es la próxima
excursión de un día?* — kwan-do es la prok-see-ma eks-koor-syon de oon dee-a

When's the next tour?

¿Cuándo es el próximo recorrido? — kwan-do es ela prok-see-mo rre-ko-rree-do

Is ... included?	¿Incluye ...?	een-kloo-ye ...
accommodation	alojamiento	a-lo-kha-myen-to
the admission charge	entrada	en-tra-da
food	comida	ko-mee-da
transport	transporte	trans-por-te

How long is the tour?

¿Cuánto dura el recorrido? — kwan-to doo-ra el rre-ko-rree-do

What time should we be back?

¿A qué hora tenemos que volver? — a ke o-ra te-ne-mos ke vol-ver

sightseeing

castle	castillo m	kas-tee-lyo
cathedral	catedral f	ka-te-dral
church	iglesia f	ee-gle-sya
main square	plaza mayor f	pla-tha ma-yor
monastery	monasterio m	mo-na-ste-ryo
monument	monumento m	mo-noo-men-to
museum	museo m	moo-se-o
old city	casco antiguo m	kas-ko an-tee-gwo
palace	palacio m	pa-la-thyo
ruins	ruinas f pl	rrwee-nas
stadium	estadio m	es-ta-dyo
statues	estatuas f pl	es-ta-twas

shopping

enquiries

Where's a ...?	¿Dónde está ...?	don·de es·ta ...
bank	el banco	el ban·ko
bookshop	la librería	la lee·bre·ree·a
camera shop	la tienda de fotografía	la tyen·da de fo·to·gra·fee·a
department store	el centro comercial	el then·tro ko·mer·thyal
grocery store	la tienda de comestibles	la tyen·da de ko·mes·tee·bles
market	el mercado	el mer·ka·do
newsagency	el quiosco	el kyos·ko
supermarket	el supermercado	el soo·per·mer·ka·do

Where can I buy (a padlock)?
¿Dónde puedo comprar (un candado)?
don·de pwe·do kom·prar (oon kan·da·do)

I'm looking for ...
Estoy buscando ...
es·toy boos·kan·do ...

Can I look at it?
¿Puedo verlo?
pwe·do ver·lo

Do you have any others?
¿Tiene otros?
tye·ne o·tros

Does it have a guarantee?
¿Tiene garantía?
tye·ne ga·ran·tee·a

Can I have it sent overseas?
¿Pueden enviarlo por correo a otro país?
pwe·den en·vee·ar·lo por ko·rre·o a o·tro pa·ees

Can I have my ... repaired?
¿Puede reparar mi ... aquí?
pwe·de rre·pa·rar mee ... a·kee

It's faulty.
Es defectuoso.
es de·fek·too·o·so

I'd like ..., please.	Quisiera ..., por favor.	kee-sye-ra ... por fa-vor
a bag	una bolsa	oo-na bol-sa
a refund	que me devuelva	ke me de-vwel-va
	el dinero	el dee-ne-ro
to return this	devolver esto	de-vol-ver es-to

paying

How much is it?
¿Cuánto cuesta esto?
kwan-to kwes-ta es-to

Can you write down the price?
¿Puede escribir el precio?
pwe-de es-kree-beer el pre-thyo

That's too expensive.
Es muy caro.
es mooy ka-ro

What's your lowest price?
¿Cuál es su precio más bajo?
kwal es soo pre-thyo mas ba-kho

I'll give you (five) euros.
Te daré (cinco) euros.
te da-re (theen-ko) e-oo-ros

There's a mistake in the bill.
Hay un error en la cuenta.
ai oon e-rror en la kwen-ta

Do you accept ...?	¿Aceptan ...?	a-thep-tan ...
credit cards	tarjetas de crédito	tar-khe-tas de kre-dee-to
debit cards	tarjetas de débito	tar-khe-tas de de-bee-to
travellers cheques	cheques de viajero	che-kes de vya-khe-ro
I'd like ..., please.	Quisiera ..., por favor.	kee-sye-ra ... por fa-vor
a receipt	un recibo	oon rre-thee-bo
my change	mi cambio	mee kam-byo

clothes & shoes

Can I try it on?
¿Me lo puedo probar?
me lo pwe-do pro-bar

My size is (40).
Uso la talla (cuarenta).
oo-so la ta-lya (kwa-ren-ta)

It doesn't fit.
No me queda bien.
no me ke-da byen

small	pequeño/a m/f	pe-ke-nyo/a
medium	mediano/a m/f	me-dya-no/a
large	grande m&f	gran-de

books & music

I'd like a ...	Quisiera un ...	kee-sye-ra oon ...
newspaper	periódico	pe-ryo-dee-ko
(in English)	(en inglés)	(en een-gles)
pen	bolígrafo	bo-lee-gra-fo

Is there an English-language bookshop?
¿Hay alguna librería en inglés?
ai al-goo-na lee-bre-ree-a en een-gles

I'm looking for something by (Enrique Iglesias).
Estoy buscando algo de
(Enrique Iglesias).
es-toy boos-kan-do al-go de
(en-ree-ke ee-gle-syas)

Can I listen to this?
¿Puedo escuchar esto aquí?
pwe-do es-koo-char es-to a-kee

photography

Can you ...?	¿Puede usted ...?	pwe-de oos-ted ...
burn a CD from	copiar un disco	ko-pyar oon dees-ko
my memory card	compacto de esta	kom-pak-to de es-ta
	tarjeta de memoria	tar-khe-ta de me-mo-rya
develop this film	revelar este carrete	rre-ve-lar es-te ka-rre-te
load my film	cargar el carrete	kar-gar el ka-rre-te

I need a ... film	Necesito película ...	ne-the-see-to pe-lee-koo-la ...
for this camera.	para esta cámara.	pa-ra es-ta ka-ma-ra
APS	APS	a pe e-se
B&W	en blanco y negro	en blan-ko y ne-gro
colour	en color	en ko-lor
slide	para diapositivas	pa-ra dya-po-see-tee-vas
(200) speed	de sensibilidad	de sen-see-bee-lee-da
	(doscientos)	(dos-thyen-tos)

When will it be ready? ¿Cuándo estará listo? kwan-do es-ta-ra lees-to

meeting people

greetings, goodbyes & introductions

Hello/Hi.	Hola.	o·la
Good night.	Buenas noches.	bwe·nas no·ches
Goodbye/Bye.	Adiós.	a·dyos
See you later.	Hasta luego.	as·ta lwe·go

Mr	Señor	se·nyor
Mrs	Señora	se·nyo·ra
Miss	Señorita	se·nyo·ree·ta

How are you?	¿Qué tal?	ke tal
Fine, thanks.	Bien, gracias.	byen gra·thyas
And you?	¿Y Usted/tú? pol/inf	ee oos·te/too
What's your name?	¿Cómo se llama Usted? pol	ko·mo se lya·ma oos·te
	¿Cómo te llamas? inf	ko·mo te lya·mas
My name is ...	Me llamo ...	me lya·mo ...
I'm pleased to meet you.	Mucho gusto.	moo·cho goos·to

This is my ...	Éste/Ésta es mi ... m/f	es·te/a es mee ...
boyfriend	novio	no·vyo
brother	hermano	er·ma·no
daughter	hija	ee·kho
father	padre	pa·dre
friend	amigo/a m/f	a·mee·go/a
girlfriend	novia	no·vya
husband	marido	ma·ree·do
mother	madre	ma·dre
partner (intimate)	pareja	pa·re·kha
sister	hermana	er·ma·na
son	hijo	ee·kho
wife	esposa	es·po·sa

Here's my ...	Éste/Ésta es mi ... m/f	es·te/a es mee ...
What's your ...?	¿Cuál es su/tu ...? pol/inf	kwal es soo/too ...
address	dirección f	dee·rek·thyon
email address	dirección de email f	dee·rek·thyon de ee·mayl
fax number	número de fax m	noo·me·ro de faks
phone number	número de teléfono m	noo·me·ro de te·le·fo·no

meeting people – SPANISH

353

occupations

What's your occupation?	¿A qué se dedica Usted? pol	a ke se de-*dee*-ka oos-*te*
	¿A qué te dedicas? inf	a ke te de-*dee*-kas
I'm a/an ...	Soy un/una ... m/f	soy oon/*oo*-na ...
artist	artista m&f	ar-*tees*-ta
business person	comerciante m&f	ko-mer-*thyan*-te
farmer	agricultor m	a-gree-kool-*tor*
	agricultora f	a-gree-kool-*to*-ra
manual worker	obrero/a m/f	o-*bre*-ro/a
office worker	oficinista m&f	o-fee-thee-*nees*-ta
scientist	científico/a m/f	thyen-*tee*-fee-ko/a
student	estudiante m&f	es-too-*dyan*-te
tradesperson	artesano/a m/f	ar-te-*sa*-no/a

background

Where are you from?	¿De dónde es Usted? pol	de *don*-de es oos-*te*
	¿De dónde eres? inf	de *don*-de e-res
I'm from ...	Soy de ...	soy de ...
Australia	Australia	ow-*stra*-lya
Canada	Canadá	ka-na-*da*
England	Inglaterra	een-gla-*te*-rra
New Zealand	Nueva Zelanda	*nwe*-va the-*lan*-da
the USA	los Estados Unidos	los es-*ta*-dos oo-*nee*-dos
Are you married?	¿Estás casado/a? m/f	es-*tas* ka-*sa*-do/a
I'm married.	Estoy casado/a. m/f	es-*toy* ka-*sa*-do/a
I'm single.	Soy soltero/a. m/f	soy sol-*te*-ro/a

age

How old ...?	¿Cuántos años ...?	*kwan*-tos a-nyos ...
are you	tienes inf	*tye*-nes
is your daughter	tiene su hija pol	*tye*-ne soo ee-*kha*
is your son	tiene su hijo pol	*tye*-ne soo ee-*kho*
I'm ... years old.	Tengo ... años.	*ten*-go ... a-nyos
He/She is ... years old.	Tiene ... años.	*tye*-ne ... a-nyos

feelings

I'm (not) ...	(No) Tengo ...	(no) ten·go ...
Are you ...?	¿Tiene Usted ...? pol	tye·ne oos·te ...
	¿Tienes ...? inf	tye·nes ...
cold	frío	free·o
hot	calor	ka·lor
hungry	hambre	am·bre
thirsty	sed	se

I'm (not) ...	(No) Estoy ...	(no) es·toy ...
Are you ...?	¿Está Usted ...? pol	es·ta oos·te ...
	¿Estás ...? inf	es·tas ...
happy	feliz m&f	fe·leeth
OK	bien m&f	byen
sad	triste m&f	trees·te
tired	cansado/a m/f	kan·sa·do/a

entertainment

going out

Where can I find ...?	¿Dónde hay ...?	don·de ai ...
clubs	clubs nocturnos	kloobs nok·toor·nos
gay venues	lugares gay	loo·ga·res gai
pubs	bares	ba·res

I feel like going	Tengo ganas de	ten·go ga·nas de
to a/the ...	ir ...	eer ...
concert	a un concierto	a oon kon·thyer·to
movies	al cine	al thee·ne
party	a una fiesta	a oo·na fyes·ta
restaurant	a un restaurante	a oon rres·tow·ran·te
theatre	al teatro	al te·a·tro

interests

Do you like ...	¿Le/Te gusta ...? pol/inf	le/te *goos*·ta ...
I (don't) like ...	(No) Me gusta ...	(no) me *goos*·ta ...
art	el arte	el *ar*·te
movies	el cine	el *thee*·ne
reading	leer	le·*er*
sport	el deporte	el de·*por*·te
travelling	viajar	vya·*khar*

Do you like to ...?	¿Le/Te gusta ...? pol/inf	le/te *goos*·ta ...
dance	ir a bailar	eer a bai·*lar*
go to concerts	ir a conciertos	eer a kon·*thyer*·tos
listen to music	escuchar música	es·koo·*char* moo·*see*·ka

food & drink

finding a place to eat

Can you recommend a ...?	¿Puede recomendar un ...?	*pwe*·de rre·ko·men·*dar* oon ...
bar	bar	bar
café	café	ka·*fe*
restaurant	restaurante	rres·tow·*ran*·te
I'd like ..., please.	Quisiera ..., por favor.	kee·*sye*·ra ... por fa·*vor*
a table for (two)	una mesa para (dos)	*oo*·na *me*·sa *pa*·ra (dos)

ordering food

breakfast	desayuno m	de·sa·*yoo*·no
lunch	comida f	ko·*mee*·da
dinner	almuerzo m	al·*mwer*·tho
snack	tentempié m	ten·tem·*pye*

What would you recommend?
¿Qué recomienda? ke rre·ko·*myen*·da

I'd like (the) ...	Quisiera ..., por favor.	kee-*sye*-ra ... por fa-*vor*
bill	la cuenta	la *kwen*-ta
drink list	la lista de bebidas	la *lees*-ta de be-*bee*-das
menu	el menú	el me-*noo*
that dish	ese plato	e-se *pla*-to

drinks

(cup of) coffee ...	(taza de) café ...	(ta-tha de) ka-*fe* ...
(cup of) tea ...	(taza de) té ...	(ta-tha de) te ...
with milk	con leche	kon *le*-che
without sugar	sin azúcar	seen a-*thoo*-kar
(orange) juice	zumo de (naranja) m	*zoo*-mo de (na-*ran*-kha)
soft drink	refresco m	rre-*fres*-ko
... water	agua ...	*a*-gwa ...
boiled	hervida	er-*vee*-da
(sparkling) mineral	mineral (con gas)	mee-ne-*ral* (kon gas)

in the bar

I'll have ...	Para mí ...	*pa*-ra mee ...
I'll buy you a drink.	Te invito a una copa. inf	le/te een-*vee*-to a *oo*-na *ko*-pa
What would you like?	¿Qué quieres tomar? inf	ke *kye*-res to-*mar*
Cheers!	¡Salud!	sa-*loo*
brandy	coñac m	ko-*nyak*
cocktail	combinado m	kom-bee-*na*-do
red-wine punch	sangría f	san-*gree*-a
a shot of (whisky)	chupito de (güisqui)	choo-*pee*-to de (*gwees*-kee)
a ... of beer	una ... de cerveza	*oo*-na ... de ther-*ve*-tha
bottle	botella	bo-*te*-lya
glass	caña	*ka*-nya
a bottle/glass of ... wine	una botella/copa de vino ...	*oo*-na bo-*te*-lya/*ko*-pa de *vee*-no ...
red	tinto	*teen*-to
sparkling	espumoso	es-poo-*mo*-so
white	blanco	*blan*-ko

self-catering

What's the local speciality?
¿Cuál es la especialidad de la zona?   kwal es la es·pe·thya·lee·*da* de la *tho*·na

What's that?
¿Qué es eso?   ke es *e*·so

How much is (a kilo of cheese)?
¿Cuánto vale (un kilo de queso)?   kwan·to *va*·le (oon *kee*·lo de *ke*·so)

I'd like …	Póngame …	pon·ga·me …
(200) grams	(doscientos) gramos	(dos·*thyen*·tos) *gra*·mos
(two) kilos	(dos) kilos	(dos) *kee*·los
(three) pieces	(tres) piezas	(tres) *pye*·thas
(six) slices	(seis) lonchas	(seys) *lon*·chas

Less.	Menos.	*me*·nos
Enough.	Basta.	*ba*·sta
More.	Más.	mas

special diets & allergies

Is there a vegetarian restaurant near here?
¿Hay un restaurante
vegetariano por aquí?   ai oon rres·tow·*ran*·te
ve·khe·ta·*rya*·no por a·*kee*

Do you have vegetarian food?
¿Tienen comida vegetariana?   tye·nen ko·*mee*·da ve·khe·ta·*rya*·na

Could you prepare a	¿Me puede preparar	me *pwe*·de pre·pa·*rar*
meal without …?	una comida sin …?	*oo*·na ko·*mee*·da seen …
butter	mantequilla	man·te·*kee*·lya
eggs	huevos	*we*·vos
meat stock	caldo de carne	*kal*·do de *kar*·ne

I'm allergic to …	Soy alérgico/a … m/f	soy a·*ler*·khee·ko/a …
dairy produce	a los productos	a los pro·*dook*·tos
	lácteos	*lak*·te·os
gluten	al gluten	al *gloo*·ten
MSG	al glutamato	al gloo·ta·*ma*·to
	monosódico	mo·no·*so*·dee·ko
nuts	a las nueces	a las *nwe*·thes
seafood	a los mariscos	a los ma·*rees*·kos

menu decoder

aceitunas rellenas f pl	a·they·*too*·nas rre·*lye*·nas	*stuffed olives*
albóndigas f pl	al·*bon*·dee·gas	*meatballs*
almejas f pl	al·*me*·khas	*clams*
arroz con leche m	a·*rroth* kon *le*·che	*rice pudding*
atún m	a·*toon*	*tuna*
bacalao m	ba·ka·*low*	*salted cod*
beicon con queso m	*bey*·kon kon *ke*·so	*cold bacon with cheese*
berberechos m pl	ber·be·re·chos	*cockles*
boquerones fritos m pl	bo·ke·*ro*·nes *free*·tos	*fried anchovies*
butifarra f	boo·tee·*fa*·rra	*thick sausage*
calamares m pl	ka·la·*ma*·res	*squid*
camarón m	ka·ma·*ron*	*shrimp • small prawn*
cangrejo m	kan·*gre*·kho	*crab*
caracol m	ka·ra·*kol*	*snail*
cazuela f	ka·*thwe*·la	*casserole*
champiñones m pl	cham·pee·*nyo*·nes	*mushrooms*
charcutería f	char·koo·te·*ree*·a	*cured pork meats*
chorizo m	cho·*ree*·tho	*spicy red or white sausage*
churrasco m	choo·*rras*·ko	*grilled meat in a tangy sauce*
churro m	*choo*·rro	*long, deep-fried doughnut*
cocido m	ko·*thee*·do	*stew of chickpeas, pork & chorizo*
cuajada f	kwa·*kha*·da	*milk junket with honey*
ensaladilla f	en·sa·la·*dee*·lya	*vegetable salad*
escabeche m	es·ka·*be*·che	*pickled or marinated fish*
estofado m	es·to·*fa*·do	*stew*

fideos m pl	fee-de-os	thin pasta noodles with sauce
flan m	flan	crème caramel
gachos m pl	ga-chos	type of porridge
gazpacho m	gath-pa-cho	cold soup with garlic, tomato & vegetables
helado m	e-la-do	ice cream
jamón m	kha-mon	ham
langosta f	lan-gos-ta	spiny lobster
langostino m	lan-gos-tee-no	large prawn
lomo m	lo-mo	pork loin • sausage
longaniza f	lon-ga-nee-tha	dark pork sausage
magdalena f	mag-da-le-na	fairy cake (often dunked in coffee)
mejillones m pl	me-khee-lyo-nes	mussels
natillas f pl	na-tee-lyas	creamy milk dessert
ostras f pl	os-tras	oysters
paella f	pa-e-lya	rice & seafood dish (sometimes with meat)
peregrina f	pe-re-gree-na	scallop
pescaíto frito m	pes-kai-to free-to	tiny fried fish
picadillo m	pee-ka-dee-lyo	minced meat
pinchitos m pl	peen-chee-tos	Moroccan-style kebabs
pulpo m	pool-po	octopus
salchicha f	sal-chee-cha	fresh pork sausage
sobrasada f	so-bra-sa-da	soft pork sausage
tortilla española f	tor-tee-lya es-pa-nyo-la	potato omelette
trucha f	troo-cha	trout
zarzuela f	thar-thwe-la	fish stew

emergencies

basics

English	Spanish	Pronunciation
Help!	¡Socorro!	so·ko·ro
Stop!	¡Pare!	pa·re
Go away!	¡Váyase!	va·ya·se
Thief!	¡Ladrón!	lad·ron
Fire!	¡Fuego!	fwe·go
Watch out!	¡Cuidado!	kwee·da·do
Call ...!	¡Llame a ...!	lya·me a ...
a doctor	un médico	oon me·dee·ko
an ambulance	una ambulancia	oo·na am·boo·lan·thya
the police	la policía	la po·lee·thee·a

It's an emergency.
Es una emergencia.
es oo·na e·mer·khen·thya

Could you help me, please?
¿Me puede ayudar, por favor?
me pwe·de a·yoo·dar por fa·vor

I have to use the telephone.
Necesito usar el teléfono.
ne·the·see·to oo·sar el te·le·fo·no

I'm lost.
Estoy perdido/a. m/f
es·toy per·dee·do/a

Where are the toilets?
¿Dónde están los servicios?
don·de es·tan los ser·vee·thyos

police

Where's the police station?
¿Dónde está la comisaría?
don·de es·ta la ko·mee·sa·ree·a

I want to report an offence.
Quiero denunciar un delito.
kye·ro de·noon·thyar oon de·lee·to

I have insurance.
Tengo seguro.
ten·go se·goo·ro

English	Spanish	Pronunciation
I've been assaulted.	He sido asaltado/a. m/f	e see·do a·sal·ta·do/a
I've been raped.	He sido violado/a. m/f	e see·do vee·o·la·do/a
I've been robbed.	Me han robado.	me an rro·ba·do

I've lost my ...	He perdido ...	e per·dee·do ...
backpack	mi mochila	mee mo·chee·la
bags	mis maletas	mees ma·le·tas
credit card	mi tarjeta de crédito	mee tar·khe·ta de kre·dee·to
handbag	mi bolso	mee bol·so
jewellery	mis joyas	mees kho·yas
money	mi dinero	mee dee·ne·ro
passport	mi pasaporte	mee pa·sa·por·te
travellers cheques	mis cheques de viajero	mees che·kes de vya·khe·ro
wallet	mi cartera	mee kar·te·ra
I want to contact my ...	Quiero ponerme en contacto con mi ...	kye·ro po·ner·me en kon·tak·to kon mee ...
consulate	consulado	kon·soo·la·do
embassy	embajada	em·ba·kha·da

health

medical needs

Where's the nearest ...?	¿Dónde está el ... más cercano?	don·de es·ta el ... mas ther·ka·no
dentist	dentista	den·tees·ta
doctor	médico	me·dee·ko
hospital	hospital	os·pee·tal

Where's the nearest (night) pharmacist?
¿Dónde está la farmacia
(de guardia) más cercana?

don·de es·ta la far·ma·thya
(de gwar·dya) mas ther·ka·na

I need a doctor (who speaks English).
Necesito un médico
(que hable inglés).

ne·the·see·to oon me·dee·ko
(ke a·ble een·gles)

Could I see a female doctor?
¿Puede examinarme una
médica?

pwe·de ek·sa·mee·nar·me oo·na
me·dee·ka

I've run out of my medication.
Se me terminaron los
medicamentos.

se me ter·mee·na·ron los
me·dee·ka·men·tos

symptoms, conditions & allergies

| I'm sick. | Estoy enfermo/a. m/f | es·toy en·fer·mo/a |
| It hurts here. | Me duele aquí. | me dwe·le a·kee |

I have (a) ...	Tengo...	ten·go ...
asthma	asma	as·ma
bronchitis	bronquitis	bron·kee·tees
constipation	estreñimiento	es·tre·nyee·myen·to
cough	tos	tos
diarrhoea	diarrea	dya·rre·a
fever	fiebre	fye·bre
headache	dolor de cabeza	do·lor de ka·be·tha
heart condition	una condición	oo·na kon·dee·thyon
	cardíaca	kar·dee·a·ka
nausea	náusea	now·se·a
pain	dolor	do·lor
sore throat	dolor de garganta	do·lor de gar·gan·ta
toothache	dolor de muelas	do·lor de mwe·las

I'm allergic to ...	Soy alérgico/a a ... m/f	soy a·ler·khee·ko/a a ...
antibiotics	los antibióticos	los an·tee·byo·tee·kos
anti-	los anti-	los an·tee·
inflammatories	inflamatorios	een·fla·ma·to·ryos
aspirin	la aspirina	la as·pee·ree·na
bees	las abejas	las a·be·khas
codeine	la codeína	la ko·de·ee·na
penicillin	la penicilina	la pe·nee·thee·lee·na

antiseptic	antiséptico m	an·tee·sep·tee·ko
bandage	vendaje m	ven·da·khe
condoms	condones m pl	kon·do·nes
contraceptives	anticonceptivos m pl	an·tee·kon·thep·tee·vos
diarrhoea medicine	medicina para diarrea f	me·dee·thee·na pa·ra dya·rre·a
insect repellent	repelente de insectos m	re·pe·len·te de een·sek·tos
laxatives	laxantes m pl	lak·san·tes
painkillers	analgésicos m pl	a·nal·khe·see·kos
rehydration salts	sales rehidratantes f pl	sa·les re·eed·ra·tan·tes
sleeping tablets	pastillas para dormir f pl	pas·tee·lyas pa·ra dor·meer

english–spanish dictionary

Spanish nouns in this dictionary, and adjectives affected by gender, have their gender indicated by ⓜ (masculine) or ⓕ (feminine). If it's a plural noun, you'll also see pl. Words are also marked as v (verb), n (noun), a (adjective), pl (plural), sg (singular), inf (informal) and pol (polite) where necessary.

A

accident *accidente* ⓜ ak-thee-*den*-te
accommodation *alojamiento* ⓜ a-lo-kha-*myen*-to
adaptor *adaptador* ⓜ a-dap-ta-*dor*
address *dirección* ⓕ dee-rek-*thyon*
after *después de* des-*pwes* de
air-conditioned *con aire acondicionado* kon *ai*-re a-kon-dee-thyo-*na*-do
airplane *avión* ⓜ a-*vyon*
airport *aeropuerto* ⓜ ay-ro-*pwer*-to
alcohol *alcohol* ⓜ al-*col*
all *a todo* a to-*do/a*
allergy *alergia* ⓕ a-*ler*-khya
ambulance *ambulancia* ⓕ am-boo-*lan*-thya
ankle *tobillo* ⓜ to-*bee*-lyo
and *y* ee
arm *brazo* ⓜ *bra*-tho
ashtray *cenicero* ⓜ the-nee-*the*-ro
ATM *cajero automático* ka-*khe*-ro ow-to-*ma*-tee-ko

B

baby *bebé* ⓜ be-*be*
back (body) *espalda* ⓕ es-*pal*-da
backpack *mochila* ⓕ mo-*chee*-la
bad *malo/a* ⓜ/ⓕ *ma*-lo/a
bag *bolso* ⓜ *bol*-so
baggage claim *recogida de equipajes* ⓕ rre-ko-*khee*-da de e-kee-*pa*-khes
bank *banco* ⓜ *ban*-ko
bar *bar* ⓜ bar
bathroom *baño* ⓜ *ba*-nyo
battery (general) *pila* ⓕ *pee*-la
battery (car) *batería* ⓕ ba-te-*ree*-a
beautiful *hermoso/a* ⓜ/ⓕ er-*mo*-so/a
bed *cama* ⓕ *ka*-ma
beer *cerveza* ⓕ ther-*ve*-tha
before *antes* *an*-tes
behind *detrás de* de-*tras* de
bicycle *bicicleta* ⓕ bee-thee-*kle*-ta

big *grande* *gran*-de
bill *cuenta* ⓕ *kwen*-ta
black *negro/a* ⓜ/ⓕ *ne*-gro/a
blanket *manta* ⓕ *man*-ta
blood group *grupo sanguíneo* ⓜ *groo*-po san-*gee*-neo
blue *azul* a-*thool*
boat *barco* ⓜ *bar*-ko
book (make a reservation) v *reservar* rre-ser-*var*
bottle *botella* ⓕ bo-*te*-lya
bottle opener *abrebotellas* ⓜ a-bre-bo-*te*-lyas
boy *chico* ⓜ *chee*-ko
brakes (car) *frenos* ⓜ pl *fre*-nos
breakfast *desayuno* ⓜ des-a-*yoo*-no
broken (faulty) *roto/a* ⓜ/ⓕ *ro*-to/a
bus *autobús* ⓜ ow-to-*boos*
business *negocios* ⓜ pl ne-*go*-thyos
buy *comprar* kom-*prar*

C

café *café* ⓜ ka-*fe*
camera *cámara (fotográfica)* ⓕ *ka*-ma-ra (fo-to-*gra*-fee-ka)
camp site *cámping* ⓜ *kam*-peen
cancel *cancelar* kan-the-*lar*
can opener *abrelatas* ⓜ a-bre-*la*-tas
car *coche* ⓜ *ko*-che
cash *dinero en efectivo* ⓜ dee-ne-ro en e-fek-*tee*-vo
cash (a cheque) v *cambiar (un cheque)* kam-*byar* (oon *che*-ke)
cell phone *teléfono móvil* ⓜ te-*le*-fo-no *mo*-veel
centre *centro* ⓜ *then*-tro
change (money) v *cambiar* kam-*byar*
cheap *barato/a* ⓜ/ⓕ ba-*ra*-to/a
check (bill) *cuenta* ⓕ *kwen*-ta
check-in *facturación de equipajes* ⓕ fak-too-ra-*thyon* de e-kee-*pa*-khes
chest *pecho* ⓜ *pe*-cho
child *niño/a* ⓜ/ⓕ *nee*-nyo/a
cigarette *cigarrillo* ⓜ thee-ga-*ree*-lyo
city *ciudad* ⓕ theew-*da*
clean a *limpio/a* ⓜ/ⓕ *leem*-pyo/a

closed *cerrado/a* ⓜ/ⓕ the-*rra*-do/a
coffee *café* ⓜ ka-*fe*
coins *monedas* ⓕ pl mo-*ne*-das
cold a *frío/a* ⓜ/ⓕ free-o/a
collect call *llamada a cobro revertido* ⓕ
  lya-*ma*-da a *ko*-bro re-ver-*tee*-do
come *venir* ve-*neer*
computer *ordenador* ⓜ or-de-na-*dor*
condom *condones* ⓜ pl kon-*do*-nes
contact lenses *lentes de contacto* ⓜ pl
  len-tes de kon-*tak*-to
cook v *cocinar* ko-thee-*nar*
cost *precio* ⓜ *pre*-thyo
credit card *tarjeta de crédito* ⓕ
  tar-*khe*-ta de *kre*-dee-to
cup *taza* ⓕ *ta*-tha
currency exchange *cambio de dinero* ⓜ
  kam-byo de dee-*ne*-ro
customs (immigration) *aduana* ⓕ a-*dwa*-na

D

dangerous *peligroso/a* ⓜ/ⓕ pe-lee-*gro*-so/a
date (time) *fecha* ⓕ *fe*-cha
day *día* ⓜ *dee*-a
delay *demora* ⓕ de-*mo*-ra
dentist *dentista* ⓕ den-*tees*-ta
depart *salir de* sa-*leer* de
diaper *pañal* ⓜ pa-*nyal*
dictionary *diccionario* ⓜ deek-thyo-*na*-ryo
dinner *cena* ⓕ *the*-na
direct *directo/a* ⓜ/ⓕ dee-*rek*-to/a
dirty *sucio/a* ⓜ/ⓕ *soo*-thyo/a
disabled *minusválido/a* ⓜ/ⓕ mee-noos-*va*-lee-do/a
discount *descuento* ⓜ des-*kwen*-to
doctor *doctor/doctora* ⓜ/ⓕ dok-*tor*/dok-*to*-ra
double bed *cama de matrimonio* ⓕ
  ka-ma de ma-*tree*-mo-nyo
double room *habitación doble* ⓕ a-bee-ta-*thyon* *do*-ble
drink *bebida* ⓕ be-*bee*-da
drive v *conducir* kon-doo-*theer*
drivers licence *carnet de conducir* ⓜ
  kar-*ne* de kon-doo-*theer*
drugs (illicit) *droga* ⓕ *dro*-ga
dummy (pacifier) *chupete* ⓜ choo-*pe*-te

E

ear *oreja* ⓕ o-*re*-kha
east *este* es-te
eat *comer* ko-*mer*

economy class *clase turística* ⓕ *kla*-se too-rees-tee-ka
electricity *electricidad* ⓕ e-lek-tree-thee-*da*
elevator *ascensor* ⓜ as-then-*sor*
email *correo electrónico* ⓜ ko-*rre*-o e-lek-*tro*-nee-ko
embassy *embajada* ⓕ em-ba-*kha*-da
emergency *emergencia* ⓕ e-mer-*khen*-thya
English (language) *inglés* ⓜ een-*gles*
entrance *entrada* ⓕ en-*tra*-da
evening *noche* ⓕ *no*-che
exchange rate *tipo de cambio* ⓜ *tee*-po de *kam*-byo
exit *salida* ⓕ sa-*lee*-da
expensive *caro/a* ⓜ/ⓕ *ka*-ro/a
express mail *correo urgente* ⓜ ko-*rre*-o oor-*khen*-te
eye *ojo* ⓜ *o*-kho

F

far *lejos* *le*-khos
fast *rápido/a* ⓜ/ⓕ *rra*-pee-do/a
father *padre* ⓜ *pa*-dre
film (camera) *carrete* ⓜ ka-*rre*-te
finger *dedo* ⓜ *de*-do
first-aid kit *maletín de primeros auxilios* ⓜ
  ma-le-*teen* de pree-*me*-ros ow-*ksee*-lyos
first class *de primera clase* de pree-*me*-ra *kla*-se
fish *pez* ⓜ peth
food *comida* ⓕ ko-*mee*-da
foot *pie* ⓜ pye
fork *tenedor* ⓜ te-ne-*dor*
free (of charge) *gratis* *gra*-tees
friend *amigo/a* ⓜ/ⓕ a-*mee*-go/a
fruit *fruta* ⓕ *froo*-ta
full *lleno/a* ⓜ/ⓕ *lye*-no/a
funny *gracioso/a* ⓜ/ⓕ gra-*thyo*-so/a

G

gift *regalo* ⓜ rre-*ga*-lo
girl *chica* ⓕ *chee*-ka
glass (drinking) *vaso* ⓜ *va*-so
glasses *gafas* ⓕ pl *ga*-fas
go *ir* eer
good *bueno/a* ⓜ/ⓕ *bwe*-no/a
green *verde* *ver*-de
guide n *guía* ⓜ/ⓕ *gee*-a

H

half *mitad* ⓕ mee-*tad*
hand *mano* ⓕ *ma*-no
handbag *bolso* ⓜ *bol*-so

happy *feliz* fe-*leeth*
have *tener* te-*ner*
he *él* el
head *cabeza* ⓕ ka-*be*-tha
heart *corazón* ⓜ ko-ra-*thon*
heat *calor* ⓜ ka-*lor*
heavy *pesado/a* ⓜ/ⓕ pe-*sa*-do/a
help v *ayudar* a-yoo-*dar*
here *aquí* a-*kee*
high *alto/a* ⓜ/ⓕ *al*-to/a
highway *autovía* ⓕ ow-to-*vee*-a
hike v *ir de excursión* eer de eks-koor-*syon*
holiday *vacaciones* ⓕ pl va-ka-*thyo*-nes
homosexual *homosexual* ⓜ/ⓕ o-mo-se-*kswal*
hospital *hospital* ⓜ os-pee-*tal*
hot *caliente* ka-*lyen*-te
hotel *hotel* ⓜ o-*tel*
hungry *hambriento/a* ⓜ/ⓕ am-bree-*en*-to/a
husband *marido* ⓜ ma-*ree*-do

I

I *yo* yo
identification (card) *carnet de identidad* ⓜ kar-*net* de ee-den-tee-*da*
ill *enfermo/a* ⓜ/ⓕ en-*fer*-mo/a
important *importante* eem-por-*tan*-te
included *incluido* een-kloo-*ee*-do
injury *herida* ⓕ e-*ree*-da
insurance *seguro* ⓜ se-*goo*-ro
Internet *Internet* ⓜ *een*-ter-net
interpreter *intérprete* ⓜ/ⓕ een-*ter*-pre-te

J

jewellery *joyas* ⓕ pl *kho*-yas
job *trabajo* ⓜ tra-*ba*-kho

K

key *llave* ⓕ *lya*-ve
kilogram *kilogramo* ⓜ kee-lo-*gra*-mo
kitchen *cocina* ⓕ ko-*thee*-na
knife *cuchillo* ⓜ koo-*chee*-lyo

L

laundry (place) *lavadero* ⓜ la-va-*de*-ro
lawyer *abogado/a* ⓜ/ⓕ a-bo-*ga*-do/a
left (direction) *izquierda* ⓕ eeth-*kyer*-da

left-luggage office *consigna* ⓕ kon-*seeg*-na
leg *pierna* ⓕ *pyer*-na
lesbian *lesbiana* ⓕ les-bee-*a*-na
less *menos* me-nos
letter (mail) *carta* ⓕ *kar*-ta
lift (elevator) *ascensor* ⓜ as-then-*sor*
light *luz* ⓕ looth
like v *gustar* goos-*tar*
lock *cerradura* ⓕ the-rra-*doo*-ra
long *largo/a* ⓜ/ⓕ *lar*-go/a
lost *perdido/a* ⓜ/ⓕ per-*dee*-do/a
lost-property office *oficina de objetos perdidos* ⓕ o-fee-*thee*-na de ob-*khe*-tos per-*dee*-dos
love v *querer* ke-*rer*
luggage *equipaje* ⓜ e-kee-*pa*-khe
lunch *almuerzo* ⓜ al-*mwer*-tho

M

mail *correo* ⓜ ko-*rre*-o
man *hombre* ⓜ *om*-bre
map *mapa* ⓜ *ma*-pa
market *mercado* ⓜ mer-*ka*-do
matches *cerillas* ⓕ pl the-*ree*-lyas
meat *carne* ⓕ *kar*-ne
medicine *medicina* ⓕ me-dee-*thee*-na
menu *menú* ⓜ me-*noo*
message *mensaje* ⓜ men-*sa*-khe
milk *leche* ⓕ *le*-che
minute *minuto* ⓜ mee-*noo*-to
mobile phone *teléfono móvil* ⓜ te-*le*-fo-no *mo*-veel
money *dinero* ⓜ dee-*ne*-ro
month *mes* ⓜ mes
morning *mañana* ⓕ ma-*nya*-na
mother *madre* ⓕ *ma*-dre
motorcycle *motocicleta* ⓕ mo-to-thee-*kle*-ta
motorway *autovía* ⓕ ow-to-*vee*-a
mouth *boca* ⓕ *bo*-ka
music *música* ⓕ *moo*-see-ka

N

name *nombre* ⓜ *nom*-bre
napkin *servilleta* ⓕ ser-vee-*lye*-ta
nappy *pañal* ⓜ pa-*nyal*
near *cerca* ther-ka
neck *cuello* ⓜ *kwe*-lyo
new *nuevo/a* ⓜ/ⓕ *nwe*-vo/a
news *noticias* ⓕ pl no-*tee*-thyas
newspaper *periódico* ⓜ pe-ryo-*dee*-ko

night *noche* ⓕ *no*-che
no *no* no
noisy *ruidoso/a* ⓜ/ⓕ rrwee-*do*-so/a
nonsmoking *no fumadores* no foo-ma-*do*-res
north *norte* ⓜ *nor*-te
nose *nariz* ⓕ na-*reeth*
now *ahora* a-*o*-ra
number *número* ⓜ *noo*-me-ro

O

oil (engine) *aceite* ⓜ a-*they*-te
old *viejo/a* ⓜ/ⓕ *vye*-kho/a
one-way ticket *billete sencillo* ⓜ bee-*lye*-te sen-*thee*-lyo
open a *abierto/a* ⓜ/ⓕ a-*byer*-to/a
outside *exterior* ⓜ eks-te-*ryor*

P

package *paquete* ⓜ pa-*ke*-te
paper *papel* ⓜ pa-*pel*
park (car) v *estacionar* es-ta-thyo-*nar*
passport *pasaporte* ⓜ pa-sa-*por*-te
pay *pagar* pa-*gar*
pen *bolígrafo* ⓜ bo-*lee*-gra-fo
petrol *gasolina* ⓕ ga-so-*lee*-na
pharmacy *farmacia* ⓕ far-*ma*-thya
phonecard *tarjeta de teléfono* ⓕ tar-*khe*-ta de te-*le*-fo-no
photo *foto* ⓕ *fo*-to
plate *plato* ⓜ *pla*-to
police *policía* ⓕ po-lee-*thee*-a
postcard *postal* ⓕ pos-*tal*
post office *correos* ⓜ ko-*rre*-os
pregnant *embarazada* ⓕ em-ba-ra-*tha*-da
price *precio* ⓜ *pre*-thyo

Q

quiet *tranquilo/a* ⓜ/ⓕ tran-*kee*-lo/a

R

rain *lluvia* ⓕ *lyoo*-vya
razor *afeitadora* ⓕ a-fey-ta-*do*-ra
receipt *recibo* ⓜ rre-*thee*-bo
red *rojo/a* ⓜ/ⓕ *rro*-kho/a
refund *reembolso* ⓜ rre-em-*bol*-so
registered mail *correo certificado* ⓜ ko-*rre*-o ther-tee-fee-*ka*-do

rent v *alquilar* al-kee-*lar*
repair v *reparar* rre-pa-*rar*
reservation *reserva* ⓕ re-*ser*-va
restaurant *restaurante* ⓜ rres-tow-*ran*-te
return v *volver* vol-*ver*
return ticket *billete de ida y vuelta* ⓜ bee-*lye*-te de ee-da ee *vwel*-ta
right (direction) *derecha* de-*re*-cha
road *carretera* ⓕ ka-rre-*te*-ra
room *habitación* ⓕ a-bee-ta-*thyon*

S

safe a *seguro/a* ⓜ/ⓕ se-*goo*-ro/a
sanitary napkin *compresas* ⓕ pl kom-*pre*-sas
seat *asiento* ⓜ a-*syen*-to
send *enviar* en-vee-*ar*
service station *gasolinera* ⓕ ga-so-lee-*ne*-ra
sex *sexo* ⓜ *se*-kso
shampoo *champú* ⓜ cham-*poo*
share (a dorm) *compartir* kom-par-*teer*
shaving cream *espuma de afeitar* ⓕ es-*poo*-ma de a-fey-*tar*
she *ella* ⓕ *e*-lya
sheet (bed) *sábana* ⓕ *sa*-ba-na
shirt *camisa* ⓕ ka-*mee*-sa
shoes *zapatos* ⓜ pl tha-*pa*-tos
shop *tienda* ⓕ *tyen*-da
short *corto/a* ⓜ/ⓕ *kor*-to/a
shower *ducha* ⓕ *doo*-cha
single room *habitación individual* ⓕ a-bee-ta-*thyon* een-dee-vee-*dwal*
skin *piel* ⓕ pyel
skirt *falda* ⓕ *fal*-da
sleep v *dormir* dor-*meer*
slowly *despacio* des-*pa*-thyo
small *pequeño/a* ⓜ/ⓕ pe-*ke*-nyo/a
smoke (cigarettes) v *fumar* foo-*mar*
soap *jabón* ⓜ kha-*bon*
some *alguno/a* ⓜ/ⓕ al-*goo*-no/a
soon *pronto* *pron*-to
south *sur* ⓜ soor
souvenir shop *tienda de recuerdos* ⓕ *tyen*-da de re-*kwer*-dos
Spain *España* ⓕ es-*pa*-nya
Spanish (language) *español/castellano* ⓜ es-pa-*nyol*/kas-te-*lya*-no
speak *hablar* a-*blar*
spoon *cuchara* ⓕ koo-*cha*-ra
stamp *sello* ⓜ *se*-lyo

stand-by ticket *billete de lista de espera* ⓜ
bee-*lye*-te de *lees*-ta de es-*pe*-ra
station (train) *estación* ⓕ es-ta-*thyon*
stomach *estómago* ⓜ es-*to*-ma-go
stop v *parar* pa-*rar*
stop (bus) *parada* ⓕ pa-*ra*-da
street *calle* ⓕ *ka*-lye
student *estudiante* ⓜ/ⓕ es-too-*dyan*-te
sun *sol* ⓜ sol
sunscreen *crema solar* ⓕ *kre*-ma so-*lar*
swim v *nadar* na-*dar*

T

tampons *tampones* ⓜ pl tam-*po*-nes
taxi *taxi* ⓜ *tak*-see
teaspoon *cucharita* ⓕ koo-cha-*ree*-ta
teeth *dientes* ⓜ pl *dyen*-tes
telephone *teléfono* ⓜ te-*le*-fo-no
television *televisión* ⓕ te-le-vee-*syon*
temperature (weather) *temperatura* ⓕ
tem-pe-ra-*too*-ra
tent *tienda (de campaña)* ⓕ *tyen*-da (de kam-*pa*-nya)
that (one) *ése/a* ⓜ/ⓕ *e*-se/a
they *ellos/ellas* ⓜ/ⓕ *e*-lyos/e-lyas
thirsty *sediento/a* ⓜ/ⓕ se-*dee*-en-to/a
this (one) *éste/a* ⓜ/ⓕ *es*-te/a
throat *garganta* ⓕ gar-*gan*-ta
ticket *billete* ⓜ bee-*lye*-te
time *tiempo* ⓜ *tyem*-po
tired *cansado/a* ⓜ/ⓕ kan-*sa*-do/a
tissues *pañuelos de papel* ⓜ pl pa-*nywe*-los de pa-*pel*
today *hoy* oy
toilet *servicio* ⓜ ser-*vee*-thyo
tomorrow *mañana* ma-*nya*-na
tonight *esta noche* es-ta *no*-che
toothbrush *cepillo de dientes* ⓜ the-*pee*-lyo de *dyen*-tes
toothpaste *pasta dentífrica* ⓕ *pas*-ta den-*tee*-free-ka
torch (flashlight) *linterna* ⓕ leen-*ter*-na
tour *excursión* ⓕ eks-koor-*syon*
tourist office *oficina de turismo* ⓕ
o-fee-*thee*-na de too-*rees*-mo
towel *toalla* ⓕ to-*a*-lya
train *tren* ⓜ tren
translate *traducir* tra-doo-*theer*
travel agency *agencia de viajes* ⓕ
a-*khen*-thya de *vya*-khes
travellers cheque *cheque de viajero* ⓜ
che-ke de vya-*khe*-ro
trousers *pantalones* ⓜ pl pan-ta-*lo*-nes

twin beds *dos camas* ⓕ pl dos *ka*-mas
tyre *neumático* ⓜ ne-oo-*ma*-tee-ko

U

underwear *ropa interior* ⓕ *rro*-pa een-te-*ryor*
urgent *urgente* oor-*khen*-te

V

vacant *vacante* va-*kan*-te
vacation *vacaciones* ⓕ pl va-ka-*thyo*-nes
vegetable *verdura* ⓕ ver-*doo*-ra
vegetarian a *vegetariano/a* ⓜ/ⓕ ve-khe-ta-*rya*-no/a
visa *visado* ⓜ vee-*sa*-do

W

waiter *camarero/a* ⓜ/ⓕ ka-ma-*re*-ro/a
walk v *caminar* ka-mee-*nar*
wallet *cartera* ⓕ kar-*te*-ra
warm a *templado/a* ⓜ/ⓕ tem-*pla*-do/a
wash (something) *lavar* la-*var*
watch *reloj de pulsera* ⓜ rre-*lokh* de pool-*se*-ra
water *agua* ⓕ *a*-gwa
we *nosotros/nosotras* ⓜ/ⓕ no-*so*-tros/ no-*so*-tras
weekend *fin de semana* ⓜ feen de se-*ma*-na
west *oeste* ⓜ o-*es*-te
wheelchair *silla de ruedas* ⓕ *see*-lya de *rrwe*-das
when *cuando* *kwan*-do
where *donde* *don*-de
white *blanco/a* ⓜ/ⓕ *blan*-ko/a
who *quien* kyen
why *por qué* por ke
wife *esposa* ⓕ es-*po*-sa
window *ventana* ⓕ ven-*ta*-na
wine *vino* ⓜ *vee*-no
with *con* kon
without *sin* seen
woman *mujer* ⓕ moo-*kher*
write *escribir* es-kree-*beer*

Y

yellow *amarillo/a* ⓜ/ⓕ a-ma-*ree*-lyo/a
yes *sí* see
yesterday *ayer* a-*yer*
you sg inf/pol *tú/Usted* too/oos-*te*
you pl *vosotros/vosotras* ⓜ/ⓕ vo-*so*-tros/vo-*so*-tras

Turkish

turkish alphabet

A a a	*B b* be	*C c* je	*Ç ç* che	*D d* de
E e e	*F f* fe	*G g* ge	*Ğ ğ* yu-*moo*-shak ge	*H h* he
I ı uh	*İ i* ee	*J j* zhe	*K k* ke	*L l* le
M m me	*N n* ne	*O o* o	*Ö ö* er	*P p* pe
R r re	*S s* se	*Ş ş* she	*T t* te	*U u* oo
Ü ü ew	*V v* ve	*Y y* ye	*Z z* ze	

■ turkish

TÜRKÇE

introduction

Turkish (*Türkçe* tewrk·che) – the language which traces its roots as far back as 3500 BC, has travelled through Central Asia, Persia, North Africa and Europe and been written in both Arabic and Latin script – has left us words like *yogurt*, *horde*, *sequin* and *bridge* (the game) along the way. But how did it transform itself from a nomad's tongue spoken in Mongolia into the language of modern Turkey, with a prestigious interlude as the diplomatic language of the Ottoman Empire?

The first evidence of the Turkish language, which is a member of the Ural-Altaic language family, was found on stone monuments from the 8th century BC, in what's now Outer Mongolia. In the 11th century, the Seljuq clan invaded Asia Minor (Anatolia) and imposed their language on the peoples they ruled. Over time, Arabic and Persian vocabulary was adopted to express artistic and philosophical concepts and Arabic script began to be used. By the 14th century, another clan – the Ottomans – was busy establishing the empire that was to control Eurasia for centuries. In their wake, they left the Turkish language. There were then two levels of Turkish – ornate Ottoman Turkish, with flowery Persian phrases and Arabic honorifics (words showing respect), used for diplomacy, business and art, and the language of the common Turks, which still used 'native' Turkish vocabulary and structures.

When the Ottoman Empire fell in 1922, the military hero, amateur linguist and historian Kemal Atatürk came to power and led the new Republic of Turkey. With the backing of a strong language reform movement, he devised a phonetic Latin script that reflected Turkish sounds more accurately than Arabic script. On 1 November 1928, the new writing system was unveiled: within two months, it was illegal to write Turkish in the old script. In 1932 Atatürk created the *Türk Dil Kurumu* (Turkish Language Society) and gave it the brief of simplifying the Turkish language to its 'pure' form of centuries before. The vocabulary and structure was completely overhauled. As a consequence, Turkish has changed so drastically that even Atatürk's own speeches are barely comprehensible to today's speakers of *öztürkçe* ('pure Turkish').

With 70 million speakers worldwide, Turkish is the official language of Turkey and the Turkish Republic of Northern Cyprus (recognised as a nation only by the Turkish government). Elsewhere, the language is also called *Osmanlı* os·man·luh and is spoken by large populations in Germany, Bulgaria, Macedonia, Greece and the '-stans' of Central Asia. So start practising and you might soon be complimented with *Ağzına sağlık!* a·zuh·na sa·luhk (lit: health to your mouth) – 'Well said!'

pronunciation

vowel sounds

Most Turkish vowel sounds can be found in English, although in Turkish they're generally shorter and slightly harsher. When you see a double vowel, such as *saat* sa-*at* (hour), you need to pronounce both vowels.

symbol	english equivalent	turkish example	transliteration
a	run	*abide*	a·bee·*de*
ai	aisle	*hayvan*	hai·*van*
ay	say	*ney*	nay
e	bet	*ekmek*	ek·*mek*
ee	see	*ile*	ee·le
eu	nurse	*özel*	eu·zel
ew	ee pronounced with rounded lips	*üye*	ew·ye
o	pot	*oda*	o·da
oo	zoo	*uçak*	oo·chak
uh	ago	*ıslak*	uhs·lak

word stress

In Turkish, the stress generally falls on the last syllable of the word. Most two-syllable placenames, however, are stressed on the first syllable (eg *Kıbrıs kuhb*·ruhs), and in three-syllable placenames the stress is usually on the second syllable (eg *İstanbul* ees·*tan*·bool). Another common exception occurs when a verb has a form of the negative marker *me* (*me* me, *ma* ma, *mı* muh, *mi* mee, *mu* moo, or *mü* mew) added to it. In those cases, the stress goes onto the syllable before the marker – eg *gelmiyorlar gel*·mee·yor·lar (they're not coming). You don't need to worry too much about this, as the stressed syllable is always in italics in our coloured pronunciation guides.

consonant sounds

Most Turkish consonants sound the same as in English, so they're straightforward to pronounce. The exception is the Turkish r, which is always rolled. Note also that ğ is a silent letter which extends the vowel before it – it acts like the 'gh' combination in 'weigh', and is never pronounced.

symbol	english equivalent	turkish example	transliteration
b	bed	*bira*	*bee·ra*
ch	cheat	*çanta*	*chan·ta*
d	dog	*deniz*	*de·neez*
f	fat	*fabrika*	*fab·ree·ka*
g	go	*gar*	*gar*
h	hat	*hala*	*ha·la*
j	joke	*cadde*	*jad·de*
k	kit	*kadın*	*ka·duhn*
l	lot	*lider*	*lee·der*
m	man	*maç*	*mach*
n	not	*nefis*	*ne·fees*
p	pet	*paket*	*pa·ket*
r	red (rolled)	*rehber*	*reh·ber*
s	sun	*saat*	*sa·at*
sh	shot	*şarkı*	*shar·kuh*
t	top	*tas*	*tas*
v	van (but softer, between 'v' and 'w')	*vadi*	*va·dee*
y	yes	*yarım*	*ya·ruhm*
z	zero	*zarf*	*zarf*
zh	pleasure	*jambon*	*zham·bon*

basics

language difficulties

Do you speak English?
İngilizce konuşuyor musunuz?   een-gee-*leez*-je ko-noo-*shoo*-yor moo-*soo*-nooz

Do you understand?
Anlıyor musun?   an-*luh*-yor moo-*soon*

I understand.
Anlıyorum.   an-*luh*-yo-room

I don't understand.
Anlamıyorum.   an-*la*-muh-yo-room

What does (*kitap*) mean?
(Kitap) ne demektir?   (kee-*tap*) ne de-*mek*-teer

How do you pronounce this?
Bunu nasıl telaffuz edersiniz?   boo-*noo* na-suhl te-laf-*fooz* e-*der*-see-neez

How do you write (*yabancı*)?
(Yabancı) kelimesini   (ya-ban-*juh*) ke-lee-me-see-*nee*
nasıl yazarsınız?   na-suhl ya-*zar*-suh-nuhz

Could you please …?	*Lütfen …?*	*lewt*-fen …
repeat that	*tekrarlar mısınız*	tek-*rar*-lar muh-suh-*nuhz*
speak more	*daha yavaş*	da-ha ya-*vash*
slowly	*konuşur musunuz*	ko-noo-*shoor* moo-soo-*nooz*
write it down	*yazar mısınız*	ya-*zar* muh-suh-*nuhz*

essentials

Yes.	*Evet.*	e-*vet*
No.	*Hayır.*	ha-*yuhr*
Please.	*Lütfen.*	*lewt*-fen
Thank you	*(Çok) Teşekkür*	(chok) te-shek-*kewr*
(very much). **pol**	*ederim.*	e-*de*-reem
Thanks. **inf**	*Teşekkürler.*	te-shek-kewr-*ler*
You're welcome.	*Birşey değil.*	beer-*shay* de-*eel*
Excuse me.	*Bakar mısınız?*	ba-*kar* muh-suh-*nuhz*
Sorry.	*Özür dilerim.*	eu-*zewr* dee-*le*-reem

numbers

0	sıfır	suh-fuhr		16	onaltı	on-al-tuh
1	bir	beer		17	onyedi	on-ye-dee
2	iki	ee-kee		18	onsekiz	on-se-keez
3	üç	ewch		19	ondokuz	on-do-kooz
4	dört	deurt		20	yirmi	yeer-mee
5	beş	besh		21	yirmibir	yeer-mee-beer
6	altı	al-tuh		22	yirmiiki	yeer-mee-ee-kee
7	yedi	ye-dee		30	otuz	o-tooz
8	sekiz	se-keez		40	kırk	kuhrk
9	dokuz	do-kooz		50	elli	el-lee
10	on	on		60	altmış	alt-muhsh
11	onbir	on-beer		70	yetmiş	yet-meesh
12	oniki	on-ee-kee		80	seksen	sek-sen
13	onüç	on-ewch		90	doksan	dok-san
14	ondört	on-deurt		100	yüz	yewz
15	onbeş	on-besh		1000	bin	been

time & dates

What time is it?	Saat kaç?	sa-at kach
It's one o'clock.	Saat bir.	sa-at beer
It's (10) o'clock.	Saat (on).	sa-at (on)
Quarter past (10).	(Onu) çeyrek geçiyor.	(o-noo) chay-rek ge-chee-yor
Half past (10).	(On) buçuk.	(on) boo-chook
Quarter to (11).	(Onbire) çeyrek var.	(on-bee-re) chay-rek var
At what time ...?	Saat kaçta ...?	sa-at kach-ta ...
At ...	Saat ...	sa-at ...
am (morning)	sabah	sa-bah
pm (afternoon)	öğleden sonra	er-le-den son-ra
pm (evening)	gece	ge-je
Monday	Pazartesi	pa-zar-te-see
Tuesday	Salı	sa-luh
Wednesday	Çarşamba	char-sham-ba
Thursday	Perşembe	per-shem-be
Friday	Cuma	joo-ma
Saturday	Cumartesi	joo-mar-te-see
Sunday	Pazar	pa-zar

January	*Ocak*	o·*jak*
February	*Şubat*	shoo·*bat*
March	*Mart*	mart
April	*Nisan*	nee·*san*
May	*Mayıs*	ma·*yuhs*
June	*Haziran*	ha·zee·*ran*
July	*Temmuz*	tem·*mooz*
August	*Ağustos*	a·oos·*tos*
September	*Eylül*	ay·*lewl*
October	*Ekim*	e·*keem*
November	*Kasım*	ka·*suhm*
December	*Aralık*	a·ra·*luhk*

What date is it today?
   Bugün ayın kaçı?   boo·gewn a·*yuhn ka*·chuh

It's (18 October).
   (Onsekiz Ekim).   (on·se·keez e·*keem*)

since (May)	*(Mayıs'tan) beri*	(ma·yuhs·*tan*) be·*ree*
until (June)	*(Haziran'a) kadar*	(ha·zee·ra·*na*) ka·*dar*
yesterday	*dün*	dewn
today	*bugün*	boo·gewn
tonight	*bu gece*	boo ge·*je*
tomorrow	*yarın*	ya·*ruhn*
last/next ...	*geçen/gelecek ...*	ge·*chen*/ge·le·*jek* ...
night	*gece*	ge·*je*
week	*hafta*	haf·*ta*
month	*ay*	ai
year	*yıl*	yuhl
yesterday/tomorrow ...	*dün/yarın ...*	dewn/ya·ruhn ...
morning	*sabah*	sa·*bah*
afternoon	*öğleden sonra*	eu·le·*den son*·ra
evening	*akşam*	ak·*sham*

weather

What's the weather like?	*Hava nasıl?*	ha·*va* na·suhl
It's ...	*Hava ...*	ha·*va* ...
cloudy	*bulutlu*	boo·loot·*loo*
cold	*soğuk*	so·*ook*
hot	*sıcak*	suh·*jak*
raining	*yağmurlu*	ya·moor·*loo*
snowing	*kar yağışlı*	kar ya·uhsh·*luh*
sunny	*güneşli*	gew·nesh·*lee*
warm	*ılık*	uh·*luhk*
windy	*rüzgarlı*	rewz·gar·*luh*
spring	*ilkbahar*	eelk·ba·har
summer	*yaz*	yaz
autumn	*sonbahar*	son·ba·har
winter	*kış*	kuhsh

border crossing

I'm here ...	*Ben ...*	ben ...
in transit	*transit yolcuyum*	tran·*seet* yol·*joo*·yoom
on business	*iş gezisindeyim*	eesh ge·zee·seen·*de*·yeem
on holiday	*tatildeyim*	ta·teel·*de*·yeem
I'm here for ...	*Ben ... buradayım.*	ben ... boo·ra·*da*·yuhm
(10) days	*(on) günlüğüne*	(on) gewn·lew·ew·*ne*
(three) weeks	*(üç) haftalığına*	(ewch) haf·ta·luh·uh·*na*
(two) months	*(iki) aylığına*	(ee·*kee*) ai·luh·uh·*na*

I'm going to (Sarıyer).
(Sarıyer'e) gidiyorum.   (sa·*ruh*·ye·re) gee·dee·*yo*·room

I'm staying at the (Divan).
(Divan'da) kalıyorum.   (dee·van·da) ka·luh·*yo*·room

I have nothing to declare.
Beyan edecek hiçbir şeyim yok.   be·yan e·de·*jek* heech·beer she·*yeem* yok

I have something to declare.
Beyan edecek bir şeyim var.   be·yan e·de·*jek* beer she·*yeem* var

That's (not) mine.
Bu benim (değil).   boo be·*neem* (de·*eel*)

transport

tickets & luggage

Where can I buy a ticket?
Nereden bilet alabilirim?
ne·re·den bee·*let* a·*la*·bee·lee·reem

Do I need to book a seat?
Yer ayırtmam gerekli mi?
yer a·*yuhrt*·mam ge·rek·*lee* mee

One ... ticket to	*(Bostancı'ya) ...*	*(bos·tan·juh·ya) ...*
(Bostancı), please.	*lütfen.*	*lewt·fen*
one-way	*bir gidiş bileti*	beer gee·*deesh* bee·le·*tee*
return	*gidiş-dönüş*	gee·*deesh*·deu·*newsh*
	bir bilet	beer bee·*let*

I'd like to ... my	*Biletimi ...*	bee·le·tee·*mee* ...
ticket, please.	*istiyorum.*	ees·*tee*·yo·room
cancel	*iptal ettirmek*	eep·*tal* et·teer·*mek*
change	*değiştirmek*	de·eesh·teer·*mek*
collect	*almak*	al·*mak*
confirm	*onaylatmak*	o·nai·lat·*mak*

I'd like a ... seat,	*... bir yer istiyorum.*	... beer yer ees·*tee*·yo·room
please.		
nonsmoking	*Sigara içilmeyen*	see·*ga*·ra ee·*cheel*·me·yen
	kısımda	kuh·suhm·da
smoking	*Sigara içilen*	see·*ga*·ra ee·*chee*·len
	kısımda	kuh·suhm·da

How much is it?
Şu ne kadar?
shoo ne ka·*dar*

Is there air conditioning?
Klima var mı?
klee·ma var muh

Is there a toilet?
Tuvalet var mı?
too·va·*let* var muh

How long does the trip take?
Yolculuk ne kadar sürer?
yol·joo·*look* ne ka·*dar* sew·*rer*

Is it a direct route?
Direk güzergah mı?
dee·*rek* gew·zer·*gah* muh

Where's the luggage locker?
Emanet dolabı nerede?
e·ma·*net* do·la·*buh* ne·re·de

My luggage has been ...	Bagajım ...	ba·ga·zhuhm ...
damaged	zarar gördü	za·rar geu·dew
lost	kayboldu	kai·bol·doo
stolen	çalındı	cha·luhn·duh

getting around

Where does flight (TK0060) arrive?

(TK0060) sefer sayılı uçak nereye iniyor? — (te·ka suh·fuhr suh·fuhr alt·muhsh) se·fer sa·yuh·luh oo·chak ne·re·ye ee·nee·yor

Where does flight (TK0060) depart?

(TK0060) sefer sayılı uçak nereden kalkıyor? — (te·ka suh·fuhr suh·fuhr alt·muhsh) se·fer sa·yuh·luh oo·chak ne·re·den kal·kuh·yor

Where's (the) ...?	... nerede?	... ne·re·de
arrivals hall	Gelen yolcu bölümü	ge·len yol·joo beu·lew·mew
departures hall	Giden yolcu bölümü	gee·den yol·joo beu·lew·mew
duty-free shop	Gümrüksüz satış mağazası	gewm·rewk·sewz sa·tuhsh ma·a·za·suh
gate (12)	(Oniki) numaralı kapı	(on·ee·kee) noo·ma·ra·luh ka·puh

Is this the ... to (Sirkeci)?	(Sirkeci'ye) giden ... bu mu?	(seer·ke·jee·ye) gee·den ... boo moo
boat	vapur	va·poor
bus	otobüs	o·to·bews
plane	uçak	oo·chak
train	tren	tren

What time's the ... bus?	... otobüs ne zaman?	... o·to·bews ne za·man
first	İlk	eelk
last	Son	son
next	Sonraki	son·ra·kee

At what time does it arrive/leave?

Ne zaman varır/kalkacak? — ne za·man va·ruhr/kal·ka·jak

How long will it be delayed?

Ne kadar gecikecek? — ne ka·dar ge·jee·ke·jek

What station/stop is this?
Bu hangi istasyon/durak?
boo *han*·gee ees·tas·yon/doo·*rak*

What's the next station/stop?
Sonraki istasyon/durak hangisi?
son·ra·*kee* ees·tas·yon/doo·rak han·gee·see

Does it stop at (Kadıköy)?
(Kadıköy'de) durur mu?
(ka·*duh*·kay·de) doo·*roor* moo

Please tell me when we get to (Beşiktaş).
(Beşiktaş'a) vardığımızda lütfen bana söyleyin.
(be·*sheek*·ta·sha) var·duh·uh·muhz·da *lewt*·fen ba·*na* say·le·yeen

How long do we stop here?
Burada ne kadar duracağız?
boo·ra·*da* ne ka·*dar* doo·ra·*ja*·uhz

Is this seat available?
Bu koltuk boş mu?
boo kol·*took* bosh moo

That's my seat.
Burası benim yerim.
boo·ra·*suh* be·*neem* ye·*reem*

I'd like a taxi ... — *... bir taksi istiyorum.* — *... beer* tak·*see* ees·*tee*·yo·room
at (9am)	*(Sabah dokuzda)*	(sa·*bah* do·kooz·*da*)
now	*Hemen*	he·men
tomorrow	*Yarın*	ya·ruhn

Is this taxi available?
Bu taksi boş mu?
boo tak·*see* bosh moo

How much is it to ...?
... ne kadar?
... ne ka·*dar*

Please put the meter on.
Lütfen taksimetreyi çalıştırın.
lewt·fen tak·*see*·met·re·yee cha·luhsh·*tuh*·ruhn

Please take me to (this address).
Lütfen beni (bu adrese) götürün.
lewt·fen be·*nee* (boo ad·re·*se*) geu·*tew*·rewn

Please ... — *Lütfen ...* — *lewt*·fen ...
slow down	*yavaşlayın*	ya·vash·*la*·yuhn
stop here	*burada durun*	boo·ra·*da* doo·roon
wait here	*burada bekleyin*	boo·ra·*da* bek·*le*·yeen

car, motorbike & bicycle hire

I'd like to hire a ...	Bir ... kiralamak istiyorum.	beer ... kee·ra·la·mak ees·tee·yo·room
bicycle	bisiklet	bee·seek·let
car	araba	a·ra·ba
motorbike	motosiklet	mo·to·seek·let

with ...		
a driver	şoförlü	sho·feur·lew
air conditioning	klimalı	klee·ma·luh

How much for ... hire?	... kirası ne kadar?	... kee·ra·suh ne ka·dar
hourly	Saatlık	sa·at·luhk
daily	Günlük	gewn·lewk
weekly	Haftalık	haf·ta·luhk

air	hava	ha·va
oil	yağ	ya
petrol	benzin	ben·zeen
tyres	lastikler	las·teek·ler

I need a mechanic.
Tamirciye ihtiyacım var.
ta·meer·jee·ye eeh·tee·ya·juhm var

I've run out of petrol.
Benzinim bitti.
ben·zee·neem beet·tee

I have a flat tyre.
Lastiğim patladı.
las·tee·eem pat·la·duh

directions

Where's the ...?	... nerede?	... ne·re·de
bank	Banka	ban·ka
city centre	Şehir merkezi	she·heer mer·ke·zee
hotel	Otel	o·tel
market	Pazar yeri	pa·zar ye·ree
police station	Polis karakolu	po·lees ka·ra·ko·loo
post office	Postane	pos·ta·ne
public toilet	Umumi tuvalet	oo·moo·mee too·va·let
tourist office	Turizm bürosu	too·reezm bew·ro·soo

Is this the road to (Taksim)?		
(Taksim'e) giden yol bu mu?		*(tak-see-me)* gee-*den* yol boo moo
Can you show me (on the map)?		
Bana (haritada)		ba-*na* (ha-ree-ta-*da*)
gösterebilir misiniz?		geus-te-*re*-bee-leer mee-seen-*neez*
What's the address?		
Adresi nedir?		ad-re-*see* ne-*deer*
How far is it?		
Ne kadar uzakta?		ne ka-*dar* oo-zak-*ta*
How do I get there?		
Oraya nasıl gidebilirim?		o-ra-*ya na*-suhl gee-*de*-bee-lee-reem

Turn ...	*... dön.*	*... deun*
at the corner	*Köşeden*	keu-she-*den*
at the traffic lights	*Trafik*	tra-*feek*
	ışıklarından	uh-shuhk-la-ruhn-*dan*
left/right	*Sola/Sağa*	so-*la*/sa-*a*

It's ...		
behind ...	*... arkasında.*	*...* ar-ka-suhn-*da*
far away	*Uzak.*	oo-*zak*
here	*Burada.*	boo-ra-*da*
in front of ...	*... önünde.*	*...* eu-newn-*de*
left	*Solda.*	sol-*da*
near ...	*... yakınında.*	*...* ya-kuh-nuhn-*da*
next to ...	*... yanında.*	*...* ya-nuhn-*da*
on the corner	*Köşede.*	keu-she-*de*
opposite ...	*... karşısında.*	*...* kar-shuh-suhn-*da*
right	*Sağda.*	sa-*da*
straight ahead	*Tam karşıda.*	tam kar-shuh-*da*
there	*Şurada.*	shoo-ra-*da*

by bus	*otobüslü*	o-to-bews-*lew*
by taxi	*taksili*	tak-see-*lee*
by train	*trenli*	tren-*lee*
on foot	*yürüyerek*	yew-rew-ye-*rek*

north	*kuzey*	koo-*zay*
south	*güney*	gew-*nay*
east	*doğu*	do-*oo*
west	*batı*	ba-*tuh*

Giriş/Çıkış	gee-reesh/chuh-kuhsh	Entrance/Exit
Açık/Kapalı	a-chuhk/ka-pa-luh	Open/Closed
Boş Oda	bosh o-da	Rooms Available
Boş Yer Yok	bosh yer yok	No Vacancies
Danışma	da-nuhsh-ma	Information
Polis Karakolu	po-lees ka-ra-ko-loo	Police Station
Yasak	ya-sak	Prohibited
Tuvaletler	too-va-let-ler	Toilets
Erkek	er-kek	Men
Kadın	ka-duhn	Women
Sıcak/Soğuk	suh-jak/so-ook	Hot/Cold

accommodation

finding accommodation

Where's a ...?	Buralarda nerede ... var?	boo-ra-lar-da ne-re-de ... var
camping ground	kamp yeri	kamp ye-ree
guesthouse	misafirhane	mee-sa-feer-ha-ne
hotel	otel	o-tel
youth hostel	gençlik hosteli	gench-leek hos-te-lee

Can you recommend somewhere ...?	... bir yer tavsiye edebilir misiniz?	... beer yer tav-see-ye e-de-bee-leer mee-see-neez
cheap	Ucuz	oo-jooz
good	İyi	ee-yee
nearby	Yakın	ya-kuhn

I'd like to book a room, please.
Bir oda ayırtmak
istiyorum lütfen.

beer o-da a-yuhrt-mak
ees-tee-yo-room lewt-fen

I have a reservation.
Rezervasyonum var.

re-zer-vas-yo-noom var

My name's ...
Benim ismim ...

be-neem ees-meem ...

Do you have a ... room?	... odanız var mı?	... o-da-*nuhz* var muh
single	Tek kişilik	tek kee-shee-*leek*
double	İki kişilik	ee-*kee* kee-shee-*leek*
twin	Çift yataklı	cheeft ya-tak-*luh*

How much is it per ...?	... ne kadar?	... ne ka-*dar*
night	Geceliği	ge-je-lee-*ee*
person	Kişi başına	kee-*shee* ba-shuh-*na*

Can I pay by ...?	... ile ödeyebilir miyim?	... ee-*le* eu-de-ye-*bee*-leer mee-*yeem*
credit card	Kredi kartı	kre-dee kar-*tuh*
travellers cheque	Seyahat çeki	se-ya-*hat* che-*kee*

I'd like to stay for (three) nights.
Kalmak istiyorum (üç) geceliğine.   kal-*mak* ees-*tee*-yo-room (ewch) ge-je-lee-ee-*ne*

From (2 July) to (6 July).
(İki Temmuz'dan)   (ee-*kee* tem-mooz-*dan*)
(altı Temmuz'a) kadar.   (al-*tuh* tem-moo-*za*) ka-*dar*

Can I see it?
Görebilir miyim.   geu-*re*-bee-leer mee-*yeem*

Am I allowed to camp here?
Burada kamp yapabilir miyim?   boo-ra-*da* kamp ya-*pa*-bee-leer mee-*yeem*

Where can I find a camping ground?
Kamp alanı nerede?   kamp a-la-*nuh* ne-re-de

requests & queries

When/Where is breakfast served?
Kahvaltı ne zaman/   kah-val-*tuh* ne za-*man*/
nerede veriliyor?   ne-re-de ve-ree-lee-*yor*

Please wake me at (seven).
Lütfen beni (yedide) kaldırın.   lewt-fen be-*nee* (ye-dee-*de*) kal-*duh*-ruhn

Could I have my key, please?
Anahtarımı alabilir miyim?   a-nah-ta-ruh-*muh* a-*la*-bee-leer mee-*yeem*

Can I get another (blanket)?
Başka bir (battaniye)   bash-*ka* beer (bat-*ta*-nee-ye)
alabilir miyim?   a-*la*-bee-leer mee-*yeem*

Is there an elevator/a safe?
Asansör/Kasanız var mı?   a-san-*seur*/ka-sa-*nuhz* var muh

The room is too ...	Çok ...	chok ...
expensive	pahalı	pa·ha·luh
noisy	gürültülü	gew·rewl·tew·lew
small	küçük	kew·chewk

The ... doesn't work.	... çalışmıyor.	... cha·luhsh·muh·yor
air conditioning	Klima	klee·ma
fan	Fan	fan
toilet	Tuvalet	too·va·let

This ... isn't clean.	Bu ... temiz değil.	boo ... te·meez de·eel
pillow	yastık	yas·tuhk
sheet	çarşaf	char·shaf
towel	havlu	hav·loo

checking out

What time is checkout?
Çıkış ne zaman?   chuh·kuhsh ne za·man

Can I leave my luggage here?
Eşyalarımı burada   esh·ya·la·ruh·muh boo·ra·da
bırakabilir miyim?   buh·ra·ka·bee·leer mee·yeem

Could I have	... alabilir	... a·la·bee·leer
my ..., please?	miyim lütfen?	mee·yeem lewt·fen
deposit	Depozitomu	de·po·zee·to·moo
passport	Pasaportumu	pa·sa·por·too·moo
valuables	Değerli eşyalarımı	de·er·lee esh·ya·la·ruh·muh

communications & banking

the internet

Where's the local Internet café?
En yakın internet kafe nerede?   en ya·kuhn een·ter·net ka·fe ne·re·de

How much is it per hour?
Saati ne kadar?   sa·a·tee ne ka·dar

I'd like to ...	... istiyorum.	... ees·tee·yo·room
check my email	E-postama bakmak	e·pos·ta·ma bak·mak
get Internet access	İnternete girmek	een·ter·ne·te geer·mek
use a printer	Printeri kullanmak	preen·te·ree kool·lan·mak
use a scanner	Tarayıcıyı	ta·ra·yuh·juh·yuh

mobile/cell phone

I'd like a ...	... istiyorum.	... ees·tee·yo·room
mobile/cell phone for hire	Cep telefonu kiralamak	jep te·le·fo·noo kee·ra·la·mak
SIM card for your network	Buradaki şebeke için SİM kart	boo·ra·da·kee she·be·ke ee·cheen seem kart
What are the rates?	Ücret tarifesi nedir?	ewj·ret ta·ree·fe·see ne·deer

telephone

What's your phone number?
Telefon numaranız nedir?
te·le·fon noo·ma·ra·nuhz ne·deer

The number is ...
Telefon numarası ...
te·le·fon noo·ma·ra·suh ...

Where's the nearest public phone?
En yakın telefon kulübesi nerede?
en ya·kuhn te·le·fon koo·lew·be·see ne·re·de

I'd like to buy a phonecard.
Telefon kartı almak istiyorum.
te·le·fon kar·tuh al·mak ees·tee·yo·room

I want to ...	... istiyorum.	... ees·tee·yo·room
call (Singapore)	(Singapur'u) aramak	(seen·ga·poo·roo) a·ra·mak
make a local call	Yerel bir görüşme yapmak	ye·rel beer geu·rewsh·me yap·mak
reverse the charges	Ödemeli görüşme yapmak	eu·de·me·lee ger·rewsh·me yap·mak

How much does		
... cost?	*... ne kadar eder?*	*... ne ka-dar e-der*
a (three)-minute call	*(Üç) dakikalık konuşma*	*(ewch) da-kee-ka-luhk ko-noosh-ma*
each extra minute	*Her ekstra dakika*	*her eks-tra da-kee-ka*

It's (10) *yeni kuruş* per minute.
Bir dakikası (on) yeni kuruş. beer da-kee-ka-*suh* (on) ye-*nee* koo-*roosh*

post office

I want to send a ...	*Bir ... göndermek istiyorum.*	beer ... geun-der-*mek* ees-*tee*-yo-room
fax	*faks*	faks
letter	*mektup*	mek-*toop*
parcel	*paket*	pa-*ket*
postcard	*kartpostal*	kart-pos-*tal*

I want to buy a/an ...	*... satın almak istiyorum.*	*... sa-tuhn al-mak ees-tee-yo-room*
envelope	*Zarf*	zarf
stamp	*Pul*	pool

Please send it (to Australia) by ...	*Lütfen ... (Avustralya'ya) gönderin.*	*lewt-fen ... (a-voos-tral-ya-ya) geun-de-reen*
airmail	*hava yoluyla*	ha-*va* yo-*looy*-la
express mail	*ekspres posta*	eks-*pres* pos-*ta*
registered mail	*taahhütlü posta*	ta-ah-hewt-*lew* pos-*ta*
surface mail	*deniz yoluyla*	de-*neez* yo-*looy*-la

Is there any mail for me? *Bana posta var mı?* ba-*na* pos-ta var muh

bank

Where's a/an ...?	*... nerede var?*	*... ne-re-de var*
ATM	*Bankamatik*	ban-ka-ma-*teek*
foreign exchange office	*Döviz bürosu*	deu-*veez* bew-ro-*soo*

I'd like to ...	... istiyorum.	... ees-tee-yo-room
cash a cheque	Çek bozdurmak	chek boz-door-mak
change a travellers cheque	Seyahat çeki bozdurmak	se-ya-hat che-kee boz-door-mak
change money	Para bozdurmak	pa-ra boz-door-mak
get a cash advance	Avans çekmek	a-vans chek-mek
withdraw money	Para çekmek	pa-ra chek-mek

What's the ...?	... nedir?	... ne-deer
charge for that	Ücreti	ewj-re-tee
commission	Komisyon	ko-mees-yon
exchange rate	Döviz kuru	deu-veez koo-roo

It's ...		
(12) euros	(Oniki) euro.	(on-ee-kee) yoo-ro
(25) lira	(Yirmibeş) lira.	(yeer-mee-besh) lee-ra
free	Ücretsiz.	ewj-ret-seez

What time does the bank open?
Banka ne zaman açılıyor?   ban-ka ne za-man a-chuh-luh-yor

Has my money arrived yet?
Param geldi mi?   pa-ram gel-dee mee

sightseeing

getting in

What time does it open/close?
Saat kaçta açılır/kapanır?   sa-at kach-ta a-chuh-luhr/ka-pa-nuhr

What's the admission charge?
Giriş ücreti nedir?   gee-reesh ewj-re-tee ne-deer

Is there a discount for children/students?
Çocuk/Öğrenci indirimi var mı?   cho-jook/eu-ren-jee een-dee-ree-mee var muh

I'd like a ...	... istiyorum.	... ees-tee-yo-room
catalogue	Katalog	ka-ta-log
guide	Rehber	reh-ber
local map	Yerel Harita	ye-rel ha-ree-ta

I'd like to see ...	... görmek istiyorum.	... geur·mek ees·tee·yo·room
What's that?	Bu nedir?	boo ne·deer
Can I take a photo?	Bir fotoğrafınızı	beer fo·to·ra·fuh·nuh·zuh
	çekebilir miyim?	che·ke·bee·leer mee·yeem

tours

When's the next ...?	Sonraki ... ne zaman?	son·ra·kee ... ne za·man
day trip	gündüz turu	gewn·dewz too·roo
tour	tur	toor

Is ... included?	... dahil mi?	... da·heel mee
accommodation	Kalacak yer	ka·la·jak yer
the admission charge	Giriş	gee·reesh
food	Yemek	ye·mek
transport	Ulaşım	oo·la·shuhm

How long is the tour?
Tur ne kadar sürer?   toor ne ka·dar sew·rer

What time should we be back?
Saat kaçta dönmeliyiz?   sa·at kach·ta deun·me·lee·yeez

sightseeing – TURKISH

sightseeing

castle	kale	ka·le
church	kilise	kee·lee·se
main square	meydan	may·dan
monument	anıt	a·nuht
mosque	cami	ja·mee
museum	müze	mew·ze
old city	eski şehir	es·kee she·heer
palace	saray	sa·rai
ruins	harabeler	ha·ra·be·ler
stadium	stadyum	stad·yoom
statue	heykel	hay·kel
Turkish bath	hamam	ha·mam

shopping

enquiries

Where's a ...?	... nerede?	... ne·re·de
bank	Banka	ban·ka
bookshop	Kitapçı	kee·tap·chuh
camera shop	Fotoğrafçı	fo·to·raf·chuh
department store	Büyük mağaza	bew·yewk ma·a·za
grocery store	Bakkal	bak·kal
market	Pazar yeri	pa·zar ye·ree
newsagency	Gazete bayii	ga·ze·te ba·yee·ee
supermarket	Süpermarket	sew·per·mar·ket

Where can I buy (a padlock)?
Nereden (asma kilit) ne·re·den (as·ma kee·leet)
alabilirim? a·la·bee·lee·reem

I'm looking for ...
... istiyorum. ... ees·tee·yo·room

Can I look at it?
Bakabilir miyim? ba·ka·bee·leer mee·yeem

Do you have any others?
Başka var mı? bash·ka var muh

Does it have a guarantee?
Garantisi var mı? ga·ran·tee·see var muh

Can I have it sent overseas?
Yurt dışına gönderebilir yoort duh·shuh·na geun·de·re·bee·leer
misiniz? mee·see·neez

Can I have my ... repaired?
... burada tamir ettirebilir ... boo·ra·da ta·meer et·tee·re·bee·leer
miyim? mee·yeem

It's faulty.
Arızalı. a·ruh·za·luh

I'd like ..., please.	... istiyorum lütfen.	... ees·tee·yo·room lewt·fen
a bag	Çanta	chan·ta
a refund	Para iadesi	pa·ra ee·a·de·see
to return this	Bunu iade etmek	boo·noo ee·a·de et·mek

paying

How much is it?
Ne kadar?

ne ka·*dar*

Can you write down the price?
Fiyatı yazabilir misiniz?

fee·ya·*tuh* ya·*za*·bee·leer mee·see·*neez*

That's too expensive.
Bu çok pahalı.

boo chok pa·ha·*luh*

Is that your lowest price?
Son fiyatınız mı bu?

son fee·ya·tuh·*nuhz* boo moo

I'll give you (30) lira.
(Otuz) lira veririm.

(o·*tooz*) lee·*ra* ve·*ree*·reem

There's a mistake in the bill.
Hesapta bir yanlışlık var.

he·sap·*ta* beer yan·luhsh·*luhk* var

Do you accept …?	… *kabul ediyor musunuz?*	… ka·*bool* e·dee·yor moo·soo·*nooz*
credit cards	*Kredi kartı*	kre·dee kar·*tuh*
debit cards	*Banka kartı*	ban·ka kar·*tuh*
travellers cheques	*Seyahat çeki*	se·ya·*hat* che·kee

I'd like …, please.	… *istiyorum lütfen.*	… ees·*tee*·yo·room *lewt*·fen
a receipt	*Makbuz*	mak·*booz*
my change	*Paramın üstünü*	pa·ra·*muhn* ews·tew·*new*

clothes & shoes

Can I try it on?	*Deneyebilir miyim?*	de·ne·*ye*·bee·leer mee·*yeem*
My size is (42).	*(Kırkiki) beden giyiyorum.*	(kuhrk·ee·*kee*) be·*den* gee·*yee*·yo·room
It doesn't fit.	*Olmuyor.*	ol·*moo*·yor
small	*küçük*	kew·*chewk*
medium	*orta*	or·*ta*
large	*büyük*	bew·*yewk*

books & music

I'd like a ...	... istiyorum.	... ees·tee·yo·room
newspaper	(İngilizce)	(een·gee·leez·je)
(in English)	bir gazete	beer ga·ze·te
pen	Tükenmez kalem	tew·ken·mez ka·lem

Is there an English-language bookshop?
İngilizce yayın satan   een·gee·leez·je ya·yuhn sa·tan
bir dükkan var mı?   beer dewk·kan var muh

I'm looking for something by (Yaşar Kemal).
(Yaşar Kemal'in) albümlerine   (ya·shar ke·mal·een) al·bewm·le·ree·ne
bakmak istiyorum.   bak·mak ees·tee·yo·room

Can I listen to this?
Bunu dinleyebilir miyim?   boo·noo deen·le·ye·bee·leer mee·yeem

photography

Can you ...?	... misiniz?	... mee·see·neez
develop this film	Bu filmi basabilir	boo feel·mee ba·sa·bee·leer
load my film	Filmi makineye	feel·mee ma·kee·ne·ye
	takabilir	ta·ka·bee·leer
transfer photos	Kameramdaki	ka·me·ram·da·kee
from my	fotoğrafları	fo·to·raf·la·ruh
camera to CD	CD'ye aktarabilir	see·dee·ye ak·ta·ra·bee·leer

I need a/an ... film	Bu kamera için ...	boo ka·me·ra ee·cheen ...
for this camera.	film istiyorum.	feelm ees·tee·yo·room
APS	APS	a·pe·se
B&W	siyah-beyaz	see·yah·be·yaz
colour	renkli	renk·lee
slide	slayt	slayt
(200) speed	(ikiyüz) hızlı	(ee·kee·yewz) huhz·luh

When will it be ready?   Ne zaman hazır olur?   ne za·man ha·zuhr o·loor

meeting people

greetings, goodbyes & introductions

Hello.	Merhaba.	mer·ha·ba
Hi.	Selam.	se·lam
Good night.	İyi geceler.	ee·yee ge·je·ler
Goodbye.	Hoşçakal. inf	hosh·cha·kal
(by person leaving)	Hoşçakalın. pol	hosh·cha·ka·luhn
Goodbye.	Güle güle.	gew·le gew·le
(by person staying)		
See you later.	Sonra görüşürüz.	son·ra ger·rew·shew·rewz
Mr	Bay	bai
Mrs/Miss	Bayan	ba·yan
How are you?	Nasılsın? inf	na·suhl·suhn
	Nasılsınız? pol	na·suhl·suh·nuhz
Fine. And you?	İyiyim. Ya sen/siz? inf/pol	ee·yee·yeem ya sen/seez
What's your name?	Adınız ne? inf	a·duh·nuhz ne
	Adınız nedir? pol	a·duh·nuhz ne·deer
My name is ...	Benim adım ...	be·neem a·duhm ...
I'm pleased to	Tanıştığımıza	ta·nuhsh·tuh·uh·muh·za
meet you.	sevindim.	se·veen·deem

This is my ...	Bu benim ...	boo be·neem ...
brother	kardeşim	kar·de·sheem
daughter	kızım	kuh·zuhm
father	babayım	ba·ba·yuhm
friend	arkadaşım	ar·ka·da·shuhm
husband	kocam	ko·jam
mother	anneyim	an·ne·yeem
partner (intimate)	partnerim	part·ne·reem
sister	kız kardeşim	kuhz kar·de·sheem
son	oğlum	o·loom
wife	karım	ka·ruhm

Here's my ...	İşte benim ...	eesh·te be·neem ...
(email) address	(e-posta) adresiniz	(e·pos·ta) ad·re·see·neez
fax number	faks numaram	faks noo·ma·ram
phone number	telefon numaram	te·le·fon noo·ma·ram

What's your ...?	Sizin ... nedir?	see-zeen ... ne-deer
(email) address	(e-posta) adresiniz	(e-pos-ta) ad-re-see-neez
fax number	faks numaranız	faks noo-ma-ra-nuhz
phone number	telefon numaranız	te-le-fon noo-ma-ra-nuhz

occupations

What's your occupation?	Mesleğiniz nedir? pol	mes-le-ee-neez ne-deer
	Mesleğin nedir? inf	mes-le-een ne-deer
I'm a/an ...	Ben ...	ben ...
artist	sanatçıyım m&f	sa-nat-chuh-yuhm
business person	iş adamıyım m	ish a-da-muh-yuhm
	kadınıyım f	ka-duh-nuh-yuhm
farmer	çiftçiyim m&f	cheeft-chee-yeem
manual worker	işçiyim m&f	eesh-chee-yeem
office worker	memurum m&f	me-moo-room
scientist	bilim adamıyım m&f	bee-leem a-da-muh-yuhm

background

Where are you from?	Nerelisiniz? pol	ne-re-lee-see-neez
	Nerelisin? inf	ne-re-lee-seen
I'm from ...	Ben ...	ben ...
Australia	Avustralya'lıyım	a-voos-tral-ya-luh-yuhm
Canada	Kanada'lıyım	ka-na-da-luh-yuhm
England	İngiltere'liyim	een-geel-te-re-lee-yeem
the USA	Amerika'lıyım	a-me-ree-ka-luh-yuhm
Are you married?	Evli misiniz?	ev-lee mee-see-neez
I'm married/single.	Ben evliyim/bekarım.	ben ev-lee-yeem/be-ka-ruhm

age

How old ...?	Kaç ...?	kach ...
are you	yaşındasın inf	ya-shuhn-da-suhn
is your son	yaşında oğlunuz	ya-shuhn-da o-loo-nooz
is your daughter	yaşında kızınız	ya-shuhn-da kuh-zuh-nuhz
I'm ... years old.	Ben ... yaşındayım.	ben ... ya-shuhn-da-yuhm
He/She is ... years old.	O ... yaşında.	o ... ya-shuhn-da

feelings

I'm/I'm not ...

cold	*Üşüdüm./*	ew-shew-*dewm*/
	Üşümedim.	ew-*shew*-me-deem
happy	*Mutluyum./*	moot-*loo*-yoom/
	Mutlu değilim.	moot-*loo* de-ee-leem
hot	*Sıcakladım./*	suh-jak-la-*duhm*/
	Sıcaklamadım.	suh-jak-*la*-ma-duhm
hungry	*Açım./Aç değilim.*	a-chuhm/ach de-ee-leem
sad	*Üzgünüm./*	ewz-gew-*newm*/
	Üzgün değilim.	ewz-*gewn* de-ee-leem
thirsty	*Susadım./Susamadım.*	soo-sa-*duhm*/soo-*sa*-ma-duhm
tired	*Yorgunum./*	yor-*goo*-noom/
	Yorgun değilim.	yor-*goon* de-ee-leem

Are you ...?

cold	*Üşüdün mü?*	ew-shew-*dewn* mew
happy	*Mutlu musun?*	moot-*loo* moo-*soon*
hot	*Sıcakladın mı?*	suh-jak-la-*duhn* muh
hungry	*Aç mısın?*	ach muh-*suhn*
sad	*Üzgün müsün?*	ewz-*gewn* moo-*soon*
thirsty	*Susadın mı?*	soo-sa-*duhn* muh
tired	*Yorgun musun?*	yor-*goon* moo-*soon*

entertainment

going out

Where can I find ...?	*Buranın ... nerede?*	boo-ra-*nuhn* ... *ne*-re-de
clubs	*kulüpleri*	koo-lewp-le-*ree*
gay venues	*gey kulüpleri*	gay koo-lewp-le-*ree*
pubs	*birahaneleri*	bee-ra-ha-ne-le-*ree*
I feel like going to a/the ...	*... gitmek istiyor.*	... geet-*mek* ees-*tee*-yor
concert	*Konsere*	kon-se-*re*
movies	*Sinemaya*	see-ne-ma-*ya*
party	*Partiye*	par-tee-*ye*
restaurant	*Restorana*	res-to-ra-*na*
theatre	*Oyuna*	o-yoo-*na*

interests

Do you like ...?	... sever misin?	... se-ver mee-seen
I like ...	... seviyorum.	... se-vee-yo-room
I don't like ...	... sevmiyorum.	... sev-mee-yo-room
art	Sanat	sa-nat
movies	Sinemaya gitmeyi	see-ne-ma-ya geet-me-yee
reading	Okumayı	o-koo-ma-yuh
sport	Sporu	spo-roo
travelling	Seyahat etmeyi	se-ya-hat et-me-yee
Do you ...?	... misin/misiniz? inf/pol	... mee-seen/mee-see-neez
dance	Dans eder	dans e-der
go to concerts	Konserlere gider	kon-ser-le-re gee-der
listen to music	Müzik dinler	mew-zeek deen-ler

food & drink

finding a place to eat

Can you recommend a ...?	İyi bir ... tavsiye edebilir misiniz?	ee-yee beer ... tav-see-ye e-de-bee-leer mee-see-neez
bar	bar	bar
café	kafe	ka-fe
restaurant	restoran	res-to-ran
I'd like ..., please.	... istiyorum.	... ees-tee-yo-room
a table for (five)	(Beş) kişilik bir masa	(besh) kee-shee-leek beer ma-sa
the nonsmoking section	Sigara içilmeyen bir yer	see-ga-ra ee-cheel-me-yen beer yer
the smoking section	Sigara içilen bir yer	see-ga-ra ee-chee-len beer yer

ordering food

breakfast	kahvaltı	kah-val-tuh
lunch	öğle yemeği	eu-le ye-me-ee
dinner	akşam yemeği	ak-sham ye-me-ee
snack	hafif yemek	ha-feef ye-mek

What would you recommend?
Ne tavsiye edersiniz?   ne tav·see·ye e·der·see·neez

I'd like (a/the)...	*... istiyorum.*	*... ees·tee·yo·room*
bill	*Hesabı*	he·sa·buh
drink list	*İçecek listesini*	ee·che·jek lees·te·see·nee
menu	*Menüyü*	me·new·yew
that dish	*Şu yemeği*	shoo ye·me·ee

drinks

(cup of) coffee ...	*(fincan) kahve ...*	(feen·jan) kah·ve ...
(cup of) tea ...	*(fincan) çay ...*	(feen·jan) chai ...
with milk	*sütlü*	sewt·lew
without sugar	*şekersiz*	she·ker·seez
(orange) juice	*(portakal) suyu*	(por·ta·kal) soo·yoo
soft drink	*alkolsüz içecek*	al·kol·sewz ee·che·jek
sparkling mineral water	*maden sodası*	ma·den so·da·suh
still mineral water	*maden suyu*	ma·den soo·yoo
(hot) water	*(sıcak) su*	(suh·jak) soo

in the bar

I'll have ...	*... alayım.*	*... a·la·yuhm*
I'll buy you a drink.	*Sana içecek alayım.*	sa·na ee·che·jek a·la·yuhm
What would you like?	*Ne alırsınız?*	ne a·luhr·suh·nuhz
Cheers!	*Şerefe!*	she·re·fe
brandy	*brendi*	bren·dee
cocktail	*kokteyl*	kok·tayl
cognac	*konyak*	kon·yak
a shot of (whisky)	*bir tek (viski)*	beer tek (vees·kee)
a bottle/glass of beer	*bir şişe/bardak bira*	beer shee·she/bar·dak bee·ra
a bottle/glass	*bir şişe/bardak*	beer shee·she/bar·dak
of ... wine	*... şarap*	*... sha·rap*
red	*kırmızı*	kuhr·muh·zuh
sparkling	*köpüklü*	keu·pewk·lew
white	*beyaz*	be·yaz

self-catering

What's the local speciality?
Bu yöreye has yiyecekler neler?   boo yeu·re·*ye* has yee·ye·jek·*ler* ne·ler

What's that?
Bu nedir?   boo *ne*·deer

How much (is a kilo of cheese)?
(Bir kilo peynir) Ne kadar?   (beer kee·*lo* pay·*neer*) ne ka·*dar*

I'd like ...	... *istiyorum.*	... ees·*tee*·yo·room
(200) grams	*(İkiyüz) gram*	(ee·*kee*·yewz) gram
(two) kilos	*(İki) kilo*	(ee·*kee*) kee·*lo*
(three) pieces	*(Üç) parça*	(ewch) par·*cha*
(six) slices	*(Altı) dilim*	(al·*tuh*) dee·*leem*
Less.	*Daha az.*	da·*ha* az
Enough.	*Yeterli.*	ye·ter·*lee*
More.	*Daha fazla.*	da·*ha* faz·*la*

special diets & allergies

Where's a vegetarian restaurant?
Buralarda vejeteryan restoran   boo·ra·lar·*da* ve·zhe·ter·*yan* res·to·*ran*
var mı?   var muh

Do you have vegetarian food?
Vejeteryan yiyecekleriniz   ve·zhe·ter·*yan* yee·ye·jek·le·ree·*neez*
var mı?   var muh

Is it cooked with ...?	*İçinde ... var mı?*	ee·cheen·*de* ... var muh
butter	*tereyağ*	te·*re*·ya
eggs	*yumurta*	yoo·moor·*ta*
meat stock	*et suyu*	et soo·*yoo*
I'm allergic to ...	... *alerjim var.*	... a·ler·*zheem* var
dairy produce	*Süt ürünlerine*	sewt ew·rewn·le·ree·*ne*
gluten	*Glutene*	gloo·te·*ne*
MSG	*Mono sodyum*	mo·*no* sod·*yoom*
	glutamata	gloo·ta·ma·*ta*
nuts	*Çerezlere*	che·rez·le·*re*
seafood	*Deniz ürünlerine*	de·*neez* ew·rewn·le·ree·*ne*

menu decoder

asma yaprağında sardalya	as-*ma* yap-ra-uhn-*da* sar-*dal*-ya	sardines in vine leaves
baklava	bak-la-*va*	pastry stuffed with pistachio & walnuts
biber dolması	bee-*ber* dol-ma-*suh*	stuffed capsicum
börek	beu-*rek*	sweet or savoury dishes with a thin crispy pastry
bumbar	boom-*bar*	sausage made of rice & meat stuffed in a large sheep or lamb gut
cacık	ja-*juhk*	yogurt, mint & cucumber mix
cevizli bat	je-veez-*lee* bat	salad of bulgur, lentils, tomato paste & walnuts
çevirme	che-veer-*me*	eggplant, chicken, rice & pistachio dish
çoban salatası	cho-*ban* sa-la-ta-*suh*	tomato, cucumber & capsicum salad
çökertme	cheu-kert-*me*	steak on potatoes with yogurt
dolma	dol-*ma*	vine or cabbage leaves stuffed with rice
erik aşı	e-*reek* a-*shuh*	plum dish with prunes, rice & sugar
gökkuşağı salatası	geuk-koo-sha-uh sa-la-ta-*suh*	salad of macaroni, capsicum, mushrooms, pickles & salami
gül tatlısı	gewl tat-luh-*suh*	fried pastry in lemon sherbet
halim aşı	ha-*leem* a-*shuh*	soup of chickpeas, meaty bones, wheat & tomato
hamsi tava	ham-*see* ta-*va*	fried, corn-breaded anchovies with onion & lemon
höşmerim	heush-me-*reem*	walnut & pistachio pudding
humus	hoo-*moos*	mashed chickpeas with sesame oil, lemon & spices
imam bayıldı	ee-*mam* ba-yuhl-duh	eggplant, tomato & onion dish

kadayıf	ka-da-*yuhf*	dessert of dough soaked in syrup with a layer of sour cream
kapuska	ka-poos-*ka*	cold dish of onion, tomato paste & cabbage
karaş	ka-*rash*	berry, grape & nut pudding
kebab/kebap	ke-*bab*/ke-*bap*	skewered meat & vegetables cooked on an open fire
keşkül	kesh-*kewl*	almond, coconut & milk pudding
köfte	keuf-*te*	mincemeat or bulgur balls
kulak çorbası	koo-*lak* chor-ba-*suh*	meat dumplings boiled in stock
lokum	lo-*koom*	Turkish delight
musakka	moo-sak-*ka*	vegetable & meat pie
pastırma	pas-tuhr-*ma*	pressed beef preserved in spices
paşa pilavı	pa-*sha* pee-la-*vuh*	potato, egg & capsicum salad
patlıcan karnıyarık	pat-luh-*jan* kar-*nuh*-ya-ruhk	eggplant stuffed with minced meat
pirpirim çorbası	*peer*-pee-reem chor-ba-*suh*	chickpea, bean & lentil soup
pişmaniye	peesh-*ma*-nee-ye	dessert of sugar, flour & soapwort
revani	re-*va*-nee	semolina, vanilla & cream cake
soğuk çorba	so-*ook* chor-*ba*	cold soup of yogurt, rice & capsicum
sucuk	soo-*jook*	spicy sausage
susamlı şeker	soo-sam-*luh* she-*ker*	sugar-coated peanuts & almonds
sütlaç	sewt-*lach*	rice pudding
şiş kebab	sheesh ke-*bab*	meat skewered on an open fire
tarhana	tar-ha-*na*	yogurt, onion, flour & chilli mix
topik	to-*peek*	chickpeas, pistachios, flour & currants topped with sesame sauce
tulumba tatlısı	too-*loom*-ba tat-luh-*suh*	fluted fritters served in sweet syrup
yuvarlama	yoo-var-la-*ma*	chickpea & mince dumpling soup

emergencies

basics

Help!	*İmdat!*	*eem*-dat
Stop!	*Dur!*	door
Go away!	*Git burdan!*	geet boor-*dan*
Thief!	*Hırsız var!*	huhr-*suhz* var
Fire!	*Yangın var!*	*yan*-guhn var
Watch out!	*Dikkat et!*	*deek*-kat et
Call ...!	... *çağırın!*	... cha-*uh*-ruhn
a doctor	*Doktor*	dok-*tor*
an ambulance	*Ambulans*	am-boo-*lans*
the police	*Polis*	po-*lees*

It's an emergency!
Bu acil bir durum.   boo a-*jeel* beer *doo*-room

Could you help me, please?
Yardım edebilir misiniz   yar-*duhm* e-de-bee-leer mee-see-*neez*
lütfen?   *lewt*-fen

Can I use your phone?
Telefonunuzu kullanabilir   te-le-fe-noo-noo-*zoo* kool-la-*na*-bee-leer
miyim?   mee-*yeem*

I'm lost.
Kayboldum.   kai-bol-*doom*

Where are the toilets?
Tuvaletler nerede?   too-va-let-*ler* ne-re-de

police

Where's the police station?
Polis karakolu nerede?   po-*lees* ka-ra-ko-*loo* ne-re-de

I want to report an offence.
Şikayette bulunmak   shee-ka-yet-*te* boo-loon-*mak*
istiyorum.   ees-*tee*-yo-room

I have insurance.
Sigortam var.   see-gor-*tam* var

I've been ...	Ben ...	ben ...
assaulted	saldırıya uğradım	sal·duh·ruh·ya oo·ra·duhm
raped	tecavüze uğradım	te·ja·vew·ze oo·ra·duhm
robbed	soyuldum	so·yool·doom

I've lost my ...	... kayıp.	... ka·yuhp
My ... was/were stolen.	... çalındı.	... cha·luhn·duh
backpack	Sırt çantası	suhrt chan·ta·suh
bags	Çantalar	chan·ta·lar
credit card	Kredi kartı	kre·dee kar·tuh
handbag	El çantası	el chan·ta·suh
jewellery	Mücevherler	mew·jev·her·ler
money	Para	pa·ra
passport	Pasaport	pa·sa·port
travellers cheques	Seyahat çekleri	se·ya·hat chek·le·ree
wallet	Cüzdan	jewz·dan

I want to contact my ...	... görüşmek istiyorum.	... geu·rewsh·mek ees·tee·yo·room
consulate	Konsoloslukla	kon·so·los·look·la
embassy	Elçilikle	el·chee·leek·le

health

medical needs

Where's the nearest ...?	En yakın ... nerede?	en ya·kuhn ... ne·re·de
dentist	dişçi	deesh·chee
doctor	doktor	dok·tor
hospital	hastane	has·ta·ne
(night) pharmacist	(nöbetçi) eczane	(neu·bet·chee) ej·za·ne

I need a doctor (who speaks English).
(İngilizce konuşan) (een·gee·leez·je ko·noo·shan)
Bir doktora ihtiyacım var. beer dok·to·ra eeh·tee·ya·juhm var

Could I see a female doctor?
Bayan doktora ba·yan dok·to·ra
görünebilir miyim? geu·rew·ne·bee·leer mee·yeem

I've run out of my medication.
İlacım bitti. ee·la·juhm beet·tee

symptoms, conditions & allergies

I'm sick.	Hastayım.	has-*ta*-yuhm
It hurts here.	Burası ağrıyor.	boo-ra-*suh* a-ruh-yor
I have a toothache.	Dişim ağrıyor.	dee-*sheem* a-ruh-yor
I have (a) ...	Bende ... var.	ben-de ... var

asthma	astım	as-*tuhm*
bronchitis	bronşit	bron-*sheet*
constipation	kabızlık	ka-buhz-*luhk*
cough	öksürük	euk-sew-*rewk*
diarrhoea	ishal	ees-*hal*
fever	ateş	a-*tesh*
headache	baş ağrısı	bash a-ruh-*suh*
heart condition	kalp rahatsızlığı	kalp ra-hat-suhz-luh-*uh*
nausea	bulantı	boo-lan-*tuh*
pain	ağrı	a-*ruh*
sore throat	boğaz ağrısı	bo-*az* a-ruh-*suh*

I'm allergic to ...	... alerjim var.	... a-ler-*zheem* var
antibiotics	Antibiyotiklere	an-tee-bee-yo-teek-le-*re*
anti-inflammatories	Anti-emflamatuarlara	an-*tee*-em-fla-ma-too-ar-la-ra
aspirin	Aspirine	as-pee-ree-*ne*
bees	Arılara	a-ruh-la-*ra*
codeine	Kodeine	ko-de-ee-*ne*
penicillin	Penisiline	pe-nee-see-lee-*ne*

antiseptic	antiseptik	an-tee-sep-*teek*
bandage	bandaj	ban-*dazh*
condoms	prezervatifler	pre-zer-va-teef-*ler*
contraceptives	doğum kontrol hapı	do-*oom* kon-*trol* ha-*puh*
diarrhoea medicine	ishal ilacı	ees-*hal* ee-la-*juh*
insect repellent	sinek kovucu	see-*nek* ko-voo-*joo*
laxatives	müsil ilacı	mew-*seel* ee-la-*juh*
painkillers	ağrı kesici	a-*ruh* ke-see-*jee*
rehydration salts	rehidrasyon tuzları	re-heed-ras-*yon* tooz-la-*ruh*
sleeping tablets	uyku hapı	ooy-*koo* ha-*puh*

english–turkish dictionary

Words in this dictionary are marked as a (adjective), n (noun), v (verb), sg (singular), pl (plural), inf (informal) and pol (polite) where necessary.

A

accident *kaza* ka-za
accommodation *kalacak yer* ka-la-*jak* yer
adaptor *adaptör* a-dap-teur
address n *adres* ad-res
after *sonra* son-ra
air conditioning *klima* klee-ma
airplane *uçak* oo-chak
airport *havaalanı* ha-va-a-la-nuh
alcohol *alkol* al-kol
all *hepsi* hep-see
allergy *alerji* a-ler-zhee
ambulance *ambulans* am-boo-*lans*
and *ve* ve
ankle *ayak bileği* a-yak bee-le-*ee*
arm *kol* kol
ashtray *kül tablası* kewl tab-la-*suh*
ATM *bankamatik* ban-ka-ma-teek

B

baby *bebek* be-bek
back (body) *sırt* suhrt
backpack *sırt çantası* suhrt chan-ta-*suh*
bad *kötü* keu-tew
bag *çanta* chan-ta
baggage claim *bagaj konveyörü*
ba-gazh kon-ve-yeu-rew
bank *banka* ban-ka
bar *bar* bar
bathroom *banyo* ban-yo
battery *pil* peel
beautiful *güzel* gew-*zel*
bed *yatak* ya-tak
beer *bira* bee-ra
before *önce* eun-je
behind *arkasında* ar-ka-suhn-*da*
bicycle *bisiklet* bee-seek-*let*
big *büyük* bew-*yewk*
bill *hesap* he-*sap*
black *siyah* see-*yah*
blanket *battaniye* bat-*ta*-nee-ye

blood group *kan grubu* kan goo-roo-*boo*
blue *mavi* ma-vee
boat *vapur* va-poor
book (make a reservation) v *yer ayırtmak*
yer a-yuhrt-mak
bottle *şişe* shee-she
bottle opener *şişe açacağı* shee-she a-cha-ja-uh
boy *oğlan* o-*lan*
brakes (car) *fren* fren
breakfast *kahvaltı* kah-val-*tuh*
broken (faulty) *bozuk* bo-*zook*
bus *otobüs* o-to-bews
business *iş* eesh
buy *satın almak* sa-tuhn al-mak

C

café *kafe* ka-fe
camera *kamera* ka-me-ra
camp site *kamp yeri* kamp ye-ree
cancel *iptal etmek* eep-*tal* et-mek
can opener *konserve açacağı* kon-ser-ve a-cha-ja-uh
car *araba* a-ra-ba
cash n *nakit* na-*keet*
cash (a cheque) v *(çek) bozdurmak*
(chek) boz-door-mak
cell phone *cep telefonu* jep te-le-fo-*noo*
centre n *merkez* mer-*kez*
change (money) v *bozdurmak* boz-door-mak
cheap *ucuz* oo-*jooz*
check (bill) *fatura* fa-too-ra
check-in n *giriş* gee-*reesh*
chest *göğüs* geu-ews
child *çocuk* cho-*jook*
cigarette *sigara* see-*ga*-ra
city *şehir* she-*heer*
clean a *temiz* te-meez
closed *kapalı* ka-pa-*luh*
coffee *kahve* kah-ve
coins *madeni para* ma-de-nee pa-ra
cold a *soğuk* so-ook
collect call *ödemeli telefon* eu-de-me-*lee* te-le-fon
come *gelmek* gel-mek

DICTIONARY

computer *bilgisayar* beel-gee-sa-*yar*
condom *prezervatif* pre-zer-va-*teef*
contact lenses *kontak lens* kon-*tak* lens
cook v *pişirmek* pee-sheer-*mek*
cost n *fiyat* fee-*yat*
credit card *kredi kartı* kre-dee kar-*tuh*
cup *fincan* feen-*jan*
currency exchange *döviz kuru* deu-*veez* koo-*roo*
customs (immigration) *gümrük* gewm-*rewk*

D

dangerous *tehlikeli* teh-lee-ke-*lee*
date (time) *tarih* ta-*reeh*
day *gün* gewn
delay n *gecikme* ge-jek-*me*
dentist *dişçi* deesh-*chee*
depart *ayrılmak* ai-ruhl-*mak*
diaper *bebek bezi* be-*bek* be-*zee*
dictionary *sözlük* seuz-*lewk*
dinner *akşam yemeği* ak-*sham* ye-me-*ee*
direct *direk* dee-*rek*
dirty *kirli* keer-*lee*
disabled *özürlü* eu-zewr-*lew*
discount n *indirim* een-dee-*reem*
doctor *doktor* dok-*tor*
double bed *iki kişilik yatak* ee-*kee* kee-shee-*leek* ya-*tak*
double room *iki kişilik oda* ee-*kee* kee-shee-*leek* o-*da*
drink n *içecek* ee-che-*jek*
drive v *sürmek* sewr-*mek*
drivers licence *ehliyet* eh-lee-*yet*
drugs (illicit) *uyuşturucu* oo-yoosh-too-roo-*joo*
dummy (pacifier) *emzik* em-*zeek*

E

ear *kulak* koo-*lak*
east *doğu* do-*oo*
eat *yemek* ye-*mek*
economy class *ekonomi sınıfı* e-ko-no-mee suh-nuh-*fuh*
electricity *elektrik* e-lek-*treek*
elevator *asansör* a-san-*seur*
email *e-posta* e-pos-ta
embassy *elçilik* el-chee-*leek*
emergency *acil durum* a-*jeel* doo-*room*
English (language) *İngilizce* een-gee-*leez*-je
entrance *giriş* gee-*reesh*
evening *akşam* ak-*sham*
exchange rate *döviz kuru* deu-*veez* koo-*roo*
exit n *çıkış* chuh-*kuhsh*

expensive *pahalı* pa-ha-*luh*
express mail *ekspres posta* eks-pres pos-*ta*
eye *göz* geuz

F

far *uzak* oo-*zak*
fast *hızlı* huhz-*luh*
father *baba* ba-*ba*
film (camera) *film* feelm
finger *parmak* par-*mak*
first-aid kit *ilk yardım çantası* eelk yar-*duhm* chan-ta-*suh*
first class *birinci sınıf* bee-reen-*jee* suh-*nuhf*
fish n *balık* ba-*luhk*
food *yiyecek* yee-ye-*jek*
foot *ayak* a-*yak*
fork *çatal* cha-*tal*
free (of charge) *ücretsiz* ewj-ret-*seez*
friend *arkadaş* ar-ka-*dash*
fruit *meyve* may-*ve*
full *dolu* do-*loo*
funny *komik* ko-*meek*

G

gift *hediye* he-dee-*ye*
girl *kız* kuhz
glass (drinking) *bardak* bar-*dak*
glasses *gözlük* geuz-*lewk*
go *gitmek* geet-*mek*
good *iyi* ee-*yee*
green *yeşil* ye-*sheel*
guide n *rehber* reh-*ber*

H

half n *yarım* ya-*ruhm*
hand *el* el
handbag *el çantası* el chan-ta-*suh*
happy *mutlu* moot-*loo*
have *sahip olmak* sa-*heep* ol-*mak*
he *o* o
head *baş* bash
heart *kalp* kalp
heat n *ısı* uh-*suh*
heavy *ağır* a-*uhr*
help v *yardım etmek* yar-*duhm* et-*mek*
here *burada* boo-ra-*da*
high *yüksek* yewk-*sek*

highway *otoyol* o-to-yol
hike v *uzun yürüyüşe çıkmak* oo-zoon yew-rew-yew-she chuhk-mak
holiday *tatil* ta-teel
homosexual *homoseksüel* ho-mo-sek-sew-el
hospital *hastane* has-ta-ne
hot *sıcak* suh-jak
hotel *otel* o-tel
hungry *aç* ach
husband *koca* ko-ja

I

I *ben* ben
identification (card) *kimlik kartı* keem-leek kar-tuh
ill *hasta* has-ta
important *önemli* eu-nem-lee
included *dahil* da-heel
injury *yara* ya-ra
insurance *sigorta* see-gor-ta
Internet *internet* een-ter-net
interpreter *tercüman* ter-jew-man

J

jewellery *mücevherler* mew-jev-her-ler
job *meslek* mes-lek

K

key *anahtar* a-nah-tar
kilogram *kilogram* kee-log-ram
kitchen *mutfak* moot-fak
knife *bıçak* buh-chak

L

laundry (place) *çamaşırlık* cha-ma-shuhr-luhk
lawyer *avukat* a-voo-kat
left (direction) *sol* sol
left-luggage office *emanet bürosu* e-ma-net bew-ro-soo
leg *bacak* ba-jak
lesbian *lezbiyen* lez-bee-yen
less *daha az* da-ha az
letter (mail) *mektup* mek-toop
lift (elevator) *asansör* a-san-seur
light n *ışık* uh-shuhk
like v *sevmek* sev-mek
lock n *kilit* kee-leet
long *uzun* oo-zoon

lost *kayıp* ka-yuhp
lost-property office *kayıp eşya bürosu* ka-yuhp esh-ya bew-ro-soo
love v *aşık olmak* a-shuhk ol-mak
luggage *bagaj* ba-gazh
lunch *öğle yemeği* eu-le ye-me-ee

M

mail n *mektup* mek-toop
man *adam* a-dam
map *harita* ha-ree-ta
market *pazar* pa-zar
matches *kibrit* keeb-reet
meat *et* et
medicine *ilaç* ee-lach
menu *yemek listesi* ye-mek lees-te-see
message *mesaj* me-sazh
milk *süt* sewt
minute *dakika* da-kee-ka
mobile phone *cep telefonu* jep te-le-fo-noo
money *para* pa-ra
month *ay* ai
morning *sabah* sa-bah
mother *anne* an-ne
motorcycle *motosiklet* mo-to-seek-let
motorway *paralı yol* pa-ra-luh yol
mouth *ağız* a-uhz
music *müzik* mew-zeek

N

name *ad* ad
napkin *peçete* pe-che-te
nappy *bebek bezi* be-bek be-zee
near *yakında* ya-kuhn-da
neck *boyun* bo-yoon
new *yeni* ye-nee
news *haberler* ha-ber-ler
newspaper *gazete* ga-ze-te
night *gece* ge-je
no *hayır* ha-yuhr
noisy *gürültülü* gew-rewl-tew-lew
nonsmoking *sigara içilmeyen* see-ga-ra ee-cheel-me-yen
north *kuzey* koo-zay
nose *burun* boo-roon
now *şimdi* sheem-dee
number *sayı* sa-yuh

I

O

oil (engine) *jağ* ya
old (object/person) *eski/yaşlı* es-*kee*/yash-*luh*
one-way ticket *gidiş bilet* gee-*deesh* bee-*let*
open a *açık* a-*chuhk*
outside *dışarıda* duh-sha-ruh-*da*

P

package *ambalaj* am-ba-*lazh*
paper *kağıt* ka-*uht*
park (car) v *park etmek* park et-*mek*
passport *pasaport* pa-sa-*port*
pay *ödemek* eu-de-*mek*
pen *tükenmez kalem* tew-ken-*mez* ka-*lem*
petrol *benzin* ben-*zeen*
pharmacy *eczane* ej-za-ne
phonecard *telefon kartı* te-le-*fon* kar-tuh
photo *fotoğraf* fo-to-*raf*
plate *tabak* ta-*bak*
police *polis* po-*lees*
postcard *kartpostal* kart-pos-*tal*
post office *postane* pos-ta-ne
pregnant *hamile* ha-mee-*le*
price *fiyat* fee-*yat*

Q

quiet *sakin* sa-*keen*

R

rain n *yağmur* ya-*moor*
razor *traş makinesi* trash ma-kee-ne-*see*
receipt n *makbuz* mak-*booz*
red *kırmızı* kuhr-muh-*zuh*
refund n *para iadesi* pa-*ra* ee-a-de-*see*
registered mail *taahhütlü posta* ta-ah-hewt-*lew* pos-ta
rent v *kiralamak* kee-ra-la-*mak*
repair v *tamir etmek* ta-*meer* et-*mek*
reservation *rezervasyon* re-zer-vas-*yon*
restaurant *restoran* res-to-ran
return v *geri dönmek* ge-*ree* deun-*mek*
return ticket *gidiş-dönüş bilet* gee-deesh-deu-*newsh* bee-*let*
right (direction) *doğru yön* do-*roo* yeun

road *yol* yol
room *oda* o-*da*

S

safe a *emniyetli* em-nee-yet-*lee*
sanitary napkin *hijyenik kadın bağı* heezh-ye-*neek* ka-duhn ba-uh
seat *yer* yer
send *göndermek* geun-der-*mek*
service station *benzin istasyonu* ben-zeen ees-tas-yo-noo
sex *seks* seks
shampoo *şampuan* sham-poo-an
share (a dorm) *paylaşmak* pai-lash-*mak*
shaving cream *tıraş kremi* tuh-rash kre-mee
she o o
sheet (bed) *çarşaf* char-shaf
shirt *gömlek* geum-lek
shoes *ayakkabılar* a-yak-ka-buh-lar
shop n *dükkan* dewk-kan
short *kısa* kuh-sa
shower n *duş* doosh
single room *tek kişilik oda* tek kee-shee-leek o-da
skin *cilt* jeelt
skirt *etek* e-tek
sleep v *uyumak* oo-yoo-mak
slowly *yavaşça* ya-vash-cha
small *küçük* kew-chewk
smoke (cigarettes) v *sigara içmek* see-ga-ra eech-mek
soap *sabun* sa-boon
some *biraz* bee-raz
soon *yakında* ya-kuhn-da
south *güney* gew-nay
souvenir shop *hediyelik eşya dükkanı* he-dee-ye-leek esh-ya dewk-ka-nuh
speak *konuşmak* ko-noosh-mak
spoon *kaşık* ka-shuhk
stamp *pul* pool
stand-by ticket *açık bilet* a-chuhk bee-let
station (train) *istasyon* ees-tas-yon
stomach *mide* mee-de
stop v *durmak* door-mak
stop (bus) n *durağı* doo-ra-uh
street *sokak* so-kak
student *öğrenci* eu-ren-jee
sun *güneş* gew-nesh

sunscreen *güneşten koruma kremi* gew·nesh·ten ko·roo·ma kre·mee
swim ∨ *yüzmek* yewz·mek

T

tampons *tamponlar* tam·pon·lar
taxi *taksi* tak·see
teaspoon *çay kaşığı* chai ka·shuh·uh
teeth *dişler* deesh·ler
telephone n *telefon* te·le·fon
television *televizyon* te·le·veez·yon
temperature (weather) *derece* de·re·je
tent *çadır* cha·duhr
that (one) *şunu/onu* shoo·noo/o·noo
they *onlar* on·lar
thirsty *susamış* soo·sa·muhsh
this (one) *bunu* boo·noo
throat *boğaz* bo·az
ticket *bilet* bee·let
time *zaman* za·man
tired *yorgun* yor·goon
tissues *kağıt mendil* ka·uht men·deel
today *bugün* boo·gewn
toilet *tuvalet* too·va·let
tomorrow *yarın* ya·ruhn
tonight *bu gece* boo ge·je
toothbrush *diş fırçası* deesh fuhr·cha·suh
toothpaste *diş macunu* deesh ma·joo·noo
torch (flashlight) *el feneri* el fe·ne·ree
tour n *tur* toor
tourist office *turizm bürosu* too·reezm bew·ro·soo
towel *havlu* hav·loo
train *tren* tren
translate *çevirmek* che·veer·mek
travel agency *seyahat acentesi* seya·hat a·jen·te·see
travellers cheque *seyahat çeki* se·ya·hat che·kee
trousers *pantolon* pan·to·lon
Turkey *Türkiye* tewr·kee·ye
Turkish (language) *Türkçe* tewrk·che
Turkish Republic of Northern Cyprus (TRNC) *Kuzey Kıbrıs Türk Cumhuriyeti (KKTC)* koo·zay kuhb·ruhs tewrk joom·hoo·ree·ye·tee (ka·ka·te·je)
twin beds *çift yatak* cheeft ya·tak
tyre *lastik* las·teek

U

underwear *iç çamaşırı* eech cha·ma·shuh·ruh
urgent *acil* a·jeel

V

vacant *boş* bosh
vacation *tatil* ta·teel
vegetable n *sebze* seb·ze
vegetarian a *vejeteryan* ve·zhe·ter·yan
visa *vize* vee·ze

W

waiter *garson* gar·son
walk ∨ *yürümek* yew·rew·mek
wallet *cüzdan* jewz·dan
warm a *ılık* uh·luhk
wash (something) *yıkamak* yuh·ka·mak
watch n *saat* sa·at
water *su* soo
we *biz* beez
weekend *hafta sonu* haf·ta so·noo
west *batı* ba·tuh
wheelchair *tekerlekli sandalye* te·ker·lek·lee san·dal·ye
when *ne zaman* ne za·man
where *nerede* ne·re·de
white *beyaz* be·yaz
who *kim* keem
why *neden* ne·den
wife *karı* ka·ruh
window *pencere* pen·je·re
wine *şarap* sha·rap
with *ile* ee·le
without *-sız/-siz/-suz/-süz* ·suhz/·seez/·sooz/·sewz
woman *kadın* ka·duhn
write *yazı yazmak* ya·zuh yaz·mak

Y

yellow *sarı* sa·ruh
yes *evet* e·vet
yesterday *dün* dewn
you sg inf *sen* sen
you sg pol & pl *siz* seez

INDEX

411

	Alb	Cro	Fre	Gre	Ital	Mac	Por	Sln	Spa	Tur
post office	27	67	107	147	186	227	267	307	347	387
problems (car & motorbike)	21	61	101	141	181	221	261	301	341	381
pronunciation	12	52	92	132	172	212	252	292	332	372

Q

	Alb	Cro	Fre	Gre	Ital	Mac	Por	Sln	Spa	Tur
quantities	38	78	118	158	198	238	278	318	358	398
queries (hotel)	24	64	104	144	184	224	264	304	344	384
queries (shopping)	30	70	109	150	189	230	270	309	350	390
queries (transport)	18	58	98	138	178	218	258	298	338	378

R

	Alb	Cro	Fre	Gre	Ital	Mac	Por	Sln	Spa	Tur
reading	32, 36	72, 76	111, 115	152, 155	191, 195	232, 236	272, 276	311, 315	352, 356	392, 396
receipts	31	71	111	151	191	231	271	310	351	391
refunds	31	70	110	150	190	230	271	310	351	391
repairs	31	70	110	150	190	230	271	310	350	390
requests (hotel)	24	64	104	144	184	224	264	304	344	384
requests (restaurant)	37	77	116	156	196	237	277	316	357	397
reservations	18, 20, 23, 36	58, 63, 76	98, 100, 103, 116	138, 140, 143, 156	178, 180, 183, 196	218, 220, 223, 236	258, 260, 263, 276	298, 300, 303, 316	338, 340, 343, 356	378, 380, 383, 396
restaurant	36	75, 76	115, 116	155, 156	195, 196	235, 236	275, 276	315, 316	355, 356	395, 396
room (hotel)	24	63	103	143, 144	183, 184	224	263	304	343, 345	383, 385

S

	Alb	Cro	Fre	Gre	Ital	Mac	Por	Sln	Spa	Tur
seasons	17	57	97	137	177	217	257	297	337	377
seating	18, 20	58, 60	98, 100	138, 140	178, 180	218, 220	258, 260	298, 300	338, 340	378, 380
self-catering	38	78	118	158	198	238	278	318	358	398
shoes	32	71	111	151	191	231	272	311	351	391
shopping	30	70	109	150	189	230	270	309	350	390
sightseeing	29	68	108	148	188	228	269	308	348	388
signs	23	62	102	142	182	223	263	303	343	383
sizes (clothes & shoes)	32	71	111	151	191	232	272	311	351	391
smoking	18, 36	58, 76	98, 116	138, 156	178, 196	218, 236	258, 276	298, 316	–	378, 396
speakers of the language	11	51	91	131	171	211	251	291	331	371
special diets	38	78	118	158	198	238	278	318	358	398
sport	36	76	115	156	195	236	276	315	356	396
symptoms (health)	43	83	123	163	203	243	283	323	363	403

festivals in mediterranean europe

The Tirana International Film Festival in December is the first and only short film festival in **Albania**. Gjirokastra is the home of the Albanian Folklore Festival, usually held in September every four years to celebrate the national traditions, folk music and dance.

In July and August, a programme of theatre, concerts and dance is presented on open-air stages at the prestigious Dubrovnik Summer Festival in **Croatia**. The Rijeka Carnival in February is a week of partying with plenty of parades and street dances.

The Cannes Film Festival in May is the world's most glitzy cinema event and a feast for the paparazzi. Another spectacle is the *Tour de France*, the famous bicycle race through **France** and the neighbouring countries, which ends in Paris in July.

The Hellenic Festival in Athens, the major summer arts festival in **Greece**, features international music, dance and theatre. Το φεστιβάλ κρασιού (the wine festival) is held in early September in Dafni, west of Athens, to celebrate the grape harvest.

The San Remo Music Festival in March has been running in **Italy** since 1951 and was the inspiration for the Eurovision Song Contest. The Italian Gran Prix, organised in September at Monza, is one of the oldest circuits in Formula One.

In July, a village in **Macedonia** hosts very popular and wildly romantic traditional weddings during the Galichnik Wedding Festival. Poets from around 50 countries take part at the Struga Poetry Evenings in August, complete with food and drink in the streets.

Festas das Cruzes (Festival of the Crosses), held in May in Barcelos, **Portugal**, is known for processions, folk music and regional handicrafts. In June, Santarém hosts the *Feira Nacional da Agricultura* (National Agricultural Fair) with bullfighting and folk music.

Kurentovanje, a rite of spring celebrated in February, is the most extravagant folklore event in **Slovenia**, held in Ptuj. Maribor hosts both the International Puppet Festival in July and August and a renowned theatre festival in the second half of October.

In June, Pamplona combines the *San Fermíne* festivities with macho posturing and running bulls, drawing TV crews from all over the world to **Spain**. *Semana Santa* (Holy Week) in April brings parades of holy images and huge crowds, notably in Seville.

Şeker Bayramı (Sweets Festival) is a three-day festival in **Turkey** at the end of the Muslim lunar month of Ramadan. *Kurban Bayramı* (Sacrifice Festival), two months after Ramadan, lasts for four days during which people make animal sacrifices.

Read it, hear it, speak it!

The right phrasebook for every trip

FAST TALK
- Perfect for a short trip
- All your essential needs covered

PHRASEBOOK & DICTIONARY
- The original
- Comprehensive
- Easy to use

Plus audio products to suit every traveller

BOOK & CD
- Read, listen and talk like a local
- Practise your pronunciation before you go

Visit
for our full language products